the Unofficial Guide™ to Quitting Smoking

Donna Howell

IDG Books Worldwide, Inc.
An International Data Group Company
Foster City, CA • Chicago, IL • Indianapolis, IN
New York, NY

IDG Books Worldwide, Inc.
An International Data Group Company
919 E. Hillsdale Boulevard
Suite 400
Foster City, CA 94404

This publication contains the opinions and ideas of its author[s] and is designed to provide useful advice to the reader on the subject matter covered. Any references to any products or services do not constitute or imply an endorsement or recommendation. The publisher and the author[s] specifically disclaim any responsibility for any liability, loss or risk (financial, personal or otherwise) which may be claimed or incurred as a consequence, directly or indirectly, of the use and/or application of any of the contents of this publication.

Certain terms mentioned in this book which are known or claimed to be trademarks or service marks have been capitalized.

IDG Books Worldwide, Inc. does not attest to the validity, accuracy or completeness of this information. Use of a term in this book should not be regarded as affecting the validity of any trademark or service mark.

Unofficial Guides are a [registered] trademark of Macmillan General Reference USA, Inc., a wholly owned subsidiary of IDG Books Worldwide, Inc.

For general information on IDG Books Worldwide's books in the U.S., please call our Consumer Customer Service department at 800-762-2974. For reseller information, including discounts and previous sales, please call our Reseller Customer Service department at 800-434-3422.

ISBN: 0-02-863342-3

Manufactured in the United States of America

10 9 8 7 6 5 4 3 2 1

First edition

With all good wishes for your health and happiness.

Acknowledgments

The author wishes to acknowledge and thank generally all those persons and organizations who provided assistance and information for this book, and to specifically acknowledge Boston University Medical Center's COHIS (Community Outreach Health Information System) project, for resources related to the history of tobacco use.

Contents

The *Unofficial Guide* Reader's Bill of Rights

We Give You More Than the Official Line

Welcome to the *Unofficial Guide* series of Lifestyle titles—books that deliver critical, unbiased information that other books can't or won't reveal—*the inside scoop.* Our goal is to provide you with the *most accessible, useful* information and advice possible. The recommendations we offer in these pages are not influenced by the corporate line of any organization or industry; we give you the hard facts, whether those institutions like them or not. If something is ill-advised or will cause a loss of time and/or money, we'll give you ample warning. And if it is a worthwhile option, we'll let you know that, too.

Armed and Ready

Our handpicked authors confidently and critically report on a wide range of topics that matter to smart readers like you. Our authors are passionate about their subjects but have distanced themselves enough from them to help you be armed and protected and to help you make educated decisions as you go through your process. It is our intent that, from having read this book, you will avoid the pitfalls everyone else falls into and get it right the first time.

Don't be fooled by cheap imitations; this is the *genuine article Unofficial Guide* series from Macmillan Publishing. You may be familiar with our proven track record of the travel *Unofficial Guides*, which have more than two million copies in print. Each year thousands of travelers—new and old—are armed with a brand-new, fully updated edition of the flagship *Unofficial Guide to Walt Disney World*, by Bob Sehlinger. It is our intention here to provide you with the same level of objective authority that Mr. Sehlinger does in his brainchild.

The Unofficial Panel of Experts

Every work in the Lifestyle *Unofficial Guides* is intensively inspected by a team of three top professionals in their fields. These experts review the manuscript for factual accuracy, comprehensiveness, and an insider's determination as to whether the manuscript fulfills the credo in this Reader's Bill of Rights. In other words, our Panel ensures that you are, in fact, getting "the inside scoop."

Our Pledge

The authors, the editorial staff, and the Unofficial Panel of Experts assembled for *Unofficial Guides* are determined to lay out the most valuable alternatives available for our readers. This dictum means that our writers must be explicit, prescriptive, and above all, direct. We strive to be thorough and complete, but our goal is not necessarily to have the "most" or "all" of the information on a topic; this is not, after all, an encyclopedia. Our objective is to help you narrow down your options to the best of what is available, unbiased by affiliation with any industry or organization.

In each *Unofficial Guide*, we give you:

- Comprehensive coverage of necessary and vital information
- Authoritative, rigidly fact-checked data
- The most up-to-date insights into trends
- Savvy, sophisticated writing that's also readable
- Sensible, applicable facts and secrets that only an insider knows

Special Features

Every book in our series offers the following six special sidebars in the margins that were devised to help you get things done cheaply, efficiently, and smartly.

1. **Timesaver**—tips and shortcuts that save you time.

2. **Moneysaver**—tips and shortcuts that save you money.

3. **Watch Out!**—more serious cautions and warnings.

4. **Bright Idea**—general tips and shortcuts to help you find an easier or smarter way to do something.

5. **Quote**—statements from real people that are intended to be prescriptive and valuable to you.

6. **Unofficially...**—an insider's fact or anecdote.

We also recognize your need to have quick information at your fingertips and have thus provided the following comprehensive sections at the back of the book:

1. **Glossary:** Definitions of complicated terminology and jargon.

2. **Resource Guide:** Lists of relevant agencies, associations, institutions, Web sites, etc.

3. **Recommended Reading List:** Suggested titles that can help you get more in-depth information on related topics.

4. **Important Documents:** "Official" pieces of information you need to refer to, such as government forms.

5. **Important Statistics:** Facts and numbers presented at a glance for easy reference.

6. **Index.**

Letters, Comments, and Questions from Readers

We strive to continually improve the *Unofficial* series, and input from our readers is a valuable way for us to do that. Many of those who have used the *Unofficial Guide* travel books write to the authors to ask questions, make comments, or share their own discoveries and lessons. For lifestyle *Unofficial Guides*, we would also appreciate all such correspondence, both positive and critical, and we will make best efforts to incorporate appropriate readers' feedback and comments in revised editions of this work.

How to write us:

Unofficial Guides
Lifestyle Guides
IDG Books
1633 Broadway
New York, NY 10019

Attention: Reader's Comments

About the Author

Donna Howell is an award-winning health and consumer journalist based in Los Angeles, California. Her background includes reporting and anchoring television news, as well as producing newsmagazine stories at the nationally syndicated television shows *Inside Edition* and *American Journal.* She holds a master's degree from Columbia University's Graduate School of Journalism, where she was a duPont Fellow and Pulitzer Traveling Fellow.

Donna is the author of *The Unofficial Guide to Coping With Menopause* and *The Unofficial Guide to Buying or Leasing a Car,* as well as a contributor to a recent business best-seller.

Donna's work in health journalism has been recognized with awards from United Press International and the Florida Medical Association (an American Medical Association state affiliate).

For more information about quitting smoking and Internet links to smoking-cessation sites, visit Donna's Web site on the topic at http://members.theglobe.com/quitsmoking or e-mail her at AuthorDonnaH@yahoo.com.

About the Author

The *Unofficial Guide* Panel of Experts

The *Unofficial* editorial team recognizes that you've purchased this book with the expectation of getting the most authoritative, carefully inspected information currently available. Toward that end, on each and every title in this series, we have selected a minimum of three "official" experts comprising the "Unofficial Panel" who painstakingly review the manuscripts to ensure: factual accuracy of all data; inclusion of the most up-to-date and relevant information; and that, from an insider's perspective, the authors have armed you with all the necessary facts you need that the institutions don't want you to know.

For *The Unofficial Guide to Quitting Smoking,* we are proud to introduce the following panel of experts:

Larry Deutsch Larry Deutsch, M.D., is a family physician and hypnotist with a large medical practice in Ottawa, Canada. Dr. Deutsch has a keen interest in the application of hypnosis to assist patients with various medical problems, including smoking cessation. He produces many self-help hypnosis materials for his own medical practice and for his growing Internet practice. His Web site is located at www.drlarry. com. He is based in Ottawa but travels around North America giving hypnosis seminars for small groups. Dr. Deutsch is a graduate of Cornell University (B.Sc., 1968). He received his M.D. from Dalhousie University, Halifax, Nova Scotia, Canada, in 1973. Dr. Deutsch's other interests include obstetrics, psychotherapy, aviation medicine, and music.

Allen R. Miller Allen R. Miller, Ph.D., is a Licensed Psychologist and is Associate Director of Behavioral Health Services for York Health in York, Pennsylvania. He has had 20 years experience treating people with addictive behavior problems. Dr. Miller was trained in Behavior Therapy at the Behavior Therapy Unit, Department of Psychiatry, Temple University under the direction of Joseph Wolpe, M.D. He was an Extramural Fellow for two years at the Beck Institute for Cognitive Therapy and Research, under the direction of Aaron Beck, M.D., and Judith Beck, Ph.D. Additionally, he has had extensive experience with people who utilize self-help treatment programs. In his current position, Dr. Miller assumes overall responsibility for clinical operations of inpatient and outpatient services. His main clinical interests are treatment of problems associated with addictive behaviors, physical and sexual abuse, and personality disorders.

Alexander V. Prokhorov Alexander V. Prokhorov, M.D., Ph.D., is an assistant professor in the Department of Behavioral Science at the

University of Texas M.D. Anderson Cancer Center. His current research projects focus on the development and testing of smoking-cessation programs for college students and smokeless tobacco prevention programs in youth. His research interests include examining smoking behavior and smoking cessation in different population groups, such as adolescents, high-risk young adults, and cancer survivors. In 1990, he was awarded the World Health Organization's certificate and medal recognizing his achievements in tobacco research. Dr. Prokhorov graduated from the first Moscow Medical Sechenov School in 1979 and received his Ph.D. from the National Cardiology Research Centre in Moscow in 1988. He completed a two-year post-doctoral training program at the Cancer Prevention Research Center at the University of Rhode Island, where he studied the application of behavioral approaches to various health-related behaviors, including cigarette smoking.

Welcome to *The Unofficial Guide to Quitting Smoking*

Did you know about half the people in America who used to smoke *no longer do?* Smokers fed up with their habit become *nonsmokers* every day, and if they can do it so can *you*. It's true that quitting is not easy! But it *can* be *done*, and spending a little time *learning how* to do it *right* is well worth the effort.

If you're like most smokers trying to quit, this isn't your first go-round. Chances are you've made a few attempts and succeeded in taking a *vacation* from smoking, but not a permanent one. This book will help you by pointing out which quitting methods are, according to studies, most effective for most people for the long term (here's a hint: cold turkey isn't).

In the most effective approach, quelling your physical craving for cigarettes is important, but so is psychological support. It makes no sense to steel yourself and try to *tough out* the difficult task of quitting. Instead, make it as *easy* as possible.

How do you do that given that tobacco has been controversially called as addictive as *heroin?* For the psychological side of the issue, quiz yourself on when and why you're really smoking, then learn about the tips, tricks, and buddy systems that are helping other people give up the habit. I'll show you what you can do on your own to stop thinking about smoking and introduce you to some formal smoking-cessation support groups that meet in your town or even on the Internet.

For the physical craving that's largely because of nicotine, you have a wide choice of mainstream treatments including patches, gum, *newer* forms of nicotine replacement, and even a pill that could help you kick the habit. You'll learn about their pluses and minuses, the cost, how long you use them, and just how effective they are, as well as alternatives.

The book will also explain just how nicotine works in your body, making you crave more and more. It's important to understand the effects of this chemical for your own health. Did you know that *in the short run*, nicotine can actually calm you down when you're anxious or raise your level of attention when you're bored? Or that studies show it modifies body weight?

By the time you decide to say goodbye to cigarettes, you need to be prepared with other, healthy ways to stay calm, cool, and collected. And you should know to watch your weight. In Chapter 4, I'll tell you which quit methods have been shown to thwart withdrawal weight gain.

You'll also learn why quitting can make you feel not so great for a short time—and provide some needed reassurance. Did you know that dizziness after stopping cigarettes is often due to the fact that your body is getting more of the oxygen it needs? That a slight cough can mean your body's working to clean up your lungs?

Cigarettes carry a government-mandated warning right on the label. While you know smoking is bad for your health, do you really know in what ways it's doing damage? Chapter 2 explains the frightening statistics clearly so you can understand how smoking increases your disease risks—and how quitting *lowers* them. Ever wonder how much longer nonsmokers live compared to smokers? *The Unofficial Guide to Quitting Smoking* will tell you.

Smoking and using tobacco in other ways is so dangerous that the World Health Organization has gone on record saying that unless tough actions are taken immediately, the tobacco epidemic will prematurely claim the lives of about 250 million children and young people alive today. And, certainly, tobacco is more and more coming under government controls to limit its use and keep it away from children.

Chapter 3 delves into the politics of tobacco, in case you wonder what's going on with smokers' lawsuits and even nonsmokers' lawsuits over *secondhand smoke*. It explains how advertising bans and warning labels got their start, and what the U.S. Justice Department's newly-instituted legal battle against the tobacco industry entails.

These things go right to your pocketbook. A huge portion of what you pay for cigarettes goes to taxes—taxes designed to curtail the habit and also to pay for the extra medical care that smokers have been needing over the years.

Oddly enough, smoking likely started as something one did for one's health. *The Unofficial Guide to Quitting Smoking* traces the tobacco timeline back to before the birth of America and explains how the habit took hold. Unfortunately, at least one important figure in the development of tobacco use died from cancer possibly caused by it—and he *thought* it was doing him *good*. Then there's the controversy over what was at one time considered a step towards making a *safer* cigarette—asbestos filters.

Most of this book concentrates on *how you can help yourself quit*. Do you know if you're really interested in quitting for yourself rather than loved ones? It's so important to have very personal reasons to kick the habit. Are your motivators health related, about your social life, about your budget? I'll show you how to move *quitting* up in your priority list.

Have you ever wondered what's in a cigarette besides tar, nicotine, and a filter? You may be surprised at how many different dangerous chemicals there are—some of them household names you'd never consider putting near your mouth—poisons straight out of movie plots. A clear picture of what smoking is and does should help your motivation to become smoke-free.

How do you plan to quit—how long should you take to wean yourself from cigarettes? This book points to guidelines and tried-and-true methods that can help you get a grip on the monster. And you'll learn what to do if you backslide!

Maybe you've wondered if you should quit gradually just by reducing the number of cigarettes that you smoke every day or by switching brands. You'll see a comparison of top brands for tar and nicotine content in Chapter 5, which also explains the pros and cons of switching. (By the way, all information given throughout this book is for the *United States* unless otherwise indicated.)

Part I of this book introduces you to the basics of quitting—why you should, what you can expect, the basic ways to go about it. In Part II, you can plan your quit and work your plan. Part III delves into the many methods you can use to help yourself kick the physical and psychological habit, and Part IV is devoted to methods to help reduce addiction—like nicotine-replacement therapy and a quit-smoking pill that's actually a popular antidepressant in disguise. Find out what you need a prescription for and what you don't. Did you know you could go buy nicotine patches at the drugstore right now?

Part V talks about using your head and health to help yourself quit. Learn about nutrition for the quitting smoker—what helps clean your system of toxins, what helps support your mood when nicotine is gone? I will also address hypnosis and other alternative quitting aides here. Can herbs help you quit? What about exercise—is that a good idea or a bad idea while you're quitting? The good news is it should be easier after you've gotten cigarettes out of your system. Another important point—what if you find it easy to get addicted to other things—alcohol, illegal drugs, even food? The book will give you some special help and tips for avoiding other addictions, so you don't replace one monkey on your back with another.

Part VI is about quitting and the special situation. What's a special situation? If you're pregnant or if you have certain medical conditions where it could be imperative for you to quit immediately rather than gradually. Which smoking-cessation aides can and can't you use then?

Smoking can have very serious consequences during pregnancy. You'll find out how soon before you're planning to get pregnant you should try to quit. You'll also learn what smoking can do to your fertility levels (impair them—women *and* men) and beauty. You probably already know smoking is hard on your skin, but did you know that it can send a woman into menopause earlier? Or that, in males, it's associated with *erectile dysfunction*? So much for the proverbial cigarette after sex.

How do you help a loved one quit smoking? This book can provide some suggested approaches that are more likely to help than alienate.

In Part VII, you'll find some points to ponder as a newly smoke-free citizen. How should you handle it when other people are smoking around you? What are your rights? Should you exercise them? In this section, I'll give you some suggestions for how nonsmokers and smokers can coexist peaceably and politely. I'll also look at where smoking is headed—could cigarettes ever be banned? Are more taxes ahead? (It could be a good reason to quit now.)

In the *glossary* you'll find some helpful definitions you'll need to know to get around quitting and medical terminology. And in the *resource guide,* you can find out where to get more specific helps for your quit-smoking quest, as well as where to read more on topics surrounding quitting that you might want to know more about—addictions, 12-step programs, health implications, or nutrition for quitting smokers, for instance. Internet users will find a collection of helpful links for information and communities on the Web you can turn to, to chat with other quitting smokers and compare notes, plus get some instant encouragement.

By the time you've read through this book, you should be well versed in the ways of quitting, and if you follow guidelines that have stood the test of time, I hope you'll be completely smoke-free by the moment you reach the last chapter, "You and Smokers," about how you as a new nonsmoker can relate to those who are still smoking. Statistically, it turns out, most of them want to quit, too. Best wishes on your journey into health.

A note to readers:

The material in this book is provided for informational purposes only. In no way should it be considered as offering medical advice, endorsement, medical opinion or diagnosis, or as constituting a replacement for medical examination or treatment. Please see your physician directly for treatment, medical advice, and questions about your medical condition. The author assumes no responsibility for how this material is used or for its accuracy. Keep in mind that health information can change quickly as new discoveries are made and as additional studies are conducted. The author encourages you to be careful when using *any* health or medical information, yet also to stay current on applicable issues and keep an open dialogue with your health-care professional about them.

So You Want to Quit Smoking

PART I

GET THE SCOOP ON...
The odds of kicking the habit for good ▪ Why
quitters succeed or backslide ▪ How to improve
your chances ▪ Your quitting method choices

Chapter 1

Just How Hard Is Quitting?

Smoking can be a pleasurable, seemingly need-fulfilling little habit, part of a lifestyle. To some people it's a statement, to some a diversion, but to many it's also a craving, one with potentially awful consequences—disease and *death*. If you're stuck on smoking cigarettes, you've got plenty of company—some even say smoking is at least as tough a habit to kick as *heroin*. It may not be just the *nicotine* that has you hooked, either, since new research suggests cigarettes might contain previously unknown addictive agents.

About 50 million Americans are smokers—more than one in every five people. In Canada more than one in four are smokers. Surveys suggest 80 percent of smokers want to quit, while 70 percent have tried to quit. Not all are successful at stopping but some *are* able to kick the habit for good. This book is dedicated to helping you find *your* best approach to quitting among the myriad ways out there. We'll provide encouragement and facts about how the methods work, and how *well* they work.

> *My best friend told me she had cancer. She had surgery and the cancer is gone. So are my cigs. I threw them down the day she called and swore I'd never pick up another. Now I feel like a new person. I can breathe so much better—it's wonderful.*
>
>   *—Jackie*

This chapter looks at the reasons people quit and some success rates. It introduces you to the most popular methods of quitting and should help you learn more about your *real* reasons for smoking and deciding to kick the habit.

Just how hard is hard?

First the bad news—those who try to quit usually don't get it right the first time. On average, people make about five attempts before quitting for good or giving up trying. Chances are you've been there. It is rather amazing, given that nearly 440,000 Americans die every year from diseases that are caused by smoking. In Canada, smoking is estimated to be responsible for about one in every five deaths. But the tug of psychological and *physical* addiction and the ease of denial perpetuate a smoking culture, despite *plenty of reasons* to quit, as we'll get to later in this chapter.

Successful quitting

There is *good news*—about 1.3 million Americans *do* quit smoking every year. The big question is *how can you be among them?* What does it take to make the cut and really quit? Among the most important factors are:

Bright Idea
Psych yourself up for the challenge of quitting—what can you do right away? Promise yourself now you're *going* to quit. And start doing healthier things—such as getting adequate exercise and eating good-for-you foods.

- Having a strong desire and commitment to quitting

- Having confidence in yourself and your ability to kick the habit

- Knowing how your quitting efforts will affect your *life*, and having a good sense of what quitting will do *for* your life

- Using a method of quitting that fits you

- Addressing both psychological and physical addiction

- Maintaining your motivation to quit

A large part of quitting involves knowing your own patterns and doing things that make it easier to quit. You can prepare ahead of time to divert attention from the desire to smoke. For example, if you always have a cigarette with breakfast, try changing your morning routine. Read the paper instead or stop for a quick breakfast on the way to work. Chapter 10 describes dozens of practical tactics.

When you make an attempt to quit smoking, keep in mind that you're facing two different roadblocks:

- Physical addiction

- The habit of smoking

Whichever methods you decide to employ to help you quit, address both the physical and psychological aspects. A combined approach offers you the easiest ride to a nonsmoking life.

Remember there are plenty of former smokers who *have successfully quit.* According to the American Lung Association, in the mid-nineties, an estimated 44.3 million adults were former smokers, and of the remaining 47 million smokers, more than 31 million reported they wanted to quit smoking, too.

Watch Out!
Pregnant and thinking of quitting? Jump to Chapter 13 for important information you need right now.

Failed attempts

What keeps people from succeeding in their attempts to give up cigarettes? In 1998, Yankelovich Partners did a study for the American Lung Association, surveying 1,001 smokers who tried to quit but failed.

The main reason people continue to smoke once they've started is *addiction*. More women than men said they smoke to relieve stress or to have something to do with their hands. Other reasons people keep smoking include feeling more comfortable in social situations and to keep from feeling hungry.

Do you know why you are still smoking? You can evaluate your reasons in the following checklist.

Why Am I Still Smoking?
_____ Addiction
_____ Stress relief
_____ Something to do with hands
_____ Social situation comfort
_____ To avoid eating
_____ Other _____
_____ Other _____
_____ Other _____
_____ Other _____

Think about how many of your answers are actually talking about a psychological smoking habit, and how many are primarily physical. For instance, are you really self-medicating by smoking to improve your mood or to settle nerves? Are cigarettes an artifact of your social environment? Do you secretly harbor a belief that your life won't be as good without smoking?

Why people quit

When people make a quit-smoking attempt, it's for their health more than for any other reason.

Women are more likely than men to try to give up cigarettes when friends and family ask them to, according to the Yankelovich survey. The cost of cigarettes is another factor people cite in their attempts to quit, and there are other motivators.

Reasons why people attempted to give up smoking, according to the Yankelovich survey, include:

Health problems/illness	34%
No reason, just wanted to quit	15%
Family/friends asked you to quit	12%
Cost/too expensive	7%
Pregnancy	7%
Doctor told you to quit	5%
Shortness of breath	4%
Tired of bad taste in mouth	3%
Tired of smelling like smoke	3%
Not socially acceptable	2%
Smoking prohibited	1%
Friend/relative died	1%
Something else	14%
Don't know	3%

Often, the decision to give up cigarette smoking is a combination of reasons, as it is for Lori—who at 33 was an 11-year veteran of smoking.

> I have tried to quit twice before—once several years ago with patches, and again last year by going cold turkey. Those quits lasted about a month. My reasons for quitting now are varied. I know that smoking has a cumulative effect. I've been smoking for years, but feel as if I'm reaching a crossroads of sorts. If I can quit soon, maybe I can avoid ending up talking through a hole in my throat. I haven't had significant

Unofficially... Women cited pregnancy as one reason for their quitting attempt. Some *men* cited pregnancy as their reason, too.

health problems yet, but give me 10 more years, and there will be no turning back.

But some of the psychological factors are even more motivating these days. I am feeling the stigma of being a "smoker." Not from others, but from myself. No one in my family smokes, and I am one of only two smokers at work— I am starting to feel like one of "those" people. Continuing to smoke makes me feel "low-class." This was not who I was supposed to be—I am better than this.

I am also a single female who would eventually like to have a family and children. Being a smoker significantly reduces my choices in men—the types of men I would like to be involved with simply wouldn't consider dating a smoker, and I can't blame them. And there is no way in the world I want to be smoking with children. I believe that smoking is an impediment to my getting some of the things I want.

Everyone has a different perception of smoking (see Chapter 3 for more about that topic and the social history of smoking). Your strongest motivators for quitting are key to successfully ending your smoking habit (so is self-confidence). If self-image is your reason, use it!

I'm quitting for my health

Smokers know smoking is very bad for their health, and many who are driven to quit do it literally to save their lives. According to the American Lung Association, over 40,000 studies have proven smoking causes disease and death. Every year, more Americans die from smoking-related diseases than die from alcohol, drugs, accidents, suicides, homicides, and AIDS—*combined.*

How's your knowledge about the health dangers of smoking? You can try the following quiz to find out.

WHAT DO YOU KNOW ABOUT SMOKING AND HEALTH?

1. Smoking is said to be directly responsible for what percentage of lung cancer cases in America each year?
   a. None
   b. 11 percent
   c. 87 percent
   d. 98 percent

2. How many Americans die each year as a result of smoking-related diseases?
   a. 59,100
   b. 121,800
   c. 430,700
   d. 1.62 million

3. Which of the following are true of cigarette smoking during pregnancy?
   a. It can prevent 25 percent of oxygen from reaching the placenta
   b. It passes nicotine to the fetus
   c. It accounts for up to 14 percent of preterm deliveries
   d. It accounts for roughly 10 percent of all infant deaths

4. Which of the following are true of secondhand smoke?
   a. It is smoke exhaled by a smoker
   b. It comes from the end of a burning cigarette
   c. It contains between 15 and 20 different poisons
   d. It can cause pneumonia or ear infections in babies

5. Which of the following are true about smoking?
   a. It causes most cases of emphysema and chronic bronchitis
   b. It is a major factor in heart disease and stroke
   c. It may be causally related to malignancies elsewhere in the body
   d. It has been linked to slowed wound healing, infertility, and peptic ulcer disease

← The information in this quiz is based in part on data from the American Lung Association. You can call (800) LUNG-USA or (800) 586-4872 for more information, or visit their Web site at www.lungusa.org.

Answers: 1. c; 2. c; 3. a, b, c, d; 4. a, b, d (not c: secondhand smoke contains about 200 poisons); 5. a, b, c, d.

Overall, smoking causes 1 in 5 deaths in the United States, through a variety of illnesses. We'll go over the problems smoking presents to health in more detail in Chapter 2 and talk about *what* makes cigarettes so dangerous. Suffice it to say for now that it's the number one reason people quit—*for* a reason.

Social quitters

Where smoking has in the past been portrayed as a glamorous affectation, these days, the image is tarnishing. Publicity about the disease impact cigarettes present has taken off much of the luster, but a general trend toward health and fitness is also probably somewhat responsible.

The more other people quit, the less social reason smokers have to continue. And there is relatively new knowledge of the dangers of secondhand smoke to take into account, as well. A "no smoking" clampdown in places like restaurants and offices makes it harder for the social smoker to keep smoking while continuing to be social.

Where once there was peer pressure to *start smoking* to be cool, intentional publicity portraying smoking as anything *but* attractive has had a noticeable effect. However, a glamorous aura unfortunately still surrounds smoking in *some* groups despite the health risks of smoking. It may be just a change in associates that prompts some smokers to try to quit.

Social quitters kick the habit for at least one of four reasons:

- Being a nonsmoker is important to their image
- Being a smoker is detrimental to their image
- Smoking is inconvenient in their social situations
- A loved one has asked them to give up cigarettes

Quitting because of secondhand smoke risks to your family may be a combination reason—if it's your family's *health* but your *social situation* at issue.

Stopping because of others or how you fit in with them carries its own psychological burden, and you would be well-advised to come up with a few valid personal reasons why *you* want to quit for your *own* well-being, too. You don't want to be susceptible to temptation whenever you experience a negative emotion related to the person who's trying to get you to quit.

If your spouse annoys you one day, subconsciously, resuming smoking could be a way of defending your ground. If you're quitting just because you usually can't smoke where you choose to socialize, you could backslide easily when you wind up in a situation where there are other smokers and where smoking *is* possible. Chapters 10, 12, and 15 deal with these issues in more depth.

Bottom-line quitters

If you smoke much at all now, you're probably aware that the cost of all those cigarettes you buy is adding up. Some smokers choose to quit for the health of their finances, as well as the health of their body. Of course, the costs of smoking includes more than the pack prices. According to the American Lung Association, firsthand smoking alone costs $97.2 billion each year in health-care costs and lost productivity in the United States.

How much do cigarettes cost you? Assuming you pay about $3.20 per pack and smoke just a single pack a day, that's $1,168 a year. At three packs a day, the annual cost is $3,504. What could you use the money for instead—a luxury vacation, a complete kitchen remodeling, a top-of-the-line computer, an

Timesaver
Even if you don't quit smoking immediately, whenever you reach for a cigarette, think about what you could be substituting for it at that time and other ways you could avoid that particular smoking situation.

Moneysaver
Curb your
cigarette
spending habits
by figuring out
how much you're
paying and what
you could buy
instead. Try the
calculator at the
Canadian Lung
Association's
Internet site, at
www.sk.lung.ca
(in the *students'*
section).

hour-long professional massage *every week*, or even lease payments on a new car?

Quitting and you

Most people quit for their health, but almost any reason can be valid. Down the line, when you're trying to avoid the temptation of another puff, it can be helpful to know exactly what your real reasons are for not giving in. The following quiz can help you assess the factors going into your decision to quit smoking.

KNOW YOUR REASONS FOR QUITTING

Quitting for Others

1. Is someone important to you actively asking you to quit?

2. Are you seriously concerned about the impact of second-hand smoke on family and friends?

3. Do you spend your time mostly with other smokers?

4. Have you felt uncomfortable in any smoking situation in the last week or had to excuse yourself in order to smoke?

Quitting for Health

5. Are you at least a little worried about your health?

6. Do you think smoking has impaired your abilities?

7. Do you have a health condition you attribute largely to smoking?

8. Are you getting regular exercise or thinking about starting a fitness program?

Quitting for Money

9. Are you on a conservative budget?

10. Do you grimace at how much you're spending on cigarettes?

11. Do you smoke more than x packs a day?

12. Are you careful how much you spend on food at the grocery store and on eating out?

Add your yes answers in each section and compare which sections have the most yes answers. A predominance of yesses in the first section means you may be a social quitter. Your efforts at avoiding cigarettes may be strongest when your personal relationships are strongest.

Having many yes answers in the second section suggests your reasons have more to do with *you*— and keeping a healthy self-image may help your progress.

Finally, if you had a large number of yesses in the third section, on money, then you're bottom-lining it. Practicality is a fine way to approach quitting, but concentrate on other reasons, too, so you don't backslide when finances are less of an issue.

Why quitting can be tough

Smokers are up against the physical addictiveness of nicotine, as well as their own habit patterns. These urges can be a lot stronger than they may look at first glance. There's also a lot of misunderstanding about smoking and quitting methods. According to the Yankelovich survey mentioned earlier, nearly 40 percent of smokers said they were confused about quit-smoking products.

Physical addiction

How addictive do you consider cigarettes to be—less than illegal drugs? More of a psychological habit? Cigarettes have been described as *very* addictive—so much so that relapse among former smokers is as high as it is among former heroin users, according to a Harvard research report. And the U.S. Surgeon General's office describes nicotine as *just as* addictive as heroin and cocaine.

Nicotine is an alkaloid chemical found in the leaves of tobacco plants that affects both the function and structure of the brain, as well as the skeletal muscles, cardiovascular system, and other systems

Unofficially...
Nicotine was declared addictive in 1986 by the U.S. Surgeon General.

throughout the body. It is psychoactive, with the ability to alter mood, behavior, cognition, and mental tension or anxiety.

In Chapter 2, I'll describe nicotine's effects in depth, but a short primer here can help to explain cigarette addiction.

- **Nicotine.** When you smoke, nicotine is absorbed into the lungs and quickly goes into the bloodstream. The nicotine in smokeless tobacco is absorbed through mouth or nasal tissues and then enters the blood. Once there, nicotine crosses the blood-brain barrier and is distributed in the brain. How long does all this take? Once inhaled in cigarette smoke, nicotine speeds into the brain in about 11 seconds or less. The quick nicotine kick comes from the release of epinephrine from the adrenal cortex. Stimulation of the nervous system results in the release of glucose, which is then followed by depression and fatigue, causing the user to seek more nicotine.

  When nicotine reaches the brain, it binds to receptors for a neurotransmitter called acetylcholine and spurs the release of other brain chemicals, producing effects on mood, alertness, and maybe even cognition. Continued use can make for an increase in the number of nicotine-binding receptors and alters both the metabolic and electrical activity of the brain.

  Nicotine's so-called *rewarding effects*, the positives that promote its continued use, happen through spurring of the release of dopamine, a brain chemical that has a big role in the regulation of pleasure sensation. Amphetamines and cocaine work this way, too. Who hasn't wondered if their tobacco craving isn't all in their head? A lot of it *is*, in bona fide chemical brain changes.

People may smoke, in part, to self-medicate, for nicotine can be a (ill-advised) mood panacea. A cigarette can be either arousal-increasing or arousal-reducing, depending on the circumstances. In a stressful situation, a little nicotine can have a calming effect as tested with an electroencephalograph (EEG) reading. But when there's not much excitement around, it can have a stimulant effect instead. While low doses of nicotine have been shown to increase blood pressure and heart rate, higher doses slow heart rate. The 1988 Surgeon General's report on smoking concluded that after smoking cigarettes or receiving nicotine, smokers perform better on some cognitive tasks than when deprived of cigarettes or nicotine, though smoking and nicotine were not found to improve general learning.

A federal government tobacco policy committee cochaired by former Surgeon General C. Everett Koop, M.D. has described the cigarette's chemical cocktail this way:

> *Nicotine makes the product addictive, the toxins make it deadly, and the additives make it more consumer acceptable, like sweetening a poison.*

But what *is* addiction? One good definition is this:

- **Addiction.** A cluster of cognitive, behavioral, and physiological symptoms indicating sustained psychoactive substance use despite substance-related problems. In addition, substance dependence is characterized by repeated

Unofficially...
Nicotine is a powerful substance. In fact, the Food and Drug Administration (FDA) says nicotine in cigarettes and smokeless tobacco products is actually a *drug* and that these products are thereby *drug delivery devices*.

self-administration that usually results in tolerance, withdrawal, and compulsive drug-taking behavior. (Source: Centers for Disease Control)

Another description is that a physical addiction is present if a physical dependence on a drug develops and if withdrawal symptoms are experienced when the dose is decreased or use of the drug is stopped. Physical symptoms of nicotine withdrawal can include:

- Depression
- Anxiety
- Irritability
- Craving
- Decrease in sensitivity to pleasure
- Cognitive and attentional deficits
- Sleep disturbances
- Increased appetite

Some of these symptoms may start within a few hours after a smoker's last cigarette, and the syndrome of nicotine withdrawal can last a month or longer, peaking in the first few days and subsiding (at least somewhat) over the first few weeks, according to the National Institute on Drug Abuse. Cravings for tobacco can last half a year or longer.

Addictiveness is typically measured using a list of criteria. While smoking nicotine-containing cigarettes doesn't offer as *dramatic* an effect as using heroin or cocaine, it ranks high in other determinants of addictiveness, such as tending to create dependence and tolerance among users. Tobacco dependence is listed by the World Health Organization (WHO) as a mental and behavioral disorder, in its *International Classification of Diseases (ICD-10)*, and the American Psychiatric Association includes nicotine dependence and nicotine withdrawal as disorders in its *Diagnostic and Statistical Manual of Mental Disorders (DSM-IV)*.

It turns out that cigarettes *may* even be *more addictive* than alcohol, pot, cocaine, or heroin. According to a CDC and National Institute on Drug Abuse review of survey data, a symptom of substance dependence is more likely to be reported by those who smoke cigarettes and those who use cocaine than by those who use alcohol or marijuana. And nicotine may not be the *only* physically addictive chemical component of cigarettes. Recent research suggests another, unknown compound in cigarette smoke also raises dopamine levels in the brains of smokers by inhibiting an enzyme that usually breaks down dopamine. Nicotine's precise level of addictiveness, however, is a matter of some debate in the scientific community.

Many people say they feel much healthier and more comfortable after they quit, but the process usually gets worse before it gets better. Quitting smokers can experience frustration, anger, anxiety, difficulty concentrating, restlessness, and decreased heart rate as they work through their physical and psychological addiction.

Psychological addiction and the habit factor

When you quit smoking, you go through physical withdrawal as your body copes with the pharmacological effects of missing a regular dose of nicotine on which it has become dependent. But you also must contend with kicking your psychological addiction—breaking the *habit*.

Watch Out!
Watch those ashes! Careless smoking is the leading cause of fire deaths, according to the U.S. Fire Administration.

Cravings for a cigarette may be related not only to the brain chemical tweaking cigarettes provide (through nicotine) but also to the feel, smell, taste, and sight of a cigarette. In large part, it may be the routine and ritual of smoking that a smoker finds comforting and compelling. Positive expectations of what will happen when a smoker smokes also play a role—for instance, feeling more comfortable in a social situation or otherwise experiencing the easing of anxieties. Earlier in this chapter the "Why Am I Still Smoking?" checklist listed some popular habitual reasons for smoking—which were yours?

It is important to realize that your body and mind are not operating independently when it comes to cigarette addiction and that psychological addiction and physical dependence often occur together. As the neural rewards of nicotine are received, they become psychological reinforcements to continue smoking. For instance, when the body perceives a cigarette helps to ease tension, it's natural to think about reaching for one in the next stressful situation—a learned behavior.

As an addiction develops, a drug whose effect was once sought only occasionally and in specific situations becomes more and more important, while the other things important in a person's life fade into the background as motivators, relatively speaking. *Motivational toxicity* usually becomes apparent, as one addictions researcher puts it.

While a desire for a drug can develop from repeatedly experiencing its rewarding effects, what may not be immediately apparent, Bozarth notes, is that cognitions and social interactions can also affect *physiological* processes.

Put simply, your psychological desire to smoke can exacerbate a physical craving (just as the physical things smoking does for you prompt you to want it psychologically). Put even more simply, *cigarette addiction is a vicious circle.*

Counting the many ways to quit

You can quit smoking using only the word "no," take part in a well-thought-out behavior modification program, or go to your pharmacist for help. Or try any of a number of other stop-smoking methods.

Timesaver
For more on specific methods of addressing psychological addiction to cigarettes *behaviorally,* turn to Chapters 6 and 10.

Since nicotine is considered addictive and habits are hard to break, a combined approach addressing both your physical need and your psychological temptations may be your best route. The Yankelovich study found of those who tried to quit and failed, three out of four flopped at a cold turkey attempt and about two out of five had tried a more gradual method.

Among your treatment options for physical dependency on cigarettes are nicotine replacement therapy products. They work by providing (at decreasing levels) the nicotine you used to get from cigarettes. You can get nicotine patches (that provide nicotine *transdermally*—through the skin) over the counter *or* by prescription, and nicotine gum over the counter. Patches and gum are available over the counter in pharmacies in Canada. A nicotine nasal spray and an inhaler are available by prescription in the United States.

Zyban is a non-nicotine pill available by prescription in both the United States and Canada. It is thought to address the biology of addiction and helps reduce withdrawal symptoms from nicotine. Its chemical name is bupropion hydrochloride, and it was first developed and marketed as an antidepressant (Wellbutrin). It works on neurotransmitters, and you'll find out more about it and other pre-scription stop-smoking aides in Chapter 6.

Beyond physical stop-smoking aides, a number of behavior-modification programs exist to help smokers quit, such as the American Lung Association's Freedom from Smoking program and others. Generally speaking, programs may seek to do some combination of the following:

- Help a smoker get to know why he or she smokes and wants to quit
- Provide information about smoking and quitting
- Establish a timetable and structure for quitting
- Help a smoker to identify and avoid situations where he or she is most likely to relapse
- Provide psychological or social support for quitting
- Create aversion to cigarette smoking
- Replace cigarette smoking with healthy activity that takes its place

You may find one or more of these programs very useful as you quit smoking, in addition to this book. Chapter 10 deals with the topic in detail, and you can also check the Resource Guide in Appendix C for information on specific programs.

There are plenty of informal quitting methods, too, such as simply cutting down by a cigarette a day (or even by a cigarette a week) or switching to brands that have progressively less nicotine content (or employing so-called smokeless cigarettes or special filters). You've probably heard about the use of hypnosis in quitting smoking. It is one of a host of alternative quit-smoking therapies in use and which is

Unofficially...
At concentrated doses, nicotine is used as an insecticide.

covered in upcoming chapters. While some may be of help to you, others present problems you should know of before you decide to try a particular aid.

The important thing at this point is that you get to know the reasons you're smoking and why you want to quit, and that you make a commitment to quitting—somehow and soon. Take time to decide which methods you'd like to use, but consider putting to work at least some of these tips from the American Lung Association *now.*

1. Make a list of your reasons for quitting and say them often.

2. Set a quit date and tell everyone you are going to quit.

3. Keep a supply of healthy snacks handy.

4. Increase your exercise. Walk more.

5. Make specific plans for what you'll do when the urge hits. For example, take a deep breath, get up and walk around, call a friend for help, keep your hands busy. Remember the urge passes in a few minutes whether you smoke or not.

6. Remove all cigarettes, ashtrays, matches, and lighters from your home, workplace, and car.

7. Consider using a nicotine-replacement product; they work best for smokers who are addicted to nicotine and are really trying to quit.

You can contact the American Lung Association at (800) LUNG-USA for additional information about their stop-smoking programs, covered in more detail in Chapter 10. Another tip is to try to start believing now that you actually *can* quit.

Health, wealth, and smokeless happiness

Quitting smoking is not easy, and like any addict, consciously staying away from whatever you've been addicted to is something you'll need to keep in mind for the rest of your life.

The adjustment from smoker to nonsmoker may not be perfectly smooth. Some quitters grapple with depression, anxiety, and the threat of weight gain. But by knowing ahead of time what the reasons are for such difficulties, you can take steps to minimize their likelihood. Many terrific things about not smoking are waiting around the corner. What happens when you quit?

Within a few hours nicotine and carbon monoxide levels in the body drop. During the days, weeks and months after a smoker puffs his last cigarette, the ability to smell and taste is enhanced, blood pressure normalizes. Circulation and lung function improve. The risk of certain diseases also starts to drop:

- **1 year:** Heart disease death rate is halfway back to that of a nonsmoker.

- **5 years:** Risk of esophageal and mouth cancer is cut in half.

- **10 years:** Lung cancer death rate drops to 30–50 percent of the risk seen in continuing smokers.

If you've been a smoker for years, you could find your health very much improved not very long after you quit smoking. It is heartening to know that the body is capable of the kind of healing and recuperation that exsmokers report. The rest of this book shows you how to get there.

Just the facts

- Nicotine has been called potentially as addictive as heroin or cocaine.

- More Americans die annually from smoking-related diseases than die from alcohol, drugs, accidents, suicides, homicides, and AIDS combined.

- Smokers trying to quit make an average of five attempts.

- Backsliding quitters say they missed the feeling smoking gave them and also having something to hold.

- Every year, about 1.3 million Americans quit smoking.

GET THE SCOOP ON...
How you can be harmed by smoking ▪ Which
components do damage ▪ Why some call cigarettes as addictive as heroin ▪ Why quitting *now*
is much better than *later*

Smoking and You

Chapter 2

Y ou've heard smoking is terrible for your
health, and if you're like most people, protecting your health is the prime reason
you're thinking about quitting. But if you're like
most smokers, you may tend to *underestimate* your
real risk of illness, and that's one thing you can stop
right now with ease.

In this chapter, we'll talk candidly about what
damage smoking *does* and what damage smoking is
suspected of doing. You should be better able to assess
how important quitting is to your well-being once
you've heard the facts.

Sorting out smoking's health risks

Does smoking cause cancer? Yes. Does smoking
cause lung disease? Of course. Is that it? No!
Smoking cigarettes can increase your chances of getting sick—or even dying—from any of a number of
different ailments. *Tobacco* is a risk factor for at least
25 different diseases.

And then there are the *other* undesirable potential consequences of smoking. For instance, that

25

Watch Out!
Freud aside, a
cigar is never
just a cigar. One
can contain as
much tobacco as
a *pack* of
cigarettes. Check
out Chapter 5 for
cigar versus
cigarette facts.

proverbial cigarette after sex *may* be ruining your
sex life, not to mention your skin.

More on that in a bit, but first the biggies—
according to the U.S. Centers for Disease Control
and Prevention, it is now well documented that
smoking can cause:

- Chronic lung disease
- Coronary heart disease
- Stroke
- Cancer of the lung, larynx, esophagus, mouth,
  and bladder

Smoking can also *exacerbate* other cancers in the
body. You can take a look at how most smoking
deaths stack up by type of disease in the following
figure.

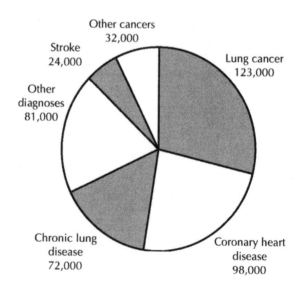

430,700 U.S. deaths are attributable each year to cigarette
smoking. (Average annual number of deaths, 1990–1994.) Source:
Based on U.S. Centers for Disease Control and Prevention, Morbidity
and Mortality Weekly Report 1997;46:448–51.

There are many ways smoking can kill, such as:

- Cancer of the lung, throat and mouth, esophagus, bladder, kidney, stomach, and pancreas, as well as leukemia

- Heart and circulatory problems such as ischemic heart disease, aortic aneurysm, myocardial degeneration, atherosclerosis, stroke

- Bronchitis and emphysema

- Pneumonia

- Ulcers of the stomach and duodenum

Even with hard figures and humble pie charts, it may be tough to get a grip on the damage cigarettes *can really do* to your body. Just 3 of 10 smokers in one survey thought they had a higher-than-average risk of heart attack, and only 2 of 5 believed they had a higher-than-average cancer risk—when of course, they *did*. The less educated respondents were, the less likely they were to have an accurate picture of their risks. *Learning* is good—it may help save your life.

The cancer question

Cancer is abnormal growth of abnormal cells. A *carcinogen* is something that causes or spurs cancer. Tobacco smoke contains at least *43* of them.

Probably because these chemicals are introduced rather directly into the lungs *by inhalation*, lung cancer is the most obvious cancer associated with smoking (about 87 percent of lung cancer cases are attributed to cigarette use). Smoking is also associated with cancers of the

- Mouth
- Pharynx

Watch Out!
Cigars and
smokeless
tobacco have
deadly
consequences,
too, such as
lung, larynx,
esophageal, and
oral cancer
(among other
diseases).

- Larynx
- Esophagus
- Pancreas
- Uterine cervix
- Kidney
- Bladder

Lung cancer most often starts in the lining of the breathing passages leading to the lungs (bronchial tubes). It is slow, typically developing over many years. Before a tumor is visible by X-ray, precancerous changes take place. If conditions continue to be right for development, malignant (*cancerous*) cells eventually begin to grow. One of the big dangers in cancer occurs when these malignant cells undergo *metastasis*, breaking away from the original tumor and spreading to other sites in the body, and lung cancer often spreads in this manner even before it is detected by X-ray.

That's part of what makes it so deadly. A patient's chances of surviving lung cancer for one year are about 38 percent, and the five-year survival rate is only about 14 percent, despite treatment with chemotherapy, radiation, or other measures. But if cancer is found and treated surgically very early, before it has spread, the five-year survival rate increases to about 50 percent. Unfortunately, most lung cancer is *not* detected early.

Some early warning signs of lung cancer include:

- A persistent cough
- Chest pain
- Hoarseness
- Weight loss and loss of appetite
- Bloody or rust-colored sputum

- Shortness of breath

- Fever without a known reason

- Recurring infections such as bronchitis and pneumonia

After lung cancer spreads in the body, it can cause bone pains, neurological changes like numbness of the limbs, or dizziness, jaundice, or masses under the skin. Bear in mind that some of these symptoms can arise from *other* causes and noncancerous diseases, but if you have *any* of these symptoms, see a doctor promptly and raise your concerns.

Very good news came out in early 1999 about the possibility of lung cancer *screening*. Preliminary results of a New York study called the Early Lung Cancer Action Program (ELCAP) suggest that *computed tomography* (CT) scans can be effective in detecting lung cancer in its early stages in those at high risk. In the study, a special low-dose CT scan detected 19 out of 24 cancers in the very early stage (only three of those cancers were picked up on X-ray).

Many smokers, not to mention *non*smokers, fear cancer—half of all men and one-third of all women will develop it in their lifetimes, but most of the time, risk can be reduced by making a lifestyle change—for instance, cutting out smoking, eliminating excessive alcohol intake, or improving your diet. If you are worried about cancer, you can turn it into a good motivator to quit because quitting helps reduce your cancer risk quickly.

According to a study at the University of Minnesota Cancer Center, certain cancer-causing substances in tobacco can stay in the body at significant levels as long as six weeks after you stop smoking, but these carcinogens eventually disappear (the

Moneysaver
The cost for a limited *lung cancer screening* CT scan should be much lower than for a full CT scan—the neighborhood of $200 has been suggested. For more info, contact the American Cancer Society.

discovery may help researchers find ways to keep carcinogens from triggering cancer to develop).

Emphysema, bronchitis, and that cough

Smoking cigarettes interrupts your lungs' round-the-clock work. It causes something known as *chronic obstructive pulmonary disease* (COPD), which consists of emphysema and chronic bronchitis. Together, these constitute the most common chronic lung disease in the U.S., affecting almost 15 million people and ranking as the number four cause of death. Most cases of emphysema and bronchitis are due to *smoking*.

Anyone can get emphysema, though it's a gradual-onset disease most often seen in older men. Severity increases with the amount of smoking and length of time one has been a smoker. In nonsmokers, emphysema is rare (though as many as 100,000 Americans may have an inherited form of emphysema due to deficiency of a specific protein).

In emphysema, the air sacs (alveoli) in the lungs overinflate as their walls break down, and the lungs can't do their respiratory job as well—their elasticity is impaired and the lungs are not able to transfer as much oxygen to the bloodstream. Some of the first symptoms are shortness of breath and a cough.

Unofficially...
There is no cure for emphysema, but researchers have been experimenting with drugs, such as metallo-proteinase inhibitors, that might help prevent some emphysema damage.

Treating emphysema typically includes a *mandate to quit smoking*. The American Lung Association calls kicking the habit the *single most important factor* for maintaining healthy lungs. Treatment may also include the use of prescription drugs, called *bronchodilators*, that relax and open airways, or antibiotics in the case of bacterial infection. Breathing exercises may be recommended, too. In severe cases, lung transplants or removal of damaged tissue in the lung may be necessary.

Some steps to help prevent worsening of emphysema noted by the American Lung Association include:

- Quitting smoking

- Getting proper nutrition, sleep, and exercise (for stamina and resistance to infection)

- Reducing your exposure to air pollution

- Consulting your doctor at the start of any cold or respiratory infection

While *emphysema* is inflammation of the air sacs in the lungs, *bronchitis* is inflammation of the lining of what connects your lungs to your windpipe—the bronchial tubes. Inflammation here reduces air flow to the lungs, and one result is the coughing up of heavy mucus.

You may get *acute bronchitis* with a serious cold, but *chronic bronchitis* occurs when the bronchial tubes have suffered irritation over a long time, such as daily onslaught of inhaled smoke from cigarettes. There is thickening of the bronchial tube lining, mucus is produced almost constantly, a persistent cough develops, and air flow can be reduced, endangering the lungs and leaving the bronchial tubes ripe for infection. Smoking also damages the small hairlike cells of the respiratory tract—known as *cilia,* making it harder to clear out mucus and other debris, further complicating chronic bronchitis.

About five percent of Americans have chronic bronchitis, making it the number seven chronic condition in the nation, according to the American Lung Association. More females than males seem to have it. Anyone can get it, but it's more common in those over 45. The most likely candidates for

Bright Idea
If you have emphysema, ask your doctor about getting flu and pneumonia vaccinations.

Moneysaver
Already quit smoking? A *room air cleaner* can help clear the air further. Look for the *Clean Air Delivery Rate (CADR)* seal to compare efficiency between units and see how powerful a device you need for your square footage.

chronic bronchitis are cigarette smokers. People who work around lots of dust or fumes—such as coal miners, grain handlers, or metal molders—also show increased risk.

If you think you may have chronic bronchitis, it's very important to *quit smoking immediately* and see your doctor now. Many people disregard it until the disease has progressed, and by the time they do see a doctor, serious damage to the respiratory system or the heart may have occurred.

The American Lung Association advises that anyone with chronic bronchitis should follow these rules for general good health:

- See your doctor or follow physician instructions at the start of a cold or other respiratory infection

- Quit smoking

- Follow a nutritious, well-balanced diet, maintain your ideal body weight, and get regular exercise

- Ask your doctor about getting influenza and pneumococcal pneumonia vaccination

- Avoid getting exposed to colds and the flu wherever you are and also avoid respiratory irritants like secondhand smoke, dust, and air pollution

Treatment of chronic bronchitis from smoking often has to do with reducing bronchial tube irritation. Bronchodilators are used to relax and open airways. Antibiotics are sometimes used in cases of acute infection. Chronic bronchitis may be disabling and advanced cases can require the daily use of a portable oxygen tank. Sufferers need to avoid air pollution and dusty conditions and *quit smoking*, as well as keep up their general health to reduce the likelihood of a respiratory infection.

Heart disease and stroke

Heart disease is *the* top killer of Americans, and *smoking* is a major risk factor—blamed for as many as 3 of 10 coronary heart disease deaths. Cigarettes almost *double* the risk of stroke.

These situations are linked—smoking creates havoc in the cardiovascular system, encouraging the clogging of arteries (or *atherosclerosis*, the top contributor to excess deaths from smoking). Clogged and compromised arteries cause circulatory problems, the most dramatic examples of which may be stroke and heart attack.

Heart disease is simply a broad term meaning an abnormal condition of the heart (or of the heart and circulation). Heart attack is its most visible sign, but certainly not the only one, happening when the blood supply to part of the heart muscle is reduced or stopped because of an obstruction, such as plaque or a clot, in the arteries that supply the heart. A *stroke* is a sudden reduction in or loss of consciousness, feeling, and voluntary motion that is caused by a rupture or obstruction in an artery of the brain.

In the case of coronary heart disease (which leads to heart attack), it appears the more you smoke, the more your risk rises. But it's a double-whammy since smoking seems to work synergistically with other heart disease risk factors, too. If you have high blood pressure, cigarette smoking exaggerates the risk factors of cardiovascular disease, according to a Scandinavian study in the *American Journal of Hypertension.*

There's good news—much of the heart risk posed by smoking is considered reversible. You can

Bright Idea
See an animation of how a heart attack occurs at www.heartpoint. com and check the rest of the HeartPoint Web site for good info about heart health.

Unofficially...
Sudden cardiac death is abrupt, unexpected, and is the unresuscitated loss of heart function (*cardiac arrest*), which is most often due to rapid or chaotic activity of the heart. It accounts for about a quarter million deaths among adults in the U.S. every year, according to the American Heart Association.

cut your danger of heart disease and stroke by quitting smoking. Stop now and your risk of heart attack and sudden death drops 50 percent right away. Quitting slows the progression of arterial blockages, which can improve with time.

Q: What if you've been a heavy smoker for a long time and wonder if quitting will do you any good?

A: According to the American Heart Association, benefits from quitting are seen in former smokers even after many years of heavy smoking.

Q: What if you already have symptoms of smoking-related diseases?

A: People already diagnosed with coronary heart disease have been found to cut by as much as *half* their risk of another heart attack, sudden cardiac death, and overall mortality.

According to the U.S. Surgeon General, smoking is the most important of the known modifiable risk factors for coronary heart disease. But you should pay particular attention to the wisdom of quitting smoking if you otherwise are in danger of heart disease. The major risk factors are:

- Cigarette and tobacco smoke

- High blood cholesterol

- High blood pressure

- Physical inactivity

- Obesity

- Diabetes

A family history of heart disease seems to significantly increase your risk. If you're a woman and you smoke, keep in mind that you greatly increase your risk of heart disease and stroke if you also use oral contraceptives (as compared to the risk run by non-smoking women who don't use birth control pills).

You can use the following checklist to look for some of the risk factors for heart attack and stroke in your own life.

Heart Attack and Stroke Risk Factors

_____ You are a man over 45 years old or a woman over 55 years old (or who has passed menopause or had your ovaries removed).

_____ You have a close blood relative who had a heart attack before age 55 (if father or brother) or before age 65 (if mother or sister).

_____ You have a close blood relative who had a brain attack (stroke).

_____ You smoke or live or work with people who smoke every day.

_____ Your total cholesterol level is 240 mg/dL or *higher* or your HDL ("good") cholesterol level is less than 35 mg/dL.

_____ Your blood pressure is 140/90 mm Hg or higher or you have been told that your blood pressure is too high.

_____ You get less than a total of 30 minutes of physical activity on at least 3 days per week.

_____ You are 20 pounds or more overweight.

_____ You have diabetes or need medicine to control your blood sugar.

_____ You have coronary artery disease or you have had a heart attack.

_____ A doctor said you have carotid artery disease or you have had a stroke.

_____ You have an abnormal heartbeat.

Source: American Heart Association.

Bright Idea
If you have risk factors at all, it's wise to discuss them with your physician. Learn more about heart attack and stroke at the American Heart Association Web site at www.americanheart.org or call (800) AHA-USA1.

Smokers of cigars or pipes appear to run higher risk of dying from heart disease (possibly stroke) than nonsmokers, but the risk is not thought to be as great as for cigarette smokers. But the American Heart Association notes that regular cigar smoking

Unofficially...
Some *circulatory disorders* are strongly linked to smoking. Peripheral vascular disease is a narrowing of leg arteries that can lead to blockage sometimes requiring limb amputation. Nine out of ten people who have the disease are smokers.

doubles risk of dying of all forms of cancer combined and of certain circulatory conditions, including heart damage that results from high blood pressure and *cardiomyopathy*—deterioration of the heart muscle.

Other smoking woes

Beyond the major diseases discussed already, smoking is linked to a number of conditions as different as slowed wound healing, infertility, and peptic ulcer disease. As the Action on Smoking and Health organization puts it, smoking has more than 50 ways of making life a misery through illness and more than 20 ways of killing you. It can be said that, generally, smokers endure poorer health than nonsmokers.

Then there's the one that male smokers (and their sex partners) may not want to hear—smoking is a risk factor for *impotence*. Perhaps you've seen anti-smoking television ads where a man in the company of a woman lights up a cigarette as a show of virility—and the cigarette immediately droops. That's the idea here.

Bright Idea
Only about half of current smokers say their doctor or other health-care professional encouraged them to quit. Bring up smoking concerns with your physician yourself and get a dialogue started.

According to a study at Britain's Bristol Heart Institute, smoking may cause *erectile dysfunction* in many different ways, including by adversely affecting blood flow in the penis. Researchers also note that quitting may restore or improve the ability to get an erection. In women, smoking has been found to hasten menopause. It is also a risk factor for osteoporosis. If you ever thought smoking was sexy, think again.

Smoking may make for reduced fertility in both women and men. One study found that women who smoked were 3.4 times more likely than nonsmokers to have taken more than a year to conceive a child. In male smokers, sperm density and motility was reduced, compared to nonsmokers.

The negative effects of smoking can be felt across the entire body. Some of the potentially debilitating medical conditions associated with smoking include those in the following table:

Timesaver
You can read more about the impact of smoking on fertility and pregnancy in Chapter 13, which is devoted to these issues.

SMOKING & DISEASE

Increased Risk for Smokers

Acute necrotizing ulcerative gingivitis (gum disease)	Macular degeneration (eyes, 2× risk)
Angina (20× risk)	Muscle injuries
Back pain	Neck pain
Buerger's Disease (severe circulatory disease)	Nystagmus (abnormal eye movements)
Duodenal ulcer	Ocular Histoplasmosis (fungal eye infection)
Cataract (2× risk)	Osteoporosis (in both sexes)
Cataract, posterior subcapsular (3× risk)	Osteoarthritis
Colon polyps	Penis (inability to have an erection)
Crohn's disease (chronic inflamed bowel)	Peripheral vascular disease
Depression	Pneumonia
Diabetes	Psoriasis (2× risk)
Hearing loss	Skin wrinkling (2× risk)
Influenza	Stomach ulcer
Impotence (2× risk)	Tendon injuries
Optic Neuropathy (loss of vision, 16× risk)	Tobacco Amblyopia (loss of vision)
Ligament injuries	Tooth loss
	Tuberculosis

Function Impaired in Smokers

Ejaculation (volume reduced)	Sperm count reduced
Fertility (30% lower in women)	Sperm motility impaired
Immune System (impaired)	Sperm less able to penetrate the ovum
Menopause (onset 1.74 years early on average)	Sperm shape abnormalities increased

Symptoms Worse in Smokers

Asthma	Chronic rhinitis (chronic inflammation of the nose)

SMOKING & DISEASE *(cont.)*

Symptoms Worse in Smokers

Diabetic retinopathy (eyes)	Multiple Sclerosis
Graves' disease (over-active thyroid gland)	Optic Neuritis (eyes)

Disease More Severe or Persistent in Smokers

Common cold	Pneumonia
Crohn's Disease (chronic inflamed bowel)	Tuberculosis
Influenza	

Source: "Smoking Statistics: Illness and Death"; Action on Smoking & Health, 1998.

If health is a serious reason why you want to quit, try looking up details about any of the illnesses above in a good medical encyclopedia whenever you feel the urge for a cigarette—it could help put off the craving.

Secondhand Health Risks

The issue of secondhand smoke is where the smoker's right to smoke runs headlong into non-smoker's right not to smoke. How big a deal is the purported health risk of just being in a room with smokers if you're not lighting up yourself?

It turns out the risk is pretty big. Secondhand smoke has been listed by the U.S. Environmental Protection Agency as a Group A known human carcinogen, putting it up there in the same category with asbestos, radon, benzene, and only a dozen other pollutants. In layman's terms, the EPA calls it responsible for about 3,000 lung cancer deaths among nonsmokers every year in the United States and 37,000 deaths from heart disease annually.

The 1993 EPA report on secondhand smoke has been instrumental in spurring clean indoor air laws around the U.S., however the tobacco industry has alleged the research is flawed. A federal judge in North Carolina in fact vacated several chapters of the EPA document "Respiratory Health Effects of Passive Smoking: Lung Cancer and Other Disorders."

The study is the basis for both the EPA's classification of secondhand smoke as a Group A carcinogen and its estimates that environmental tobacco smoke causes 3,000 lung cancer deaths in nonsmokers annually. According to the EPA, the court ruling—which is being challenged, was largely based on procedural grounds, and none of the findings concerning the serious respiratory health effects of secondhand smoke in children were challenged.

A number of studies show secondhand smoke can lead to lung cancer—for instance, Florida researchers found wives had a 60 percent overall increased risk of lung cancer from exposure to their husband's smoke.

How do you gauge whether someone has been exposed to secondhand smoke, and how much? There is one cancer-causing chemical out of 43, known as *NNK-1-butanone* (short for NNK 4-methyl-nitrosamino-1-butanone), which is thought to originate from only tobacco—it cannot be attributed to another source. At the University of Minnesota Cancer Center, a researcher has found traces of that carcinogen in the urine of nine nonsmokers who work in an area of a Canadian veterans hospital where smoking is allowed. This research is a step in the direction of accurately measuring how much exposure people have had to tobacco carcinogens.

Secondhand smoke packs a wallop in many of the same ways actual smoking does, beyond lung

Unofficially...
Secondhand smoke is sometimes called *environmental tobacco smoke (ETS),* and inhaling it is often described as *passive smoking* or *involuntary smoking.*

> **"**
> If a nonsmoker is around a person who smokes a pack of cigarettes during the day, the nonsmoker's exposure is so great that it's almost comparable to his or her smoking half of that pack of cigarettes.
> —Aubrey Taylor, Ph.D., American Heart Association
> **"**

cancer. A study at Wake Forest University (Winston-Salem, N.C.) in 1998 found dramatic, cumulative, and potentially irreversible effects of secondhand smoke on heart disease. According to the American Heart Association, it is the first study to link secondhand smoke to an important marker for heart problems—narrowing in the neck's carotid arteries indicating other blood vessels are similarly affected, including those in the heart.

There are some special situations where it may be particularly dangerous to smoke around others, such as when a pregnant mother smokes and puts her unborn baby at risk, and also when children are recipients of secondhand smoke. Smoking during pregnancy accounts for an estimated 20 to 30 percent of low birth-weight babies, as many as 14 percent of preterm deliveries, and about 10 percent of all infant deaths, according to the American Lung Association. You can read more about smoking—and quitting—as it relates to pregnancy and children in Chapter 13, which is devoted to the topic.

It is not enough to quit just while you are pregnant. Smoking by parents has been associated with a number of problems in their children—worsened asthma conditions, more colds and ear infections, and sudden infant death syndrome. According to the American Lung Association, between 150,000 and 300,000 lower respiratory tract infections in children under 18 months are caused by secondhand smoke, and a 1992 study found significant levels of cotinine, a major metabolite of nicotine, in the urine of hundreds of children exposed to smoke.

Some of the more immediately noticeable effects of exposure to secondhand smoke include those in the following lists.

EXPOSURE TO ENVIRONMENTAL TOBACCO SMOKE (SECONDHAND SMOKE)

Key Signs/Symptoms in Adults

Rhinitis/pharyngitis	Headache
Nasal congestion	Wheezing (bronchial constriction)
Persistent cough	
Conjunctival irritation	Exacerbation of chronic respiratory conditions

Key Signs/Symptoms in Infants and Children

Asthma onset	Persistent middle-ear effusion
Increased severity of or difficulty in controlling asthma	Snoring
	Repeated pneumonia, bronchitis
Frequent upper respiratory infections and/or episodes of otitis media	

Source: Indoor Air Pollution—An Introduction for Health Professionals.

It's often fairly easy to know when you're being exposed to secondhand smoke. As a rule of thumb, avoid it when possible and at least take whatever steps you can to seek good ventilation—fresh air—when secondhand smoke is unavoidable. Chapter 3 talks more about the push to ban smoking in public areas, and Chapter 17—the last chapter in the book—looks at how you can deal with secondhand smoke as a new nonsmoker yourself.

Which cigarette ingredients are so bad

Most smokers have probably heard about the dangers of tar and nicotine, at least in passing, but have you ever wondered what exactly in your cigarettes is doing the damage? About 4,000 chemicals have been identified in cigarette smoke, though only a relatively small percentage has been found related to specific health risks. More than 40 are carcinogens, and many spur havoc in the respiratory system.

Watch Out! Secondhand smoke is a widespread problem. About 37 percent of nonsmoking adults are exposed at home or work, and 43 percent of children (ages 2 months to 11 years) are exposed at home, according to the American Heart Association.

Unofficially...
"Sidestream smoke" comes from the burning tip of a cigarette and "mainstream smoke" from the end that is put in the mouth.

Among the many ingredients identified in the chemical cocktail of a cigarette are the pesticide DDT, the poison arsenic, and the toxic preservative formaldehyde. Smoke coming from the burning end of a cigarette has been found to contain the dangerous ingredients shown in the table on the following page.

About 85 percent of the smoke in a room comes from the burning end of a cigarette, not the end the smoker is inhaling directly. This smoke carries many toxins in *greater* concentration.

Tar

Tar is one of the toxic substances in cigarettes that can cause cancer, as well as hurt your lungs and cause breathing problems. It's a brown, sticky substance that winds up being deposited in your lungs and other areas of your respiratory system where it is gradually absorbed by the body. It is what stains smokers' teeth and fingertips.

Tar is actually a chemical cocktail all on its own, made up of chemicals that can be toxic on their own:

- Formaldehyde
- Arsenic
- Cyanide
- Benzopyrene
- Benzene
- Toluene
- Acrolein

A substance in cigarette tar, benzopyrene diol epoxide (BPDE for short), has been found to damage DNA in a tumor-suppressing gene. That's one cellular link between smoking and lung cancer.

TOXIC AND CARCINOGENIC AGENTS
IN UNDILUTED SIDESTREAM SMOKE

Ingredient	Toxicity & Carcinogenicity
Carbon Monoxide	T
Carbonyl Sulfide	T
Benzene	C
Formaldehyde	C
3-Vinylpyridine	SC
Hydrogen Cyanide	T
Hydrazine	C
Nitrogen Oxides	T
N-Nitrosodemethylamine	C
N-Nitrosylpyrrolidine	C
Tar	C
Nicotine	T
Phenol	TP
Catechol	CoC
o-Toluidine	C
2-Naphthylamine	C
4-Aminobiphenyl	C
Benzanthracene	C
Benzopyrene	C
Quinoline	C
N-Nitrosonornicotine	C
NNK	C
N-Nitrosodiethanolamine	C
Cadmium	C
Nickel	C
Polonium-210	C

Key:
C = Carcinogenic
CoC = Cocarcinogenic
SC = Suspected Carcinogen
T = Toxic
TP = Tumor Promoter

Source: NIOSH Current Intelligence Bulletin 54, "Environmental Tobacco Smoke in the Workplace," June 1991, National Institute for Occupational Safety and Health.

← A *co-carcinogen* is an agent able to cause cancer when combined with another substance. A *tumor promoter* is something that can increase the sensitivity of tumor formation after a *primary carcinogen* has been introduced.

Watch Out!
According to a 1998 Gallup survey, two-thirds of smokers believe they are likely to die of a smoking-related disease if they do not quit.

Nicotine

Cigarettes contain *nicotine*. It has been described as their major pharmacologically active substance and is the main addictive substance they contain, though scientists are looking for other things in cigarettes that may also get you hooked. Nicotine is a *psychoactive* drug that affects the brain, the skeletal muscles, the cardiovascular system, and other systems throughout the body.

When nicotine is inhaled in cigarette smoke, it is absorbed into the lungs and then rapidly enters the bloodstream. Once there, it can cross the blood-brain barrier where it's rapidly distributed. Once you've inhaled, nicotine can reach the brain in 11 seconds or less.

In the brain, nicotine creates effects by binding to receptors in the brain that are intended to receive the neurotransmitter acetylcholine. When activated by nicotine, they cause the release of other chemicals in the brain that produce effects on mood, alertness, and possibly cognition. Nicotine stimulates the release of dopamine in the brain, which is a major pleasure-regulating neurotransmitter. Continuing to use nicotine leads to an increase in the number of receptors that can bind to nicotine and literally changes the electrical and metabolic activity of the brain.

The nicotine in cigarettes also increases your chances of getting heart disease. It is a suspected cause of neural birth defects and, in large quantity, is considered poisonous. It stimulates your central nervous system, increasing heart rate and blood pressure, when taken in low doses. Higher doses slow heart rate. Depending on the circumstances, nicotine from cigarette smoking can stimulate or soothe—for instance, the former in times of boredom or the latter when one is under stress. These effects have been measured by electroencephalographic (EEG) analysis.

Gases

When you smoke, you take in carbon monoxide, the same gas that could kill you if you left the car motor running in a closed garage. Carbon monoxide reduces the amount of oxygen in your bloodstream and tissues because it binds to hemoglobin in the blood more easily than oxygen, basically replacing it. It is one of the tobacco smoke constituents most likely to contribute to the development of heart disease.

Actually, cigarette smoke can be divided into two types of constituents—those in the particulate phase, like tar and nicotine, and those in the gas phase, which includes the following, among others:

- Carbon monoxide
- Ammonia
- Dimethylnitrosamine
- Formaldehyde
- Hydrogen cyanide
- Acrolein

Some of the gases in cigarette smoke are irritants, and dozens (including benzopyrene and dimethylnitrosamine) have been shown to cause cancer or worsen other ailments. For instance, nitrogen oxides contribute to acute and chronic obstructive pulmonary diseases and emphysema.

What makes smoking addictive?

So nicotine is the main physically addictive substance in cigarettes—but how does the addiction work? When you inhale smoke from a cigarette, I mentioned the nicotine it contains quickly enters your bloodstream through the lungs—more quickly than, say, if you were wearing a nicotine patch. From there, nicotine does a lot to moderate stress and produce pleasure. In essence, some people who smoke are self-medicating without even knowing it, taking nicotine to treat their edginess or depression.

The pathway through which nicotine lifts the spirits is believed to be the pathway by which it is physically addictive—through *dopamine*. Dopamine is a major pleasure-oriented brain chemical—it plays a big role in creating feelings of bliss, such as when you are "falling in love."

Recent research by American, French, and Swedish scientists has found that drugs of abuse, such as nicotine (or alcohol, cocaine, or heroin, and so on), appear to increase levels of the neurotransmitter dopamine in a similar route in the brain. Put simply, they may have found the exact way addiction to nicotine is tied to the production of pleasurable sensations in your body (this knowledge may help in the development of medications to treat nicotine addiction).

As nicotine enters the blood stream and spurs the elevation of dopamine levels, the smoker begins to feel pleasure. The problem—and the addiction—is that taking away this pleasure-boost (such as when you try to quit smoking) decreases the dopamine pathway's sensitivity to pleasure sensations. In other words, it's harder to feel jazzed about anything.

When you don't get a regular smoke, you begin to go through withdrawal and can experience changes in:

Unofficially...
Dopamine levels that are too low are associated with the tremors of Parkinson's Disease, while too-high levels are sometimes implicated in mental and emotional disorders.

- Body temperature
- Heart rate
- Digestion
- Muscle tone
- Appetite

You can also experience specific withdrawal symptoms, such as:

- Irritability
- Anxiety
- Sleep disturbance
- Nervousness
- Headache
- Fatigue
- Nausea
- Depression
- Tobacco cravings

Put simply, the more you take in nicotine, the more you want it and the less effect it has, so the more your body thinks it needs.

Are there any pluses from smoking?

You may have heard about a cancer study that both surprised and embarrassed the researchers who conducted it—the results certainly made news. Smoking cigarettes apparently reduced the risk of breast cancer in some women—those with an unusual gene mutation. That's no reason to smoke, regardless of your breast cancer risk, though the study's unexpected results may help researchers develop an appropriate treatment for those with the gene mutation in question—about 1 in every 250 women.

Watch Out!
According to the U.S. Centers for Disease Control and Prevention, there is no safe tobacco product. The use of any—including cigarettes, cigars, pipes, and chewing tobacco or mentholated, "low-tar," "naturally grown," or "additive-free" cigarettes—can cause cancer and other adverse health effects.

The study, published in the *Journal of the National Cancer Institute,* looked at what aspects of lifestyle could affect cancer development in these women, who have a high risk of developing breast cancer. Researchers discovered breast cancer among the heavy smokers in the group was 54 percent lower than among those in the group who didn't smoke, and the more a woman smoked, the less likely she was to develop breast cancer.

Why? Researchers think a compound in cigarettes interferes with how a woman's body uses estrogen—a necessary hormone that is tied to breast cancer development. (There are estrogen-modifying treatments available for women with breast cancer that do not have the same health risks as cigarettes!)

Why is this study significant? Women should take heed that while this research suggests smoking may interfere with estrogen in breast tissue, there could be estrogen-interfering ramifications for the rest of the body. And adequate estrogen is vitally important for fertility, your bones, and a host of other things—even maintaining the healthy appearance of your skin.

Prolonged smoking seems to reduce risk in certain other diseases—but they are few and far between, well-outweighed by the increased risk of other ailments from smoking. One of the diseases with such a negative risk correlation is Parkinson's disease, which produces uncontrollable tremors and movements and progressive muscle stiffness, and which is intimately tied to brain dopamine levels (which, if you recall, are greatly affected by nicotine).

According to a 1992 study, a history of smoking up to 20 years earlier was associated with a risk of developing Parkinson's disease about half that in nonsmokers. Other studies that have looked at the lesser risk in smokers note theories on why this may be: Perhaps a genetic predisposition that increases the risk for Parkinson's disease (such as defective detoxification enzymes) might also decrease the likelihood of smoking; or inherently lower dopamine levels in those predestined to get Parkinson's could cause them to be less prone to addiction; or in the case of Parkinson's, smoking may simply be neuroprotective.

Oddly enough, a similar situation exists with Alzheimer's Disease. According to a 1991 study in the Netherlands, risk of Alzheimer's disease decreased with an increasing daily number of cigarettes smoked (before the onset of the disease). Nicotine is thought possibly to play a role in the risk reduction for both Alzheimer's disease and Parkinson's disease. This knowledge helps researchers looking into these ailments, but it's no reason to smoke, given the huge risk it poses in other categories.

Smoking's cumulative effects

The life costs of smoking are huge. In the U.S. alone, smoking-related diseases kill more than 430,000 Americans annually. And it's not just the smokers who are included in that number—some are babies born prematurely because their mothers smoked, and some are victims of the very real dangers of secondhand smoke. The dollar cost of smoking is daunting as well—first-hand smoke costs the U.S. an estimated $97.2 billion a year in health-care costs and lost productivity.

The biggest cost is to the individual who finds his or her life impaired—or lost—because of smoking.

Unofficially...
Who smokes? Roughly 1 in 3 people aged 15 and older worldwide, according to the World Health Organization. About 47 percent of men smoke and 12 percent of women.

How much do you really know about the risks? Try the following quiz.

1. Smoking deaths in the U.S. are highest in which two disease categories?
   a. Stroke and Parkinson's disease
   b. Chronic lung disease and lung cancer
   c. Lung cancer and coronary heart disease
   d. Alzheimer's disease and coronary heart disease

2. Nicotine reduces fertility in females but cannot hasten menopause.
   TRUE or FALSE

3. Lifestyle changes can reduce risk of getting cancer.
   TRUE or FALSE

4. Smoking cigarettes can do what to your risk of a stroke?
   a. Increase it by 16 percent
   b. Almost double it
   c. Oddly, reduce it
   d. None of the above

Answers: 1. c; 2. False (it reduces fertility and can hasten menopause); 3. True; 4. b.

According to the American Lung Association, tobacco as a risk factor is expected to make a bigger claim on health worldwide than any one disease. It is estimated to kill 3.5 million people around the world every year, with the death toll rising to 10 million annually by the early 2020s or 2030s—about the current population of the greater Los Angeles area.

Multiple whammies

Smoking may be reducing your intake of fresh air, but no one's living in a vacuum—that is, tobacco may not be the only risk factor you've got going. Smoking can have a detrimental impact on a host of other illnesses, such as by exacerbating heart risk if you have high blood pressure.

Smoking can also combine with other, rarer risk factors, such as these environmental examples, to greatly increase your chances of illness. Radon, for example, is a colorless, odorless gas and the second leading cause of lung cancer (after smoking). Exposure to radon and tobacco smoke is synergistic, and some scientists believe the increased risk to smokers or former smokers is as great as 10 to 20 fold over someone who has never smoked. In cases of exposure to asbestos, a carcinogen, exposure to tobacco smoke is thought to raise lung cancer risk about five fold.

What are my odds?

How likely are you to die from smoking? On average, smokers die about seven years earlier than non-smokers. If you're a man who smokes 10 or more cigarettes daily for a quarter century, you could face an 80 percent higher likelihood of dying from heart disease or lung cancer (if it's less than 10 a day, you could face a 30 percent higher risk). The following figure shows an approximate comparison between smoking deaths and other causes of death.

Lung cancer kills more women every year than any other type of cancer, and females 35 and over are a dozen times more likely to die prematurely from lung cancer if they smoke, according to the American Lung Association.

It has been said that smoking is a major cause of statistics, but every statistic boils down to an individual, human bottom line:

My father had a three-pack-a-day cigarette habit. He started smoking when he was 15 years old and smoked the last day he was conscious. While I was growing up, we lived in a house

Bright Idea
Check out *Tobacco Explored*, a well-illustrated interactive "game" about the supply, demand, and consequences of smoking, at the Web site of Action on Smoking and Health (www.ash. org.uk).

Actual causes of death.

➡

Percentages are for United States, 1990. The percentages used in this figure are composite approximations derived from published scientific studies that attributed deaths to these causes. Source: Centers for Disease Control and McGinnis JM, Foege WH. Actual causes of death in the United States. JAMA 1993; 270:2207-12.

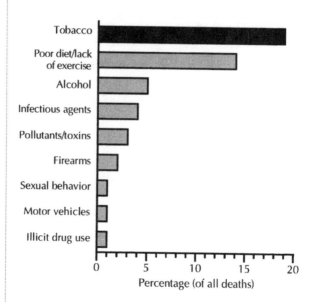

where my bedroom was just off the kitchen. He would wake up before I did, come out into the kitchen, light a cigarette, and start making his coffee. We lived in that house for 16 years, and the first thing I remember hearing every morning was the sound of him coughing that smokers' cough, and then the sound and the smell of the butane lighter flicking on and him lighting another cigarette.

These and others are powerful memories. I spent a lot of effort in my mid-twenties to mid-thirties sorting out these memories and their myriad of effects on me.

According to the American Cancer Society, every year, three million people die of smoking worldwide. If each of these smoker's lives and deaths affected one or two other people, that is a lot of people like me with strong memories and emotions, love, anger, and grief.

Nancy Garman's memories of her father led her to start a fledgling Web site, www.remembrance.org, in commemoration of him and for others to post to, remembering loved ones who died because they smoked. If everyone in the world had access to her Web site and wanted to, a remembrance for a new casualty of smoking-related disease could theoretically be posted every 10 seconds (the annual tobacco-related toll amounting to more than three million people a year, according to the World Health Organization)!

Just the facts

- Nicotine is the major addictive component of cigarettes.

- Tobacco use is a risk factor for at least 25 different diseases.

- Smoking can cause cancer, heart and lung disease, and stroke, among other ailments.

- Smokers die about seven years earlier than nonsmokers, on average.

GET THE SCOOP ON...
Who lit up way back when (and why) ▪ How we
found out it's dangerous ▪ The impact of all
these tobacco lawsuits ▪ All the ways
we've been trying to quit

An Unofficial History of Smoking (and Kicking the Habit)

Chapter 3

Smoking through the ages

An article in *New Scientist* magazine once described smoking as an epidemic *of medieval proportions*. But, ironically, smoking appears to have started out as something you did *for* your health. Nevermind that today, smoking-related diseases kill more people annually than the *Black Death did* during any one year of its four-year rampage through fourteenth-century Europe (half again as many by some accounts).

Tobacco's roots may go back as far as 6,000 B.C., when the first such plants are thought to have sprung up somewhere in the Americas. Around the time when B.C. changed into A.D., natives of the Americas started using tobacco for a variety of medicinal and religious purposes. It was thought to be a panacea and was used to treat wounds and as an anesthetic. Chewing tobacco may have had its start as a toothache remedy.

Centuries passed and then, just as Marco Polo brought spices from faraway lands to Europe, explorers to the New World discovered and delighted in tobacco. They found that the natives in Cuba, Mexico, and Central and South America smoked twisted bunches of tobacco leaves wrapped in dried palm leaves or corn husks. The Mayan word for smoking—*sik'ar*—is thought to have been adapted by the Spaniards as *cigarro*, out of which we get *cigar* and *cigarette*.

In 1492, when Christopher Columbus sailed the ocean blue and arrived in America, the natives offered him dried tobacco leaves as a gift. Sailors brought tobacco back to Europe where its popularity as a medicine sprouted since it was thought an excellent treatment for maladies from cancer to bad breath, ironically enough. Nicolas Monardes, a Spanish physician of the sixteenth century, included tobacco among the medicinal plants recovered from the New World and claimed it could cure 36 health problems.

Soon afterward, cigar smoking grew to popularity in Spain. It held smoky court as a status symbol in that country, and the allure eventually caught on in other European countries. There is some evidence to suggest that in the latter 1500s, recreational smoking was catching on in England, courtesy of the country's sailors, who were exposed to the Spanish custom (which was also becoming a Portuguese, French, and Flemish custom).

Tobacco was first classified by European botanists of the day under the genus *hyoscyamus* or *henbane*, while the French named it after their ambassador Jean Nicot, who had introduced them to it. And so it was known as *nicotiane*, and that terminology was by

Unofficially...
Tobacco is from the same plant family as peppers, poison nightshades, and the potato.

the end of the 1500s accepted as the scientific name, according to the notes of Elizabeth Wyckoff for the New York Public Library exhibition "Dry Drunk: The Culture of Tobacco in 17th- and 18th-century Europe." Eventually, nicotine was officially adopted as the name for tobacco's major psychoactive alkaloid (which wasn't isolated and identified until the late 1820s). Tobacco has also been called by the Native American names *petun(m)* and *picietl*, as well as *the divine* or *holy herb*, *the Queen's herb*, and *herba panaceam*, so esteemed was its repute.

Timesaver
View "Dry Drunk" tobacco history among the New York Public Library's digital collections on the Internet at digital.nypl.org.

Variants of the word *tabaco* were also widely adopted. It is a Native American term that probably identifies one of the instruments through which tobacco was traditionally consumed, according to Wyckoff. Early smokers were sometimes called *tobacconists*.

Tobacco use in the United States is thought to have developed as New England was being settled. When English explorer Sir Francis Drake returned from Virginia to his homeland in 1586 with colonists in tow, he brought back tobacco plants and pipes. Sir Walter Raleigh, who was the first Englishman to establish an American colony, also brought stores of tobacco back to England and helped set the trend there. But the first person to introduce tobacco to England is thought, by some accounts, to have been either Sir John Hawkins around 1564 or 1565, or Raleigh's employee, the mathematician Thomas Hariot, who is also credited with bringing the potato to Europe.

Hariot wrote *A Briefe and True Report of the New Found Land of Virginia* in 1588 and therein described tobacco in a list of salable goods from the New World:

> *There is an herb which is sowed apart by it*
> *self & is called by the inhabitants* vppówoc....
> *The leaves thereof being dried and brought into*
> *powder: they use to take the fume or smoke*
> *thereof by sucking it through pipes made of clay*
> *into their stomach and head; from whence it*
> *purgeth superfluous phlegm & other gross*
> *humors, openeth all the pores & passages of the*
> *body.*

Hariot described tobacco as of such precious estimation among the natives that "they think their gods are marvelously delighted therewith." He described hallowed fires and tobacco sacrifices—to win divine appeasement and give thanks for escape from danger, conducted amid ceremonial ritual, dancing, and chanting. He also described taking tobacco himself:

> *We ourselves during the time we were there*
> *used to suck it after their manner, as also since*
> *our return, and have found many rare and*
> *wonderful experiments of the virtues thereof; of*
> *which the relation would require a volume by*
> *itself. The use of it by so many of late, men and*
> *women of great calling as else, and some*
> *learned physicians also, is sufficient witness.*

The custom of the time was to drink tobacco smoke, by inhaling and then swallowing it. Indeed, to a great extent, imbibing was thought to spur a kind of drunkenness. Hariot did suggest taking tobacco by smoking it, exhaling through the nostrils. Incidentally, he is reported to have died of nose cancer. Quitting may also have had its roots around this time, as some dangerous effects of smoking tobacco were beginning to be noticed. Sir Francis Bacon observed in 1610 that trying to quit was difficult, and by 1632, just a dozen years after the arrival of the Mayflower, public smoking was illegal in Massachusetts for moral reasons.

There is no doubt that tobacco had gained in popularity. Tobacco was so much in use during the seventeenth century that it was often used as money. Rather than being smoked in the proverbial peace pipe of the American Indians, in the next century, tobacco actually comprised a war chest—American tobacco was used as collateral to back up French loans financing the Revolutionary War. This same century saw the rise of the first official tobacco firm in the British colonies, as Pierre Lorillard opened the P. Lorillard Company in New York City for the processing of tobacco, cigars, and snuff. His company is still in business.

For the first three centuries of its European heyday, pipes were frequently used to ingest tobacco smoke, with the old Native American method of taking tobacco as *snuff* catching on during the seventeenth and eighteenth centuries and cigars, which had also been around earlier, becoming a phenomenon of the nineteenth century.

As time passed, scientists began taking a closer look at tobacco and taking heed of its potential dangers. In the late 1820s they discovered the pure form of nicotine and shortly thereafter described it as a dangerous poison, as tobacco was thus similarly described. But the tobacco industry kept growing.

And Europe was being introduced to tobacco from another front. Shortly before the midpoint of the nineteenth century, a British company named Phillip Morris began selling hand-rolled Turkish

Unofficially...
During the 1950s, Lorillard marketed Kent cigarettes with asbestos filters. Scientific data at the time showed they helped cut tar. But cases have gone to court involving the filters and mesothelioma, a rare asbestos-linked form of lung cancer.

Bright Idea
For a sarcastic
look at cigarette
advertising of
decades past,
check the
Web site
www.chickenhead.
com.

cigarettes, which caught on in Europe during the Crimean War in the 1850s. Phillip Morris would grow to become the world's largest tobacco business, controlling roughly half the U.S. market for tobacco and owning what has been described as the second most valuable brand name on the planet: Marlboro.

Cigarettes had still not become the dominant form of tobacco use, and during the 1800s in the U.S., they were reportedly made largely with the leftovers of tobacco processing. Instead of cigarettes, it was chewing tobacco that had become popular, a hallmark of the rough-and-tumble American West, of the cowboy, of the literal "Marlboro man."

With the advent of the twentieth century came the dawn of smoking's golden days. It became the main way to take in tobacco. At the turn of the century, cigars were tops. For every five cigars sold, only three cigarettes were bought. Those tables would eventually turn, and as the popularity of cigarettes grew during the early twentieth century, so did the backlash against all forms of tobacco. Some states even proposed banning tobacco altogether. The NonSmokers' Protective League of America was up and running, extolling the right of each person to breathe and enjoy fresh and pure air uncontaminated by tobacco odors and fumes.

But the demand for cigarettes escalated wildly during the first World War when they became known as the "soldier's smoke." In the next decade, during the Flapper era, cigarette marketing to women began in earnest, with he-man ads giving way to a smooth, silky, sophisticated tone for the gals. From the mid-1920s through the mid-1930s, smoking rates among teenage girls tripled. By the time World War II was in full swing, cigarette sales had exploded—the smoke sticks so ubiquitous as to be included in a soldier's C-rations (like food), with tobacco companies providing millions of cigarettes free to American soldiers overseas.

By the 1950s, links to lung cancer were surfacing, though they were downplayed and denied by the tobacco industry, despite the existence of internal documents discussing potential dangers. These documents later became ammunition in litigation against the tobacco industry. For instance, Pennsylvania's attorney general notes in the complaint of a 1997 lawsuit that back in 1946, a scientist for the Lorillard tobacco company, H.B. Parmele, wrote a memo saying:

> *Certain scientists and medical authorities have claimed for many years that the use of tobacco contributes to cancer development in susceptible people. Just enough evidence has been presented to justify the possibility of such a presumption.*

Though the Surgeon General's landmark report on the dangers of smoking wouldn't be issued for more than another decade, purportedly "safer" cigarettes were coming about in response to a new health consciousness. They sported lower tar and filters. Unfortunately, some of these filters were made from asbestos, of all things, which had been touted as a "material of the future" and as the "magic mineral" at the New York World's Fair of 1939. Asbestos wouldn't be identified by the Environmental Protection Agency as a hazardous pollutant itself until 1971. It can cause lung cancer and other diseases, particularly when asbestos fibers are inhaled.

Unofficially...
Though asbestos use has been promoted throughout much of the twentieth century, reports of suspected asbestos-related injury have been traced back at least as far as 1899.

(Originally intended as a building insulation material, its use in cigarette filters and in hair dryers sounds particularly ill-advised.)

In 1953, tar was found to cause tumors when applied to the backs of mice, and eleven years later, U.S. Surgeon General Luther L. Terry released a landmark report on Smoking and Health. This was the first substantial official American government recognition that smoking causes cancers and other serious diseases, and the advisory committee behind the report declared:

> *Cigarette smoking is a health hazard of sufficient importance in the United States to warrant appropriate remedial action.*

The government knew the 1964 report would be earthshaking—reportedly it was purposely released on a quiet Saturday morning to guard against mayhem on Wall Street, at a State Department auditorium with good security. The report was issued at a sensitive time in modern American history— President John F. Kennedy had been assassinated less than two months earlier.

With the issuance of this report, regulation of the sale and advertisement of cigarettes began in earnest. Congress adopted the Federal Cigarette Labeling and Advertising Act in 1965 and the Public Health Cigarette Smoking Act in 1969. This legislation slapped health warnings on cigarette packs and stripped cigarette ads from the airwaves. It called for a yearly report on what the health consequences of smoking were. It wasn't long until the big tobacco companies started branching out into other, purportedly safer industries, and the largest firms are still well-diversified today.

In 1972 all passenger airlines were required to have separate smoking and nonsmoking sections on their flights. More than a decade and a half later, smoking would be prohibited on short domestic flights, and by the spring of 1999, 97 percent of all flights to and from the United States would be smoke-free.

According to the Department of Transportation, all U.S. air carriers have now banned smoking systemwide. Smoking is prohibited by statute on nearly all U.S. domestic flights, and is prohibited by international agreement on nonstop flights operated by Australian, Canadian, New Zealand, and U.S. carriers between their territories. Foreign carriers are increasingly going smoke-free—more than 50 have enacted complete smoking bans.

But do nonsmoking flights mean hostile passengers? In the wake of an apparent dramatic increase in so-called "air rage" incidents, airline officials have been quoted as saying that many of the instances, even a preponderance, have to do with smoking prohibitions. What to do about passengers going through nicotine withdrawals on a long flight on which they're not allowed to light up? Pilots have suggested that smokers carry nicotine gum or patches with them when traveling, and that these items could potentially be provided on request by flight attendants.

In 1982, another pivotal Surgeon General's report was issued, stating that secondhand smoke may cause lung cancer. By the middle of the decade, lung cancer had surpassed breast cancer as the top fatal cancer in women. Throughout the 1980s, lawsuits related to the harmful effects of smoking began to trickle in, and smoking was increasingly

Unofficially...
About 30 years ago the non-nicotine, non-tobacco cigarette *Bravo* was introduced. Made largely of lettuce, it didn't catch on. The brand recently came back on the scene, no doubt in hopes smokers will turn over a new leaf this time.

banned in public places. In 1988, the Surgeon General declared nicotine an addictive drug.

The push to persuade smokers to save themselves is worldwide. From 1970 to 1995, the World Health Assembly adopted 14 resolutions, which, taken together, strongly urge Member States to implement comprehensive tobacco control measures.

Back in 1996 the Food and Drug Administration began regulating cigarettes and smokeless tobacco products as drugs. But cigars weren't included— they have historically come under fewer federal government regulations than cigarettes and smokeless tobacco. For instance, warning labels are not required on cigars, whereas they are required on cigarettes and smokeless tobacco, even though cigars carry sizable health risks. The Federal Trade Commission recently recommended to Congress that warning labels be required for cigars as they are with other tobacco products.

Public health officials are proud of how anti-smoking efforts have turned out, particularly given that tobacco is addictive and that there are major economic forces promoting its use. In the mid-1990s, the Centers for Disease Control and Prevention estimated that while 48 million American adults were smokers, approximately 42 million more would have smoked without smoking prevention campaigns. Case in point is Florida's comprehensive anti-tobacco campaign, deemed effective in reducing teen tobacco use. The campaign combines media counter-marketing, community-based activities, education and training, plus an enforcement program. Tobacco use in Florida among middle school students declined from

18.5 percent to 15.0 percent and among high school students from 27.4 percent to 25.2 percent between 1998 and 1999.

Who smokes in America

Just how many smokers are there in the United States? The number runs close to the combined populations of California and New York, the two most populous states in the Union. As noted in Chapter 1, about 50 million of us are smokers—nearly one out of every four people. The percentages are close no matter what age group, but more men smoke than women—25.5 percent compared to 21.3 percent. There are also some differences depending on where you live and socioeconomic factors.

Where are you most likely to find a smoker? Kentucky, a lush green land of 88,000 farms and prize horses where, according to 1997 figures, almost 31 percent of adults smoke and fully 47 percent of youths do. It should be no surprise, since Kentucky ranks among the very top tobacco-producing states in the nation.

Where is smoking at its lowest ebb? Also, not surprisingly, in Utah, where conservative Mormon pressure against tobacco has pressed smoking down to under 14 percent of the adult population, less than half the smoking rate seen in Kentucky. Among youths, the difference is even more dramatic, with about a third the proportion of Utah kids and teens partaking (16 percent) as compared to Kentucky, which, by the way, sold a whopping 186.8 cigarette packs per person in 1997.

You're most likely to smoke if you live in:

1. Kentucky
2. Missouri

Watch Out! Remember to think about your community's history and acceptance of tobacco among the temptation factors you'll have to deal with when quitting.

3. Arkansas

4. Nevada

5. West Virginia

You are least likely to smoke if you reside in:

1. Utah

2. California

3. Hawaii

4. District of Columbia

5. Idaho

PREVALENCE OF CIGARETTE SMOKING AMONG ADULTS AND YOUTHS—UNITED STATES, 1997

State	Adults	Youth
Alabama	24.7	35.8
Alaska	26.7	n/a
Arizona	21.1	n/a
Arkansas	28.5	43.2
California	18.4	26.6*
Colorado	22.6	36.6*
Connecticut	21.8	35.2
Delaware	26.6	35.0*
District of Columbia	18.8	22.7
Florida	23.6	33.6*
Georgia	22.4	n/a
Hawaii	18.6	29.2
Idaho	19.9	n/a
Illinois	23.2	n/a
Indiana	26.3	n/a
Iowa	23.1	37.5
Kansas	22.7	n/a
Kentucky	30.8	47.0
Louisiana	24.6	36.4
Maine	22.7	39.2
Maryland	20.6	n/a
Massachusetts	20.4	34.4

State	Adults	Youth
Michigan	26.1	38.2
Minnesota	21.8	n/a
Mississippi	23.2	31.3
Missouri	28.7	40.3
Montana	20.5	38.1
Nebraska	22.2	n/a
Nevada	27.7	29.4
New Hampshire	24.8	39.6*
New Jersey	21.5	37.9*
New Mexico	22.1	n/a
New York	23.1	32.9
North Carolina	25.8	35.8*
North Dakota	22.2	45.0*
Ohio	25.1	34.5
Oklahoma	24.6	n/a
Oregon	20.7	n/a
Pennsylvania	24.3	n/a
Rhode Island	24.2	35.4
South Carolina	23.4	38.6
South Dakota	24.3	44.0
Tennessee	26.9	38.6*
Texas	22.6	n/a
Utah	13.7	16.4
Vermont	23.2	38.3
Virginia	24.6	n/a
Washington	23.9	n/a
West Virginia	27.4	41.9
Wisconsin	23.2	36.0
Wyoming	24.0	37.4
United States	**23.2**	**36.4**

Source: Centers for Disease Control.

The use of smokeless tobacco is highest among men in West Virginia (18.4 percent), followed by men in Wyoming (14.7 percent).

Canadian smoking rates have declined over recent decades and vary somewhat by province. In the mid-1960s about every other Canadian was a smoker. But by the mid-1990s, the rate dropped to not quite one in three (31 percent of men and 28 percent of women). The highest rates of smoking are seen in Quebec (34 percent) and the lowest in British Columbia (25.5 percent), according to 1996 government figures.

Smokers of color

Statistically speaking, if you're a member of one or another minority group in the U.S., you might be more likely to smoke. American Indians and Alaska Natives have the highest rates of tobacco use. African-American and Southeast Asian men also smoke a lot on the whole, while Asian-American women and Hispanic women smoke the least. The following figure takes a comparative look at how smoking among different ethnic groups in the U.S. is changing.

How smoking affects different ethnic groups.

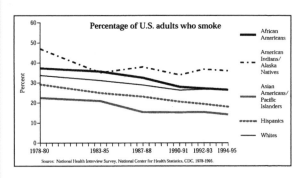

Taking a simpler look at the proportion of smokers in America's minority populations (according to 1995 data):

- African Americans: 26.5 percent
- American Indians and Alaska Natives: 39.2 percent
- Asian Americans and Pacific Islanders: 15.3 percent
- Hispanics: 18.9 percent

While African Americans are currently less likely to smoke than are whites in this country, you can see that it hasn't always been the case and may not always be the case. Cigarette smoking among African-American teens has increased 80 percent over the last six years—three times as fast as among white teens according to the Surgeon General's 1998 report on smoking and minorities (during the 1970s and 1980s, smoking among African-American youths had shown an admirable decline). This new upswing is literally cause for alarm, the Surgeon General says, describing the situation as "a time-bomb" for minority health with "severe health consequences" that will start to be felt in the early 2000s.

Tobacco companies have received a lot of negative press for vigorously marketing toward minorities and youths, but is that the reason for any increases in smoking among either? According to the Surgeon General, no single factor determines patterns of tobacco use among ethnic minority groups, and, instead, the smoking patterns "are the result of complex interactions of multiple factors, such as socioeconomic status, cultural characteristics, acculturation, stress, biological elements, targeted advertising, price of tobacco products, and varying capacities of communities to mount effective tobacco control initiatives."

> **❝**
> We are witnessing the first steps of a potentially tragic reversal for the health of American minorities...we now see striking increases in smoking by minority youth. Unless we can reverse these trends, they are bound to result in more lung disease and early death.
> —Dr. David Satcher, Surgeon General of the United States
> **❞**

Bright Idea
If you're interested in reading the Surgeon General's 1998 report on smoking among minorities, you can find it on the Internet at www.cdc.gov.

Researchers found other notable points that describe likelihood of smoking among different cultural or racial groups, such as:

- **African Americans.** Declines in smoking have been greater among African-American men with at least a high school education than among those with less education.

- **American Indians and Alaska Natives.** Many tribes consider tobacco a sacred gift and still use it during religious ceremonies and as traditional medicine, but the tobacco-related health problems this group suffers are caused by chronic cigarette smoking and the use of spit tobacco.

- **Asian Americans and Pacific Islanders.** Factors associated with smoking include having recently moved to the U.S., poverty, limited English proficiency, and little knowledge about how tobacco use affects health.

- **Hispanics.** Smoking in the Mexican-American adult population increases as people learn and adopt the values, beliefs, and norms of American culture. Factors associated with smoking among Hispanics include drinking alcohol, working and living with other smokers, having poor health, and being depressed. Declines in smoking have been greater among Hispanic men with at least a high school education than among those with less than the same schooling.

What *is* clear is that most people want to quit smoking, regardless of racial or ethnic group. Motivation varies among different groups but runs high in all.

PERCENTAGE OF U.S. ADULT SMOKERS WHO WOULD LIKE TO STOP SMOKING

	African Americans	American Indians/ Alaska Natives	Asian Americans/ Pacific Islanders	Hispanics	Whites
Total	71.4	65.0	60.2	68.7	70.4
Men	68.6	57.3	58.3	63.8	67.8
Women	74.9	70.3	65.3	79.3	72.4

Source: National Health Interview Survey, National Center for Health Statistics, CDC, 1993.

Unofficially...
Aboriginal Canadians smoke at among the highest rates in the world.

According to a 1998 study published in the *Journal of the American Medical Association,* levels of serum cotinine, a nicotine metabolite, were found to be higher among black smokers than among white or Mexican-American smokers. That could indicate higher nicotine intake or a different action of it in the body—possibly helping to explain why blacks find it harder to quit and experience higher lung cancer rates than white smokers.

Just a cigar

Back in the early 1990s, cigarette smoking had been mildly on the decline for a few years while interest in cigars had been dropping for two decades. But something happened in 1993—cigars became hip in some circles, taking their place in the land of trends alongside gourmet coffee and microbrewed beer. Since then, their use has risen almost 50 percent— 70 percent if you count only the big and fat variety— or a huge 250 percent if you count only premium cigars, the pricey handmade and imported types.

Cigar use ballooned among teens and young men who didn't smoke them every day. According to a 1996 survey in Massachusetts, students who claimed they smoked cigars ranged from 3.2 percent

Watch Out!
Secondhand
smoke from a
cigar contains
many of the
same toxins and
carcinogens as
cigarette smoke,
but in higher
concentrations.

in sixth grade to as much as 30 percent in high school. Even 6 to 7 percent of the girls in grades 9 to 11 at least said they had used cigars in the past month. However, women are, as you might expect, more likely to smoke cigarettes than other forms of tobacco. Among women, smokeless tobacco use is 1.7 percent or less.

Remember, cigars have not been as regulated as cigarettes—for instance, they have been exempt from regulations restricting minors' access to them. Despite this seeming federal oversight, all states have laws that either address youth access to cigars or to all tobacco products, the American Cancer Society notes. Makers of cigars haven't had to report their levels of tar, nicotine, or carbon monoxide to any federal agency, either. And while cigarettes and smokeless tobacco are taboo on television (or radio or any other FCC-regulated form of electronic communication), the ad ban simply has not included cigars. Tighter restrictions have been proposed.

Another loophole (or lack of a loop at all) exists with regard to American Indians and Alaska Natives—who, as described earlier, have high rates of tobacco consumption. American-Indian and Alaska-Native lands are sovereign nations not subject to state laws that prohibit the sale and promotion of tobacco to minors, so youth have had access to tobacco at a young age. Plus, tobacco companies have sometimes funded cultural events like pow-wows and rodeos to build their image.

Smoking around the world

America is not the likeliest nation to light up. Even just across the Atlantic in Britain, smoking rates are a few percentage points higher for both sexes. According to 1996 British government figures,

28 percent of women and 29 percent of men smoked cigarettes (though back in 1974, the rate had been a huge 41 percent and 51 percent, respectively). There's also a youth smoking trend in Britain, with those aged 20–24 more likely to smoke than any other age group (43 percent of young men and 36 percent of young women). As in the United States, in Britain, there are many would-be quitters—two-thirds of smokers say they'd like to give up the habit. At one time, the U.K. had the highest rate of smoking-related deaths among males in the world, but that rate has been falling since 1975.

Unofficially...
In Britain, 15 percent of smokers have their first cigarette within 5 minutes of waking up, and fully a third light up within 15 minutes.

Billions of dollars in U.S. tobacco is sold abroad, and markets in Asia, Eastern Europe, and other areas are described as explosive, such is the demand for cigarettes and other tobacco products. One international study on smoking in developed countries posits that between 1950 and the year 2000, 60 million people will have died due to smoking.

The World Health Organization (WHO) expects about 10 million annual tobacco-related deaths by the year 2030. Based on current smoking trends, it is predicted to be the leading cause of disease burden worldwide, causing about one out of every eight deaths, 70 percent of which will be in developing countries.

In China alone, there are about 300 million smokers—90 percent of which are males. China has now overtaken the United States as the country with the largest number of deaths from smoking, with tobacco expected to kill a third of all young men in China if current rates of new smokers persist. Generally speaking, males in developing countries smoke much more than females—about 48 percent compared to 7 percent.

GLOBAL SMOKING TRENDS
(AGES 15+, 1980–82 TO 1990–92)

World Health Organization Regions	Cigarettes per person (1990–92)	Annual % Change (1980–82 to 1990–92)
African	590	0.3
American	1900	-2.8
Eastern Mediterranean	930	-0.1
European	2340	-0.7
Southeast Asian	1230	0.8
Western Pacific	2010	2.2
World	1660	0.1

Source: The Tobacco Epidemic: A Global Public Health Emergency; Tobacco Alert; April 1996; World Health Organization (WHO).

Among the disturbing facts and projections about global tobacco use from the World Health Organization:

- Globally, about one-third of the adult population smokes.

- Tobacco accounts for 14 percent of all deaths in the European region.

- The life expectancy gap between men and women is growing significantly because of a larger number of men who smoke and die of tobacco-related diseases.

- Sections of Eastern and Central Europe are projected in 2020 to have the highest adult male risk of death, even higher than that in sub-Saharan Africa.

- About two-thirds of Russian men and one-third of Russian women smoke.

Tobacco rationing in the early 1990s because of a shortage of raw tobacco and other supplies in the former Soviet Union led to disastrous results—riots with cars overturned and roads blocked. This led to allowing cigarette imports and massive amounts of advertising.

Progress has been made in efforts to curb smoking around the world. Smoke-free areas in public places have been introduced in many countries, and several have lowered tar levels in cigarettes. Some countries, like Australia, New Zealand, and Singapore, have a long history of action against tobacco use and have seen declines in smoking rates, and the World Health Organization exerts a global effort to cut smoking.

Unofficially...
Singapore's first tobacco advertising ban was instituted in 1971, and China made the historic decision to ban smoking on domestic airplane flights in 1983.

Tobacco wars

Smoking is so bad for you—and members of the American public so convinced of it—that at least in some cases juries are awarding huge sums to estates of people who took up puffing but paid with their lives. A sizable tide has turned against smoking in recent years.

Will smoking be outlawed? Given smoking's popularity and the lobby in support of the personal choice to smoke, probably not. Alcohol prohibition didn't work in America, and among the last things many think we need is another popular illegal drug, particularly one that is legal now. The anti-smoking war instead is being waged in the theater of public opinion, the courts, and the short-of-a-ban regulatory arena.

A federal case

In early 1999, before President Bill Clinton knew he was off the impeachment hook (and indeed on a day when his trial was underway in the Senate), he laid out an ambitious agenda for the United States. It involved a bit about protecting Social Security, a rallying cry about the state of the Union being strong—and among other wholesome topics, the announcement that the government would sue the tobacco industry for smokers' health costs, plus seek a 55-cent-a-pack cigarette tax. That led to speculation the tobacco industry might want to reconsider a $516 billion federal settlement that it rejected in 1998.

February 1999 found the Justice Department asking for $20 million as a sort of down payment for launching a civil lawsuit against the tobacco industry, most of the money expected to pay for 40 attorneys, though $5 million would be for expert witness costs. Then on September 22, 1999, the Department of Justice made good on its preparatory work, filing an 88-page complaint against the largest cigarette companies—to recover billions of dollars the federal government spends each year on smoking-related health-care costs.

> *Each year, American taxpayers spend billions of dollars due to the actions of the cigarette companies. Today's suit seeks to recover those expenses... Smoking is the nation's largest preventable cause of death and disease, and American taxpayers should not have to bear the responsibility for the staggering costs.*
> —Attorney General Janet Reno

Unofficially...
You can read the text of the government's lawsuit complaint at the Department of Justice Web site at www.usdoj.gov.

The complaint, filed in U.S. District Court in Washington, D.C., alleges that cigarette companies have conspired since the 1950s to defraud and mislead the American public and to conceal information about the effects of smoking—among other things that the companies:

- Made false and misleading statements to create a false controversy about whether smoking causes disease, even though they knew that smoking did cause disease

- Made false promises that they would undertake or sponsor research to determine whether smoking causes disease

- Sponsored research that was designed not to answer the question of whether smoking caused disease, promoted biased research that would assist in defending lawsuits brought by injured smokers, and suppressed research that suggested that smoking causes disease

- Denied that nicotine was addictive, despite the fact that they knew nicotine was addictive

- Failed to warn consumers about the effects of smoking, including that cigarettes are addictive

- Refrained from developing, testing, and marketing potentially less hazardous products

- Denied that they marketed and/or targeted products to children, although they actively sought to capture the youth market

Defendants in the case include Philip Morris, Inc., Philip Morris Companies, R.J. Reynolds Tobacco Co., American Tobacco Co., Brown & Williamson Tobacco Corp., British-American Tobacco, P.L.C., British-American Tobacco (Investments) Ltd., Lorillard Tobacco Co., Inc., Liggett and Myers, Inc., The Council for Tobacco Research U.S.A., Inc., and the Tobacco Institute, Inc. The attorney general said that for more than 45 years the firms have conducted their business without regard to the truth, the law, or the health of Americans. Tobacco industry lawyers call the government's suit political and hypocritical.

States against tobacco

The Justice Department's lawsuit is reminiscent of those filed and settled by state governments for more than $200 billion. American states have been suing tobacco since 1994, when Mississippi filed a lawsuit seeking compensation from tobacco companies for smokers' Medicaid bills. It was followed by Minnesota, then West Virginia. Eventually, tobacco lawsuit fever spread throughout the country. Individual settlements were reached with Mississippi, Florida, Texas, and Minnesota. Then in late 1998, a general settlement was reached for the remaining states. Overall, the tobacco industry agreed to pay a total of $246 billion to the states, stop outdoor advertising, and restrict other kinds of marketing, as well as fund a research foundation and campaign to educate the public. Around the time of the states' settlement, debate thundered away about whether cities and other local governments should be able to sue.

If states have already sued, why should the federal government jump on the bandwagon? While state suits recovered funds paid out under the Medicaid program, which is a joint state and federal program, they did not recover funds from a different hefty price tag borne by taxpayers—money paid out under solely federal programs such as Medicare.

Other tobacco lawsuits

Groups have also sued tobacco interests—with mixed results. One type of suit is that filed on behalf of a labor union health fund, seeking compensation for treating smokers, just as the states did on behalf of Medicaid in their own suits. In March 1999, an Ohio jury ruled against 114 union health funds in their $2 billion bid. It was the first of about three dozen suits filed by union health funds to actually reach a jury verdict. In part, attorneys for the labor unions argued that the tobacco industry concealed the dangers of smoking and marketed to less-educated blue-collar workers with the Marlboro Man and other tactics.

The first class action tobacco lawsuit to actually reach a verdict did so in Florida in July 1999. It was filed on behalf of as many as 50,000 smokers statewide. Jurors found against large tobacco for conspiring to hide information about how dangerous and addictive cigarettes are. But in September 1999 a state appeals court decided class action damage claims need to be considered a single smoker at a time. That ruling severely dampens prospects of a single multibillion-dollar verdict in the non-government cases that go to trial.

The Florida suit was brought by a Miami attorney known for a previous tobacco industry case—one in which flight attendants exposed to secondhand smoke reached a settlement totaling hundreds of millions of dollars. The so-called flight attendants' lawsuit began when nonsmoker Norma Broin, an American Airlines employee, was diagnosed with aggressive lung cancer in 1989. Other plaintiffs joined in the class action suit, and a settlement was approved by a Florida judge in 1998 on behalf of 60,000 flight attendants. It was the first secondhand smoke tobacco industry case to go to trial. While the plaintiffs did not get the $5 billion they were seeking, the deal stipulated tobacco companies would spend $300 million to begin a foundation to research effects of secondhand smoke on flight attendants and provide $49 million to the flight attendants' attorneys, while not prohibiting individual flight attendants from suing on their own.

Timesaver
Curious about the tobacco lawsuits? Check Court TV's coverage, with video and articles, on the Web at www.courttv.com.

A legal war has actually been waged on tobacco interests in the United States since around the mid-point of the twentieth century. A lung cancer victim filed the first liability lawsuit in 1954, but it was dropped after more than a decade. Other suits followed. In 1983, a smoker dying of lung cancer filed suit and won a verdict for $400,000, which was later overturned. The case went to the Supreme Court but was eventually dropped because of the cost of continuing to press it.

More cases came, and close to two dozen went to jury by the mid-'90s. In a notable recent lawsuit, what has been described as a very angry jury in San Francisco awarded $50 million in punitive damages and $1.5 million in compensatory damages to Patricia Henly, a former Marlboro smoker with inoperable lung cancer after 35 years of smoking. It is the largest jury verdict ever decided against a tobacco firm. Many, many more smokers are lined up to try their hand in court against tobacco.

What has been at issue in much of the tobacco warring is whether the warning labels on cigarette packs are enough, whether the consumer really assumes the responsibility of his or her decision to smoke, whether tobacco companies knew early on that their products could cause cancer and were addictive, and whether they suppressed that information. Much evidence has been presented to illustrate that yes, dangers were known, and that consumers were lied to. It's important to note, though, that in many cases the tobacco industry has prevailed in court.

Despite the societal importance of huge federal and state tobacco lawsuits, it's a single case involving one family that is perhaps among the most haunting by simple mention. In 1996 a widow filed suit against tobacco firms alleging the wrongful death of her husband, David McLean, from lung cancer. McLean was an actor who, according to his widow's lawsuit, routinely smoked up to five packs of cigarettes daily in the course of his work role since the early 1960s— shooting long-running television and print advertising campaigns where he appeared as "The Marlboro Man."

Unofficially...
Actor David McLean was the second "Marlboro Man" to die of lung cancer.

Tobacco taxes

Among those who would prefer to see laws against marijuana dropped, a common suggestion is to legalize the stuff—and tax it! Cost is a deterrent to cigarette use, and taxes are used to try to cut the use of cigarettes—with proceeds often going toward health funding.

Looking at 1997 statistics, every cigarette pack sold in the U.S. was taxed at a bit more than 50 cents—adding around a 50 percent hike to the cost. Almost half of the tax is a federal levy, with the rest of it coming from state and local sources. Is that too much? Some say it's not enough. A 1993 government study notes that for each of the 24 billion packs of cigarettes sold in the U.S. that year, about $2 was spent on avoidable medical costs due to smoking (granted that *some* of those costs are borne by the smoker rather than society at large).

The possibility of raising the federal cigarette tax was under discussion in early 1999—either 50 cents, $1, or perhaps even $1.50. Economists expect that, given such an act of Congress, a 10 percent increase in the price of cigarettes would cause a 4 percent drop in demand. All told, assuming 1996 tax rates and consumption, upping the price of cigarettes by $1.50 a pack with a federal tax could theoretically cut into state revenues by $2 billion, so the idea of

Moneysaver
Large tobacco
settlements may
lead to higher
cigarette prices,
too—kick the
habit before it
becomes more
expensive!

increased federal tax is a hot potato, even in government itself.

States have their own options when it comes to taxing tobacco and deciding where the money goes. In 1998, voters in California approved Proposition Ten, a 50-cent tax on every pack of cigarettes, with proceeds headed toward early childhood development programs. In early 1999, efforts were underway by opponents to repeal the measure. In March 1999, Maryland's House of Delegates gave preliminary approval to a $1 hike in the cost of a pack of cigarettes. If the tax passes, Maryland would have the highest such tax in the nation.

As has been mentioned, cigars have led a bizarrely charmed regulatory life in comparison with cigarettes, and it extends to their tax status. The highest federal tax on a cigar is 3 cents, regardless of the price of the cigar.

Tobacco tomorrow

The rate of smoking in the U.S. declined slightly every year in the early 1990s, but that drop leveled off late in the decade. Will the future bring fewer smokers or more? According to World Health Organization figures, smoking levels have been remarkably stable over quite a few years—because declines in smoking in developed countries is offset by increases in developing countries. The WHO says that by the 2020s or early 2030s, if current trends continue, tobacco will kill 10 million people each year, with 70 percent of these deaths occurring in developing countries.

What other predictions are there? According to tobacco state policy analysts, those in the know suspect more tobacco tax and that cigarette manufacturing will be increasingly moved out of the U.S.

STATE CIGARETTE TAX RATES, JANUARY 1, 1999

State	Tax Rate (¢ per pack)	Rank
Alabama [1]	16.5	43
Alaska	100	1
Arizona	58	13
Arkansas	31.5	29
California	87	3
Colorado	20	37
Connecticut	50	17
Delaware	24	32
Florida	33.9	27
Georgia	12	46
Hawaii	100	1
Idaho	28	31
Illinois [1]	58	13
Indiana	15.5	44
Iowa	36	23
Kansas	24	32
Kentucky [2]	3	50
Louisiana	20	37
Maine	74	8
Maryland	36	23
Massachusetts	76	6
Michigan	75	7
Minnesota	48	18
Mississippi	18	39
Missouri [1]	17	41
Montana	18	39
Nebraska	34	26
Nevada	35	25
New Hampshire	37	22
New Jersey [1]	80	5
New Mexico	21	36
New York [1]	56	15
North Carolina	5	49

STATE CIGARETTE TAX RATES *(cont.)*

State	Tax Rate (¢ per pack)	Rank
North Dakota	44	19
Ohio	24	32
Oklahoma	23	35
Oregon [3]	68	10
Pennsylvania	31	30
Rhode Island	71	9
South Carolina	7	48
South Dakota	33	28
Tennessee [1] [2]	13	45
Texas	41	21
Utah	51.5	16
Vermont	44	19
Virginia [1]	2.5	51
Washington	82.5	4
West Virginia	17	41
Wisconsin	59	12
Wyoming	12	46
Dist. of Columbia	65	11
U.S. Median	34.0	

Source: Compiled by the Federation of Tax Administrators from various sources.

(1) Counties and cities may impose an additional tax on a pack of cigarettes in AL, 1¢ to 6¢; IL, 10¢ to 15¢; MO, 4¢ to 7¢; TN, 1¢; and VA, 2¢ to 15¢.

(2) Dealers pay an additional enforcement and administrative fee of 0.1¢ per pack in KY and 0.05¢ in TN.

(3) In OR, the tax rate will decrease to $0.58 per pack effective 1/1/00.

Regardless of what happens in the political and economic arena and to the economic bottom line of tobacco, the most important bottom line is an individual one. Americans have freedom to smoke, just as they have freedom to eat junk food or to not exercise or to ignore their doctor's recommendations for avoiding disease. If you want to take smoking's risks, you *may* (although where you light up is now limited to protect others from secondhand smoke, and the price you pay for cigarettes includes deterrent taxes). You also have the choice to quit.

Just the facts

- A San Francisco jury awarded more than $50 million in damages to a smoker with lung cancer.

- The Justice Department filed suit against the tobacco industry in September 1999.

- The Food and Drug Administration began regulating cigarettes and smokeless tobacco products as drugs in 1996.

- Reports of cancer linked to cigarettes surfaced as early as the 1950s.

Getting to Quitting

PART II

GET THE SCOOP ON...
Whether you're really ready ▪ Filling *other* needs
to make quitting easier ▪ How to pick a quit
method ▪ Weight gain after quitting

Chapter 4

Taking the First Steps to Quitting

Everyone knows a journey of a thousand miles begins with a single step, and so it is with quitting smoking. Taking one tiny action toward stopping a lifelong problem, and then another, and another, can lead you to freedom from a nagging habit. Some people do quit smoking just by saying, "That's it—no more," but you're more likely to succeed at quitting if you've done your homework first and if you use certain quit-smoking aides.

This chapter takes a look at those baby steps that will help prepare you properly and provides some tools you can use to get started on the right foot in your journey, including a series of quizzes to get to know your smoking self a bit better. Our first stop is figuring out where you're at now.

Assessing your habit—and your commitment to quitting

The longer you've been smoking and the more you smoke, the harder you may find it to quit, but half the battle is being truly ready. How close are you?

The "Are You Ready to Quit Smoking?" quiz can help you find out.

Are You Ready to Quit Smoking?

1. Do I want to quit smoking for myself?
   YES or NO

2. Is quitting smoking a #1 priority for me?
   YES or NO

3. Have I tried to quit smoking before?
   YES or NO

4. Do I believe that smoking is dangerous to my health?
   YES or NO

5. Am I committed to trying to quit, even though it may be tough at first?
   YES or NO

6. Are my family, friends, and coworkers willing to help me quit smoking?
   YES or NO

7. Besides health reasons, do I have other personal reasons for quitting smoking?
   YES or NO

8. Will I be patient with myself if I backslide?
   YES or NO

Answer Key: If you answered YES to four or more of these questions, you are ready to quit smoking.

Source: *Freedom from Smoking* program, American Lung Association.

Every YES ➜ answer is one more thing that can help you quit effectively. Look at your NO answers for places where you can make improvements and get ready to quit smoking.

Do you really believe you *can* quit, and that you can cope with life's good and bad times *without cigarettes*? No matter who is telling you to quit smoking—your physician, your friends, your spouse, parents, or children—you're not likely to succeed if you feel you'd just be going along with the idea to please someone else. If you're not there yet, make it a point to think about reasons to quit that could benefit *you*, reasons *you* could take to heart, like these health-related points:

▪ Better health as soon as you quit

- Not having to fear the extra risk smoking poses in terms of cancer, lung, and heart disease, or other awful ailments

- Simply feeling better once you've kicked the addiction—easier breathing, movement, and so on

Perhaps though you're concerned about the health impact of smoking, your primary motivation to quit comes from another place—such as the social ramifications of being a smoker or the cost. Take a look back at your answers to the "Know Your Reasons for Quitting" quiz from Chapter 1—which kind of quitter did you turn out to be?

If you want to quit smoking because you don't like having the image of a smoker, that *is* a personal reason to quit (rather than just quitting because your friends would like you to). Generally speaking, the more external your reasons, the more you would be well-advised to look for very personal reasons to quit to bolster your effort. After all, your financial situation could change for the better, and you could wind up spending time around different people than you do now, but no one gets away from their own health (at least not until it is too late).

Is quitting a top priority in your life? Realistically speaking, you probably have healthful priorities that are higher. To help figure out where smoking ranks on your to-do list, go back to Psychology 101 from high school or college. Remember something called Maslow's *Hierarchy of Needs*? Abraham Maslow posited that human beings are motivated by unsatisfied needs. He thought that some *lower needs* had to be satisfied before *higher needs* could be satisfied, and whenever an unsolved lower need popped up, humans would go back and fill that more primary need.

From the most primary to the highest, needs include those that are:

1. Physiological

2. Safety-related

3. To do with love and belonging

4. Tied to esteem

5. Relating to self-actualization

Getting enough food, water, and air to survive is more important to a person than quitting smoking. Being safe from a hailstorm or being financially solvent may be more important to you than giving up cigarettes if you are in a hailstorm or worried about finances. Being cared for and loved is certainly important, but where does your desire to quit smoking rank?

If it's a pie-in-the-sky want, one that comes after the desire for a luxury car or a vacation home, then it sounds related to your self-actualization and being all you can be—or perhaps it relates to the higher levels of the *esteem* category. The problem with that is that whenever a chink develops in your armor, whenever something threatens your comfort in the lower levels of the need hierarchy, your higher level needs are easily put on hold or even forgotten.

If quitting smoking is just a nice ideal, like the vacation home or the luxury car, aren't you going to turn to a cigarette out of fear and frustration if you're suddenly threatened with losing your job or if a love affair turns sour? Chances are the words "vacation home" or "luxury car" wouldn't cross your mind during a crisis—let alone would the words "quit smoking," especially since it is so easy to use smoking as a crutch for crises and since nicotine may seem to alleviate anxiety in the short term.

Bright Idea
Unlike some psychology pioneers before him, Abraham Maslow believed in studying healthy, happy people in order to develop a philosophy (explained in his book *Motivation and Personality*). Take the hint when forming your own (and quitting smoking)!

How do you get around this little dilemma? Think of the ways smoking can fit higher into your priority list. Those with breathing difficulties from years of cigarettes may already have noted that their basic physiological need to *get enough air to breathe* is compromised by cigarette use. An emphysema patient may still have to fight addiction, but often has no problem figuring quitting smoking into the most basic *physiological needs* category.

Taking steps out of fear isn't the ideal answer, though having a realistic view of smoking's consequences may help spike *quitting cigarette smoking* into priority. Maybe a trip to the medical library or a visit with a lung cancer patient can help put things in perspective. Maybe just the thought of going into menopause earlier or suffering erectile dysfunction is enough. Using your imagination and the "Making Quitting a Priority" quiz, what realistic ways can you think of to help move quitting into your most basic needs categories (as well as the others)?

MAKING QUITTING A PRIORITY

In what ways can quitting smoking fit into each of these needs categories in your life?

Needs	How Quitting Fits
1. Physiological	_____
2. Safety	_____
3. Love and belonging	_____
4. Esteem	_____
5. Self-actualization	_____

Here's an example of possible answers:

Needs	How Quitting Fits
Physiological	Easier breathing; feel better
Safety	Less risk of debilitating disease

Needs	How Quitting Fits
Love and belonging	Won't put off nonsmoking loved ones
Esteem	Won't be thought of as a "smoker"
Self-actualization	Will be living up to a higher ideal for myself

Remember, your goal is to move quitting to a place in your mind where it equates with a pretty basic need. Quitting is not supposed to take the place of your other basic needs—in fact, the more you're able to satisfy those other primary needs, the better prepared you'll be to quit smoking without a hitch. Are there other areas you need to get a plan together for—improving your finances, strengthening relationships, getting appropriate treatment for illness? Find healthy ways to fill your needs and look after *yourself*. Quitting isn't about denying yourself something—it's about providing for yourself.

How much, when, and why you smoke

Are you an occasional smoker, a pack-a-day woman, a menthol-lights-only-kind-of-guy, an inveterate chain-smoker? This week, try to keep tabs on your habit. Turn a slip of paper into a cigarette diary you can slide inside your box of smokes (maybe with a short pencil). Note when you smoke a cigarette and a quick word about why—even if it's just the word "desperate" or "routine" or even "sex" (or "headache" for that matter).

Along with taking note of how much you're smoking, knowing the reasons you're smoking can help you as you kick the habit. Your approach can be different depending on why you light up. At the end of a week, tally up how much you smoked and the major reasons. The "Smoker, Know Thyself" checklist can also help you project some of those answers now.

Smoker, Know Thyself

____ I smoke at specific times of the day, out of habit

____ I smoke to control anxiety

____ I smoke to alleviate boredom

____ I smoke when I see my friends smoking

____ I smoke when an ad or movie shows smoking

____ I smoke when I'm out socially in the evening

____ I smoke to avoid or annoy someone

____ I smoke when I'm trying to impress someone

____ I smoke when I get specific cigarette cravings

____ I smoke when I have caffeine

____ I smoke when I'm drinking alcohol

____ I smoke when _____

← Use numbers 1–5 to rank how well you fit the checklist questions—1 for not at all, 5 for definitely.

checklist

Wherever you discover your strongest pull to smoke, do some advance planning about how you'll handle that cigarette when you quit. For instance, if you're most likely to smoke out of routine, think about ways you can change your daily routine a little where a different activity could take the place of smoking. Things like the following:

- Taking a walk in the park on a short break

- Drinking decaf instead of caffeinated coffee

- Bringing a healthy but tasty snack when seeing a smoking friend

- Practicing stress-relieving meditation

What could you do that you'd like to instead of having a cigarette? Make a list! If flavored (preferably decaf) coffee can supplant a cigarette, buy some that you like. Get carrot sticks (or at least reduced-calorie chips). Pick up a few magazines to read, breath mints—whatever it takes (within reason)! Do be careful about replacing cigarettes with anything but the healthiest, lowest-calorie foods.

About quitting

As you prepare to quit—and hopefully this time it will be for good—you need to set a timetable. Right now, you're investigating quitting. Before you truly do it, take the steps in the "Your Quit-Smoking Plan" checklist.

Your Quit-Smoking Plan

_____ 1. Make a commitment to yourself that you will quit

_____ 2. Set a date on which you'll stop smoking

_____ 3. Decide the smoking cessation method you want to use

_____ 4. Set quit-smoking goals—decide how many fewer cigarettes you'll have each day or week, and when you'll be smoke-free

_____ 5. Write down your goals

_____ 6. Seek out friends and other supportive people

_____ 7. Plan to reward yourself with something specific for each week and month you meet your quit-smoking goals

You can do steps 1 and 2 right now. Give yourself a little breathing room and time to get ready, but *do* set a quit date. Now, you need to figure out what quitting method you'd like to use.

Cold turkey versus step-by-step

Quitting cold turkey is harder and statistically less successful than step-by-step quitting methods, such as progressive nicotine replacement therapy (the patches and gum route). Some people *do* quit cold turkey and successfully refrain from smoking forever. If willpower has never been much of a problem for you, perhaps cold turkey is worth trying. There are two things going for this method:

▪ It's cheap

▪ It's incredibly simple

You just stop smoking, period. Much of the remainder of this book is devoted to explaining the other quit-smoking methods, which have a higher chance of success and should be easier on you. They do require more planning, varying degrees of expense, and sometimes a prescription. However, successfully quitting will pay you back in spades, regardless of a little extra cost during the time you're actually kicking the habit.

Nicotine replacement therapy (discussed briefly in Chapter 1 and dealt with fully in Chapters 6, 8, and 9) can just about double cessation rate. A typical program of over-the-counter nicotine patch use runs several weeks (10 in the case of NicoDerm CQ), at the end of which you should be nicotine free if you don't touch the smokes. Nicotine gum is also available, as are nicotine inhalers and nasal sprays in the U.S. (the latter two by prescription only). Various nicotine-replacement products provide plans that may allow you to quit in as little as a few weeks or take as long as a few months to reduce your nicotine intake more gradually.

Some of the choices before you include:

- Cold turkey
- Gradually reducing cigarettes smoked
- Nicotine replacement (patch, gum, inhaler, nasal spray)
- A quit-smoking pill (Zyban)
- Alternative methods
- Attending a support group (in addition to the above)

If you have a preference for a particular type of quit method, flip to the chapter that deals with it and learn more on the topic. Or read through at your leisure and evaluate all the different methods before you choose. Chapter 6 goes over them in detail, and check Chapter 7 for the experiences other people have had with a variety of quitting methods (and also about support groups).

What method should you try first?

What ways have you already tried to quit? Many people have at one time or another attempted a cold-turkey quit and found it too difficult. As we've mentioned, nicotine replacement therapy offers good success rates compared to no quit aid (though neither it nor other cessation methods constitute a sure-fire smoking-stopper).

Would you be more comfortable wearing a patch on your arm every day, using a nasal spray, chewing gum, or using a new kind of nicotine inhaler that looks a bit like a plastic cigarette?

It's true you can always try the simplest methods and if they don't work, move on to more elaborate or expensive ones—*but*.... Given that quitting smoking is a monumental effort for many people, no matter the method they try, why not go for the best odds of successful cessation and use a combination method—for instance, nicotine replacement or Zyban paired with one of the group programs in Chapter 7?

Whichever method(s) you choose, don't forget the psychological component—the more support you have, the better. So whether you join a weekly or monthly quitters' meeting or receive extra encouragement and care from a loved one, get some moral support. Chapters 10 and 15 should be of particular help here.

Overcoming fear of failure

Since smokers on average have tried to quit about five times already, you know you can always try again, but the disillusionment of not successfully meeting your goal—of backsliding—can become a disenchanting bugaboo if you let it.

The best way to overcome fear of failure is to have a quit plan that you stick to, with support mechanisms in place. In other words, look out for places where you might fail and make sure you know exactly what to do when a craving hits—call a particular friend, undertake a specific activity instead of smoking. And have a plan for what you'll do if you backslide. If you've gone three days without a cigarette and have one, it doesn't mean you're a smoker again. It means you're a backsliding quitter who should pick up quitting again right where he or she left off. Later in this book you'll find a number of ways to support your quit plan during tough willpower moments. Some counselors, for instance, suggest literally putting together rudimentary flash cards with an *alternative* to a smoking thought or action on each. These can be a good visual intervention (and flash cards *do* give you something to do with your hands).

Not quite quitting

If you're under a great amount of stress and quitting seems like too much effort, don't give up on the idea—with nicotine replacement therapy or Zyban (or perhaps an alternative quit method), it may be easier than you realize. However, if you just cannot go the distance, you can at least do things to mitigate the danger of cigarettes:

- Make an effort to cut down on how much you smoke
- Make one day a week, or weekends, smoke free
- Switch to cigarettes with less tar and nicotine (but read up on how smoking these can be misleading, in Chapter 5)

Bright Idea
Don't be afraid to treat yourself like a schoolkid on occasion—put gold stars on your calendar for each day or week you're smoke-free rather than a black mark for every cigarette you've snuck.

Bright Idea
What's on your mind? Check your thoughts frequently and steer them toward a can-do attitude.

You may be well advised to make a real plan to take care of whatever in your life is preventing you from being able to make a full commitment to quitting smoking, give *that* a timetable, and set a quit smoking date for soon afterward.

What to expect from kicking the habit

We didn't say it would be easy, but with gradual nicotine reduction systems, pharmaceutical aids, nutrition, social support, and some stick-to-it-iveness, you can make quitting smoking less tough. Here are some of the things you can expect from quitting.

Pros and cons

Here's what happens when you quit smoking: Within a couple of days, your sense of taste and smell is enhanced; within three days, breathing should be easier; and within a couple weeks to a few months, walking should become easier as circulation improves, among other things. Also, in the months after you quit, coughing and fatigue lift.

But then there are the cravings, largely prompted by nicotine. You will want to smoke and will need to distract yourself and show willpower. Withdrawal from nicotine can also cause a host of symptoms (also mentioned in Chapter 1), ranging from depression to insomnia to having the munchies (psychological cravings can also hang around long after the physical cigarette craving has passed).

Irritability can be part of the body's craving for nicotine and often lasts a few weeks. So does fatigue, which can occur because of the lack of nicotine (a stimulant). In the week after you quit smoking, particularly the first 72 hours, insomnia is common—nicotine affects brain wave function, and you may dream about smoking.

If you've heard "it gets worse before it gets better," you can apply that to quitting. Coughing and nasal problems can be your body's way of getting rid of mucus that before may have been blocking your airways—and it may persist a few days. The extra oxygen your body gets when the carbon monoxide of cigarette smoke is absent can cause a little dizziness during the first 48 hours after you quit.

Also, you may find you have difficulty concentrating (nicotine withdrawal again), a little tightness in your chest, potential stomach pain or constipation for a week or two, and increased hunger. Be aware of the possibilities but also contact your physician if you experience symptoms of concern.

The truth about smoking and your weight

The good news is that after you quit, you'll wind up with more energy and an easier time breathing and exercising. The bad news is that you may have to work to keep from gaining weight. Animal studies show nicotine withdrawal brings on weight gain and, according to some research, an increased tendency to eat, whereas taking nicotine leads to a weight and fat loss—and, some research shows, more modest eating. Interestingly, other studies find nicotine's ability to reduce body weight happens in the absence of a significant decrease in food consumption. They point to the ability of nicotine (and some other types of drugs, such as amphetamines), to regulate the body's *set point*—a specific level of weight at which, some scientists believe, your system seeks to stabilize.

Women who have tried to quit sometimes say they relapse and go back to smoking when they find pounds piling on. Sadly, in a 1997 Tennessee study, more than 1 in 10 *seventh-grade* smokers said weight control was among the reasons they smoked.

Unofficially... It's a popular belief that smoking makes you lose weight by suppressing your appetite, but *some* studies suggest smokers *don't* eat less than nonsmokers or former smokers. According to a 1992 study at the University of Pittsburgh School of Medicine, they tend to eat a bit *more*.

Although smoking is no reasonable way to try to control your weight, nicotine research in animals has found that females are more susceptible to nicotine-withdrawal weight gain and eating changes than are males. And according to a 1998 study at the University of Toronto, women who dieted reported a comparatively higher weight gain when they stopped smoking, as compared to women who didn't diet. So if you're a woman prone to weight gain already, be aware that you may have double duty to do—quitting smoking and battling the bulge.

Weight gain from smoking cessation is typically described as minor—often not much more than a few pounds. But it may actually be a larger problem than researchers have thought, according to relatively recent research reported in the *American Journal of Epidemiology*. A Tennessee study focusing on nearly 6,000 smokers found that over five years of sustained smoking cessation, women gained an average of 19.2 pounds and men 16.7, with the greatest proportion of those gains occurring in the first year of kicking the habit. Around one in five of the study participants was actually deemed a sustained quitter (not smoking for five years), and fully a third of those subjects gained 22 pounds or more over the five-year span, versus just six percent of those who continued to smoke.

You might want to keep a lid on the cookie jar. Rats allowed access to Oreos, potato chips, lab chow, and water changed their consumption to just the sweet goodies when nicotine was given and then taken away. Will you get a sweet tooth? Some quitting smokers say they do, but the jury's still out. One study in humans found that neither quitting smoking nor using nicotine patches led to a change in the percentage of carbohydrates or sweets consumed.

Why would nicotine encourage weight loss? Remember that it works on dopamine, a main pleasure neurotransmitter, among myriad other body factors. And nicotine doesn't *always* cause weight loss. In one animal study, a very high-dose nicotine injection actually caused a weight gain, whereas lower doses caused a loss.

Is there anything you can do to mitigate nicotine-withdrawal weight gain? If you have a tendency to put on pounds, the unfortunate truth about nicotine may be a good reason to consider quitting with a nicotine patch or gum so that you're weaned more slowly away from it. A 1996 Harvard study of 79 quitting smokers found the use of nicotine gum suppressed weight gain—and the higher the dose, the greater the suppression. Meanwhile, a 1989 study found that quitting smokers gained an average of 3.8 pounds over 10 weeks if they used nicotine gum, and an average of 7.8 pounds if they didn't. Transdermal nicotine patches cut weight gain, too, of course.

The quit-smoking pill Zyban (bupropion hydrochloride) could offer relief in this department, as well; a 1997 Mayo Clinic study found sustained-release bupropion helped fend off quitting-related weight gain. While members in a group given placebos gained an average of 6.4 pounds over seven weeks, those in a group taking 100mg or 150mg doses of bupropion gained only an average 5.1 pounds, and those taking 300mg doses gained just an average of 3.3 pounds.

If you don't want to go the nicotine-replacement route or the Zyban route, you can do other things to help keep down the pounds. Embarking on a healthy weight-loss plan before or around the same time you quit might not be a bad idea—if you're feeling strong in the willpower department.

Bright Idea
Take an interactive quiz to check how dependent you are on the nicotine in cigarettes at the NicodermCQ nicotine patch Web site, www.nicodermcq. com.

Conversely, what about getting some fresh air and exercising a bit more? Have a plan in place, and work your plan.

Ready, set, quit

The rest of this book discusses specifics of how to quit smoking *and to do it right.* The "Preparing to Quit" quiz goes over some important questions (from the American Lung Association's *Freedom from Smoking* program) about skills, techniques, and information often used to help kick the habit. Included is a quick cross-reference to where you can find items in this book.

PREPARING TO QUIT

1. Have you identified your reasons for wanting to stop smoking?
   YES or NO (This chapter and Chapter 1)

2. Do you feel you are addicted to nicotine?
   YES or NO (Chapter 2)

3. Do you know how to cope with withdrawal symptoms?
   YES or NO (Chapters 6 and 10)

4. Are you informed about nicotine gum and the nicotine patch?
   YES or NO (This chapter and Chapters 6 and 9)

5. Do you know how to use deep breathing as a technique to stay free of smoking?
   YES or NO (Chapter 11)

6. Do you know how to develop social support to help keep you free from cigarettes?
   YES or NO (Chapter 10)

7. Have you planned strategies for dealing with temptations to start smoking again?
   YES or NO (Chapter 10)

8. Have you planned a reward for yourself once you have quit smoking?
   YES or NO (Chapter 10)

9. Do you know how to manage weight gain, which sometimes occurs when people stop smoking?

   YES or NO (This chapter and Chapter 11)

10. Do you have other strategies to handle stress without smoking?

    YES or NO (Chapter 10)

11. Do you feel stopping smoking is your top health improvement priority?

    YES or NO (This chapter and Chapter 2)

Now might be a good time to think about other things you can do for your health and lifestyle along with quitting smoking. Rather than embark on other difficult endeavors at the same time (strict dieting, for instance), think about pleasurable positive changes that you can make—a spring cleaning, a new leaf, better nutrition, more weekend trips. Remember, if it cuts down on anxiety, it may cut down on your need to *smoke*.

Just the facts

- Seeing quitting as a basic safety need may help you succeed

- The more personal your quit reasons, the better

- Dizziness when quitting can occur because you're getting more oxygen

- Watch the scale during nicotine withdrawal

GET THE SCOOP ON...
Switching to low tar safely ▪ Finding your
brand's tar and nicotine content ▪ Changing the
way you smoke to reduce tar and nicotine ▪
Considering smokeless cigarettes

Is There a Safe Cigarette?

Chapter 5

After lung cancer surgery, nearly half of smokers return to their habit. Among smokers who suffer a heart attack, more than a third resume smoking before they leave the hospital. And two of five smokers who have had their larynx removed try smoking again. Clearly, smoking is a powerful addiction, and while many smokers keep smoking despite health problems, many more consider quitting only because they realize the dire health risks posed by cigarettes. But what if a safe cigarette could be developed?

It turns out there are big differences in the level of tar, nicotine, and carbon monoxide delivered by various cigarettes (technically, anyway). But alas, there is no absolutely safe smoke, nor any promise of one on the horizon.

This chapter compares many of the most popular brands for their tar, nicotine, and carbon monoxide numbers and looks at the push toward the development of a "safe" cigarette. If you're not completely

Bright Idea
Use this chapter as a *step* in kicking the habit gradually, but remember that nothing beats quitting altogether.

ready to quit yet, you may find it helpful to move to a light cigarette, though you should be aware that "light" can be a misleading term, as you'll find out. You can also look at some tobacco smoking alternatives.

Searching for a safer smoke

The adverse impact of smoking on health has been known for a long time, and for decades, scientists have been trying to find ways to give the public a safe or, at least, less dangerous smoke. The push started in the 1950s with efforts to reduce tar content. As to the idea of less nicotine, well, too little, and people might not come back for more. And while the stated nicotine content of the average cigarette has dropped, government documents show that in some cases, nicotine levels in cigarettes have been purposely increased. There also has been plenty of research on ways that nicotine might deliver a more powerful punch to the user.

How did nicotine boosting come about? During the forties and fifties, tobacco makers experimented with ways to use more of the tobacco plant and waste less in the manufacturing process—better for the bottom line. This "reconstituted tobacco" combined a reduced number of tobacco leaves with a mixture of previously unusable stems and scraps to stretch the product. It was this process that gave rise to manipulation of nicotine levels as manufacturers sought to make reconstituted tobacco just as appealing to the consumer.

Clearly, a lot of industry attention has been devoted to the topic. Patents exist for increasing nicotine content by adding it to the tobacco "rod," the cigarette filter, wrapper, or other parts of the cigarette, and even the glue used to hold it together.

There are patents using advanced technology to change the levels of nicotine in tobacco, to extract nicotine from tobacco, and even to develop new chemical variants of nicotine. One patent has the object of providing a cigarette that can deliver a larger amount of nicotine in the first few puffs than in the last few.

As smokers grew increasingly concerned about health matters, scientists increased their efforts to accommodate those concerns. But in the 1960s, consultants to the tobacco industry warned that because of cancer-causing chemicals produced simply by the burning of tobacco, an entirely safe cigarette was impossible.

Consumers do have a choice concerning the strength of a cigarette they smoke, however. The Federal Trade Commission (FTC) records and publicizes data about the levels of harmful smoke constituents, like tar, nicotine, and carbon monoxide in various cigarette brands, so you can choose a brand that delivers less of those chemicals if you wish.

You can find some important information right on a cigarette package; you'll learn what to look for in a moment, but first you can try the "Know Your Tobacco Labels" quiz to find out how well you know your labels.

While cigarette makers do voluntarily disclose the amount of tar and nicotine their products contain, you won't necessarily see specific numbers listed on the cigarette package—perhaps "lowered tar and nicotine" in the case of brands touting that they are light cigarettes. In fact, a 1990 study of cigarette package labels found tar yield was progressively less likely to be shown on the package the higher it was and was not disclosed on the package of any cigarette yielding 11mg or more of tar.

> **"**
> In many cigarettes today, the amount of nicotine present is a result of choice, not chance.
> —David A. Kessler, M.D. (former FDA Commissioner)
> **"**

KNOW YOUR TOBACCO LABELS

1. Which of the following cautionary statements appear on cigarette packages?

   a. SURGEON GENERAL'S WARNING: Smoking Causes Lung Cancer, Heart Disease, Emphysema, and May Complicate Pregnancy.

   b. SURGEON GENERAL'S WARNING: Quitting Smoking Now Greatly Reduces Serious Risks to Your Health.

   c. SURGEON GENERAL'S WARNING: Smoking By Pregnant Women May Result in Fetal Injury, Premature Birth, and Low Birth Weight.

   d. SURGEON GENERAL'S WARNING: Cigarette Smoke Contains Carbon Monoxide.

2. Cigarette packages are the only place the Surgeon General's warning is required.

   TRUE or FALSE?

3. Smokeless tobacco packages require what warning?

   a. WARNING: THIS PRODUCT MAY CAUSE MOUTH CANCER

   b. WARNING: THIS PRODUCT MAY CAUSE GUM DISEASE AND TOOTH LOSS

   c. WARNING: THIS PRODUCT IS NOT A SAFE ALTERNATIVE TO CIGARETTES

   d. Any one of the above

4. Cigarette manufacturers voluntarily disclose the amount of tar and nicotine their products contain.

   TRUE or FALSE?

Answers: 1. a, b, c, and d (any one of the four is required); 2. False (most related advertising requires a warning too); 3. d; 4. True.

So what's in your smokes? Maybe a lot more tar, nicotine, and carbon monoxide than you realize. The upcoming set of tables will help you figure out how much of those chemicals you may be getting, as well as identify brands that test lower in them.

Comparison shopping

While many cigarettes on the market today deliver reduced tar and nicotine amounts compared to the early days of the smoke, there are still high-strength brands doing well on the market. The "Cigarette

Varieties Highest in Tar" table lists cigarettes tested that were found to have the highest tar content and also provides their nicotine and carbon monoxide levels.

If your brand of smokes is shown here, you may find a way to cut tar significantly by switching to a different brand or possibly to a light version of the same brand. You'll learn how to interpret the specific tar, nicotine, and carbon monoxide numbers shortly (and also how to make sure you're not over-smoking light cigarettes, since it's easy to do and can negate the purpose of going "light" in the first place). While these tables may be helpful for some comparison, please note that according to the FTC "tar" and nicotine ratings were never intended to reflect what any individual consumer would get from any particular cigarette.

How low can you go in terms of tar content? The "Cigarette Varieties Lowest in Tar" table shows the brands ranked with the least tar yield. You can use this list if you want to switch from higher-tar smokes temporarily as you wean yourself away from cigarettes altogether. Check the label of your present brand to compare all three categories—tar, nicotine, and carbon monoxide—or visit Appendix E, where results of testing on more than 1,200 cigarette varieties can be found.

Who smoked all these cigarettes to find out which ones ranked highest or lowest in tar, nicotine, and carbon monoxide? A machine, actually. The FTC gathered results of tar, nicotine, and carbon monoxide tests on no less than 1,252 varieties of cigarettes sold in the United States in 1997 to compile its report. To get a broad sample of cigarettes sold, two packages were bought of every variety of cigarettes in

Watch Out!
How you smoke "light" cigarettes can change the amount of tar, nicotine, and carbon monoxide you take in, as you'll learn later in this chapter.

CIGARETTE VARIETIES HIGHEST IN TAR

Brand Name	Description	Tar	Nic	CO
Bristol	King NF SP	27	1.7	16
Commander	King NF SP	27	1.7	15
Basic	King NF SP	26	1.7	15
English Ovals	King NF HP	25	2.0	15
Old Gold	King NF SP Straight	25	1.8	17
Pyramid	King NF SP FF	15	1.5	17
Camel	Reg NF SP	24	1.7	16
All American Value*	King NF SP	24	1.6	NA
Best Buy*	King NF SP Generic	24	1.6	NA
Bronson*	King NF SP Generic	24	1.6	NA
Genco*	King NF SP Generic	24	1.6	NA
Generals*	King NF SP Generic	25	1.6	NA
Gridlock*	King NF SP Generic	24	1.6	NA
Premium Buy*	King NF SP Generic	24	1.6	NA
Shenandoah*	King NF SP Generic	24	1.6	NA
Shield*	King NF SP Generic	24	1.6	NA
Top Choice*	King NF SP Generic	24	1.6	NA
Lucky Strike	Reg NF SP	24	1.5	17
Chesterfield	King NF SP FF	24	1.4	17
Tareyton	King NF SP	24	1.4	16

Key:
NIC = Nicotine
CO = Carbon Monoxide
NF = Non-Filter
FF= Full Filter
HP = Hard Pack
SP = Soft Pack

* indicates brand tested by the manufacturer rather than by the Tobacco Institute Testing Laboratory.

Source: Federal Trade Commission Report of "Tar," Nicotine, and Carbon Monoxide of the Smoke of 1252 Varieties of Domestic Cigarettes for the Year 1997.

50 different locations around the United States. The data comes from the five largest cigarette makers in the United States, and most of the testing was conducted at the industry-affiliated Tobacco Institute

CIGARETTE VARIETIES LOWEST IN TAR

Brand Name	Description	Tar	Nic	CO
Carlton	King F HP Ultra-Lt	<0.5	<0.05	<0.5
Now	King F HP	<0.5	<0.05	<0.5
Now	100 F HP	<0.5	<0.05	<0.5
Carlton	King F SP Lt	<0.5	0.1	1
Cambridge	King F SP Lowest	1	0.1	1
Carlton	100 F HP Lt-Men	1	0.1	1
Carlton	King F HP	1	0.1	1
Carlton	King F SP Lt-Men	1	0.1	1
Carlton	100 F HP Lt	1	0.1	1
Bristol	King SP Lowest	1	0.1	2
Merit	King F HP Ultra-Lt	1	0.1	2
Now	King F SP	1	0.1	2
Now	King F SP Men	1	0.1	2
Merit	King F SP Ultra-Lt	1	0.1	3
Carlton	100 F SP Lt	1	0.2	2

Key:
Nic = Nicotine
CO = Carbon Monoxide
F = Filter
HP = Hard Pack
SP = Soft Pack
Lt = Light
Men = Menthol

Source: Federal Trade Commission Report of "Tar," Nicotine, and Carbon Monoxide of the Smoke of 1252 Varieties of Domestic Cigarettes for the Year 1997.

Testing Laboratory according to exacting standards prescribed by the FTC.

Tar, nicotine, and carbon monoxide numbers

Now that you know generally which brands are high in tar and nicotine and which are low, at least technically speaking, how do you interpret the numbers? One way is to look at averages. Weighted for sales, the average tar delivered by a cigarette sold in 1997 was 12mg. Incidentally, that's not much over half the tar delivered by the average cigarette sold back in 1968 (21.6mg). Consumers and cigarette manufacturers have clearly become conscious of the need to reduce tar intake. Generally speaking, absent hard-and-fast government guidelines, "low tar" is often used by cigarette manufacturers to describe a tar rating of 5mg to 15mg, and "ultra low tar" usually means 6mg or less.

The typical amount of nicotine delivered by cigarettes has declined over the years just as tar has. The average amount of nicotine for a cigarette sold in 1997 is just about two-thirds what it was in 1968—.89mg instead of 1.35mg. Remember in the case of both tar and nicotine numbers, the levels represent the intake when a cigarette was machine-smoked. A human intent on getting as much nicotine as possible could draw higher levels of chemicals from the same cigarette.

Dangerous is as dangerous does

Timesaver
While on the topic of nicotine amounts, you may want to check Chapters 8 and 9 to note the level provided by nicotine replacement quit-smoking aides. One patch, for instance, starts at an initial strength of 21mg of nicotine released over a day.

Unfortunately these numbers aren't the whole story. How a person smokes can and does affect the amount of tar, nicotine, or carbon monoxide he or she gets from a cigarette. Smokers often compensate for choosing a light cigarette by taking more puffs, deeper puffs, or by blocking the ventilation holes in the filter—either inadvertently or on purpose—as they unconsciously seek to reach a certain level of nicotine fix.

Added filter ventilation holes are a major way that cigarette makers turn their smokes into "low tar" and "low nicotine" varieties, allowing mostly air to be inhaled along with a reduced amount of cigarette smoke. However, a smoker who is blocking ventilation slits can drastically reduce or reverse the benefit of having chosen a low-tar, low-nicotine cigarette whose lightness comes from its filter. The smoking machine used to test cigarettes for tar and nicotine yield does not cover ventilation slits—but then it, unlike a human smoker, is not craving nicotine. And there are other ways that humans can get more tar-and-nicotine punch for their puff inadvertently when smoking lights.

Polls show some smokers do consider light brands less harmful than regular cigarettes, but health experts have gone on record saying that light cigarettes offer no real benefits to smokers because of the false reassurance they seem to offer. Many smokers may not know about the ways they become more aggressive in their smoking behavior when they switch to light. In 1994, then-FDA commissioner David A. Kessler, M.D., offered insightful comments to a congressional subcommittee about the lengths to which smokers go to get their nicotine fix. He stated:

> It is a myth that people who smoke low-nicotine cigarettes are necessarily going to get less nicotine than people who smoke high-nicotine cigarettes. There are several reasons for this. One reason is that there are differences between the smoking habits of a machine and a human. The way in which a cigarette is smoked is probably the most important determinant of how much tar and nicotine is inhaled. Humans can compensate—and do compensate—when smoking low-yield cigarettes by altering puff volume, puff duration, inhalation frequency, depth of inhalation, and the number of cigarettes smoked. As a result of these compensatory mechanisms, a low-yield cigarette can actually result in a relatively high intake of nicotine.

Watch Out!
Ventilation holes
can be hard to
see. They are
sometimes made
with laser cuts,
and smokers may
not realize
they're covering
them.

Just how much impact can altered smoking behavior have? According to Kessler's report to Congress, scientific demonstrations show 32 to 69 percent of low-tar smokers have blocked cigarette ventilation holes with their fingers or lips, giving them greater nicotine yields. And when increased amounts of nicotine are taken in, so it usually goes with tar.

In 1998, the U.K.-based organization Action on Smoking and Health (ASH) and *The Observer* newspaper commissioned tests to check on the amount of tar and nicotine inhaled when ventilation holes are blocked. The tests were conducted using a cigarette-testing machine called the Filtrona SM400 at a government laboratory near London. Three tests were carried out to simulate how someone compensating for having "gone light" might smoke. Filter holes were purposely blocked completely in one test; in another, the holes were blocked halfway; and in the third test, holes were left unblocked. Results are shown in the "Filter Blocking" table.

Before you begin to think you're actually getting a good handle on what can happen when you block cigarette filter slits, consider a pair of studies that shed light on just how complex the issue is. Reported in the journal *Pharmacology, Biochemistry and Behavior* in 1998, these studies showed that when humans smoked ultralight cigarettes (1mg tar) with vents blocked, their carbon monoxide intake was doubled, but when they smoked light cigarettes (10mg tar) with vents blocked, the levels of carbon monoxide inhaled remained similar to unblocked levels. The authors concluded 1mg-tar cigarettes differ from other cigarettes, at least with respect to their susceptibility to increased yields as a result of blocking vents.

FILTER BLOCKING

		Silk Cut Ultra		Marlboro Lights	
		Tar	Nicotine	Tar	Nicotine
Displayed on Pack		1 mg	0.1 mg	6 mg	0.5 mg
Measured	No Blocking	1.4mg	0.16mg	6.3mg	0.54mg
	Half Blocked	4.5mg	0.56mg	7.6mg	0.62mg
	Fully Blocked	12.3mg	1.21mg	10.5mg	0.77mg

Source: Action on Smoking and Health (ASH); "Why Low Tar Cigarettes Don't Work and How the Tobacco Industry Has Fooled the Smoking Public" (1999).

← For comparative purposes, testers note that Benson & Hedges Special Filter, the best-selling cigarette in the U.K., where these tests were conducted, has 12mg tar and 1.0mg nicotine yield displayed on the pack.

Because of the possibility of smokers smoking light cigarettes more aggressively, the FTC has proposed a new way of testing and ranking tar, nicotine, and carbon monoxide content. One set of smoking conditions would reflect testing as it's currently done; the other would reflect more intensive smoking.

What does all this mean to you, a smoker who's getting ready to quit? That you should be *aware* of this dilemma and use common sense. Making the switch to a light cigarette may help you curtail your smoking behavior, but only if you:

- Don't compensate by taking bigger, longer, or deeper puffs

- Don't compensate by smoking more of the cigarette

- Don't compensate by smoking more cigarettes

- Take care not to cover filter holes (with fingers, lips, or saliva)

- Don't rely on the numbers for absolutes about how much tar, nicotine, and carbon monoxide you'll take in

Remember, if you're a "power puffer," you may be getting more hazardous chemicals from each cigarette than a laid-back smoker. If you can "psych" yourself up to actually quit now instead of just switching to a lighter cigarette, remember that a nicotine-replacement form of cessation aide can supply the nicotine you crave without the other dangerous chemicals even a light cigarette contains, even when smoked correctly. Also, nicotine-replacement aides come in graduated strengths with specific instructions, so weaning yourself away from nicotine is more of a no-brainer than trying to figure out the intricacies of low-tar, low-nicotine cigarettes (Chapter 6 covers the varieties of prescription and nonprescription nicotine-replacement aides available).

Matters of taste

When public worries about the health hazards of smoking intensified in the 1960s, the tobacco industry started marketing "low-yield" cigarettes. But they weren't as flavorful, which presented the industry with a problem. In the words of tobacco industry patent no. 4,830,028, for a nicotine salt said to improve the flavor of low-tar cigarettes:

> *The perceived taste or strength of the cigarettes classified as having lower levels of "tar" and nicotine are progressively less than that of the cigarettes which are classified as approaching the characteristics of the "full flavor" cigarettes.*

Smokers tend to pick up on nicotine kick as an important part of their brand choice, as attested to in tobacco industry patent no. 4,595,024 C1:33-36, for a "segmented" cigarette that varies levels of nicotine delivered:

> *It also has been generally recognized that the smoker's perception of the "strength" of the*

cigarette is directly related to the amount of nico-
tine contained in the cigarette smoke during
each puff.

This is to say that a cigarette with high levels of nicotine delivery may come across as more satisfying to the smoker—that is, more satisfying to the *addiction* the smoker has.

And then there is the dilemma just emerging with menthol cigarettes. According to new research conducted at Ohio State University and reported in the journal *Addictive Behaviors*, women who smoke menthol cigarettes may be more likely to inhale more deeply and potentially take in more nicotine than smokers of nonmenthol cigarettes. Menthol cigarette smokers tended to smoke their first cigarette of the day earlier than nonmenthol smokers, which is important because the sooner a person smokes the first cigarette of the day, the more nicotine-dependent they are thought to be.

High-tech cigarettes

What about a cigarette you *don't smoke?* Various attempts have been made to design so-called "smokeless" cigarettes. For instance, in the mid-'90s, R.J. Reynolds Tobacco Company started marketing the Eclipse, which looks like a regular cigarette but simply heats tobacco instead of burning it, which cuts down drastically on the amount of secondhand smoke compared to regular cigarettes.

The tip is comprised of a carbon rod wrapped in glass fibers. It is lit, and the user inhales, pulling heated air over the tobacco—which releases a nicotine-containing vapor—and through a filter, into the mouth. While lauded for its ability to cut down on secondhand smoke, the Eclipse was not

Unofficially...
Studies show 65 percent or more of African-American smokers choose menthol cigarettes, as compared to only 25 to 30 percent of whites.

Moneysaver
If you're just
cutting down on
cigarettes, try
smoking just half
a cigarette at a
time.

without its critics nor its drawbacks in terms of science. According to 1998 study that appeared in the journal *Cancer Epidemiology, Biomarkers, and Prevention*, a study of Eclipses still in their packs showed 95 percent or more of the filters were contaminated with glass fibers, which the authors concluded could invariably be inhaled, posing a potential health hazard.

You may recall from Chapter 3 that in the 1950s, filters designed to improve the safety of a cigarette at one point contained the carcinogen asbestos. A 1997 study in the publication *Tobacco Control* noted that charcoal granules incorporated into some cigarette filters, to help remove toxins, can be released during smoking.

A 1995 study reported in the journal *Cancer Research* showed fibers were released from cigarette filters and could be inhaled. The tests used 12 popular brands of cigarettes made by six companies. Although smoking filtered cigarettes instead of unfiltered cigarettes has been found to cut risk of diseases like lung cancer, it's clear that more needs to be learned about the filters themselves.

Exotic smokes and other ways to take tobacco

In addition to the typical brands of light cigarettes on the market these days, other choices have appeared, from organic-tobacco cigarettes to tobacco-free herbal cigarettes. So what's the story? Is there any safer cigarette to be found, or, for that matter, what about smokeless tobacco? Is there a good way to segue into nonsmoking using these products? As you've probably guessed, there's no simple answer, but there are some things you should know.

Exotic cigarettes often combine tobacco with a variety of spices and flavorings, from cloves, which have gained some popularity in the United States, to cinnamon, strawberry, lemon-lime, vanilla, chocolate, or any of a host of herbs. Some exotic varieties of cigarettes are available that contain no tobacco at all, but a blend of botanicals that may include ginseng, rose, or cloves, among many other ingredients.

Are these a realistic alternative to conventional cigarettes as you're trying to quit? Probably not. It's important to remember that many types of exotic cigarettes are blended with tobacco. For instance, certain varieties sold in China have been found to contain between 11mg and 15mg of tar and about 1.5mg of nicotine. In the case of tobacco-free cigarettes, the lack of tobacco does not mean a lack of danger. Tar and particulate matter can pose a danger when smoked, regardless of the presence of nicotine.

As noted by the organization Action on Smoking and Health (ASH), herbal cigarettes are not recommended as an aide to quitting smoking because they produce both tar and carbon monoxide, and some brands have a tar content equal to that of tobacco cigarettes. However, some herbal or flavored cigarettes (with or without tobacco) are available with laser-cut filters designed to cut down on intake of tar and other chemicals.

The bottom line on herbal cigarettes is difficult to assess. These nonstandard smokes have received much less scientific scrutiny than widely sold tobacco brands, though there is some data. Taking a look at popular clove cigarettes (which, in actuality, are often more than half tobacco), for example, the American Medical Association concluded:

Watch Out!
Using any kind of cigarette in your quitting efforts—be it a light blend or herbal cigarette—doesn't do anything to help you overcome the habit of smoking, which you'll still have to confront when you quit for good.

1. Clove cigarettes are tobacco products. Therefore, they possess all the hazards associated with smoking.

2. Inhaling clove cigarette smoke has been associated with severe lung injury in a few susceptible individuals. For example, people with asthma appear to be at increased risk from inhalation of clove cigarette smoke.
Respiratory tract infections may increase the risk from inhalation of clove cigarette smoke.

In 1992, an article in the *Western Journal of Medicine* commented that the active ingredient in the clove part of a clove-and-tobacco cigarette (an anesthetic chemical called eugenol) appears to be safe when applied topically, but that inhaling it is a new issue. Cited were two fatalities and a reported case of lung inflammation.

Long-term health effects of many of the constituents of alternative cigarettes have not been studied, especially not when *smoked*. For the quitting smoker concerned about his or her health, it makes sense to steer clear of tobacco alternatives that are really an unknown commodity.

Makers of organic tobacco cigarettes have done phenomenal business in recent years, but organic tobacco does not mean safe tobacco. These cigarettes are often made from whole-leaf tobacco and may profess to contain no chemical additives, preservatives, reconstituted tobacco, flavorings, moisteners, or burning aides. However, they can have even higher levels of tar and nicotine than conventional cigarettes.

What about rolling your own tobacco cigarettes? Because of the difficulty of assessing what makes up an "average" self-rolled cigarette, there is a lack of useful data on tar, nicotine, and carbon monoxide content. As noted by the Australian organization Quit, the paper used in rolling and any filter added would need to be assessed too, as that has a great effect on how much tar, nicotine, and carbon monoxide is inhaled.

What about smoking marijuana instead of tobacco cigarettes? Not only is it illegal in the United States and Canada, it won't win you points toward respiratory health either. Beyond the constituents of *cannabis* that provide a high, marijuana smoke contains dangerous chemicals, some of which are carcinogens.

Marijuana is usually smoked unfiltered and is inhaled deeply, then held in the lungs for a few seconds. Those factors have led to concern about its potential effects on the respiratory system. Marijuana smoke contains carbon monoxide, nitrosamines, benzopyrene, and dozens of cannabinoid compounds. All of these are irritating to the respiratory tract and are potentially cancer-causing.

Some studies have shown marijuana smoking can lead to lung cancer. It can impair respiration, change lung cells, and increase heart rate, beyond its psychoactive effects. Other reported symptoms of use include:

- Hoarseness

- Coughing

- Laryngitis

- Bronchitis

Some studies suggest that chronic use can impair the immune system and may damage the reproductive system, reducing sperm production in men and estrogen production in women. In pregnancy, marijuana use *may* be sufficient to lead to abnormalities in a developing fetus, although more research is needed in this area. A 1988 study in the *New England Journal of Medicine* comments that smoking marijuana results in a substantially greater respiratory burden of carbon monoxide and tar than smoking a similar quantity of tobacco.

Switching from cigarettes to cigars, a pipe, or smokeless tobacco is not a recommended way to quit smoking. These all carry serious health risks, as discussed in Chapter 2, and should never be used as a long-term replacement for cigarettes. Also, the nicotine dependence and psychological addiction that develops with these forms of tobacco is similar to that with cigarettes.

Cigarette smokers who switch to a pipe or cigar may even be at increased risk compared to those who have always only smoked pipes or cigars. The issue goes right back to smoking behaviors. According to Action on Smoking and Health (ASH), cigarette smokers who switch usually continue to inhale the smoke when they are using a cigar or pipe. Most long-time pipe and cigar smokers, however, do not inhale and take in less tar than an average cigarette smoker, even though the smoke from most cigars and pipe tobaccos has a higher tar content than cigarettes do.

The latest smoking rage among teens are *bidis*, rudimentary flavored tobacco rolls that in India have been known as the poor man's cigarette. Available data shows they pose risks akin to cigarettes, and the CDC notes these unfiltered smokes release three to five times more tar and nicotine than a regular cigarette despite containing less tobacco. Bidis may contain higher concentrations of other dangerous chemicals too.

Just the facts

- Filter-blocking behavior and deeper inhalation can negate the benefit of choosing a low-tar, low-nicotine cigarette.

- Smokers tend to extract more nicotine and tar from ultralight cigarettes than expected through compensatory behavior, such as taking deeper and longer puffs.

- Many kinds of "herbal" cigarettes are blended with tobacco and are still bad for your health.

- Organic-tobacco cigarettes can have as much nicotine and tar as conventional cigarettes, or even more.

Many Ways to Quit Smoking

PART III

GET THE SCOOP ON...
What method needs a prescription ▪ Success
rates compared ▪ Drawbacks to look out for ▪
How much will it cost

A Look at Popular Quitting Options

*Habit is habit, and not to be flung out of
the window by any man, but coaxed downstairs
a step at a time.*
—Mark Twain, *Puddn'head Wilson's
Calendar*

How are you going to quit smoking? If one is to heed Mark Twain's advice and the results of scientific studies, quitting cold turkey is the first choice likely to go out the window. Remember, a review of those who tried to quit and failed found that three of four flopped at a cold turkey attempt.

If you are a person of exceptional willpower, quitting on the spot is certainly the simplest and quickest, not to mention least expensive cessation method (though if you're a person of exceptional willpower, why have you been smoking all along?).

This chapter compares highlights of the most popular mainstream quitting methods you can use—nicotine replacement and the stop-smoking pill. Their potential drawbacks are covered, as well as how expensive they are or how difficult they are to obtain—do you need a prescription?

Quit aids and how they work

There are two types of assists for quitting smoking—those that help with physical cravings and those that help you break the psychological habit. Your best bet for success in quitting is to address both issues. In this chapter, you'll read about quit aids designed to work primarily on the physical addiction.

Nicotine replacement

Nicotine-replacement aids include transdermal patches (such as the brands NicoDerm CQ, Nicotrol, and ProStep) and nicotine gum (Nicorette). These patches and gum are available over the counter in the United States. Other types of nicotine replacement are available by prescription only in the U.S., including the Nicotrol inhaler and Nicotrol nasal spray, as well as the Habitrol patch. In Canada, patches and gum are available over the counter in pharmacies, near the pharmacy desk—no other nicotine-replacement products are currently available.

Some of the benefits of using nicotine replacement include a better chance you'll succeed in quitting than if you simply stopped smoking, as numerous studies show. Also, you should be reducing the severity of withdrawal symptoms you would otherwise experience, since you'll be weaning yourself away from nicotine gradually.

Remember that a nicotine addict (which you can usually consider yourself if you're a smoker) who goes too long without nicotine can become irritable, frustrated, anxious, angry, restless, and distracted.

Bright Idea
Are you nicotine dependent? You can take an interactive test to help assess that possibility at www.mentalhealth.com.

During the time you take a nicotine replacement, you can expect to experience the short-term positive effects of nicotine as you may have experienced them when you smoked—this can include stimulation, relaxation, calming during stress, improved memory, and improved concentration.

The dose of nicotine provided in nicotine replacement generally provides less nicotine than a smoker would get from cigarettes, and the amount provided declines over time until use of the aid is finally stopped. For instance, with nicotine patches, you often begin with a higher-dose patch and end with a lower-dose patch toward the end of the treatment period. When using gum, you may chew more pieces (or higher-dose pieces) for the first several weeks of treatment before cutting down to fewer pieces (or lower-dose pieces and *then* fewer pieces).

You can expect to experience some symptoms of nicotine withdrawal, just of more manageable intensity than if you were to quit cold turkey. Since withdrawal symptoms are not altogether eliminated with nicotine replacement and because you'll still be parting with a psychological smoking habit, it pays to prepare in advance by knowing what you'll do when a craving hits. You'll read more about them throughout Part V of this book.

Another thing to remember when using nicotine replacement is that you really shouldn't also smoke. It could result in higher levels of nicotine in your system than you're used to, and that can make you ill (though studies *are being conducted* to explore the use of gradual reduction of smoking along with nicotine replacement therapy). However, as I'll explain in Chapter 8, a combination of nicotine replacement aids *may* be desirable to provide both continual

Watch Out!
Caution is needed if you are considering using nicotine replacement therapy and you are elderly, pregnant, or have certain health conditions. See Chapters 8 and 9 for more specifics, check product package inserts, and, of course, ask your physician and pharmacist before use if you have any questions.

nicotine replacement (as with a patch), as well as occasional relief of cravings (with nicotine nasal spray or another fast-acting aid). This should only be done with a physician's supervision. Remember, nicotine in very high doses can be fatal. Nicotine replacement is for sale only to those 18 and older.

Nicotine patches

Nicotine patches look something like oversized adhesive bandages, and their generic name is nicotine transdermal system. They are worn on the body, usually the upper arm, for most of the day or around the clock. The side that sticks to your skin has adhesive around the edges. The center of the sticky side contains nicotine that can be absorbed in a continual manner.

Nicotine patches come in different strengths, depending on whether you are a heavy or light smoker, and depending on what stage of quitting you are at. NicoDerm CQ, Nicotrol, and ProStep patches are available over the counter, though when the first patch was approved by the FDA in 1992, it was available by prescription only, with the first over-the-counter availability coming four years later. The Habitrol patch is available in the United States by prescription. Habitrol patches are available in Canada without a prescription. Other patch brands available in Canada include Nicoderm, Nicotrol, and ProStep.

The "Nicotine Patches" table is a quick guide to the strengths of nicotine patches that are available, and how they're typically used.

One of the biggest benefits of patch use is that it requires little more than remembering to put the patch on and to switch patches daily. Also, the continual dose of nicotine it provides may mean for fewer highs and lows. However, nicotine does not

Timesaver
More nicotine patch information can be found at these manufacturer Web sites:
Habitrol: www.habitrol.com
NicoDerm CQ: www.nicodermcq.com
Nicotrol: www.nicotrol.com

NICOTINE PATCHES

Patch	Nicotine Dose (Daily)			Step Duration
NicoDerm CQ (24-hour use)	Step 1 21mg	Step 2 14mg	Step 3 7mg	Heavier smokers (10+ cigarettes per day) Step 1: 6 weeks Step 2: 2 weeks Step 3: 2 weeks
				Lighter smokers (<10 cigarettes per day) (Begin at step 2) Step 2: 6 weeks Step 3: 2 weeks
Nicotrol patch (16-hour use)	15mg			6 weeks
Habitrol (24-hour use)	Step 1 21mg	Step 2 14mg	Step 3 7mg	Heavier smokers (20+ cigarettes per day) 3 to 4 weeks each step
				Lighter smokers (<20 cigarettes per day) (Begin at step 2) Step 2: 6–8 weeks Step 3: 3–4 weeks
ProStep (24-hour use)	Step 1 22mg	Step 2 11mg		Step 1: 4–8 weeks Step 2: 2–4 weeks

← This table is only a general informational guideline to dosing. *Always* check the package insert for complete and up-to-date usage information, and go by your physician's instructions.

make it into a smoker's system as quickly as it does when smoking a cigarette. Instead of a near-instant hit of nicotine absorbed into the blood through the lungs, transdermally provided nicotine seeps into the bloodstream more gradually and may take as long as three hours. This is one reason it is important to maintain a regular patch-switching schedule. Nicotine keeps seeping into your bloodstream for several hours after you take off a patch, too, so don't think about removing the patch and then having a cigarette.

What are patch drawbacks? The most common side effects are a skin rash in the area the patch adhered to and some sleep disturbances. A rash is most often due to either a reaction to the adhesive

Timesaver
Find out more
about Nicotrol
nicotine patches,
nasal spray, and
inhaler at the
Web site
www.nicotrol.
com.

or to the nicotine itself. Sleep problems (including vivid dreams) can be due to receiving nicotine while you're asleep and not used to getting it and are more likely to occur with the 24-hour patch than the 16-hour patch. A trade-off is that users of 16-hour patches sometimes wake up in the morning craving a cigarette. You can read more about these side effects in Chapters 8 and 9.

You should advise your physician before trying a nicotine patch whether you have or have had any of the following conditions:

- Allergy to adhesive plasters
- An allergic or unusual reaction to nicotine, other medicines, foods, dyes, or preservatives
- Angina
- Asthma
- Depression
- Diabetes
- Heart attack
- Heart disease
- High blood pressure
- Irregular heartbeat
- Overactive thyroid
- Pheochromocytoma (a type of adrenal tumor)
- Skin problems
- Stomach ulcers

Pregnant women, those who are trying to get pregnant, and breast-feeding mothers should advise their physician before trying nicotine patches or using any form of nicotine replacement therapy. You should really discuss with your physician whether *any* present or past medical condition, or current use of any drug or supplement, could affect your use of nicotine replacement therapy.

Nicotine gum

The FDA approved the use of *nicotine polacrix* gum as a prescription drug in 1984. In 1996, it became the first smoking cessation aid allowed for sale over the counter in the U.S.—it is also available over-the-counter in Canadian pharmacies. Nicotine gum works a little differently than cigarettes or transdermal patches. To use nicotine gum, you chew a piece until you experience a peppery taste in your mouth, and then you "park" it between your cheek and gum for a minute or so (until the peppery taste is gone), and then chew it again, park it again, and so on, for up to half an hour. Nicotine is absorbed through the mouth tissues into the bloodstream.

Like patches, each piece of nicotine gum provides lower levels of nicotine than the typical 6mg to 8mg provided by a cigarette. Nicorette gum is available in two strengths:

- 2mg for those who smoke less than 25 cigarettes daily

- 4mg for those who smoke 25 or more cigarettes daily

Nicorette is also available in *mint* flavor. (In Canada, the 4mg gum is called Nicorette Plus.)

About 90 percent of the nicotine in nicotine gum is released in 20 to 30 minutes. Using nicotine gum is more like smoking a cigarette than patches are in that you chew gum when a nicotine craving occurs. Also, the action of chewing may provide oral gratification. Acidic foods and beverages can interfere with nicotine absorption, so try to avoid them at the times you're using nicotine gum.

Bright Idea
You can read up on Nicorette gum at the Web site www.nicorette. com.

The basic recommended usage schedule for Nicorette is shown in the "Nicorette Nicotine Gum" table.

NICORETTE NICOTINE GUM

Weeks 1 through 6	Weeks 7 through 9	Weeks 10 through 12
1 piece every 1 to 2 hours	1 piece every 2 to 4 hours	1 piece every 4 to 8 hours

Do not use ➡ more than 24 pieces per day.

If you have any of the following conditions, discuss matters with your physician before using nicotine gum:

- An allergic or unusual reaction to nicotine, other medicines, foods, dyes, or preservatives

- Angina

- Dental disease

- Diabetes

- Irregular heartbeat

- Overactive thyroid

- Pheochromocytoma (a type of adrenal tumor)

- Previous heart attack

- Stomach problems or ulcers

If you are pregnant or trying to get pregnant, or are breast-feeding, you should also discuss this with your physician before using nicotine gum. Chapter 13 discusses pregnancy and smoking cessation concerns. Again, it's wise to talk to your physician about any medical conditions that could affect your use of nicotine gum, and ditto for any drugs or supplements you may be taking.

Nicotine inhaler

Another nicotine replacement aid for smoking cessation is the nicotine inhaler. It is available in the

United States by prescription only under the brand name Nicotrol. (The inhaler is not currently available in Canada.) The inhaler looks vaguely like a cigarette, and the quitting smoker inhales nicotine through a mouthpiece attached to a plastic nicotine cartridge. Nicotine used in this way is typically absorbed through the mucous membranes of the mouth and throat.

The inhaler is a device that not only replaces nicotine, but provides some sense of the ritual of smoking and the tactile feel of a cigarette. Among the drawbacks are possible cough and irritation of the mouth or throat, which, according to one study, was experienced by 40 percent of patients who used the inhaler. Some 32 percent of inhaler users reported experiencing a cough, and 18 percent reported an upset stomach. Most of the patients who had a cough and mouth or throat irritations described the symptoms as mild and decreasing with continued use.

Before you are prescribed a nicotine inhaler, you should tell your doctor whether you have any of the following conditions:

- Asthma or wheezing

- Diabetes (requiring insulin)

- Drug allergies

- Heart problems (recent heart attack, irregular heartbeat, and severe or worsening heart pain)

- High blood pressure

- Kidney or liver disease

- Overactive thyroid

- Stomach ulcers

Ask your physician whether *any* medical conditions or use of drugs or supplements could affect your use of the inhaler.

Unofficially...
Despite its addictive characteristics, scientists are finding that nicotine may be useful in the treatment of certain diseases. A preliminary study found a nicotine injection followed by use of nicotine patches improved motor function and cognition in several Parkinson's disease patients.

The nicotine cartridges provide about 20 minutes of puffing and deliver 8 to 10 times less nicotine per puff than a typical cigarette. Users of Nicotrol Inhalers are advised not to use more than 16 cartridges per day unless directed to do so by their doctor. Recommended treatment is up to three months and, if needed, gradual reduction from there over the following 6 to 12 weeks, with treatment not exceeding 6 months.

Nicotine nasal spray

Another type of nicotine replacement currently available only by prescription in the U.S. (currently not available in Canada) is nicotine nasal spray. It was approved by the FDA in 1996 and is marketed under the brand name Nicotrol NS (patches and a nicotine inhaler are also marketed under the brand name Nicotrol).

Instead of smoking cigarettes, a person inhales nicotine nasal spray into the nose from a pump bottle. Nicotine is then absorbed through the nasal lining into the bloodstream almost as quickly as when smoking a cigarette, in contrast with the speed of patches or nicotine gum. There can be drawbacks, including nasal and sinus irritation, so it's not recommended for people with nasal or sinus conditions, asthma, or allergies.

Advise your doctor before requesting nasal spray if you have a history of any of the following:

- An allergic or unusual reaction to nicotine, other medicines, foods, dyes, or preservatives
- Angina
- Dental disease
- Diabetes
- Heart attack

- Irregular heartbeat
- Overactive thyroid
- Pheochromocytoma (a type of adrenal tumor)
- Stomach problems or ulcers

Advise your doctor if you are pregnant, trying to get pregnant, or breast-feeding. Discuss with your physician whether any health conditions or use of drugs or supplements could affect your use of nicotine replacement therapy.

Nicotine sublingual tablets

The first sublingual nicotine tablet was recently introduced under the brand name Nicorette, though it is not yet available in the United States or Canada. This tiny tablet, Nicorette Microtab, is designed to dissolve while held under the tongue, allowing relatively speedy nicotine absorption through the lining of the mouth into the bloodstream.

The Microtab's recommended use (in areas where it is approved) is for a span of at least 12 weeks (not more than 6 months) with gradual reduction in the number of Microtabs used daily. A quitting smoker may choose to use as many as 40 a day, with smokers of less than 20 daily cigarettes recommended to take one sublingual tablet every hour, and smokers of more than 20 daily cigarettes recommended to use two Microtabs an hour.

Neurotransmitter support

You may have heard of a stop-smoking pill called Zyban. It is bupropion HCl, an antidepressant that turned out to be useful in smoking cessation. It does not contain nicotine. Bupropion HCl is also marketed as Wellbutrin when prescribed for depression. Zyban contains no nicotine itself. Instead, it seems to reduce nicotine withdrawal symptoms and the urge to smoke by having an effect on chemicals in the brain that are associated with nicotine addiction. Zyban is available by prescription in both the U.S. and Canada.

Among the symptoms of nicotine withdrawal Zyban was found to alleviate are:

- Irritability
- Frustration
- Anger
- Anxiety
- Difficulty in concentrating
- Restlessness
- Depressed mood or negative affect

If you are depressed as well as addicted to nicotine, Zyban *may* help both conditions. But studies found no noticeable mood changes in people who were addicted to nicotine but who were not depressed (beyond alleviation of nicotine withdrawal symptoms).

The beginning Zyban dose is usually one 150mg sustained-release tablet daily for the first three days. After that, the dose is usually doubled to 300mg per day for the rest of the 7-to-12-week course of therapy. And unlike nicotine-replacement quit aids, you can still smoke while on Zyban—the usual recommendation is to set a quit date one to two weeks from when you begin taking it.

The most common side effects of the pill are dry mouth and difficulty sleeping, though they often subside or disappear after the first few weeks. If you experience insomnia, adjusting the dosing schedule so the pill is not taken close to bedtime can help.

Bright Idea
A support package called the Zyban Advantage Plan is available at no charge; it provides tips on how to counter the psychological tug to smoke. Check package inserts or the Internet at www.zyban.com or call (800) 822-6784 to enroll.

You shouldn't take Zyban if you have a seizure disorder since risk of seizure is associated with its use and risk is increased in some patients. Nor should you take Zyban if you're already taking Wellbutrin or any medicines containing bupropion HCl, nor if you are taking or have recently taken a monoamine oxidase (MAO) inhibitor. Those who have or have had eating disorders shouldn't take Zyban, nor should women who are pregnant or breast-feeding. Discuss with your physician whether any medical conditions and drug or supplement use may affect your use of Zyban.

Comparing success rates and costs

How do these mainstream quitting methods stack up against each other? They all hold advantages over quitting cold turkey, but there are some differences in tested effectiveness and cost.

The expense of quit aids is minor compared to the health cost that continued smoking can bring, so it's best to choose whichever options you believe will give you the best chances of successfully quitting. That said, here's how some of the major quit aids can stack up in terms of comparative cost. The "Quit Aid Costs" list shows some wholesale (before pharmacy markup) prices at typical usage rates. (Check your pharmacy, as prices may vary.)

QUIT AID COSTS

Smoking Cessation Therapy	Price Per Day (average)	Price Per Course of Therapy
ZYBAN Sustained-Release Tablets 300mg per day for 7 weeks	$2.80	$137.20
Nicotrol NS 8mg per day for 12 weeks	$3.20	$268.80

QUIT AID COSTS *(cont.)*

Smoking Cessation Therapy	Price Per Day (average)	Price Per Course of Therapy
Habitrol Patch		$263.06
21mg per day for 4 weeks	$4.88	
14mg per day for 2 weeks	$4.64	
7mg per day for 2 weeks	$4.39	
Nicorette (gum 2mg/piece) for 12 weeks:		$216.72
18mg per day for 6 weeks	$3.87	
8mg per day for 3 weeks	$1.72	
4mg per day for 3 weeks	$.86	
Nicoderm CQ Patch		$188.72
14mg per day for 6 weeks	$3.37	
7mg per day for 2 weeks	$3.37	
Nicotrol		$130.20
15mg per day for 6 weeks	$3.10	

*Average wholesale price from First DataBank, Inc. as of 10/1/99.

Source: Reproduced with permission of Glaxo Wellcome, Inc. and First DataBank, Inc.

Note that wholesale acquisition costs may not represent the actual prices paid by pharmacists or consumers. In the absence of a pharmacoeconomic study, lower acquisition cost alone does not necessarily reflect a cost advantage in total cost of care. Costs are based on the shortest duration of treatment recommended by the manufacturer.

One of the most important criteria in choosing a quit aid is which one you feel most comfortable using. If you like the ritual of smoking, nicotine gum or an inhaler might be best for you. If you don't want to indulge that side of your smoking habit but prefer to keep your quit aid out of sight and out of mind, you might do better to consider a nicotine patch or Zyban pill.

Studies of nicotine-replacement therapy suggest that it can help about 15 percent of quitting smokers who seek assistance to give up the habit, though

Moneysaver
Check current smoking cessation product prices on the Internet at an online drugstore, such as www.drugstore.com, where there's often a discount.

it's important to note that most research has included some form of counseling alongside nicotine replacement. The newer forms of nicotine replacement therapy—inhalers and nasal spray—haven't been extensively studied, but they appear to be at least as effective as gum or a patch.

Almost half of those who use Nicorette nicotine gum reportedly are able to quit smoking for at least a few days. Studies have found smokers most heavily dependent on nicotine experienced better success rates with higher-dose nicotine gum (4mg) rather than the lower-dose gum (2mg) or nicotine patches. Smokers less dependent on nicotine (such as those who smoke a relatively small number of cigarettes daily) have had comparable success rates whether they were using a nicotine patch or nicotine gum.

How helpful are nicotine patches for quitting? An analysis of studies found that at the end of at least four weeks of treatment, 27 percent of users were no longer smoking, and at the six-month point, about 22 percent remained smoke free.

This 1994 look at quitting success rates in the *Journal of the American Medical Association* also found that 16-hour patches worked about as well as patches worn around the clock and that treatment with patches for longer than eight weeks didn't appear to improve results. Don't underestimate the power of suggestion either. Intensive behavioral counseling did increase success rates, albeit modestly.

A California survey goes further. It found that at the two-month mark, patch use was not any more effective than quitting without a patch unless a doctor's supervision and advice was part of the deal. Reported in the *Journal of the National Cancer Institute*

Unofficially...
In the California survey, patch users were found more likely to be female, white or Asian, and middle-aged, as well as heavier smokers.

in 1995, this study of more than 3,200 quitting smokers in California found that of the 11 percent who used the patch, only about 30 percent sought help from their physician. Those who did fared much better at quitting.

The nicotine inhaler has shown good quitting results, too. A 1997 Swedish study reported in the *Annals of Internal Medicine* found that after a year, nearly one out of three who quit smoking using the device remained smoke free. When compared to a placebo inhaler in clinical studies, the Nicotrol Inhaler as much as doubled the likelihood that a smoker would remain completely abstinent from smoking for a year. Subjects who used the nicotine inhaler were about half as likely as those using a placebo inhaler to miss smoking, feel impatient and irritable, and have difficulty concentrating, too.

Research on nicotine nasal spray has shown that 41 to 45 percent of those who used it were abstinent from smoking after three months. Between 23 and 27 percent remained abstinent after a year.

To compare the different nicotine replacement methods, a 1994 analysis appearing in the journal *Lancet* is helpful. It found that in studies where quitting behavior was tracked six months or more, using patches, gum, an inhaler, or nasal spray increased the chance of smoking abstinence by these odds:

- Inhaler: more than 3 to 1
- Nasal spray: almost 3 to 1
- Patch: more than 2 to 1
- Gum: more than 1½ to 1

Zyban has also helped many people quit. A 1997 Mayo Clinic study appearing in the *New England Journal of Medicine* found that at the end of seven weeks of treatment, nearly 39 percent of those receiving 150mg of buproprion HCl daily were smoke free, and among the group that took 300mg daily, more than 44 percent were abstinent.

Bupropion HCl was compared to a patch in a 1999 study funded by Zyban manufacturer Glaxo Wellcome and reported in the *New England Journal of Medicine.* Some 30 percent of those who used bupropion were smoke free after a year, compared with 16 percent of those who used the patch. Research suggests that combined use of Zyban *with* a nicotine patch may lead to heightened success rates.

Just the facts

- Nicotine nasal spray delivers a quick burst of nicotine, while nicotine patches deliver nicotine continuously.

- Costs for popular smoking cessation products can run from under a dollar a day to over five dollars a day.

- Nicotine nasal sprays, nicotine inhalers, and some patches (in the U.S.) require a prescription.

GET THE SCOOP ON...
Finding a support group ■ Starting a
quit-smoking journal ■ Getting to quitting on
the Internet ■ Keeping costs down

Chapter 7

How Other People Kick the Habit

S tatistics showing which cessation methods have the highest success rates don't tell the whole quit-smoking story, though they're certainly a factor. Now that you're armed with some hard data on what works, ask friends and acquaintances how *they* quit smoking. The insights and tips you can get from one person's subjective experience may have an impact on you that no double-blind, placebo-controlled study ever could.

This chapter introduces you to some ready ways to explore other people's quitting experiences so you can learn from them. You may want to find a support group of other quitters, employ the help of friends, or seek stop-smoking resources on the Internet.

Stories of what worked and why

Ask three people how they quit smoking successfully, and you'll get three answers. One may tell you the patch worked wonders and she quit with no second thoughts, another may tell you everything failed until he tried acupuncture, and the third person you asked may reflect for a moment and say that absolutely nothing worked until she changed her thinking, her environment or some other factor. Who will you be most like in your quitting experience? Chances are you already have many little stories about your own attempts in the past.

Think about your own smoking and quitting history: What would you tell a quitting smoker who asked how you have tried to quit? Take a moment and start a journal about your smoking habit and quitting efforts. Whether it's a few lines or several pages, write something down about what you have been through and where you are going. You may decide to share this with other people who are trying to kick the habit or keep it as a private reference.

Make writing in your stop-smoking journal a ritual and a habit, just like smoking a cigarette. Maybe it can replace one of your usual daily cigarettes—the one you smoke over morning coffee or before going to bed at night. If you want to get into the project, you can decorate the cover of your book, paste in pictures from magazines representing what you think of the "before" and "after," perhaps a photo of sunny blue skies or a healthy model for the latter. And maybe a smoky bit of burned cigarette paper or a "surgeon general's warning" box for the former or the most unflattering picture available of you holding a cigarette.

Not everyone has the attention span for or interest in compiling their quitting journal with all the flair of a third-grade art project. But it can be therapeutic, and no one else has to see it if you'd rather they didn't. The "Quit-Smoking Journal Questionnaire" may reveal some things you may want to include.

QUIT-SMOKING JOURNAL QUESTIONNAIRE

1. How did you start smoking?

2. What has smoking done to you?

3. What has it helped you cope with?

4. How much has smoking cost you?

5. Have you been smoking longer than you've been in school?

6. Have you been smoking longer than you've been married?

7. Have you been smoking longer than you've been driving your current car?

8. Have you been smoking longer than
   _____ ?

9. How many times have you tried to quit before?

10. Why did you try to quit when you did?

11. How did you try to quit before?

12. How long was it until you started smoking again?

13. What prompted you to resume smoking?

14. What quit method did you use each time?

15. Why didn't it work before?

16. What's different about this time?

17. What preparations are you making for quitting?

18. What are your quit-smoking goals?

19. What words, images, and feelings are linked to what you hate about being a smoker?

20. What words, images, and feelings describe your hopes for life as a nonsmoker?

21. Who and what do you expect to be a help in quitting?

22. Who and what do you expect to be a hindrance to quitting?

23. Who do you need to be to succeed now? (Describe the psychological traits you want to emphasize.)

Timesaver
Looking for a prepackaged approach? You can buy *My Smoking Cessation Journal* by Michael D. Johnson (Petals of Life, 1998), which also includes quotes and affirmations to help you address emotional issues about quitting.

If you've set a quit date already, put that in your journal, too. So much the better if the journal is a dated diary so you can track progress day to day and week to week. At the end of each entry (whether you decide to make one daily, weekly, or on another schedule), consider adding a note to yourself about how many days you've gone smoke free, how many cigarettes you've given up that you otherwise would have smoked, and how much money you've saved by not smoking them. Also note dosages of any quitting aids you're using and how you're feeling—whether it's a withdrawal symptom or a positive aspect from not having smoke filling your lungs every day.

It would be ideal to share your journal with a trusted friend, someone who knows you well, will take the time to read it, and who can give you feedback. Perhaps she's noticed you look healthier when you've gone a while without cigarettes or can point to stressors you hadn't thought of as triggers for past smoking relapses. Ask her what she thought of your past quitting attempts. Look to other people's experiences for pointers and pitfalls to beware.

Bright Idea
Health-care workers can find guidelines on talking to patients about quitting through the Agency for Healthcare Policy and Research at (800) 358-9295 or visiting their Web site's page on the topic at www.ahcpr.gov.

Doctors are in a prime position to discuss quitting smoking with their patients, but surveys have shown that fewer do than you might expect despite the big health risk reduction that quitting brings. In a 1991 government survey, just 61 percent of smokers reported that a doctor ever advised them to quit. A push is on to encourage more doctors to open a dialogue with their patients about kicking the habit. Remember that quit aids have also been shown more effective when accompanied by a physician's assistance.

Interventions by physicians to help patients quit smoking have been shown to be particularly effective—whether that's because it helps smokers take quitting more seriously; doctors provide an authority figure; patients are better-informed about quit-smoking methods; or another reason. The evidence supporting the usefulness of health-care counseling against smoking is rated as excellent by both the *Guide to Clinical Preventive Services* in the U.S. and the *Canadian Guide to Clinical Preventive Health Care*. So bring up the topic of smoking cessation with your doctor and don't be shy about suggesting quit aids he or she might be able to prescribe, if you're interested in trying one.

There's a potential part of quitting smoking that researchers are starting to learn more about— withdrawal-associated depression. Many, many smokers report going through a bout of it as they leave cigarettes behind, and often it's a more pronounced funk than they expected would occur. Indeed, many quitting smokers don't expect depression at all.

But unrecognized depression (or anxiety) is why some people begin smoking regularly in the first place. The health-care community recognizes it is sometimes a form of almost instinctual self-medication which can temporarily lift mood. While some start the habit to address their blues, others who have never knowingly experienced serious depression find themselves going through it when they're trying to quit smoking.

A 1997 study reported in the *American Journal of Psychiatry* took a closer look at the issue. Among 126 patients who had successfully finished a 10-week smoking cessation program, nine wound up with a new episode of major depression within the three following months. Two out of 91 patients who didn't have a history of depression experienced it. So did 4 of 24 patients who had only one prior episode of

Watch Out!
Don't combine nicotine replacement aids without a doctor's instructions.

major depression, along with 3 out of 10 patients who had a history of recurring major depression.

To some extent, the worse the withdrawal symptoms, the greater the chance of experiencing depression, researchers found. They noted that among those patients who didn't have significant withdrawal difficulties, symptoms dwindled about 10 weeks after quitting. Those whose withdrawal problems were moderate or severe turned out more likely to have a new episode of major depression, not surprisingly.

Being observant about what's happening to you and taking steps to help yourself get through withdrawal and deal with depression and anxiety is very important. Remaining as positive as possible is vital to your quitting success. But rather than denying or trying to squash negative emotions you may have about smoking and quitting, look at them plainly and see if you can turn them into fuel for the good fight.

You can find psychological support and tips to help yourself deal with the difficult times through stop-smoking programs and local or online resources that I'll describe in this chapter. If you join a group program, consider sharing aspects of your journal to help others trying to quit.

Stop-smoking programs and places

There are many smoking-cessation resources, programs, and clubs—from local community and church-based efforts to plans associated with a particular brand of commercial quit aid to Internet-based support communities. The ones described here are among the most widely known and accessible. Whether you use support resources individually or join into a group setting, do seek support. And company of some sort. About 33 percent of smokers who participate in group programs are successful at the one-year mark.

Bright Idea
See Chapter 10 for more on the buddy system approach to quitting.

Freedom from smoking

The American Lung Association's *Quit Smoking Action Plan* was developed in response to a survey about why people smoked and what happened when they tried to quit before. Guidebooks, videotapes, and audiotapes are available. And there is a group support counterpart to the program, too.

A 46-page *Freedom from Smoking* guide covers issues like building your support system, controlling your weight, controlling your addiction, and coping with urges to light up. A quitting calendar and record-keeping system is included. Another guide, *A Lifetime of Freedom from Smoking*, helps quitting smokers battle relapse.

The group meetings are comprised of eight sessions led by experts who help you focus on understanding why you smoke, and how to develop your own quit plan and deal with the symptoms of withdrawal. The clinic program's steps are shown in the "Freedom from Smoking" table.

AMERICAN LUNG ASSOCIATION
FREEDOM FROM SMOKING CLINIC PROGRAM

Introduction— Thinking About Quitting	Preparing to Quit, Q&A
1. On the road to freedom	Knowing your smoking patterns, smoking's health effects, are you addicted?
2. Wanting to quit	Your reasons for quitting, building social support, your plan of action
3. Quit day	Help and support, contracts and rewards, ex-smokers panel, quitting ceremony

AMERICAN LUNG ASSOCIATION
FREEDOM FROM SMOKING CLINIC PROGRAM *(cont.)*

Introduction—Thinking About Quitting	Preparing to Quit, Q&A
4. Winning strategies	Symptoms of recovery, benefits of quitting, coping with stress, reviewing your plan of action
5. The new you	Fitness and exercise, new self-image, learning to assert yourself
6. Staying off	Lifestyle changes, weight control, handling social situations
7. Let's celebrate	Preventing relapse, passive smoking, graduation

Source: American Lung Association.

You can find out about where *Freedom from Smoking* programs are offered in your area or find out about other quitting resources from the American Lung Association by calling (800) LUNG-USA or (800) 586-4872. Some information is also available at their Web site at www.lungusa.org. If you would rather not go the group meeting route, there are other options from the American Lung Association.

For a lighter look at quitting smoking, the *Alive and Kicking* audiocassette program goes heavy on behavioral change with a less-than-heavy-handed approach. The tape features a group of recent quitters discussing their problems battling the urge for a cigarette, and from that angle introduces coping strategies and techniques to prevent relapse. And the *Freedom from Smoking* audiocassette program is an 18-minute-long stop-smoking program that covers topics including addiction, social support, coping strategies, rewards, ways to build your self-confidence, and ways to control your weight. It also includes 15 minutes of relaxation exercises.

You can also learn about classes through the American Cancer Society. Call (800) ACS-2345 for more information or check their Web site at www.cancer.org. You can find out about resources from the American Heart Association at (800) 242-8721 or www.americanheart.org.

The Great American Smokeout

The Great American Smokeout is an annual event organized by the American Cancer Society and first held more than two decades ago. It has helped millions of people quit by first asking them to commit to one smoke-free day, and the American Cancer Society says more people quit smoking on this day than on any other day of the year—even considering New Year's Day when many people make resolutions.

The Great American Smokeout is held on the third Thursday in November each year. You can find out more about it by calling the American Cancer Society at (800) ACS-2345 or visiting their Web site at www.cancer.org. Be sure to check out their succinct *Commit to Quit* plan while you're there, which includes a formal contract certificate you can write to yourself committing to quitting.

Twelve-stepping tobacco

A stop-smoking program based on the principles of Alcoholics Anonymous (AA) takes the 12-step addictions-recovery approach to quitting. Nicotine Anonymous is contribution supported but requires no dues or fees. Meetings consists of two or more people getting together with a common desire to be free of nicotine—and sharing experience, strength, and hope.

If you're familiar with the 12 steps of recovery that are the cornerstone of Alcoholics Anonymous,

Unofficially...
In 1971, Arthur P. Mulvaney staged the first smokeout in Randolph, Massachusetts. He asked smokers to give up the habit for a day and donate the money that would have been spent on cigarettes to a high school scholarship fund.

then the tenets of overcoming nicotine addiction according to the suggestion of Nicotine Anonymous, and its spiritually based approach, will look familiar. If you are not acquainted with AA, it may be a surprise.

1. We admitted we were powerless over nicotine—that our lives had become unmanageable.

2. Came to believe that a Power greater than ourselves could restore us to sanity.

3. Made a decision to turn our will and our lives over to the care of God, as we understood Him.

4. Made a searching and fearless moral inventory of ourselves.

5. Admitted to God, to ourselves, and to another human being the exact nature of our wrongs.

6. Were entirely ready to have God remove all these defects of character.

7. Humbly asked Him to remove our shortcomings.

8. Made a list of all persons we had harmed and became willing to make amends to them all.

9. Made direct amends to such people wherever possible, except when to do so would injure them or others.

10. Continued to take personal inventory, and when we were wrong, promptly admitted it.

11. Sought through prayer and meditation to improve our conscious contact with God as we understood Him, praying only for knowledge of His will for us and the power to carry it out.

12. Having had a spiritual awakening as the result of these steps, we tried to carry this message to other nicotine users and to practice these principles in all our affairs.

Source: Reprinted with permission of the A.A. Grapevine.

If you are in an area where a local meeting isn't available or if you can't attend, Nicotine Anonymous offers online help, regional networking, and pen pals programs. You can find out more by visiting their

Web site at www.nicotine-anonymous.org, calling (415) 750-0328, or writing to Nicotine Anonymous World Services at P.O. Box 126338, Harrisburg, PA 17112-6338. You can also check the White Pages of your telephone directory for a local meeting contact number. Subscriptions to the quarterly *Seven Minutes,* which lists meeting schedules for Nicotine Anonymous worldwide, are available for $7 annually ($9 in Canada). Send check or money order payable to *Seven Minutes,* with your complete address, to the address above.

Commercial programs

SmokEnders is one commercial quit program available, with plans geared toward either those using nicotine replacement or those who don't want to or can't use nicotine replacement (for instance, pregnant women or those with medical conditions preventing advisable nicotine use). You can order a *Learn How to Quit Kit* for $125 (plus shipping) that contains a workbook, audiocassette sessions, a relaxation tape, and other helps. SmokEnders has counselors on call for tough moments.

SmokEnders seminars have been used for group cessation classes in many large companies and are often available in community settings. A seminar program lasts six to seven weeks, with attendees smoking for the first four or five while they learn how to quit. Individual seminar enrollment runs $395, though in a corporate setting the cost varies between $250 and $295. You can order SmokEnders products by calling (800) 828-HELP or visiting them at www.smokenders.com. While less expensive alternatives can often be found, SmokEnders boasts a high quit rate and carries the advantage of a very structured program.

Unofficially... Nicotine Anonymous stresses that it is not allied with any denomination and is not a religious organization. Though it emphasizes a spiritual approach to overcoming nicotine addiction, members form their own ideas about the meaning of life.

Moneysaver
Check with your insurer to see if coverage may be available for attending group quit-smoking sessions.

Quit-aid makers to the rescue

The major pharmaceutical quit aids offer their own support programs to go alongside treatment, such as the *Zyban Advantage Plan*, which you can receive materials about when you fill a prescription for Zyban. The makers of Nicorette gum and NicoDerm CQ patches have the *Committed Quitters* program, with enrollment materials enclosed in product packages. You can see a sample of the *Committed Quitters* program at www.committedquitters.com. With it, you go through a quick interview about your smoking habits, quit motives and barriers to quitting, and then receive personalized materials geared to your quit effort throughout the course of therapy. Among the things you'll receive: a calendar, newsletter, postcards, and letters. Nicotrol, makers of a patch, an inhaler, and a nasal spray, provides a booklet about their *Pathways to Change* program, available when you fill your prescription or from your doctor.

Canadian programs

Canadians have a wide choice of quitting programs, too, such as the *Stop Smoking Program* available through the Canadian Public Health Association. Geared toward a woman's needs in smoking cessation, it consists of four sessions of awareness raising, six to eight sessions of goal setting, and five sessions of follow-up support. You can find out more about it by contacting:

> Canadian Public Health Association
> 1565 Carling Avenue, Suite 400
> Ottawa, Ontario K1Z 8R1
> (613) 725-3769
> Fax: (613) 725-9826
> www.cpha.ca

For information about other Canadian programs, contact the following:

> *Oui, J'arrete (Yes I Quit)*
> Centre de documentation
> Direction de la santé publique de Montréal-Centre
> 4835, avenue Christophe Columb
> Montréal, Québec, H2J 3G8
> (514) 528-2400 (poste 3486)
> www.santepub-mtl.qc.ca

and

> *Catching Our Breath*
> Women's Health Clinic
> 419 Graham Avenue, 3rd Floor
> Winnipeg, Manitoba R3C 0M3
> (204) 947-1517
> Fax: (204) 943-3844
> www.crm.mb.ca/crm/health/whclinic.html

The Canadian Lung Association has materials available, as well. You can call them (in Canada) at (888) 566-LUNG or visit their Web site at www. lung.ca.

Picking a plan

What should you look for in a quitting group or class? The right environment for *you* in terms of support, encouragement, and philosophy. Generally speaking, the more intense the program, the greater the statistical chances you'll succeed in quitting. Think about how you prefer to get your intensity—more sessions, longer sessions, or keeping up sessions for a longer period of time? The American Cancer Society suggests when considering a program, you should look for one that has:

Unofficially...
Not every occasional smoker develops an addiction to cigarettes. Non-addicted Ann remembers, "When I was in college, I used to bum cigarettes while out at bars. I wasn't addicted as there were days or weeks that I went without."

- Sessions at least 20 to 30 minutes in length
- At least four to seven sessions
- Sessions for at least two weeks

You should also check to make sure that the leader of the group has been trained in tobacco cessation, and be careful of plans that say you can have instant success with no effort, as well as those that charge an unreasonably high fee, use injections or pills, or refuse to put you in touch with others who've gone through the program, as a reference.

Other resources

Check your local daily or weekly newspaper's clubs and meetings pages to locate other support groups meeting in your area—or form your own with a few friends or coworkers who want to quit. You can also contact a nearby hospital's wellness center or your HMO for information about quit-smoking programs. The HMO may either sponsor its own free or fee classes or provide a listing of stop-smoking classes meeting in your area. If you work for a large employer, help may be available through the human resources department, as well.

While some health insurers do fund limited smoking cessation efforts, it's not routine to do so. The major medical expense insurance plans often allow coverage for mental illness or substance abuse treatment (alcoholism and drug use, for instance). However, a higher coinsurance payment (for instance, 50 percent) often applies. If you have depression, are secondarily interested in quitting smoking, and wish to try Zyban, you may do better to discuss a Wellbutrin prescription with your health-care provider (since it is the same drug), in terms of the coverage that may be allowed if treatment is for

Unofficially...
The philanthropic Robert Wood Johnson Foundation has funded collaborative HMO efforts to cut tobacco use among young people. Look for help in quitting from progressive HMOs. Check your insurance booklet or call your HMO or other medical insurer about new options.

your mental health and not specifically for smoking cessation. Discuss the issue with your physician or insurer ahead of time.

Despite the health benefits of quitting, the Internal Revenue Service says the following about stop-smoking programs, in Publication 502, *Medical and Dental Expenses*:

> *You cannot include in medical expenses the cost of a program to stop smoking that you join for the improvement of your general health, even if your doctor suggests the program.*

You can read the publication online at the IRS Web site at www.irs.gov or order it by calling (800) 829-3676.

While it's a little daunting that tax codes and insurers don't typically go out of their way to cover the costs of quitting, many programs are available which are free, and if you're determined to do so, you can keep costs to a minimum. Check with your local health department if cost is a huge issue for you, as assistance may be available there that is geared toward your needs.

How much do classes cost? There are free sessions such as those provided by Nicotine Anonymous, and some classes listed by the American Lung Association or other organizations are also free. Programs with a cost often run up to around $100 for the full series, to cover expenses. Of course, you can spend as much as you want on smoking cessation, with individual weekly treatment by a psychiatrist, or other means. But you can do it on the cheap, too, if you seek out appropriate resources.

What if every adult smoker in the United States was willing to get help to quit? How much would that cost government, industry, or the individual? The "Cost of Quitting Interventions" table gives an idea of the cost of each intervention, on average, though cost would vary according to the amount of counseling, nicotine replacement therapy, and the intervention's effectiveness. Across all types, the estimated per-smoker cost is $165.61.

COST OF QUITTING INTERVENTIONS (TOTAL COST PER SMOKER OF SMOKING CESSATION INTERVENTIONS WITH AND WITHOUT NICOTINE REPLACEMENT)

Intervention	Without Nicotine Replacement	With Transdermal Nicotine	With Nicotine Gum
Minimal counseling (<3 min duration)	$33.20	$167.11	$172.18
Brief counseling (>3 min to <10 min)	$56.48	$185.57	$192.40
Full counseling	$94.24	$231.30	$246.34
Individual intensive counseling	$123.19	$255.01	$271.01
Group intensive counseling (7 1-hour sessions)	$71.83	$203.65	$219.65

Source: Agency for Health Care Policy and Research.

Quit support on the Internet

If you have access to the Internet, a wealth of help in quitting smoking is at your fingertips. Among the places you can turn to for general information and stop-smoking support are:

- **Quit Smoking Support** (www.quitsmokingsupport.com). Also known as Blair's Quitting Smoking Resource Pages, this site provides a wealth of information about quitting from virtually every aspect and features everything from self-assessment questionnaires to bulletin boards, an e-mail discussion group, a newsletter, and chat.

- **About.com** (www.quitsmoking.about.com). The Smoking Cessation section features articles and links collected from around the Internet, as well as a community of its own. You'll find personal stories, and a place to chat with other quitting smokers, as well as message boards and the option to sign up for a topical newsletter.

- **The Centers for Disease Control and Prevention's TIPS** (Tobacco Information and Prevention Source) site (www.cdc.gov/tobacco/). Here you'll find access to a number of publications about quitting, video clips of publicity campaigns to reduce smoking, and a host of other information.

- **The QuitNet** (www.quitnet.org). This community built around smoking cessation features a number of tools to help you quit and interactive forums with chat, bulletin boards, online support groups, and other ways of communicating with other quitting smokers for support.

- **Transformations** (www.transformations.com). A site for self-help, support, and recovery, not just from smoking. Transformations has message boards, chat, and other features.

- **Freedom Program** (www.ucanquit.com). This is an Internet-based but regimented quitting program that consists of 18 daily 15-minute online sessions, two weeks of "nonsmoker training," counseling, a personal journal, and other features. There is a fee to enroll.

Beyond traditional Internet resources, you can find Nicotine and Tobacco Addiction at keyword "smoking" on America Online. This AOL section features support for quitting, with message boards, chat, and other helps. You can take part in an active community of quitting smokers simply by joining an Internet newsgroup. These three are geared toward smoking cessation:

- alt.quit.smoking.support (you can also find a Web site and archive at www.swen.uwaterloo.ca/ ~bpekilis/as3/as3.html)

- alt.recovery.nicotine

- alt.support.stop-smoking

E-mail mailing lists geared toward quitting are available too, such as:

- **Ex-Smokers listserve.** To subscribe, send an e-mail with the words "subscribe exsmkr-l" (no quotes) in the body of the message to listserv@psuvm.psu.edu news:alt.smokers.

- **Former Smokers listserve.** To subscribe, send an e-mail with the words "subscribe smokfree" (no quotes) in the body of the message to listserv@cms.cc.wayne.edu.

When joining a mailing list, it can be helpful to use an alternate e-mail address so your mailbox won't be flooded with postings. Many free e-mail addresses are available; check your favorite search engine for more information. Also, check the first replies you get after you've sent your subscribing e-mail for information on how to set the list to "digest," a feature that compiles posts into a single e-mail rather than sending every posting to you individually.

Timesaver
New to newsgroups? Check your Internet browser's menu for "news." America Online users, type keyword "newsgroup."

Just the facts

- Many quitting courses are free, though some may cost up to or beyond $100.

- Personal stories from successful quitters can tell you things scientific studies cannot.

- The Great American Smokeout is held on the third Thursday of November each year.

- Go in-depth with support groups or classes to maximize your quitting success.

Medical Methods of Quitting

GET THE SCOOP ON...
Talking with your doctor effectively ▪
Combining cessation aids ▪ Watching out for
side effects ▪ Acupuncture—is it an alternative?

Chapter 8

Prescription-Strength Quitting Aids

So you're quitting smoking and you've decided to check in with your physician to kick the whole project off. Maybe it's time for an annual physical anyway, perhaps you want to be on the safe side before employing any quit aids (a very good idea), or you may know just what you want but need a prescription and a doctor's approval to take it.

This chapter goes into more detail about quit aids discussed in Chapter 6 for which you will need a doctor's okay, and addresses that "I want to quit smoking" talk you're going to be having with your physician. You can also find out about combinations of different quit aids your doctor may recommend, for instance, patches to provide nicotine on a continual basis and nasal spray to overcome spontaneous cravings. Plus, you can learn about treatments that aren't specifically for quitting smoking but that can be recommended by your doctor for that purpose. You'll learn about acupuncture, too, which has become a popular alternative medicine treatment (though its value in smoking cessation *is* debated).

Timesaver
In Canada, nicotine patches are an over-the-counter product in pharmacies.

Your prescription options

When a physician writes a scrip for a smoking cessation product, it could be for a patch, a pill, nasal spray, or an inhaler, or your doctor could recommend an over-the-counter product. Increasingly, studies are showing the value of a combination of smoking-cessation aids, so you very well could walk out with more than one prescription sheet. But *don't* combine nicotine replacement therapies independent of your physician's advice.

Currently available smoking-cessation aids available by prescription in the United States include:

- Habitrol Patch
- Nicotrol Inhaler
- Nicotrol NS (nasal spray)
- Zyban (bupropion HCl)

Zyban is the only non-nicotine prescription aid in both the U.S. and Canada that is specifically for smoking cessation. It and nicotine replacement therapies are all relatively recent developments. Patch technology is the oldest among them and is actually a spin-off of the space program.

Scientists working on the problem of motion sickness found injections were impractical—under weightless conditions, some medications can froth—and oral administration wasn't the best idea given that the problem dealt with queasy stomachs to begin with. The solution? Put the medicine into a patch in a manner so that it could be slowly absorbed through the skin and into the bloodstream.

Motion sickness patches are actually available for use on Earth now, and beyond nicotine delivery, patches are used in some other situations, such as nitroglycerin patches to relieve chest pain.

How they work

The idea behind nicotine replacement aids is that they deliver the substance a smoker craves, but not the other harmful chemicals contained in smoke. The emphasis is on small nicotine doses that help relieve symptoms of going without cigarettes, while minimizing as much of the addictive potential as possible. The use of a nicotine replacement type of quit aid can roughly double one's chances of quitting successfully.

Zyban, the stop-smoking pill, does not contain nicotine but seems to reduce nicotine withdrawal effects and the craving to light up. This new option (approved in 1997) has very good effectiveness rates, though researchers aren't sure exactly how it does what it does, just that it seems to have an effect on the brain chemicals that control addiction. That's not uncommon with pharmaceutical treatments, however.

Patches are the option providing the most continual dose of nicotine—for instance, 21mg released over a day. Regular-strength nicotine gum, an over-the-counter option, provides 2mg of nicotine with each piece (compared with a typical cigarette's 6 to 8mg) and its effect is released over 20 minutes to half an hour. Nicotine nasal spray gives users a dose of .5mg of nicotine with each spray and acts quickly. It's considered a 1mg dose since you use one squirt into each nostril. The nicotine inhaler is another option. Ten puffs provides about the same amount of nicotine as one puff on a typical cigarette.

Don't focus *too* much on the stated nicotine levels of replacement therapy products, since they're handled by your body somewhat differently than nicotine from a cigarette (but *do* follow product guidelines). They are different from each other in that respect as well. To look even more closely at the dynamics of absorbing nicotine from a patch, take a peek at a 1991 study appearing in the journal *Clinical Pharmacology and Therapeutics*. Researchers tested 11 people using a nicotine patch and traced how nicotine entered their bloodstreams. They found that about 82 percent of the nicotine contained in the patch turned out to be *bioavailable*, usable by the body, on average. The rate of nicotine absorption was highest between 6 and 12 hours after the patch was put on, and it declined after that, plateauing between 16 and 24 hours at about 62 percent of the top rate at which it was absorbed. Interestingly, 10 percent of nicotine was absorbed after the patch was removed since it remained in the skin and eventually made its way into the bloodstream.

If you started on one patch and switched to another brand of the same dosage, you *could theoretically* notice a difference if you were *very* sensitive to nicotine levels since rates and time frames of nicotine absorption vary by type of patch. Each is constructed slightly differently. For instance, a 1997 study in the *Journal of Clinical Pharmacology* reported that when participants exercised with a patch on, the mean delivered dose of nicotine was higher in Nicoderm patches compared with Habitrol patches. Bear in mind that exercise can increase the blood flow at your patch site.

Nicotine nasal spray was developed to give smokers nicotine in a way that more closely approximates the way cigarettes deliver nicotine, though it's not a continual dosing as provided by a patch. With this form of nicotine replacement, maximum blood content of nicotine is reached in around 11 to 13 minutes

Moneysaver
Using a quit aid, like nicotine patches, can save money in the long run. A 1997 study at Emory University School of Medicine found that the average cost per year of life saved ranged from $965 to $2,360 when a patch was combined with counseling.

(for 1mg doses tested), according to a 1996 study in the journal *Clinical Pharmacokinetics*. That's a slower rise than cigarettes provide but faster than other forms of nicotine replacement. A 1998 study in the journal *Psychopharmacology* found a 1mg dose of nicotine nasal spray gave more immediate relief for cigarette cravings than a 4mg dose of nicotine gum—but between 5 and 10 minutes, effects were comparable, while levels were *higher* with nicotine gum at a half hour or two hours after administration.

Instead of leading to nicotine absorption through the nasal passages, the nicotine inhaler, which you put to your mouth and draw air through, leads to nicotine absorption through your mouth. The nicotine in nicotine gum is absorbed through mouth and throat tissues, and the patch provides nicotine absorbed through the skin.

The usefulness of Nicotrol NS nasal spray has proven out in a trio of clinical trials. In one study, participants used the nasal spray with individual counseling, while in the other two studies, the nasal spray was used along with group support.

Patients were allowed to use as much Nicotrol NS as they wanted within a range between the minimum dose of 8mg per day to a maximum dose of 40mg daily. Though the recommendation was for treatment to continue for three months, in two studies, some patients were allowed to continue using the spray for up to a year if they wished. Of those patients who remained cigarette free at the year mark, 36 percent were still using the spray.

In all the studies, Nicotrol NS was found more effective than a placebo several weeks and months from the start date, through the year mark. Participants who used Nicotrol NS had more relief of the craving to smoke and withdrawal symptoms than those on a placebo. In the two studies where some patients kept using nicotine nasal spray beyond six months, the outcome was no better than among those whose nicotine spray treatment stopped at six months.

Nicotine nasal spray underwent review by the Food and Drug Administration's Drug Abuse Advisory Committee in 1994 just because of the comments of study participants who chose to keep using nicotine nasal spray for a year. Some users reported that they felt dependent on it, had some withdrawal symptoms when they stopped using it, and sometimes used it in larger amounts and more often than the study required. That was despite problems it caused for some participants in the study, such as nasal ulcers. Other studies have found that most symptoms—runny nose, nasal irritation, throat irritation, watering eyes, and sneezing—go away after about a week of use.

The Nicotrol Inhaler is made up of a mouthpiece and a plastic cartridge that provides 4mg of nicotine from a plug that contains 10mg, when about 80 deep inhalations are taken over a 20-minute period. Most of the nicotine released is deposited in the mouth, and less than 5 percent reaches the lower part of the respiratory tract. About 2mg of the nicotine is absorbed by your system with the highest blood content occurring about 15 minutes.

A pair of clinical trials established the Nicotrol Inhaler as a helpful quit-smoking aid. Patients were allowed to use between a minimum dose of four cartridges a day up to a maximum dose of twenty. While the recommendation for treatment duration was three months, patients were allowed to keep using the inhaler as long as six months if they liked.

Bright Idea
For more on studies and quit rates, refer to Chapter 6.

The Nicotrol Inhaler was found more effective than a placebo at six weeks, three months, and six months into the study. The "Nicotrol Inhaler versus Placebo" table compares the quit rates.

NICOTROL INHALER VERSUS PLACEBO

Quit Rate	Nicotrol Inhaler	Placebo
6 weeks	44–45%	14–23%
3 months	31–32%	8–15%
6 months	20–21%	6–11%
1 year	11–13%	5–10%

Each of the prescription quit aids has different characteristics that may appeal to you, such as:

- **Nicotine inhaler:** For the sensation and ritual of smoking a cigarette

- **Nicotine nasal spray:** To quell periodic, intense nicotine cravings

- **Nicotine patch:** To provide continuous nicotine replacement with little fuss

- **Zyban:** To address depression as well as nicotine addiction or for the simplicity of just taking a pill rather than fiddling with nicotine delivery devices

Zyban (bupropion HCl) can also be useful in some cases when nicotine replacement isn't recommended.

Tips and cautions

Your physician and your pharmacist can answer many questions about using nicotine replacement products or Zyban. It's important if you are using any nicotine replacement product to keep it out of

Watch Out!
In addition to contacting a poison control center, if a child comes into contact with the sticky side of a nicotine patch, you may flush the area with water and pat dry. Don't use soap, as that can increase absorption.

the reach of children and pets, and that goes for used patches and plugs (in the case of the nicotine inhaler). Of course *any* medical products should be kept out of the reach of children and pets. Contact a poison control center or doctor immediately if a child comes into contact with an exposed nicotine product.

Some nicotine-replacement products are not advised for those with certain medical conditions. Refer to Chapter 6 for more on the topic (and *check with your physician*). Keep in mind that if you have skin problems, a patch may not be the best option. Likewise, if you have sinus problems, a form of nicotine replacement other than nasal spray may be more appropriate. If you are pregnant, planning a pregnancy, or are breast-feeding, discuss cessation therapies with your doctor since nicotine may be harmful to an unborn baby or nursing infant.

What side effects could you experience? The "Quit Aid Side Effects" table details some possible ones associated with each form of prescription aid discussed in this chapter.

QUIT AID SIDE EFFECTS

Nicotine patch	Headache, insomnia, dizziness, anxiety, irritability, fatigue, nightmares, stomach upset, diarrhea, and constipation
Nicotine inhaler	Mouth or throat irritation, coughing, runny nose, indigestion, nausea, diarrhea, hiccups
Nicotine nasal spray	Nasal irritation, watering eyes, sneezing, runny nose, throat irritation, coughing, nausea, headache
Zyban (bupropion HCl)	Restlessness, agitation, dizziness, dry mouth, difficulty sleeping, headache, nausea, vomiting, constipation, change in weight, tremor

Don't combine nicotine replacement therapies or smoke while you are using them unless otherwise instructed by your physician. Too much nicotine can be harmful or fatal. How do you know if you've had too much? Symptoms of nicotine overdose can include severe headaches, dizziness, stomach upset, drooling, vomiting, diarrhea, cold sweats, blurred vision, hearing problems, confusion, weakness, fainting, and rapid or irregular heartbeat. You should call your doctor right away if you experience any of these symptoms. When using Zyban, contact your doctor if you experience confusion, rash, itching, seizures, or any side effect not noted in the table above, likewise if *any* symptom is more than minor.

It's best to ask your physician to review your medical history for any red flags that could prevent the wise use of smoking cessation products; also, ask your pharmacist for a package insert containing full prescribing information and use directions.

Beyond the basic prescription

As stated, quitting smokers should not take it upon themselves to combine different nicotine replacement aids, but a physician can prescribe a combination, which may be more helpful to you than a single form of aid—nasal spray with a patch, for instance. Or your doctor may recommend nicotine gum with a patch. With severe quitting difficulties, clinical experience has extended to combining as many as four different therapies, although there is no extensive research support for the safety or effectiveness of such ambitious combinations, at least not *yet.*

Top cessation rates have been achieved by combining Zyban with a nicotine patch. A study reported in the *New England Journal of Medicine* found that not only did Zyban test as more effective than a nicotine patch in clinical trials, combining the two helped more than 35 percent of smokers stay abstinent for a year, while the abstinence rate was 30 percent for those on bupropion alone. Among patch users, 16.4 percent were smoke free, while 15.6 percent of those who used placebo patches and pills remained abstinent.

A 1997 study at the University of Arizona compared the effects of using different nicotine replacement treatments—24-hour patches, 16-hour patches, or nicotine gum. Withdrawal symptoms reported were highest when no aid or just nicotine gum was used and most people preferred 24-hour patches or a double patch. These options led to less severe withdrawal symptoms. The morning urge to smoke was greater among those using the 16-hour patch than among those using a 24-hour variety. Double-patch use led to worse insomnia.

Nicotine nasal spray is sometimes used along with patches to provide relief from cravings. And studies show that abstinence rates are better than when a patch is used alone. A 1999 study reported in the *British Medical Journal*, for instance, concluded that a nicotine patch for five months and nicotine nasal spray for a year was more effective than patch use only.

Unofficially...
The $450 million market for smoking cessation therapies is expected to more than triple over the next decade.

After hearing about smoking cessation aids being used only for a matter of weeks, a course of many months or even years of therapy may sound odd. However, long-term nicotine replacement, still under investigation, is an idea gaining in popularity.

Many quitting smokers appear to be lengthening treatment time on their own using over-the-counter nicotine replacement, in contrast to package directions. A federally funded study of 6,000 smokers and former smokers discovered that nearly one out of five was still chewing the gum after five years. But any long-term cessation therapy should be supervised by your physician.

Why nicotine *maintenance* therapy? Some smokers, especially heavy smokers, find it much tougher to quit than others do. Part of the reason *may* lie in genetic predisposition to certain addictions. Also, long-term, heavy smoking appears to change the way the brain works, increasing its number of nicotine receptors. That helps to explain the emotional lift and focus ex-smokers experience when they use nicotine.

If you have a particularly difficult time quitting despite using nicotine replacement therapy for a recommended length of time, discuss with your physician the possibility of continuing use as needed—but bear in mind that nicotine is a *drug* and that there can be merit in the idea of being *conservative* where your health is concerned. Although the medical community has concerns about perpetuating a nicotine addiction, nicotine *not* delivered along with the other constituents of tobacco and tobacco smoke appears to be much safer than continuing a cigarette habit.

Beyond nicotine replacement therapies, antidepressants other than Zyban *may* offer help in smoking cessation, and pharmacological treatment could come from other drug areas, as well. Please remember these pharmaceuticals have not gone mainstream for use in smoking cessation—nicotine replacement therapy and Zyban are the standard.

A 1998 study reported in the *Archives of Internal Medicine* took a look at the use of nortriptyline, a

Moneysaver
Your physician may be able to get you started with samples of smoking-cessation products before you fill a prescription and purchase it at the pharmacy.

tricyclic antidepressant, in smoking cessation therapy along with a behavioral program. It led to short-term abstinence rates better than the effects of a placebo and could be a promising new option in the treatment of nicotine addiction. In another study, nortriptyline was found to help post-quit depression, as well.

Studies have yielded some helpful results for smoking cessation from other antidepressants, such as doxepin. Fluoxetine (for example, Prozac) has also been shown in small studies to help smokers quit. Buspirone (for example, BuSpar) is an antianxiety agent that has undergone studies for possible use in smoking cessation therapy. The results have been conflicting, with some showing it doesn't help, and some research showing it apparently does. More study is needed.

If you're interested in learning more about one of these pharmaceuticals beyond Zyban, you may want to go directly to a psychiatrist or psychopharmacologist who is experienced in the characteristics of different antidepressant medications and their applicability (or lack thereof) to your situation.

Mecamylamine is an old antihypertensive (blood pressure) medication that has been studied for possible use as a quit-smoking aid. It is a nicotine antagonist—that is, it works *against* nicotine or blocks its effect. Some research suggests that mecamylamine can augment the success of a nicotine replacement aid when used in conjunction with it.

Use of mecamylamine with a nicotine patch has been described as a "chemical one-two punch" against smoking addiction. Mecamylamine can take away some of the pleasures that nicotine provides, theoretically making nicotine less interesting to the body's addictive mechanisms on many levels. It binds to nicotine receptors in the brain so nicotine cannot bind there, thus blocking nicotine's effect. Because of that, when used alone, it can actually make a smoker crave nicotine, as well as lead to dizziness and drowsiness. When combined with nicotine, however, these effects are reduced. Though it sounds contradictory, the nicotine can help curb craving while the mecamylamine can help reduce the reward the body gets from receiving it.

In a study of 48 smokers, those who took mecamylamine capsules and used a nicotine patch before and after the date they planned to quit smoking had an abstinence rate of 40 percent after six months, compared with 15 percent for those who used only a standard nicotine patch, Rose said. The results were similar at one year. More studies are needed of this and other drug areas with *potential* applicability to smoking cessation.

Going to the doctor

Should you go to your family doctor for help in quitting smoking or should you see a specialist? The answer depends on your cessation needs. To some degree, the answer may also depend on your insurance plan. While you want the best advice and help in quitting, you probably also want to save money. If your HMO allows a free checkup every year, use that opportunity to bring up the cessation question with your primary care doctor. Likewise, if you need to see your family physician about some other problem.

There's usually no reason you can't piggyback a talk about quitting at the same appointment along with another issue. However, if you do, keep open to the idea that this may be just your first discussion.

When you call to make your initial appointment, it helps to be clear about your reasons for the visit. Tell the receptionist you are coming to see the doctor for two different reasons—name your first reason, then say, "And my second reason is that I'd like to get started in a smoking cessation plan with Dr. So-and-so's help."

If a smoking-cessation plan was not your chief reason to make an appointment, remember when you're checking out of the office that the diagnosis codes your doctor writes down on your bill should accurately reflect that. It can make a difference when you ask for an insurance reimbursement. The best policy is to find your health insurance papers and review the policy for language discussing benefits for smoking cessation. It *may* be covered under a section on wellness. Then call your insurer to see what approaches you can take toward physician-assisted smoking cessation without significant cost.

If your insurance is with an HMO or PPO that requires you to see a primary physician before referral to a specialist, that primary physician should be competent to discuss your medical chart and any cautions against taking a specific form of prescription aid. If you have a smoking-related disease for which you should be seeing a specialist—emphysema, for instance—a referral to a specialist could land you in the office of a physician who sees tobacco-induced problems every day and who is particularly focused on helping smokers quit. Ask around. Don't be shy. But do check coverages before you expend money that may not be easily reimbursed if it is just for smoking cessation. Likewise, if you have significant depression or anxiety, a referral to a psychiatrist, psychopharmacologist, or other mental health professional who can prescribe medicines may be the first step you need to take, bringing up quitting smoking in conjunction with other issues affecting your life.

Perhaps you've wrestled with attempts to quit before and are increasingly concerned about the impact smoking is having on your health. If a support group or other program doesn't seem like enough to you, you can always choose individual counseling for smoking cessation—almost like having a medically qualified personal trainer for kicking the habit.

This is not the cheapest option. Hour sessions can run from $80 to double that or higher, depending on where you live and what kind of a therapist you're going to. Psychiatrists and psychopharmacologists (who are experts on psychiatric medications) typically charge the most. Psychologists or other health professionals may offer less costly rates. To keep expenses in range, you might see if a qualified therapist in your area holds group sessions that you could augment with individual treatment, or discuss fees for a combination of short visits, longer ones, and periodic telephone check-ins. You can combine periodic visits to your prescribing physician or psychiatrist with a less expensive form of community-based smoking cessation support, too. Check with your county health department or a major teaching hospital in your area for details on any reduced-fee plans.

If you're going for individual cessation sessions, you may choose to limit them to five or six, a typical number for classes on quitting smoking in the outside world. This should give you enough time to choose a quit aid, get started on it, and address your smoking and withdrawal issues. But longer terms of treatment are also common, and everyone has individual needs on this count.

A is for acupuncture

Another therapy smokers turn to when trying to quit is *acupuncture*. The 3,000-year-old Chinese medical practice involves inserting very thin needles into the skin at select points on the body, and sometimes gently manipulating them by twirling or even light electrical stimulation. Will it help you quit smoking? *Maybe.* The data's not all in, and U.S. experts note that some studies suggest it's *not* helpful in quitting smoking. Yet other authorities maintain it could indeed be of use.

What *do* we know?

Along with hypnosis, acupuncture has become a relatively popular *alternative* treatment for nicotine addiction. However, acupuncture is beginning to go mainstream in the West, now deemed by experts to be effective treatment for a variety of conditions. A panel of outside specialists convened in 1997 to study acupuncture for the National Institutes of Health, and in a consensus statement concluded that:

> *"Promising results have emerged, for example, efficacy of acupuncture in adult postoperative and chemotherapy nausea and vomiting and in postoperative dental pain. There are other situations such as addiction, stroke rehabilitation, headache, menstrual cramps, tennis elbow, fibromyalgia, myofascial pain, osteoarthritis, low back pain, carpal tunnel syndrome, and asthma for which*

acupuncture may be useful as an adjunct treatment or an acceptable alternative or be included in a comprehensive management program. Further research is likely to uncover additional areas where acupuncture interventions will be useful."

—*NIH Consensus Statement Online 1997 Nov 3–5.*

Acupuncture was deemed to be effective, but not *more effective* than conventional treatment for a number of conditions—particularly those that are pain-related. However, the NIH's panel of outside experts *did* cite "...evidence that acupuncture does not demonstrate efficacy for cessation of smoking and may not be efficacious for some other conditions." Yet remember that acupuncture was seen as promising in treatment of other addictions areas beyond smoking.

Research into acupuncture's treatment success rates is in its fledgling stages in the West. While U.S. researchers stopped far short of saying acupuncture could be useful in smoking cessation, the World Health Organization lists addictions to alcohol, tobacco, and other drugs as among the medical conditions that may be helped by the use of acupuncture or *moxibustion* (which most often involves the warming of the needle with the smoke of burning *mugwort*, a plant).

Some of the medical conditions the World Health Organization says may benefit from the use of acupuncture and moxibustion include prevention and treatment of nausea and vomiting; treatment of pain and addictions to alcohol, tobacco, and other drugs; treatment of pulmonary problems

Moneysaver
Larger cities may have schools for acupuncture that offer intern clinics with reduced treatment prices.

such as asthma and bronchitis; and rehabilitation from neurological damage such as that caused by stroke.

Western investigators are starting to catch a glimpse of what acupuncture does. A number of studies have shown that it can stimulate biological responses both at the site of the needle prick or elsewhere in the body. Messages sent through the nervous system can lead to the activation of pathways that affect a range of physiological systems in the brain and surrounding tissues. For instance, opioids may be released and assist in pain control, blood flow to an area may be stimulated, or immune function modulated.

East meets Western research

Existing Western research on acupuncture has proved equivocal in many areas—nicotine addiction included. As the NIH's expert panel noted, the standard method of treatment in Chinese medicine does not lend itself to testing by the type of double-blind, placebo-controlled studies on which Occidental medical research is based.

In Chinese medicine, treatment for a condition—such as the placement of acupuncture needles, may differ *substantially* among patients depending on other health and life factors. However, in the West there is much more tendency to address a specific ailment with a specific treatment. The Western need for placebo studies also poses a perplexing problem. Since acupuncture involves needle pricks, the question, "What is the placebo alternative to a needle prick?" arises. A third point complicating the compilation of research on acupuncture is that exact needle placement is crucial to treatment success. (Here the talents of the acupuncturist come into play.) A fourth factor is that Eastern concepts such as *qi* (also spelled *chi*) don't translate easily into Western medical parlance and evaluation methods.

Qi—by the way, is a foundation of Chinese traditional medicine (and is pronounced "chee"). It can be very generally described as the *life force* of all living things, an energy considered to exist throughout the universe. Try putting *that* in your petri dish to examine.

On a practical level, hitting the perfect spot for an acupuncture needle prick to solicit the desired effect is known as *obtaining the qi*. It is an art as well as a science among acupuncturists. Chinese medicine posits that channels of energy known as *meridians* run through the body and that a disruption in energy flow is what gives rise to disease. Tapping in at the right spot tweaks the energy flow and may have a desired effect on a particular organ system. It is important to note that the area being treated may not seem to the Western eye to be anywhere near the points an acupuncturist chooses. For instance, the ear is a spot often needled in addictions treatment.

Acupuncture in smoking cessation

More than a million people in the U.S. have tried acupuncture. In addictions treatment it is widely used to cut cravings for drugs and alcohol, mitigate symptoms of withdrawal, ease tension, and assist detoxification. The ear is a common site for acupuncture needles to be inserted, for their actions on the liver and kidney organ systems.

If you go to an acupuncturist for assistance in smoking cessation you will likely find yourself being queried extensively about not only your addiction to nicotine, but also the rest of your health status, your diet, and your life and emotions generally. You will

Unofficially...
While acupuncture is often ascribed to Chinese medicine, it has traditionally been used in Japan and throughout Asia.

Watch Out!
If you try acupuncture, make sure your acupuncturist meets standards. Most states provide licensing or registration for practitioners.

probably be asked to stick out your tongue—tongue color and coating is seen as indicative of health status. Likewise your pulses will be taken—yes, pulse*s* *plural,* as Chinese medicine recognizes a variety of pulse types at different points in the wrist. Once the practitioner has had a chance to evaluate you, a diagnosis will be made in specific Chinese medicine terms, indicating what needs to be done for you to achieve *balance.* Along with recommendations on lifestyle and diet, you may be prescribed herbs, in addition to undergoing an acupuncture treatment session.

Typically patients are asked to lie down, single-use, *very thin* needles will be tapped gently into your skin at specific body points (such as your ears but possibly including a number of other points as well), and you may be asked to rest for the better part of an hour. Though you may feel a tiny needle zing upon needle insertion, the sensation can indicate that an acupuncture point has been properly located. Acupuncture may hurt a little bit during needle application. It should *not* hurt a *lot.* An experienced and deft acupuncturist can often apply needles (and manipulate them) with little or no discomfort to the patient.

More than one acupuncture session is usually desirable—your practitioner may recommend that you return more often than weekly. A few to several sessions, or even a longer course of treatment, may be desirable.

Will acupuncture help *you* quit smoking? Again the answer is *maybe,* with the caveat that Western research on which the NIH's expert panel based its conclusions did not, overall, indicate that acupuncture does help in smoking cessation. However some who have used acupuncture insist it *can* help a smoker quit—and the practice is used relatively widely in treating other addictions—including addictions believed to work through pathways *similar* to that of nicotine addiction.

Just the facts

- Zyban and nicotine patches have shown top combined therapy effectiveness in major clinical trials.

- Antidepressants beyond bupropion (Zyban) *may* be helpful in quitting smoking, and other classes of drugs are under investigation.

- The value of acupuncture in smoking cessation is a matter of debate, and more studies are needed.

- If you're using a nicotine replacement aid, keep it away from children and pets as it can be dangerous (keep all medications away from kids and pets).

- Nicotine nasal spray is currently the quickest-acting prescription nicotine replacement product.

Unofficially...
It is not uncommon for patients undergoing acupuncture to notice increased warmth in their body as energy circulates.

GET THE SCOOP ON...
Buying nicotine without a
prescription ▪ Matching your habit up with the
right product ▪ Frequently asked questions
about nicotine replacement ▪ Over-the-counter
aids beyond nicotine

Over-the-Counter Options

Chapter 9

If you've tried to quit smoking cold turkey, and that hasn't worked, and you don't want to deal with the hassle of a prescription for a smoking cessation aid, you may be on your way to the corner drugstore, where, for under $50, you can walk away with enough nicotine to keep you satisfied for weeks, minus the tar and other toxins.

Nicotine replacement patches and gum are easy over-the-counter options, and many people try them. In this chapter, I'll brief you on using those products, as well as introduce you to some quit-smoking gadgets available without a prescription.

Nicotine patches

If you know you want nicotine replacement to continuously help keep you from experiencing cravings, then nicotine patches may be your over-the-counter drug of choice. Stick one on in the morning, and, ideally, you should remain relatively craving-free through the whole day. Conversely, with nicotine gum, you may experience cravings throughout the

191

day, which can be addressed by using another piece of gum. Patches, however, provide continuous relief, seeping nicotine into your system through your skin.

Not all patches are available over the counter in the United States, as discussed in Chapters 6 and 8, though these are:

- Nicoderm CQ

- Nicotrol

- ProStep

Habitrol patches require a prescription in the United States, but are available without one in Canada. For more information on Habitrol, see Chapter 8.

According to clinical guidelines from the Agency for Health Care Policy and Research, while the patch and gum are each effective, people are typically better at using the patch the right way, and learning how to requires less effort.

The following figure shows what a nicotine patch looks like.

Nicotine patch.

Source: Nicotine CQ product courtesy SmithKline Beecham.

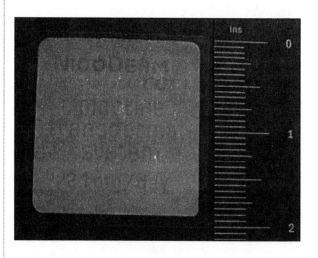

Patch directions may be slightly different, though they basically work the same way. In the case of NicoDerm CQ, you'll likely use patches for about 10 weeks, 8 weeks if you're a light smoker. Basic instructions for applying a NicoDerm CQ patch consist of the following seven items:

1. Do not remove the NicoDerm CQ patch from its sealed protective pouch until you are ready to use it. NicoDerm CQ patches will lose nicotine to the air if you store them out of the pouch.

2. Choose a non-hairy, clean, dry area of skin. Do not put a NicoDerm CQ patch on skin that is burned, broken out, cut, or irritated in any way. Make sure your skin is free of lotion and soap before applying a patch.

3. A clear, protective liner covers the sticky silver side of the NicoDerm CQ patch—the side that will be put on your skin. The liner has a slit down the middle to help you remove it from the patch. With the silver side facing you, pull half the liner away from the NicoDerm CQ patch starting at the middle slit. Hold the NicoDerm CQ patch at one of the outside edges (touch the silver side as little as possible), and pull off the other half of the protective liner. Place this liner in the slot in the disposal tray provided in the NicoDerm CQ package where it will be out of reach of children and pets.

4. Immediately apply the sticky side of the NicoDerm CQ patch to your skin. Press the patch firmly on your skin with the heel of your hand for at least 10 seconds. Make sure it

sticks well to your skin, especially around the edges.

5. Wash your hands when you have finished applying the NicoDerm CQ patch. Nicotine on your hands could get into your eyes and nose, and cause stinging, redness, or more serious problems.

6. After 24 or 16 hours, remove the patch you have been wearing. Fold the used NicoDerm CQ patch in half with the silver side together. Carefully dispose of the used patch in the slot of the disposal tray provided in the NicoDerm CQ package where it will be out of the reach of children and pets. Even used patches have enough nicotine to poison children and pets. Wash your hands.

7. Choose a different place on your skin to apply the next NicoDerm CQ patch and repeat Steps 1 to 6. Do not apply a new patch to a previously used skin site for at least one week.

No matter what brand you choose, always check package directions for specifics.

The upper arm is typically a good spot for patch use. Ideally, you should put the patch on at around the same time each morning. You should remember not to smoke at all after your quit date since that plus the patch could put too much nicotine in your system. You will be wearing your patch either 16 hours at a stretch, taking it off before you go to sleep and then applying a new one in the morning, or for 24 hours at a stretch, leaving it on around the clock but replacing it each morning.

Check your brand's directions for the length of time to keep the patch on. If you have trouble sleeping, a 16-hour schedule may be best for you, but if

Bright Idea
Putting your patch on first thing in the morning is a good idea—the earlier the better to avoid nicotine cravings if you've gone without a dose of nicotine overnight.

you wake up craving a cigarette, the around-the-clock version may be better. NicoDerm CQ and ProStep state that patches may be left on for 24 hours. Nicotrol states theirs should be removed after 16 hours.

Be sure to read Chapters 6 and 8 for more important safety and usage information about patches. Here are more answers to commonly asked questions about using a patch:

- **Will patches irritate my skin?** Some people do experience mild irritation—either itching, tingling, or burning during the first hour. This is often mild, and symptoms go away after a day. If they are bad or prolonged, remove the patch and consult your physician.

- **Should I put the patch on the same spot every day?** No. Rotate use of patches to new areas of skin, particularly if you experience mild irritation from using the patch.

- **Can I shower with the patch on?** You can usually bathe, swim, or shower for short periods as long the patch is affixed firmly on your body. Slippery bath oils or overuse of soap in the area could make it less adhesive, though.

- **What do I do if my patch comes off?** If your patch cannot be firmly reaffixed, dispose of it and use a new patch, taking it off at the same time that you would have removed the other patch had it stayed on.

- **When I progress from one step to another, with a lower level of nicotine, will I notice a difference?** Probably not, since your body can more easily adapt to lowering nicotine levels as long as it's a gradual process.

Watch Out!
If quantities of
nicotine are
seeping into
your bloodstream
after bedtime,
you may have
vivid dreams or
other sleep
disruptions. If
this happens
while you're
wearing the
patch round the
clock, you can
try taking it off
at bedtime (after
about 16 hours)
and putting on a
new one when
you wake up in
the morning.

▪ **How does a patch work?** Nicotine is delivered continuously transdermally (through the skin) and into your bloodstream. Since it takes a while for nicotine to get all the way into your bloodstream, nicotine is still being absorbed for awhile even after you remove the patch.

More medications are being developed that are delivered transdermally. In many cases, transdermal delivery may be preferable to pills because it provides a more direct route to the bloodstream.

Nicotine gum

If you're hesitant to be strapped to a patch every day or just like the idea of replacing smoking with another activity—chewing—then nicotine gum (*Nicorette*) could be for you. You can read more details about nicotine gum in Chapter 6.

The following figure shows what nicotine gum looks like.

Nicotine gum.

Source: Nicorette
photo courtesy
SmithKline
Beecham.

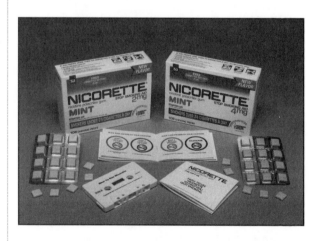

Gum usage is often up to 12 weeks, with average smokers recommended to use the 2mg variety and heavy smokers the 4mg variety. Many people chew the gum when they get a nicotine craving. However, since it takes a little time for nicotine in the gum to get into your system, a better idea may be to chew a piece of gum at regular intervals. Clinical guidelines from the Agency for Health Care Policy and Research suggest that patients often do not use enough gum to get maximum benefit and recommend a piece of gum every one or two hours when beginning therapy.

You should chew each piece of gum slowly and only intermittently. As soon as you notice a tingling or peppery sensation (often following about 15 chews), "park" the gum between your cheek and gum until after the sensation goes away. Then chew again. Repeat the process, parking the gum in a different area of your mouth each time, until you get no more tingle or peppery sensation. Typically, each piece of gum can be used for 20 to 30 minutes.

Here are some answers to frequently asked questions about nicotine gum use:

- **What happens if I chew too much or too frequently?** You may get hiccups. Too much nicotine can be released with too frequent or too vigorous chewing, and it can prompt nausea and throat irritation.

- **Can I drink something while I'm chewing the gum?** It's best not to eat or drink for 15 minutes before or after chewing the gum since it may decrease effectiveness.

- **Do I need to take special care in disposing of nicotine gum?** You should dispose of the gum in its wrapper and make sure dogs and children do not come into contact with either new or used pieces of gum.

Bright Idea
If you experience mouth soreness when chewing nicotine gum, try sucking on hard sugarless candy between pieces of gum. Brushing your teeth at regular intervals may also help.

∎ **Why doesn't it taste like regular gum?** Many people are not crazy about the taste of nicotine gum. It's important to remember that although nicotine gum is available over the counter, it's still a drug and is meant to appeal to the quitting smoker, for the purpose intended. If you don't like the taste of regular nicotine gum, try the mint-flavored version.

In January 1999, the FDA approved the sale of Nicorette Mint gum over the counter (available in the same strengths as regular Nicorette).

Other over-the-counter options

While nicotine patches and nicotine gum have been shown to help smokers achieve higher success rates when making a quit attempt, they are not the only over-the-counter options available. Nicotine patches and gum, however, *have* been widely tested and found beneficial in smoking cessation. You may find the following products useful when kicking the habit, though they are not a replacement for the efficacy of nicotine-replacement therapy or Zyban.

One Step At A Time is a device that is actually a filter system—makers say it allows you to remove much of the tar and nicotine in cigarettes. The One Step At A Time device comes with four filters that fit onto the ends of your cigarettes, which are designed to progressively block more tar and nicotine. The idea is to use each one a week or two before moving on to a "stronger" filter. One Step At A Time and its filters are shown in the following figure.

According to advertising literature, the first filter eliminates up to 25 percent of nicotine and tar, the second up to 50 percent, the third up to 70 percent, and the fourth up to 90 percent. The device, from

How the Filters Work.

EACH FILTER

REMOVES

A GREATER PERCENTAGE

OF TAR AND NICOTINE

The One Step At a Time system reduces your addiction two ways. First, a restriction passage in each filter traps tar and nicotine before they reach you. Then, additional air vents on filters 2, 3 and 4 dilute the concentration of tar and nicotine in the cigarette smoke. Each filter reduces the concentration more, gradually reducing your intake as you smoke.

Step One. Reduce Nicotine 25%

Step Two. Reduce Nicotine 50%

Step Three. Reduce Nicotine 70%

Step Four. Reduce Nicotine 90%

Percent reductions based on independent laboratory studies.

One Step At A Time (and filters).

Source: Numark Laboratories.

Numark Laboratories, Inc., of Edison, N.J., retails for around $20.

Although cutting down on tar and nicotine through a filter sounds like a great idea, if you're interested in trying a product that works this way, you should be sure not to use *compensatory* smoking behaviors. That is, not smoking more cigarettes, inhaling more deeply, or inhaling more frequently to make up for the reduced amount of nicotine you get when extra filtering is in place.

Among the many gadgets associated with cutting down on smoking is something called the LifeSign. You program this credit-card-sized computer by pressing a button every time you start to smoke a cigarette. Then, when you want to begin cutting down, it beeps to let you know when your next cigarette is allowed. In this way you "schedule" your smoking and are prevented from *not* cutting down.

You can gradually cut down over one or four weeks by scheduling your smoking in this no-brainer way. Some people have used LifeSign to schedule their nicotine gum dosing, as well. The following figure shows what a LifeSign looks like.

You can find out more about LifeSign on the Internet at www.lifesign.com or by calling the

LifeSign
computer.

Source: LifeSign.

company at (800) 543-3744. LifeSign devices are available for under $130. Check your local drugstore for other over-the-counter smoking cessation aids as well, in the pharmacy-adjacent area where nicotine patches and gum can be found.

Just the facts

- Nicotine patch use is usually for 16 or 24 hours at a time.

- Clinicians suggest using nicotine gum at regular intervals rather than just when you get a craving.

- Nicotine products should be kept away from pets and children.

- Nicotine gum isn't designed to taste terrific, though a new mint flavor is available.

Using Health and
Your Head to Quit

GET THE SCOOP ON...
What part of your smoking habit is
psychological ▪ Methods of treating
psychological addiction ▪ Simple willpower
tips ▪ How to use the buddy approach

Chapter 10

Psyching Yourself to Stop Smoking

That physical in-your-mouth craving you get for a cigarette as soon as you get up in the morning is one thing. But how much of the morning cigarette is part of your *routine*, like brushing your teeth, making the coffee, and reading the paper? This is where *psychological addiction* begins to enter the picture, making a habit tough to kick.

In this chapter, I'll help you distinguish between what is a physical symptom you can treat with nicotine replacement, a pill, or with other aids, and what is a psychological factor, something you'll need to defuse using your head. Then I'll introduce you to some tools to use for that purpose.

Research shows that smokers who use some kind of nicotine-replacement therapy and take part in a behavior change program can double their chances of quitting for good. Whenever using a product designed to help you overcome physical addiction, you still need to break the pattern of psychological addiction, or habit.

Is it a psych thing?

Remember the last time you tried to quit smoking? What happened? When did you give in? If you experienced the shakes, insomnia, or anything beyond simply wanting to have a cigarette (albeit badly), it's likely you were physically addicted.

Even if you use nicotine-replacement therapy, you still need to come to grips with psychological pressure to smoke. It may occur:

- At a social occasion
- Within a peer group of smokers
- When you feel anxious
- When you feel bored
- When you are tired

Or it may be a particular part of your daily routine:

- The morning coffee cigarette
- The work break cigarette
- The lunchtime cigarette
- The afternoon commute cigarette
- The before-or-after-dinner cigarette
- The late-night, before-bed cigarette

You may experience the psychological craving as a feeling that you need to have something to do with your hands, that you're hungry or thirsty (an oral fixation), or you may simply reach for your cigarettes without realizing it, when a situation or time cue occurs.

Think also about changes in your routine. On the weekends, do you crave cigarettes at the same times you do during the week? For instance, if you usually have a midmorning coffee break cigarette at work during the week, do you automatically crave a

Unofficially...
More women than men say they sometimes crave cigarettes to have something to do with their hands.

cigarette midmorning on the weekends when you're not at work?

Use the "Why I Smoke When I Do" checklist to keep track of when you usually light up (or, if you've just begun to kick the habit, of when you used to), and note what you think prompts you to smoke at that time, using terms like *nicotine craving, others smoking, daily ritual, stress relief, need a lift, something to do with hands, concentration aid, diversion,* and so on.

Why I Smoke When I Do

____ First thing in a.m.   _____

____ With morning coffee   _____

____ Midmorning break   _____

____ Lunch   _____

____ Afternoon   _____

____ After work   _____

____ Around dinner   _____

____ Before bed   _____

____ When reading   _____

____ Out with friends   _____

____ While waiting   _____

____ Around specific people   _____

____ Other_____   _____

____ Other_____   _____

____ Other_____   _____

____ Other_____   _____

← Example:

✔ With morning coffee *(daily ritual)*

Think about your answers and which daily cigarettes you think are mostly due to your need for nicotine, and which are due to the psychological setting. A bit later in this chapter, I'll show you specific ways to help avoid reaching for a cigarette that's tied to a specific event or situation.

The use of nicotine-replacement therapy is one way to tell whether your cravings are more likely to be psychological than physical. If you chew nicotine

checklist

gum, wear a patch, or use another form of nicotine replacement and experience craving at a specific time when there's plenty of nicotine in your system, it sounds like a psychological craving may be occurring.

When you're wearing the patch, the most common physical cravings occur first thing in the morning when a patch has not been on overnight. Switching from a 16-hour patch to a 24-hour patch may help you with this, as could adjusting the time you put on and take off a 24-hour patch.

With nicotine gum, the effect is released over 20 to 30 minutes, so nicotine cravings can persist for a short time after you've begun chewing the gum or some time after the nicotine effect is worn off. This is why it's often suggested you use nicotine gum on a regular basis when you would usually otherwise smoke before an actual craving occurs.

The other forms of nicotine replacement are not continuous like the patch, so they need to be used intermittently throughout the day to fend off nicotine hunger. Users of the Zyban pill might discuss adjusting the dosing schedule with their physician if first-thing-in-the-morning nicotine cravings are a problem.

Psych 101: methods to quit

What sorts of psychological aids can you use to assist yourself in quitting, even if you're already taking nicotine replacement or the stop-smoking pill Zyban? You should always use little strategies and tips throughout the day to combat cravings, but more formal methods may help.

Having a cohesive plan of attack on your smoking problem is important. In Chapter 7, I introduced some of the most well known stop-smoking programs, such as the American Lung Association's Freedom from Smoking plan, which includes printed guides, as well as listings of support groups meeting in local areas. This and the other step-by-step plans noted in Chapter 7 can be very helpful in methodically taking you down the road to a smoke-free life.

Addiction recovery systems

Any formal quit plan recognizes that smoking is indeed an addiction, but you may find some good help in quitting from those who deal with other types of addictions. If you have had a problem with alcohol, for instance, and have been to Alcoholics Anonymous, you probably understand how kicking an addiction involves the whole person and his or her lifestyle, rather than just the goal "I'm going to try to quit drinking."

Nicotine Anonymous uses the *12-step* approach to quitting adapted from Alcoholics Anonymous, beginning with the admission you've found yourself powerless over nicotine and that your life had thusly become unmanageable. There are other 12-step groups which may be of help beyond Nicotine Anonymous. For instance, Chemically Dependent Anonymous deals with a variety of addictions and doesn't make distinctions in the recovery process based on any particular substance. Group tenets include that the addictive-compulsive usage of chemicals is the core of the disease of addiction, and the use of any mood-changing chemical will result in relapse. You can find out about meetings and the like via their Web site at www.cdaweb.org.

A wealth of 12-step programs, one of which may suit your quitting needs, can be found on the Internet at the Twelve-Step Cyber Café at www. 12-step.org (at their Menuboard of Recovery link).

Timesaver
The Twelve Steps of recovery as adapted by Nicotine Anonymous appear in Chapter 7.

Groups exist specifically for women, for instance, and some groups are geared toward specific faiths. Another great Internet resource for finding out more about 12-step programs is Yahoo's subsection on 12-step groups. You can type in "twelve-step" at Yahoo's main search page (www.yahoo.com) and find it easily.

The heart of the 12-step concept is that an addiction, something that you have great difficulty shaking, is *not simply* a habit (though cigarette use is informally described as a *habit*) but is integrated into and can affect your entire lifestyle. The approach to overcoming addiction is a spiritual one, which can address not only the fact that there *is* an addiction present, but also the root reason why.

The 12-step concept originated in the 1930s when three alcoholics—one a stockbroker and the other two physicians—formed Alcoholics Anonymous. In a little more than four years, the first AA groups accounted for the sobering of 100 alcoholics. A textbook also called *Alcoholics Anonymous* was published, and at its core were the now well-known Twelve Steps of recovery.

Hypnosis

In hypnosis, you are encouraged to reach a state of relaxation and concentration and then to listen to a hypnotherapist's suggestions. When used for smoking cessation, the suggestions may include affirmations that you are happy and at ease with your life, descriptive imagery about the joys of fresh air, verbal support that you will be able to easily pass up a cigarette, and sometimes negative associations to do with smoking.

You are not entirely unconscious when under hypnosis. Practitioners describe it as an alternative state of consciousness in which you allow things to happen through your subconscious mind rather than trying to make them happen consciously. The state of deep relaxation allows suggestions given to you by the hypnotist to be more easily acted on by the subconscious. It is similar to that state experienced when you daydream or concentrate and don't notice distractions.

While hypnosis isn't accepted wholesale by everyone and while many studies don't support that hypnosis is efficient in curbing smoking addiction—some do, and research does show electrical changes in the brain during hypnosis, as compared to the normal awake state. Hypnosis is used often in behavior therapy (such as smoking cessation) to help people quit undesired habits. In alternative medicine, hypnosis is sometimes used for anesthesia and pain relief, and, in some forms of psychotherapy, it is used to help patients recall past traumas and to help overcome them.

Old-fashioned willpower

You can utilize some of the same methods informally and go the willpower route to avoiding cigarettes. Willpower often springs from a deep source, it doesn't work well when it's not backed up by passionately held beliefs. No one ever stood up to truly adverse circumstances for a cause they hadn't taken to heart. What is a passionately held belief? In part it's where you have a very clear concept of how something, say smoking cessation, is likely to affect your life. You may believe, for instance, that you'll find breathing and exertion easier after you've quit, and look forward to a healthy future with determination. After visiting someone who has lung cancer, too, you may come away with a passionately held

Moneysaver
Some hypnotists say multiple sessions are not needed in smoking cessation, so you can try just one (or buy a hypnosis tape and hear the message as often as you want).

belief that quitting is something you urgently need to do for your health. Deep belief can help give you the drive you need to quit.

To boost your willpower, think about surrendering some will—observe the 12 steps used in addiction recovery. The first step for Alcoholics Anonymous is, "We admitted that we were powerless over alcohol—that our lives were unmanageable." As a smoker summoning willpower to help yourself quit, coming to terms with past failures and the monumental task at hand is something like that first step. You know something has to change. But you also have to accept the past, and where you are right now.

Instead of *simply* trying to use your willpower as a force field against taking that next puff from a cigarette, dig deeply. Think about all the reasons you've not been able to quit in the past. What are your deepest fears in life and the things you're not happy with? How does smoking either perpetuate them or seem to help ease them?

Accepting that you have not *yet* been successful quitting is important. Whatever frustration and sadness you feel about it, come to terms with it instead of hitting yourself over the head. Yes, you did not reach your goal (but you made progress toward it by trying). And do you still love yourself? Spend a few minutes thinking about all the things you adore about life and the best parts of you as a person. The goal here is to get reacquainted with that wonderful self who isn't just a mirror of difficulties experienced while quitting smoking.

Try a day of doing things differently. Through each action from morning through bedtime, connect with yourself and reflect on something wonderful about yourself. Try to push other cares out of the way for now. Notice that it feels good to stretch when you wake up in the morning. When you're in the shower, reflect on how good the water feels and how fresh you feel when you get out. Smile at your own reflection and think about something you've done in the past you're really happy with.

At work, take a minute to pride yourself on your competencies and drive. If you're actually dissatisfied in your job, think about what you do well that you would rather be doing. Be glad you recognize that you want a change and feel that it's in your control to take steps toward a good future.

The idea, put simply, is to see the glass is half full rather than half empty, to turn a negative into something positive so that it fuels your drive. It's all about a good future, and to have that you first must love yourself, take care of yourself, and accept wherever it is that you are in your life. It is not your final destination. If you've been feeling bad about yourself, recognize that this a pain message, and pain messages are what the body sends to tell us that something isn't right and could be better. Be glad you're not complacent!

By reacquainting yourself with the core you—perhaps you'll liken it to you as a child when you had big dreams or at least more fun—you can delve deep enough to tap into a wellspring of willpower. It's the inner you that acts on something you vitally believe in, that provides the *will* in willpower. Anything other than the most intrinsic and instinctively proud and caring part of you is not the part you can draw willpower from.

Throughout the rest of your day, notice how you are in social situations. Notice who reacts warmly to

Bright Idea
You might choose to help out your willpower by listening to affirmation tapes designed to help you believe in your willpower. Check your library or audiobook sections of your favorite bookstore.

you, think about the good that you provide to others in your life. Go where you are appreciated and where you become happy. These are interactions to cherish, and they will make you stronger.

The 12-step method relies on a spiritual approach to quitting smoking. Those who do the steps are asked to "ask God" to help them with their resolve and pilot the way. Whether you are religious or not, calling on your own *highest power* is important. Whatever the deepest and most positive aspect of yourself and any higher power you believe in is, that's where to put your trust for willpower. Don't sweat the wording. Go for the feeling.

Quitting smoking may not be just about quitting smoking for you. This is a good time to retreat inward and do some emotional and spiritual house-cleaning. If you're religious, go on a new exploration of the most personal and enriching aspects of your beliefs. Use this time as a time to go explore the deepest good you can find.

As you summon willpower, do some life rearrangement. What can you get rid of that you don't like? How can you start concentrating, doing at least once a day and in a larger way once a week, those things you most enjoy? Get reacquainted with pleasurable things and seek them out. Make sure these are not deceptively pleasurable things that turn out to be bad for you, like smoking. In other words, don't substitute one bad habit—or addiction—for another.

When you're thoroughly reacquainted with yourself and feeling accepting of who you are, with hope for finding a happy future, then you can begin calling on your willpower to help you keep away from cigarettes. Because you love yourself and your life and will naturally want to sculpt a healthy future, cigarettes don't fit into the picture. This is the difference between thinking "cigarettes—that's something I want that I'm not going to let myself have" and "cigarettes aren't part of what I want for my life, so I'm going to disregard their call to me right now." Which do you think provides the best chances for success?

It may help to know a bit about how people really make transitions in their lives. Clinical concepts of change often involve the idea of a patient moving from chronic and unhealthy behavior to a more stabilized healthy behavior pattern. But that can lead to expectations of *quick* change.

How *do* alterations in behavior take place? Researcher J.O. Prochaska's observations about the *stages of change* are widely referred to in smoking cessation therapy—that is to say that smokers progress through periods of *precontemplation, contemplation, preparation, action* and *maintenance.* Further, data suggests it can take three to four serious quit attempts over as long as a decade before someone does finally quit smoking for good. Smoker, know thyself, and learn to recognize what stage you're in.

One key phrase to tell yourself over and over is that "coming from a positive point of view is always better than coming from a negative one." That's not to say that associating cigarettes with pictures of blackened lungs won't give you some mileage to help yourself quit. What it does is push you away from smoking through aversion. Much better is to find yourself pulled away from smoking by lessening your emotion about it. Indifference is said to be the opposite of love or hate, and when emotions are running high, love and hate can be closely linked. Indifferent is how you should wind up feeling about

Timesaver
Keeping busy in itself is one way to avoid smoking because it prevents you from even *thinking* about it. Start some new projects or a hobby, make some progress, and see how many better ways you actually have to spend your time than obsessing about smoking!

cigarettes after you've successfully quit—with cigarettes holding no strong emotions or associations for you. Then it is easier to avoid them out of simple knowledge of how bad they are for you. Attaining indifference is breaking the grip of addiction.

As you're digging deep for your strongest inner voice to support you by saying "I want something better for myself" right through those cigarette cravings, you can borrow tools from hypnosis. To reinforce positive feelings and behaviors, use music of whatever style you find relaxing as much as possible in your day, and spend some time thinking of something other than exactly what's in front of you. Daydream about vacations, paint, surround yourself with beauty, take care of yourself.

During those times, use a few regular affirmations that are personal to you, supporting your decision not to smoke. Speak them out loud or softly to yourself or even in time to the music. Silly as this seems, it is an informal approach to hypnosis. Music and a happy, relaxed state puts you in a more receptive mode for suggestion, and giving yourself positive messages during that time may well help those messages stick.

If you doubt this, think about how many negative messages you've run over and over and over in your head and how difficult those beliefs are to shake. Replace them with something new! Here are a few affirmations, though you may wish to write your own:

- I love myself and I am taking care of myself.

- I am happy and fulfilled being a nonsmoker.

- Cigarettes are not part of my life from now on.

- I feel energetic and at ease without cigarettes.

- My body is healing and making itself better already.

One of the keys to successfully using willpower is to fortify yourself on a daily basis with these good messages and, indeed, to look out for yourself before you find yourself confronted with a cigarette craving. Getting enough sleep at night and not overextending yourself or putting yourself in a situation where your willpower could be compromised are all parts of the willpower equation.

For some people, this may mean arranging not to be around smokers. For others, it could mean limiting contact with smokers and having a substitute for smoking when you're with them—be it chewing gum or carrot sticks. Willpower, then, does not mean steeling yourself against incredible odds, but rather the foresight to prevent yourself from getting into situations with bad odds, and then when you are faced with a difficult situation, doing your best to avoid smoking at that time.

If you increase confidence in other areas of your life, you may find your willpower for quitting smoking easier to summon. Regular exercise after even a few sessions has a remarkable ability to make you feel stronger in any situation. Even something as simple as cleaning and organizing your garage may lend you a feeling of accomplishment you can carry over to other areas of your life. Think about ways to nurture your resolve and willpower as well as happiness and excitement in your life.

Some ideas for bolstering your willpower include:

- Starting a fitness program
- Organizing your home or at least a closet
- Taking up a challenging hobby

Unofficially...
The portion of the brain that is responsible for processing pleasurable and exciting sensations is the same part that comes into play in nicotine addiction. Give your head some real replacement pleasure instead of nicotine.

- Setting and accomplishing any goal

- Looking out for and standing up for yourself

- Assisting a loved one with something they need to do

Some ideas for increasing the pleasure and excitement in your life include:

- Listening to music you really love

- Learning to *play* an instrument (it gives you something to do with your hands *and* is potentially stress-relieving as well as a good thing to focus on to keep your mind off cigarettes)

- Doing at least one new fun thing each weekend

- Finding ways to say no to things you don't like

- Going out with friends during the week instead of staying home

- Exercising in a pleasant setting—such as walking or jogging in a pretty park nearby instead of the gym

It may also help to think about times in the past when you've successfully employed your willpower. Call that memory to mind when you feel desire to smoke. What have you used your willpower for? To lose weight? To get a good job? To continue a fitness program? Memory of past successes can help you achieve another one.

The buddy system

Sometimes, things are easier to do if you have help from a partner. In many ways, a good friend who knows you want to quit can be the biggest help you'll find. When you're seeking encouragement, it almost always sounds better when you're not just reciting it to yourself.

Ideally, your buddy should be another quitting smoker. Ask around if any smoking friends or coworkers are interested in quitting with you. If you don't know anyone who wants to give cessation a go, you may well find a buddy to pair up with at a support group for quitting smokers.

The buddy system has been studied and found to help smokers quit. In a 1998 study in London, smokers in a support group were paired up with buddies. They attended a smokers' clinic one week prior to their quit date, another on their quit date, then a week later and three weeks following. Buddies were encouraged to keep contact and offer support between the sessions. At four weeks from the quit date, those smokers who had been paired with buddies were significantly more likely to be smoke-free as compared to those who had no quitting buddies.

A 1994 study of the buddy system among older smokers found that about a quarter of quitters used buddies to help them. Having a buddy resulted in better use of the American Lung Association quit-smoking manual that was provided to study participants, and among those who had tried at least once to quit during the prior year, those who engaged a buddy were more than twice as likely to quit as those without a buddy. In this study, those under 60 were more likely to use a buddy than those 60 or over.

In another 1994 study reported in the *American Journal of Health Promotion,* almost a third of participants in a Chicago-based cessation program engaged a buddy. Those most likely to were female, under 30, educated beyond high school, and highly determined to quit. More than half of the buddies chosen were nonsmokers.

Bright Idea
If you can't find a buddy to quit with, engage your spouse, significant other, or a friend. Try to make sure you don't choose someone who will be overly sympathetic and condone relapse.

Those most likely to be smoke-free at the end of the program were those who chose their spouse or partner as their buddy. And among those who ranked lower in determination, the quit rate was more than three times greater among those with buddies than among those without. Clearly, having a buddy aids resolve.

Tell your buddy what you would like him or her to do for you. You want an understanding ear, someone who can remind you when you have an urge to smoke that you've made a commitment not to. Your buddy can offer suggestions on ways to avoid smoking, possibly accompany you on smoke-free activities, help you with affirmations, and generally coach you into becoming a nonsmoker.

Someone who knows you well may be invaluable in providing insight about why you're smoking (in general, or particular cigarettes). If your buddy is someone you look up to and whose opinions you trust, all the better. An authority figure that you choose may be just the ticket you need to quit.

Should you tell everyone you're planning to quit? Not necessarily until afterward. Think carefully about whether friends who are smokers are likely to be supportive of your efforts or more likely to lead you into the "one won't hurt" trap. Tell whoever you feel confident with about your plans, though.

Practical tactics—affirmations, tricks, and tools

You can out-psych your psychological need for a cigarette. The key is to have the right arsenal of substitutions at the ready for every time you feel a craving. Look back to the checklist you completed at the beginning of this chapter. Which cigarettes you smoked during each day had to do with the social setting you were in, which had to do with stress, which with daily ritual? You can change your daily ritual to reduce its association with a cigarette.

Here are some tips associated with common smoking situations through the day.

The morning coffee cigarette

If you feel obliged to smoke with your morning coffee, try taking your coffee with you on the way to work, instead, since commuting may be distraction enough to prevent an all-consuming craving. If you don't eat breakfast, try having a light, healthy breakfast along with your coffee rather than a cigarette. Or make a treat out of your morning coffee. Add whipped cream and enjoy it on the porch with music or morning television.

The midmorning break cigarette

If you usually take your morning work break in a room populated by smokers, go to a nonsmoking break room instead. Since many people pick up a cigarette for a little lift at this time, eating a healthy complex-carbohydrate snack instead may give you some energy, which is what you really need. If you can take a walk and get some fresh air, terrific. At least visit a different part of your building or get out from behind your desk.

The lunchtime cigarette

Instead of having a smoke after lunch, order a modest portion of your favorite dessert and coffee. Identify, too, why exactly you're smoking at that time. Is it because you're eating in public alone, to have something to hold in your hand at all times? Take lunch with a friend and talk instead, or bring a newspaper to read. You can also use part of your lunch hour to run errands, get exercise, or breathe some fresh air. When you're choosing what to eat, make sure you get some complex carbohydrates to energize you through the afternoon.

The afternoon cigarette

If you find yourself reaching for a smoke in the afternoon because you're tired, rethink your sleep schedule. Go to bed a little earlier in the evening. Think about what you're eating for breakfast and lunch. Sugary products will only make your afternoon desire for a cigarette worse. Meals with balanced complex carbohydrates, protein, and fat are less likely to leave you wanting in the afternoon. It's also important to watch your caffeine intake. Too much of it early in the day can lead to an afternoon letdown.

Try getting some afternoon fresh air, go to the rest room and splash a little cool water on your face, stretch at your desk, and concentrate on relaxing and breathing. Have a daydream. Take a 10-minute nap. Just don't reach for your pack of cigarettes.

The commuter's cigarette

If being stuck in traffic prompts you to want a cigarette, you could be reacting out of stress, boredom, or a combination of the two. Listen to CDs or a good radio station. Keep your car's interior in perfectly clean condition and use an air freshener with a pleasant scent. If you have a mobile telephone with an inexpensive calling plan, use the time to catch up on conversations instead of cigarettes. If the problem is traffic, see if you can rearrange your day to drive earlier or later and avoid some rush. Consider taking a slightly longer route if it's less stressful.

The dinnertime cigarette

Identify whether you're having this cigarette when you dine in or out or both. If it's when you're out,

Moneysaver
If you're tempted to smoke while commuting, carpool instead so you'll have someone to talk to instead of smoking.

purposely leave your pack of cigarettes at home and resolve to have something instead—a favorite appetizer, after-dinner coffee, or the like. If dining in is your difficulty, change your routine. If you routinely smoke right after dinner and before doing the dishes, put off dishwashing until later in the evening, take a walk, call a friend, or go to the gym or out for a drive. If television will keep you away from smoking, try that. If it won't, stay away until the craving has passed.

The late-night cigarette

Up late again? If you can't sleep and need a cigarette both to wind you down and bide the time, try instead the proverbial glass of warm milk instead. Or a herbal relaxer (see Chapter 11). Or a warm bath. It can help to make a ritual out of whatever you're using to replace the cigarette with, so if you decide to try the warm bath route, consider candles, some good music, and nicely scented bath salts. A midnight snack can also take the edge off a cigarette craving. Unbuttered popcorn is one option, since you should always take care not to overeat when you're trying to quit smoking.

More kick-the-habit hints

There are things you can do every day that should help you kick the habit more easily. These are addressed thoroughly in Chapter 11:

- Get enough rest so you'll be alert through the day and less likely to rely on cigarettes to alleviate fatigue

- Get regular exercise—it will help keep your energy level at a higher level and more even keel through the day—it may even help you sleep more soundly

- Eat to properly feed your body and your mind—learn what good nutrition is and use it—don't skip meals, either

- Drink plenty of water—along with helping to detoxify your body from cigarettes, it helps in numerous ways

- Do what you can to cut down on stress in your life and do more of what you enjoy—resolve to have fun

When you're in a specific situation where you desperately want a cigarette—you can feel having one in your hand and putting it up to your mouth, try these cheats:

- Nibble raw carrots (yes, pack some up and take them with you—packages of baby carrots from the produce section are good ready-to-eat options)

- Munch on tiny salted pretzel sticks (which are fairly easy on the calorie count)

- Lick lollipops, even if you feel silly (try the sugar-free kind and stock up)

- Sip mineral water

- At a bar, persuade the bartender to supply you with celery sticks usually used as Bloody Mary garnishes.

- Write in your diary and nibble a little on the pen if you must—or jot down your reasons for quitting

- If you can't stand it, try putting an unlit cigarette to your lips

- Buy a GameBoy machine and play games to have something to do with your hands

- Play with your keys or your ring or a coin (or worry beads or rosary beads, if you have them)

- Take your pocket organizer with you and check over your to-do list when you feel the need for a smoke

- Bring a paperback book with you and read instead of smoke

- Do crosswords

- Try chewing gum

- Plan to keep your hands busy a lot—take up crochet, breadmaking, pottery, painting

- Do in-your-seat exercises instead of smoking

In other words, focus your energy away from smoking into other activities, no matter how mundane or trivial. The trick is to take your mind off smoking. You can take a number of other tactics, too, like keeping your cigarettes in a different location, one not so readily available. Make yourself wait two minutes before each new cigarette. Or make yourself *only smoke* when you smoke, so it's not associated with any other enjoyable activity. You can take this a step further and make yourself smoke only in places you don't like or that are associated with something negative. For instance, if you smoke in the bathroom, do it in the stall instead of by the sink. Or make yourself stand in your garage to smoke instead of in the kitchen.

Negative behaviors associated with smoking may help you gradually. Find a type of pickle you don't like the taste of and make yourself take one bite of it for each puff on a cigarette. You may be done sooner than you expected. If not eating a less-than-tasty pickle while smoking, you can make yourself do an exercise in between each puff. Or, if the cost of

> **“**
> My Dad has always smoked, and he let me have a drag when I was about three. It was so unpleasant that I have never felt the urge to start smoking. Rather like eating liver.
> —Ken
> **”**

cigarettes bothers you, take out as much change as one cigarette costs and put it in an envelope of money you vow not to spend but give away.

If you're still smoking, you can also cut down gradually. Allow yourself one less cigarette every day or only smoke them halfway. It all boils down to *smoker, know thyself.* By making advance preparations to help yourself avoid smoking, you're in a much better position to succeed. You can take this quiz to see which tactics you might particularly want to emphasize.

WHICH TACTICS WORK FOR YOU?

1. I'm most comfortable being a spur-of-the-moment person rather than a planner.
   TRUE or FALSE?

2. I'm an extrovert more than an introvert—I prefer to be with groups of people.
   TRUE or FALSE?

3. I find it hard to self motivate.
   TRUE or FALSE?

4. I believe my smoking has to do with deep issues in my life rather than being just a habit.
   TRUE or FALSE?

Answers: 1. If you answered true, consider tips and tricks mentioned in this chapter that don't require advance planning—for instance, playing with your keys as a diversion or ordering a mineral water instead of smoking. If you answered false, you may do well not only with these tips, but with others that involve planning—use the buddy system, for instance, and bring sugar-free lollipops with you when you leave the house. 2. If you answered true, take advantage of your extroversion—join a support group, use the buddy system. If you're an introvert, hypnosis may be more up your alley, as may props (like pretzel sticks) to keep you from smoking in social situations where you may feel ill at ease. 3. If you answered true, be sure to employ someone else's help—the buddy system or a smoking cessation group. 4. If you answered true, consider group quit therapy—such as the 12-step programs— and be sure to use affirmations and work on the rest of your life as you're quitting. If you answered false, you may do best just using hints and tips to trick yourself out of smoking that next cigarette.

You can think of your own ways to get out of smoking specific cigarettes. Refer to your answers in the "Why I Smoke When I Do" checklist at the beginning of this chapter, and think of how you might avoid each of those cigarettes, using the tips in this chapter and any other way you can think of. Whenever you feel compelled to smoke, ask yourself what the real reason is—are you simply craving nicotine, are you nervous, hungry, or is it a matter of established routine. Thinking about why you smoke each cigarette is a good way to avoid the next one.

Just the facts

- Identifying the specific circumstances in which you smoke can help you learn to avoid them.

- Research shows using the buddy system helps smokers quit.

- Twelve-step programs consider spiritual aspects important in overcoming addictions.

- Using substitutes for cigarettes—carrot sticks, pretzels, lollipops—can help you when you're smoking out of a need to have something in your mouth or something to do with your hands.

GET THE SCOOP ON...
Why antioxidant vitamins are vital to smokers ■
How the way you eat may be complicating
your quitting ■ Herbs to support stopping
smoking ■ What to eat to quell specific
kinds of cigarette cravings

Chapter 11

Nutrients, Herbs, and Healthy Living to Help You Quit

A foundation of good health and nutrition is necessary to effective quitting. Without it, you can experience stress that can worsen your cravings. Also, getting everything you need nutritionally should help you more easily and perhaps quickly rebuild from the damage smoking has done.

Because of the way nicotine addiction works, quitting actually *is* a body stressor, and you should be at your strongest when you guide yourself to a new smoke-free way of life. In this chapter, you can check out the basics of good nutrition, as well as find out which nutrients may help you particularly in quitting. Don't forget that fitness is important. We'll discuss that and some great, healthy stress reducers.

Basic nutrition

To a large extent, "you are what you eat" is true— if you don't eat healthily, you can't expect to be healthy. How adequate is your diet? Do you go relatively easy on sugar and flour products, on caffeine? It's important to maximize the healthful things you're eating and to minimize junk foods. You could be surprised at how much better you feel within a week.

Nutrition science has advanced far from the introduction of the Basic Food Groups by the U.S. government back in 1956. But it's still being sorted out. For instance, despite everything you may have heard in recent years about how a low-fat diet is so good for you, researchers are now finding it could increase risk of heart disease and potentially compromise the immune system of very active people. As well, the great importance of essential fatty acids in the diet is becoming more familiar. The right fats in the right proportion may actually help you quit smoking by stabilizing mental functions—the brain, in fact, is largely comprised of fat, just not the type around your midsection.

Common sense is a good guide. Favor a variety of basic, healthy, and naturally occurring, not-too-processed foods. Take supplemental vitamins and minerals where you need to, but don't use them to replace healthy foods, which have lots of probably helpful chemical components not necessarily found in supplements. Seek a good balance of protein, carbohydrates, and fat.

> **"**
> Good health and good sense are two of life's greatest blessings.
> —Publius Syrus (42 B.C.)
> **"**

So what is a good balance? The U.S. Department of Agriculture's 1995 dietary guidelines suggest:

- Eat a variety of foods.

- Balance the food you eat with physical activity to maintain or improve your weight.

- Choose a diet that contains plenty of grain products, vegetables, and fruits.

- Choose a diet that is low in fat, saturated fat, and cholesterol.
- Choose a diet that is moderate in sugars.
- Choose a diet that is moderate in salt and sodium.
- If you drink alcoholic beverages, do so in moderation.

Watch Out!
Stress and smoking can easily increase your body's need for many nutrients.

According to this guideline, most of your calories should come from grain products, vegetables, fruits, low-fat milk products, lean meats, fish, poultry, and dry beans, with fewer calories coming from fats and sweets.

Balancing protein, carbohydrates, and fat

According to a popular diet philosophy explained by Barry Sears, Ph.D., in his best-seller *The Zone* (HarperCollins, 1995), optimal nutrition is attained when you eat in a 30–40–30 balance. That is, when 30 percent of your caloric intake is protein, 40 percent carbohydrates, and 30 percent fat, at each meal. Whether you adhere strictly to this or try to keep the ratios in mind, it's a good policy.

Fats contain more calories per gram than either proteins or carbohydrates, so you can't just eat three grams of fat, four grams of carbohydrate and three grams of protein to have the equation work out correctly. If you're going for 30 percent protein calories, 40 percent carbohydrate calories, and 30 percent fat calories, it helps to think about how many grams of each you should have for each 100 calorie "block" of your diet (this is the way the *Zone* diet calculates meals). Each 100 calories you eat should be comprised of about 10 grams of carbohydrate, 7.5 grams of protein, and 3.33 grams of fat.

If you'd like to try following this plan closely, you will probably find it helpful to locate a cookbook or meal planner following the *Zone* philosophy. But think about your diet right now. If it's not optimal, simply eating healthier proteins, fats, and carbohydrates, and attempting a good balance between them at each meal, may do wonders.

What does a balance of protein, carbohydrates, and fats do for you? Eating some fat at each meal where you consume carbohydrates can reduce the glycemic response that food evokes. That is, carbohydrates alone, particularly simple carbohydrates like sugars and starches, tend to cause more fluctuation in your blood sugar levels than do more slowly digested carbohydrates, fats, or proteins by stimulating the hormone insulin to a degree that other foods do not.

Stable blood sugar levels are important for good health, the prevention of diabetes and other diseases, and it has quite a bit to do with how you feel. If you find yourself craving a cigarette an hour or two after a jelly doughnut, you could be answering the call of a destabilized blood sugar level, which, in turn, affects hormone and neurotransmitter balance.

When you eat a jelly doughnut or similar sweet, the sugar it contains causes your blood sugar to rise quickly. This is why you feel so good while you're eating one and immediately afterward. But a quick rush of sugar into the bloodstream tells the body that it needs to modulate that and keep any excess blood sugar under control.

Insulin rushes in and escorts the sugar out of your bloodstream, essentially to storage in the fat cells if the sugar is not being used to generate energy needed immediately (for instance, if you

Moneysaver
An inexpensive way to familiarize yourself with the protein, fat, and carbohydrate content of the foods you eat is to read labels. Just like you used to read the cereal boxes as a kid.

were doing heavy exercise). So much insulin may be released at this sudden rush of sugar into the system that it reduces your blood sugar level to a point lower than before you ate the jelly doughnut. This can leave you fatigued, spacey, and ready to reach for another jelly doughnut. Or a cigarette.

More complex carbohydrates—whole grains instead of very processed flours or vegetables instead of sweets—are digested more slowly, allowing for a steadier entry of sugar into your blood to actually give you energy without spurring such drastic insulin release. Thus by making wiser choices as to which carbohydrates you eat, you can increase and sustain your energy through the day rather than eating goodies that will fatigue you or make you crave a cigarette to lift your mood.

Proteins are necessary to build and sustain lean tissue in your body, and the amino acids they are made up of are important for a host of functions in the body, such as manufacturing and supporting neurotransmitters that regulate your mood—a very important point when you're fighting cravings for a cigarette.

Proteins are digested quite slowly in the body, and, if needed, a portion of them can be converted into glucose (sugar) to provide energy. Don't skimp on protein at breakfast. If you didn't have protein for breakfast this morning, note how you feel, then try having some tomorrow morning and see if you can tell the difference in your energy level.

The skinny on fats

Fats are essential to survival, but the wrong kind or the right kind in the wrong quantity can be detrimental. There are three kinds of fatty acids:

Timesaver
Buy a pocket *food gram counter* guidebook and familiarize yourself with the proportion of carbohydrate, fat, and protein in the foods you eat.

- Saturated

- Polyunsaturated

- Monounsaturated

We've all heard these terms, but do you know what they mean? It is the chemical structure of the fat—particularly, the number of hydrogen atoms—that determines which category a fat falls into. Saturated fats are usually animal fats, and they become solid at room temperature. There are some tropical oils like palm and coconut that become solid at room temperature, and they are high in saturated fat, too. The body uses saturated fats to make cholesterol, from which many important hormones are also made, though saturated fats are implicated in high cholesterol.

The polyunsaturated fats are seed, nut, or vegetable oils. Soybean oil, corn oil, and sunflower oil are in this group. They have been shown to lower cholesterol counts, though they may lower the levels of the good HDL (high-density lipoprotein) as well as the bad LDL (low-density lipoprotein) cholesterol. Monounsaturated fats, however, have been shown to cut levels of LDL cholesterol but apparently have no effect on HDL, or good cholesterol. Examples of monounsaturated fats are olive oil, peanut oil, and canola oil.

If you're a smoker with high cholesterol, increasing the proportion of olive oil you use to other types of oil could be an easy way to help bring down cholesterol levels safely. Many health experts advise taking it quite easy on saturated fats by comparison.

But saturated fats aren't the only kind nutritionists advise you to minimize in your diet. Research is shedding new light on the dangers of trans-fats. These are

Bright Idea
If you want to learn more about fats, consider reading *Fats That Heal, Fats That Kill: The Complete Guide to Fats, Oils, Cholesterol and Human Health*, Revised Edition (Alive Books, 1999), by Udo Erasmus.

made when the chemical structure of a fat is changed, adding hydrogen atoms, which makes the fat more "saturated." Hydrogenated fats allow a longer shelf life and turn liquid oil into solid forms, like shortening. Trans-fats can worsen cholesterol levels and increase heart disease risk. It's hard to stay away from them if you eat many processed foods. Eating healthily partly means eating less processed food.

Beyond these major categories of fats, there's something else you should know about: essential fatty acids. Sometimes called vitamin F, these are fatty acids that the body cannot make and therefore must get from elsewhere.

Essential fatty acids (EFAs) are the cornerstone for a number of processes in the body, from fat-burning itself to the construction of hormones that greatly influence our body's development and day-to-day life, not to mention our emotions. Essential fatty acids can even help prevent damage from the bad fats, that is, the fats that lead to elevated cholesterol levels and a wide range of damage. Ensuring your diet contains enough of the vital Omega 3 and Omega 6 fats is important.

Omega 3 fatty acids (also called alpha linolenic acid) can be found in supplement form as fish oil or flax seed oil (among others) and in these foods: raw nuts and seeds and fatty fish. Omega 6 fatty acids (also called linoleic acid) can be found in supplements of evening primrose oil or black currant oil (among others). Safflower, sesame, sunflower, walnut, and soybean oils are also good sources of Omega 6 fatty acids.

To obtain Omega 3 fats in your diet, try to fit in at least three servings a week of fatty, cold-water fish (such as salmon or tuna). Some nutrition experts

Unofficially...
Essential fatty acids are easily destroyed by heat. If you're supplementing, select cold-pressed oil (from the health food store) if you can, keep it refrigerated, and use it on salads or in other recipes that require minimal, if any, cooking.

believe the Omega 3 fats are what we are most in need of, with Omega 6 sources showing up elsewhere in the typical American diet. Other experts suggest we're in need of better Omega 6 supplementation, too.

For smokers and their increased risk of some diseases, essential fatty acids may be particularly important. For instance, Omega 3 fatty acids have been found to reduce fatty triglyceride levels in blood, which can impair circulation. Omega 3s may also help prevent clots. Omega 6 oils have also been found to help with regard to heart and circulation issues. Studies have found them useful in preventing hypertension and lowering cholesterol and triglycerides.

Could the right essential fatty acids actually help you quit? Flax seed oil, with its high Omega 3 content, has been found useful in treating attention deficit disorder. Could it be useful for those who smoke to gain focus on a task at hand?

Vitamins and minerals

The human body has an amazing ability to adapt when we don't have proper nutrition, but to function optimally it is very important to give your system the resources it needs to function properly. You may not be getting enough of certain vitamins and minerals if you're not consciously trying to eat a very healthy and very natural diet.

Many people choose to use a supplement, but how do you tell what you actually need? Scientists are finding out their old estimates of the nutrients people need require revision, so the standard of *Recommended Dietary Allowances (RDAs)* is being phased out and new *Dietary Reference Intakes (DRIs)* are being set. This is a work in progress, and DRIs have not been set for all nutrients. The first set of

Bright Idea
You can ask your doctor for a blood test called a fatty acid profile "EFA Status Report (EFA-SR)," if you suspect you have an imbalance or deficiency of essential fatty acids (EFAs).

tables shows the new DRIs for vitamin D, calcium, phosphorus, magnesium, fluoride, thiamin, riboflavin, niacin, vitamin B_6, folate, vitamin B_{12}, pantothenic acid, biotin, and choline. The second set of tables shows RDAs for other nutrients that don't have DRIs yet.

FOOD AND NUTRITION BOARD, INSTITUTE OF MEDICINE-NATIONAL ACADEMY OF SCIENCES DIETARY REFERENCE INTAKES: RECOMMENDED INTAKES FOR INDIVIDUALS

Life-Stage Group	Calcium (mg/d)	Phosphorus (mg/d)	Magnesium (mg/d)	Vitamin D (μg/d)[a,b]	Fluoride (mg/d)
Infants					
0–6 mo	210*	100*	30*	5*	0.01*
7–12 mo	270*	275*	75*	5*	0.5*
Children					
1–3 yr	500*	460	80	5*	0.7*
4–8 yr	800*	500	130	5*	1*
Males					
9–13 yr	1,300*	1,250	240	5*	2*
14–18 yr	1,300*	1,250	410	5*	3*
19–30 yr	1,000*	700	400	5*	4*
31–50 yr	1,000*	700	420	5*	4*
51–70 yr	1,200*	700	420	10*	4*
> 70 yr	1,200*	700	420	15*	4*
Females					
9–13 yr	1,300*	1,250	240	5*	2*
14–18 yr	1,300*	1,250	360	5*	3*
19–30 yr	1,000*	700	310	5*	3*
31–50 yr	1,000*	700	320	5*	3*
51–70 yr	1,200*	700	320	10*	3*
> 70 yr	1,200*	700	320	15*	3*
Pregnancy					
≤ 18 yr	1,300*	1,250	400	5*	3*
19–30 yr	1,000*	700	350	5*	3*
31–50 yr	1,000*	700	360	5*	3*

FOOD AND NUTRITION BOARD, INSTITUTE OF MEDICINE-NATIONAL ACADEMY OF SCIENCES DIETARY REFERENCE INTAKES: RECOMMENDED INTAKES FOR INDIVIDUALS (cont.)

Life-Stage Group	Calcium (mg/d)	Phosphorus (mg/d)	Magnesium (mg/d)	Vitamin D (μg/d)[a,b]	Fluoride (mg/d)
Lactation					
≤ 18 yr	1,300*	1,250	360	5*	3*
19–30 yr	1,000*	700	310	5*	3*
31–50 yr	1,000*	700	320	5*	3*

Life-Stage Group	Thiamin (mg/d)	Riboflavin (mg/d)	Niacin (mg/d)[c]	Vitamin B_6 (mg/d)	Folate (mg/d)[d]
Infants					
0–6 mo	0.2*	0.3*	2*	0.1*	65*
7–12 mo	0.3*	0.4*	4*	0.3*	80*
Children					
1–3 yr	0.5	0.5	6	0.5	150
4–8 yr	0.6	0.6	8	0.6	200
Males					
9–13 yr	0.9	0.9	12	1.0	300
14–18 yr	1.2	1.3	16	1.3	400
19–30 yr	1.2	1.3	16	1.3	400
31–50 yr	1.2	1.3	16	1.3	400
51–70 yr	1.2	1.3	16	1.7	400
> 70 yr	1.2	1.3	16	1.7	400
Females					
9–13 yr	0.9	0.9	12	1.0	300
14–18 yr	1.0	1.0	14	1.2	400[g]
19–30 yr	1.1	1.1	14	1.3	400[g]
31–50 yr	1.1	1.1	14	1.3	400[g]
51–70 yr	1.1	1.1	14	1.5	400
> 70 yr	1.1	1.1	14	1.5	400
Pregnancy					
≤ 18 yr	1.4	1.4	18	1.9	600[h]
19–30 yr	1.4	1.4	18	1.9	600[h]
31–50 yr	1.4	1.4	18	1.9	600[h]

Life-Stage Group	Thiamin (mg/d)	Riboflavin (mg/d)	Niacin (mg/d)[c]	Vitamin B_6 (mg/d)	Folate (mg/d)[d]
Lactation					
≤ 18 yr	**1.5**	**1.6**	**17**	**2.0**	**500**
19–30 yr	**1.5**	**1.6**	**17**	**2.0**	**500**
31–50 yr	**1.5**	**1.6**	**17**	**2.0**	**500**

Life-Stage Group	Vitamin B_{12} (mg/d)	Pantothenic Acid (mg/d)	Biotin (mg/d)	Choline (mg/d)[e]
Infants				
0–6 mo	0.4*	1.7*	5*	125*
7–12 mo	0.5*	1.8*	6*	150*
Children				
1–3 yr	**0.9**	2*	8*	200*
4–8 yr	**1.2**	3*	12*	250*
Males				
9–13 yr	**1.8**	4*	20*	375*
14–18 yr	**2.4**	5*	25*	550*
19–30 yr	**2.4**	5*	30*	550*
31–50 yr	**2.4**	5*	30*	550*
51–70 yr	**2.4**[f]	5*	30*	550*
> 70 yr	**2.4**[f]	5*	30*	550*
Females				
9–13 yr	**1.8**	4*	20*	375*
14–18 yr	**2.4**	5*	25*	400*
19–30 yr	**2.4**	5*	30*	425*
31–50 yr	**2.4**	5*	30*	425*
51–70 yr	**2.4**[f]	5*	30*	425*
> 70 yr	**2.4**[f]	5*	30*	425*
Pregnancy				
≤ 18 yr	**2.6**	6*	30*	450*
19–30 yr	**2.6**	6*	30*	450*
31–50 yr	**2.6**	6*	30*	450*
Lactation				
≤ 18 yr	**2.8**	7*	35*	550*
19–30 yr	**2.8**	7*	35*	550*
31–50 yr	**2.8**	7*	35*	550*

FOOD AND NUTRITION BOARD, INSTITUTE OF MEDICINE-NATIONAL ACADEMY OF SCIENCES DIETARY REFERENCE INTAKES: RECOMMENDED INTAKES FOR INDIVIDUALS *(cont.)*

Note: This table presents Recommended Dietary Allowances (RDAs) in **bold type** and Adequate Intakes (AIs) in ordinary type followed by an asterisk (*). RDAs and AIs may both be used as goals for individual intake. RDAs are set to meet the needs of almost all (97 to 98 percent) individuals in a group. For healthy breastfed infants, the AI is the mean intake. The AI for other life-stage and gender groups is believed to cover needs of all individuals in the group, but lack of data or uncertainty in the data prevent being able to specify with confidence the percentage of individuals covered by this intake.

[a] As cholecalciferol. 1 µg cholecalciferol = 40 IU vitamin D.

[b] In the absence of adequate exposure to sunlight.

[c] As niacin equivalents (NE). 1 mg of niacin = 60 mg of tryptophan; 0–6 months = preformed niacin (not NE).

[d] As dietary folate equivalents (DFE). 1 DFE = 1 µg food folate = 0.6 µg of folic acid from fortified food or as a supplement consumed with food = 0.5 µg of a supplement taken on an empty stomach.

[e] Although AIs have been set for choline, there are few data to assess whether a dietary supply of choline is needed at all stages of the life cycle, and it may be that the choline requirement can be met by endogenous synthesis at some of these stages.

[f] Because 10 to 30 percent of older people may malabsorb food-bound B_{12}, it is advisable for those older than 50 years to meet their RDA mainly by consuming foods fortified with B_{12} or a supplement containing B_{12}.

[g] In view of evidence linking folate intake with neural tube defects in the fetus, it is recommended that all women capable of becoming pregnant consume 400 µg from supplements or fortified foods in addition to intake of food folate from a varied diet.

[h] It is assumed that women will continue consuming 400 µg from supplements or fortified food until their pregnancy is confirmed and they enter prenatal care, which ordinarily occurs after the end of the periconceptional period—the critical time for formation of the neural tube.

FOOD AND NUTRITION BOARD, NATIONAL ACADEMY OF SCIENCES-NATIONAL RESEARCH COUNCIL RECOMMENDED DIETARY ALLOWANCES,[a] REVISED 1989 (ABRIDGED)

Category	Age (years) or Condition	Weight[b] (kg)	(lb)	Height[b] (cm)	(in)
Infants	0.0–0.5	6	13	60	24
	0.5–1.0	9	20	71	28
Children	1–3	13	29	90	35
	4–6	20	44	112	44
	7–10	28	62	132	52
Males	11–14	45	99	157	62
	15–18	66	145	176	69
	19–24	72	160	177	70
	25–50	79	174	176	70
	51+	77	170	173	68
Females	11–14	46	101	157	62
	15–18	55	120	163	64
	19–24	58	128	164	65
	25–50	63	138	163	64
	51+	65	143	160	63

Category	Age (years) or Condition	Protein (g)	Vitamin A (μg RE)[c]	Vitamin E (mg α-TE)[d]	Vitamin K (μg)
Infants	0.0–0.5	13	375	3	5
	0.5–1.0	14	375	4	10
Children	1–3	16	400	6	15
	4–6	24	500	7	20
	7–10	28	700	7	30
Males	11–14	45	1,000	10	45
	15–18	59	1,000	10	65
	19–24	58	1,000	10	70
	25–50	63	1,000	10	80
	51+	63	1,000	10	80
Females	11–14	46	800	8	45
	15–18	44	800	8	55
	19–24	46	800	8	60

FOOD AND NUTRITION BOARD, NATIONAL ACADEMY OF SCIENCES-NATIONAL RESEARCH COUNCIL RECOMMENDED DIETARY ALLOWANCES,[a] REVISED 1989 (ABRIDGED) *(cont.)*

Category	Age (years) or Condition	Protein (g)	Vitamin A (μg RE)[c]	Vitamin E (mg α-TE)[d]	Vitamin K (μg)
Females	25–50	50	800	8	65
	51+	50	800	8	65
Pregnant		60	800	10	65
Lactating	1st 6 months	65	1,300	12	65
	2nd 6 months	62	1,200	11	65

Category	Age (years) or Condition	Vitamin C (mg)	Iron (mg)	Zinc (mg)	Iodine (μg)	Selenium (μg)
Infants	0.0–0.5	30	6	5	40	10
	0.5–1.0	35	10	5	50	15
Children	1–3	40	10	10	70	20
	4–6	45	10	10	90	20
	7–10	45	10	10	120	30
Males	11–14	50	12	15	150	40
	15–18	60	12	15	150	50
	19–24	60	10	15	150	70
	25–50	60	10	15	150	70
	51+	60	10	15	150	70
Females	11–14	50	15	12	150	45
	15–18	60	15	12	150	50
	19–24	60	15	12	150	55
	25–50	60	15	12	150	55
	51+	60	10	12	150	55
Pregnant		70	30	15	175	65
Lactating	1st 6 months	95	15	19	200	75
	2nd 6 months	90	15	16	200	75

Note: This table does not include nutrients for which Dietary Reference Intakes have recently been established (see *Dietary Reference Intakes for Calcium, Phosphorus, Magnesium, Vitamin D,* and *Fluoride* [1997] and *Dietary Reference Intakes for Thiamin, Riboflavin, Niacin, Vitamin B$_6$, Folate, Vitamin B$_{12}$, Pantothenic Acid, Biotin, and Choline* [1998]).

[a] The allowances, expressed as average daily intakes over time, are intended to provide for individual variations among most normal persons as they live in the United States under usual environmental stresses. Diets should be based on a variety of common foods in order to provide other nutrients for which human requirements have been less well defined.

[b] Weights and heights of Reference Adults are actual medians for the U.S. population of the designated age, as reported by NHANES II. The median weights and heights of those under 19 years of age were taken from Hamill et al. (1979). The use of these figures does not imply that the height-to-weight ratios are ideal.

[c] Retinol equivalents. 1 retinol equivalent = 1 µg retinol or 6 µg β-carotene.

[d] α-Tocopherol equivalents. 1 mg d-α tocopherol = 1 α-TE.

Here's a primer on what vitamins and minerals do for you. Remember that while it's important to get enough, *too* much can often pose risks.

Vitamin A

Vitamin A isn't just good for your vision. It's necessary for your body's growth and repair, as well as the health of your mucous membranes. It's also an antioxidant that can help clean up your system as you quit smoking. Be careful of getting too much vitamin A, however—in excess, it can damage the liver and cause other problems.

B vitamins

Thiamine (vitamin B$_1$) is used by the body in the metabolism of foods into energy. It's also vital to the heart, nervous system and muscle tissue. Riboflavin (vitamin B$_2$) works in metabolism, in the formation of red blood cells, and for the maintenance of vision and healthy hair.

Niacin (vitamin B_3) is essential to your body's production of energy. It works in the metabolism of carbohydrates, protein, and fat. Niacin plays an important role in lowering cholesterol and can be helpful in the treatment of insomnia and depression. Too much niacin can cause serious problems, including elevated blood sugar, liver damage, and irregular heartbeat. Niacin can cause facial flushing (reddening) and a feeling of heat in some individuals. *Nonflushing* niacin (inositol hexanicotinate) supplements are available.

Vitamin B_5 (pantothenic acid) helps regulate the body's use of energy and assists its use of other vitamins. This vitamin is important in regulating your body's response to stress and in ensuring smooth functioning of the nervous system and adrenal glands.

Vitamin B_6 (pyridoxine) aids metabolism, especially protein metabolism, and assists in regulating the nervous system. Vitamin B_{12} (cobalmin) is vital to the production of red blood cells and is necessary to prevent anemia. Cobalmin also helps the nervous system function smoothly. It is found in meat, fish, eggs, and milk. Vegetarians may need supplements. Vitamin B_{12} has a strong reputation as an energy vitamin.

Vitamin C

Vitamin C (ascorbic acid) is a potent antioxidant and can help clean up what's left in your system from smoking. Vitamin C aids in the healing of wounds and may help prevent cancer as well. It is important to the health of your bones, teeth, gums, and other tissues.

Vitamin D

Vitamin D (calciferol) helps your body use calcium and other minerals, so it's important to healthy

Watch Out!
Too much of one B vitamin can throw off ratios of others. If you're supplementing, look for a balanced B formulation.

bones, teeth, and gums, as well as your cardio-vascular and nervous systems. An excess of vitamin D can cause health problems and be hard on the kidneys.

Vitamin E

Vitamin E (tocopherol) is a very important antioxidant, which helps counter damage to cells. It has been found in studies to alleviate tiredness, brighten mood, and help protect the heart and brain (especially against stroke and heart attack).

Biotin, folic acid, inositol, choline

Biotin and folic acid are key words for healthy hair and nails, with folic acid helping in the growth of all body cells. Too little folic acid can be responsible for prematurely gray hair. Inositol aids in the metabolization of fats and can reduce cholesterol. Choline helps with this, as well as with nerve transmission and memory. Choline is found in liver, eggs, and some beans and other vegetables. Inositol is widely found in fruits, whole grains, vegetables, meats, and dairy products. Folic acid can be gotten from green leafy vegetables, beans, asparagus, citrus fruits and juices, whole grain foods and liver, and biotin from yeast, liver, kidney, and eggs.

Calcium and magnesium

Just about everyone knows that calcium is important for healthy bones and teeth, but it's also vital to your heart and nerves, and to alleviate certain kinds of muscle cramps. Calcium has been found helpful for insomnia and for lowering blood pressure and cholesterol. Magnesium is important to heart function and in the proper use of calcium, as well as the metabolization of sugars. Too much calcium can throw off magnesium levels and vice versa, so if

Moneysaver
Vitamin D can be absorbed from sunshine, so get some fresh air and sunlight, but don't overdo it—skin cancer (not to mention photoaging of the skin) are real risks.

Watch Out!
Supplementing iron can lead to constipation. If you have this problem, look for a more easily absorbed time-release version.

you're supplementing, it's best to find a balanced combination of the two.

Iron

Important to the creation of red blood cells and oxygenation of tissues, iron is necessary to prevent anemia and fatigue, as well as to support immunity. An excess can be dangerous to kidneys, heart, and liver.

Iodine

Iodine is necessary for healthy functioning of your thyroid gland, which regulates the body's energy levels, among other things. Iodine is added to most brands of salt due to a deficiency of it in certain soils in the United States.

Copper and zinc

Copper is important in the building of bone and formation of red blood cells. It also helps the body repair tissue, metabolize iron, and use vitamin C. Zinc is important to healthy functioning of the reproductive system and to wound healing. It is an antioxidant and helps clean up cellular damage. Some studies have found it may help reduce the duration of a cold. It is important for zinc and copper ratios to remain in balance, so again, a balanced supplement including both is ideal if you are not relying on food to provide your mineral requirements.

Manganese and fluoride

Manganese helps bone growth by working with copper and zinc. It is also necessary to keep muscles and nerves functioning properly. Manganese is found in red meat, and vegetarians may need to supplement this mineral. Fluoride is important to healthy teeth and bones, and in many areas it is added to water supplies for that purpose.

Nutrients for smokers

Which vitamins and minerals can be helpful to a smoker kicking the addiction and cleaning up his or her body?

1. First, make sure you're getting an adequate across-the-board supply of nutrients and a combination of carbohydrates, fat, and protein to sustain your tissues and energy supply.

2. Then consider supplementation with these nutrients in particular.

Antioxidant vitamins for cleanup

You've probably heard of *free radicals*, which can damage cells. They are the result of changes in the atoms that make up cells and can be created during exposure to toxins such as those found in pollution, cigarette smoke, or radiation. However, some free radicals are created normally during metabolism or when the immune system needs them to counteract invaders. The damage from excess free radicals mounts with age.

Free radicals are actually rogue atoms that must poach electrons from other atoms in order to complete their own stable atomic structure. But when they steal an electron, the donor atom itself becomes unstable and in need of an electron, and so the free radical problem is self-perpetuating. Antioxidants, such as vitamins C and E and beta-carotene (the vitamin A precursor), are nutrients that help to counter free radical damage and the oxidation of tissues. They do their work by being ready electron donors and thus prevent electron-poaching from the body's cells.

Supplemental vitamin C can be beneficial to smokers. Not only does it help to prevent and clean

Bright Idea
Choose your meals to replenish the water-soluble vitamins (such as the Bs and C) daily since they can wash out of your body. Your body can store fat-soluble vitamins (like A, D, E, and K) for later use, so it's not as important to get them every day.

up cellular damage from smoking, but smokers have less vitamin C, since oxidants in smoke increase the metabolism of the vitamin. A 1993 study found smokers and those exposed to secondhand smoke had lower body levels of vitamin C than nonsmokers not exposed to smoke. Research has matched high vitamin C intake with reduced risk of certain cancers, such as that of the mouth, larynx, and esophagus.

Beta-carotene, the vitamin A precursor, is an important antioxidant. Studies show that plasma levels of carotenes including beta-carotene are reported to be lower in cigarette smokers than in nonsmokers. Research has found beta-carotene to help protect the body from cancer, heart attack, and cataracts, and vitamin A to be cancer-preventative. You can find vitamin A in milk, liver, butter, and eggs, and beta-carotene in carrots, leafy green and dark yellow or orange vegetables, broccoli, and cantaloupe. Vitamin A plays an important role in keeping breathing passages healthy, and, therefore, adequate quantities are very important to a quitting smoker.

Smokers have also been found to have lower levels of vitamin E than nonsmokers. Vitamin E is another important antioxidant vitamin. It can help repair damaged tissue and prevent heart attacks, stroke, the arteries, and high cholesterol. Vitamin E exists in some vegetable oils, nuts, and seeds. It is often included in multivitamin supplements in respectable quantities. When you're choosing a vitamin E supplement, look for words such as "mixed tocopherols." You can also find dry E and water soluble E for better absorption.

While smokers seem to need greater levels of antioxidants to deal with cigarette toxins, research has shown smokers to be less likely to get them. A 1996 Dutch study found that men who smoked more than 20 cigarettes a day had significantly lower intakes of beta-carotene, particularly of vitamin C, than those who had never smoked. Why? It turns out the smokers had nearly a 60 percent lower intake of fruit. Considering that a good intake of fruits and vegetables has been found to reduce some cancer risks, and, in light of all their benefits, it makes an immense amount of sense to get more vegetables and fruits into your diet, particularly if you are a smoker or a quitting smoker.

Stress vitamins for smokers

Since the B vitamins are associated with keeping energy levels up and reducing stress, they are ideal for a quitting smoker to supplement. An inadequate supply of Bs in your body can worsen the fatigue and stress associated with nicotine withdrawal. Making sure you get enough of the B vitamins could potentially keep you from reaching for a cigarette when you're tired and need a lift, if you have a borderline deficiency. To get a good range of Bs in your diet, include bananas, potatoes, nuts, seeds, and whole grains in your meal planning.

B_{12} is particularly important for smokers since they may have lower blood levels of this vitamin than the general population.

So-called stress vitamin supplements can be ideal for quitting smokers, as these often concentrate on adequate B-complex formulations. Additionally, a number of vitamin companies put out special smokers' formulations that include antioxidants and stress vitamins, which may also contain a combination of herbs for detoxification and support.

Minerals for smokers

If you have unexplained fatigue, headaches, and pallor, you could be deficient in *iron*—particularly if

Watch Out!
It's best to check with your physician before taking any unusually *high* doses of supplemental nutrients, particularly if you are on medication or have a medical condition requiring monitoring, or if you are pregnant.

you're female. Could your craving for a cigarette lift really be an inadequate supply of this mineral in your system? If you suspect so, you can try increasing protein sources in your diet since iron can be found in meat, fish, and poultry. You can also get good supplies of iron from peas and beans, spinach and other leafy dark green vegetables, potatoes, whole grains, and fortified cereals. Animal sources of iron may be most easily absorbed, however. Adequate levels of vitamin C also help your body absorb iron. Too much supplemented iron can lead to toxicity. Effects can include arthritis, diabetes, and liver damage but may not be noticed for many years.

Selenium is a trace mineral with antioxidant properties. It protects cell membranes and helps to prevent the generation of free radicals. Studies have found increased intake of selenium correlates with lowered risk of breast, colon, lung, and prostate cancer. The National Cancer Institute recommends from 50 to 200 micrograms of selenium daily to prevent cancer. However, doses above that can be toxic. You can get dietary selenium through consumption of organ and other meats (particularly chicken) and vegetables (such as cabbage, celery, and cucumber) and grains.

Amino acids in quitting

Amino acids, the building blocks of protein, have different roles, and knowing when to emphasize one of the 22 known amino acids may be helpful to your quit-smoking plan. *Tryptophan*, for instance, can be calming. If you've felt sleepy after Thanksgiving dinner, it may be partly due to the high tryptophan content of turkey. Next time you can't sleep, a turkey sandwich may do the trick. Beyond fowl, other dietary sources of tryptophan include yogurt, pineapple, and bananas. Tryptophan may also reduce anxiety, alleviate depression, and resolve migraines. Including plenty of tryptophan-rich foods in your diet isn't a bad plan to head off nicotine withdrawal symptoms and cravings.

If you smoke to stay sharp, *phenylalanine* may help. This amino acid is a precursor to the neurotransmitter *norepinephrine*, which is greatly responsible for alertness and response to stress. It can help curb depression, better memory, and improve focus. You can find phenylalanine in meats and cheeses. The amino acid *methionine* (present in meat, eggs, cottage cheese, yogurt, and sardines) may also alleviate fatigue.

The amino acid *valine* not only calms emotions but also improves alertness. It can be found in cottage cheese, meats, chickpeas, mushrooms, and nuts. Leucine and isoleucine, as well as tyrosine, help the body create energy and support brain function. They can be found in meat and dairy foods.

As you can see, amino acids play important energy-regulating roles. It should be obvious that skimping on the level of protein in your diet is unwise and could make it harder to quit. Actually making a point to include healthy protein, carbohydrate, and fat sources in your diet in appropriate quantities could surprise you—smoking may not seem quite as necessary as when you had an unhealthy diet.

Herbs for quitting smoking

Beyond basic nutrients, some quitting smokers utilize herbs for an assist in reducing craving for cigarettes, detoxification, or mood support. Herbal teas and supplements are even available in drugstores,

Timesaver
Many amino acids are available in supplement form.

not just health food stores. Here are some major herbs you may find useful in kicking the habit and supporting your health while you quit.

Smokers' formulas

An inquiry at your local health food store will undoubtedly turn up mentions of herbal supplements geared specifically for quitting smokers. You may find it easiest to choose one of these preparations (in capsules or tea form) rather than seeking out individual herbs. But you can go that route, and whether you choose a combination or single remedy, these are some of the popular herbal ingredients you're likely to find and their functions.

Lobelia or "Indian tobacco" is a plant native to Canada that, at one time, was smoked like tobacco is today. It contains an the alkaloid *lobeline*, which is used in some anti-smoking lozenges. It is a partial nicotine agonist and may give some of the effects of nicotine. It is known as something of a sedative, with muscle relaxing effects, but is also something of a stimulant, as well as a detoxifier and treatment for a number of respiratory problems. It can help rid phlegm from the lungs. Research doesn't support its effectiveness in smoking cessation; nevertheless, its reputation as an aid remains, and you're likely to find it in many smokers' formula.

St. Johns Wort is among those herbs regarded as a natural antidepressant and antianxiety agent and is widely prescribed in Europe for depression. It is commonly used in conjunction with lobelia in smoking cessation and has the ability to loosen phlegm and assist in the relief of minor respiratory maladies. Together, St. Johns Wort and lobelia can help remove smoking toxins from the lungs.

A number of herbs have the reputation of being blood purifiers, and *milk thistle* is among them. A natural antioxidant, milk thistle has been found by herbal practitioners to help the body recover from exposure to a wide variety of chemicals. *Alfalfa* is another popular purifier and herbal treatment for asthmatic conditions.

Echinacea is a flower popularly used to stimulate the immune and lymph systems and may help clear phlegm from respiratory passages. Echinacea is generally used for a few days or weeks at a time, rather than in continual fashion, to avoid overstimulation of the immune system.

Plantago major, literally "great plaintain," is a plant used in lung disorders and smoking cessation preparations for its expectorant and toxin-ridding qualities, but particularly for its long-reputed ability to create an aversion to smoking tobacco.

Bright Idea
Beyond common ingredients in smoking cessation herbal formulas, a number of herbs are good for relaxing or treating insomnia—among them *valerian, hops,* and *kava kava.*

Adaptogens for energy and well-being

Adaptogens are substances that herbal practitioners believe can help modulate the body's response to stress—essentially to strengthen it. Adaptogenic herbs are said to offer increased energy and stamina, help stabilize blood sugar levels, improve immune response and healing, and help mood. Some of the most popular adaptogens include:

- Ginseng (including Asian varieties, as well as Siberian and American ginseng)
- Astragalus
- Licorice
- Schizandra
- Reishi mushroom

Asian ginseng is not the same botanical as its cousins *Siberian ginseng* and *American ginseng*. The word *ginseng*, which means "man root," is used to describe those plants with similar adaptogenic qualities. Asian ginsengs range from the "warmer" or more energy-producing *Korean red ginseng* to the somewhat milder *Chinese white ginseng*, which may be more easy on the system, particularly for women. American ginseng is a step "cooler" for anyone who finds even Chinese white ginseng too stimulating. Siberian ginseng is also a mild form.

The Asian ginsengs have been found to have antidepressant, antidiabetic, and antihypertensive qualities. They are reputed to be strengthening and calming (though the "hotter" the ginseng, the less its calming effect). Research has found a lower incidence of cancer among those who have taken Asian ginsengs regularly.

American ginseng possesses similar qualities, though it may be more appropriate than Asian varieties if someone is easily agitated, nervous, or anxious. Siberian ginseng has been shown in studies to normalize stress reactions when used regularly for months. A study of over 2,000 men and women who took Siberian ginseng for up to two months found users experienced greater mental alertness, improved work output and quality, and better athletic performance. Participants were also less rattled by adverse conditions like noise, heat, and physical stress.

Astragalus is a Chinese herb reputed for its ability to strengthen compromised organs. It is frequently given to those who are weak and ill to improve vitality and strengthen the immune system.

Licorice root is one item routinely added to herbal formulations in Chinese medicine. It is known as

Timesaver
If you have trouble locating any of the *adaptogenic* herbs at your health food store, look for a formula containing several or check with an Asian grocer or an acupuncturist since tonic herbs like these are often prescribed with acupuncture.

"great harmonizer" for its purported ability to moderate the effects of other herbs. Licorice root can be soothing to irritated mucus membranes (which makes it ideal for the quitting smoker), and it has a reputation for nourishing the adrenal glands and producing a calm feeling.

Schizandra is another Chinese plant that has been used for centuries. Its berries grow on a low-creeping bush. Schizandra has been long reputed to improve energy, vitalize the abdominal organs, aid vision, and sooth coughs and digestion. Studies have found it to aid breathing and circulation and to alleviate fatigue and help normalize sleep patterns.

Reishi mushroom is another Asian adaptogen, reputed for boosting the immune system, helping insomnia, and reducing cholesterol and stress levels.

Whether you use herbs to address the craving to smoke itself or to support your general health and stress resistance as you quit, you may find them of great assistance. Everyone is an individual, however, and different herbs may fit your constitution better than others. Seek high-quality herbs from reputable companies for good potency and remember that effects may take weeks or longer to show up.

Watch Out!
If you have a medical condition, are pregnant, or are taking medication, check with your physician before using herbs. Always follow manufacturer usage guidelines to avoid overdose since some herbs can be dangerous in large quantities.

Just the facts

- Antioxidants such as vitamins C, E, and A are important to cleaning up toxicity from smoking.

- Tryptophan, an amino acid found in fowl (among other sources) can help insomnia, as can the hormone melatonin.

- Adequate protein plays a big role in how calm and alert you stay, so make sure you're getting enough as you quit smoking.

- Herbal smokers' formulas often contain plantago major, which may cause aversion to tobacco, and lobelia, which in some ways may act like nicotine.

- Stress and smoking can increase your need for some nutrients.

Chapter 12

GET THE SCOOP ON...
Causes of addiction ▪ Avoiding switching
addictions ▪ Whether you have an addiction ▪
Ridding your life of addiction

Avoiding Other Addictions

Some people have a harder time kicking habits than others. Do you know someone who was able to give up smoking cold turkey and found it no big deal? Chances are that's not you. Hopefully, neither is yours the story of someone who became a raging alcoholic after his or her first drink or a drug addict after a prescription for painkillers.

The mechanisms of addiction are fascinating. What compels some people to do what they do? How do you clarify whether you are susceptible to addictive behaviors? If so, how do you stop? This chapter looks at common addictions and the patterns seen in addictive behavior so you can sort out for yourself whether you're at risk. As you quit smoking, it's important not to unwittingly wind up replacing your tobacco addiction with another potentially more harmful habit.

Getting a handle on your habits

Take a moment to think about how you began smoking in the first place, and, more importantly, why you continued to. People often smoke as a form of self medication, since the nicotine in tobacco can help calm anxiety, provide a lift to depression, improve focus, reduce stress, and give pleasant feelings.

You could say that the urge to continue to smoke is really instinct. Just as humans and animals eat to quell hunger and drink to stop thirst. The problem is that many substances—nicotine included—only provide a better state of affairs as long as they are in use and leave the taker in a worse state of affairs afterward, a state that can be alleviated for a time by resuming use of the substance. Worse yet, *tolerance* builds, so that more is required to get the same rush.

In this way, nicotine and other substances of abuse are *tricksters*, perpetuating a vicious circle when all the user wanted in the first place was for things to become better. How do you tell an addiction from a normal, healthy instinct? Why is the desire for sleep when you are tired not an addiction if the desire for nicotine when you're fatigued is an addiction? Sleep is a normal physiological process, which doesn't carry adverse consequences, induce compulsion for it, or lead to tolerance. Many addictions work with an intricate stimulation-reward pathway in the brain that perpetuates use.

You may have an addiction if:

- You're preoccupied with the substance between times that you use it
- You feel compelled to use a substance and crave it
- You use more of the substance than you intend
- You keep using a substance despite its adverse consequences
- You develop tolerance to the substance

- You may tend to be in denial that you have a problem
- You experience withdrawal symptoms when trying to quit and return to using the substance
- You've tried more than once to quit but haven't succeeded
- You use the substance at inappropriate times to quell withdrawal symptoms
- You reduce other activities in order to use the substance

Unofficially...
In the 1800s, heroin was marketed as a cure for coughing.

"Feeling strong desire to use something for its positive effects despite its drastic negative effects" is a good working description of addiction—experiencing a nagging need for something that's bad for you.

Is tobacco your only vice? Think long and hard about what other compulsions you may experience—some possibilities are in the "Addictions" checklist.

Addictions
____ Nicotine
____ Caffeine or other legal stimulants, such as some diet pills
____ Alcohol
____ Tranquilizers, sleep aids, or pain medication
____ Marijuana, cocaine, heroin, ecstasy, or other illegal drugs
____ Sweets, carbohydrates, or other foods
____ Love, sex, or relationship addiction
____ Being a workaholic
____ Thrillseeking
____ Gambling

This checklist may have included some entries that are a surprise to you. Remember that nicotine addiction works largely through dopamine pathways in the brain—the "pleasure center," which figures prominently in myriad types of addictions. This is the same brain area activated when you pursue a dangerous and exciting sport, embark on an intriguing new romance, or generally are very turned on by an activity.

A perceived need for frequent stimulation is what in research circles is referred to as *novelty seeking*. Anywhere you feel compelled to search for a new buzz may have addiction potential. Such sensation seeking could also make you more likely to have an addiction to more than one substance—addictions frequently do go hand-in-hand. For instance, one research study found addicts who abused different categories of drugs were more likely to have novelty seeking traits than addicts who abused only opiates or other depressants. Another study noted that among 9,216 deaths attributed to nonmedical use of other drugs in 1995, 39 percent involved alcohol, too.

Think about whether your use of substances or pursuit of certain situations is a *healthy balance* or *pathological*, the result of compulsion. Answering the questions in the following quiz can clue you in to possible addictive behavior in your life beyond your relationship with nicotine.

POTENTIAL ADDICTIONS

1. Rather than just drinking coffee in the morning, do cappuccinos get you through the day?

2. Do you drink alcohol occasionally in social situations or do you turn to it to soothe yourself?

3. Are you eating sweets, chocolate, or other carbohydrates when you're tired, lonely, bored, or can't sleep?

4. Do you feel you are reliant on prescription drugs for mood enhancement?

5. Are you absorbed in your work to the exclusion of other activities? Do you use it to avoid other activities or thoughts?

> "
> Behavior is a mirror in which every one displays his image.
> —Johann Wolfgang von Goethe
> "

6. Do you think about your need for sex or romantic love almost constantly and find it difficult to function without a good dose of either in your life?

7. Are you the most adventurous person you know, engaging in risky behaviors or participating in games of chance?

Answers: Every yes answer indicates a potentially addiction-oriented situation in your life.

Drug and alcohol abuse are widespread addictions, ones that carry dire consequences. Alcohol has been described as the most widely used psychoactive drug, one that contributes to about 100,000 deaths annually. It is actually listed as the number three leading cause of preventable death in the United States, following tobacco and diet/activity patterns. According to figures from the early 1990s, more than 7 percent of adult Americans (nearly 13.8 million) have problems with drinking, and 8.1 million are described as alcoholics. While alcohol is sometimes distinguished from drugs in describing it ("drugs and alcohol"), it's important to remember that alcohol has mind-altering properties that make it an important player in addictions issues.

Drug abuse kills 14,000 Americans and costs taxpayers nearly $70 billion annually. Data from the mid-1990s indicates some 13 million Americans are users of illicit drugs. About 9 million are regular marijuana smokers, out of approximately 67 million Americans who have tried marijuana at least once.

Clearly not everyone who once tried pot became addicted since the vast majority are not current users, nor is everyone who has ever taken a sip of alcohol a drunk. But the potential for addiction is always there, along with health risks, not to mention the danger of arrest and imprisonment for use of

Watch Out!
Use of mild drugs or alcohol may put you closer to using *harder* drugs—any time your judgment is impaired you run a greater risk of potentially trying and becoming addicted to another substance.

illicit drugs. If you use alcohol or drugs, how do you know when you've stepped over the line from purely recreational use to something you can't easily pull yourself out of? If any of the statements in the following checklist apply to you, then you could have a problem with drugs or alcohol.

Identifying a Drug or Alcohol Problem

____ I can't predict whether or not I will use drugs or get drunk.

____ I believe in order to have fun I need to drink and/or use drugs.

____ I turn to alcohol and/or drugs after a confrontation or argument or to relieve uncomfortable feelings.

____ I drink more or use more drugs to get the same effect that I got with smaller amounts.

____ I drink and/or use drugs alone.

____ I remember how last night began, but not how it ended, so I'm worried I may have a problem.

____ I have trouble at work or in school because of my drinking or drug use.

____ I make promises to myself or others that I will stop getting drunk or using drugs.

____ I feel alone, scared, miserable, and depressed.

Source: *Straight Facts About Drugs and Alcohol,* National Clearinghouse for Alcohol and Drug Information (NCADI).

You can further assess for yourself whether your behavior with certain substances leans toward addiction using the next two quizzes. The first quiz includes questions from Alcoholics Anonymous designed to clarify whether you may have a drinking problem.

Addiction recovery organizations readily recognize the dangers of cross-addiction—becoming dependent on another abusable substance when attempting to give up the drug of choice. Marijuana Anonymous, for instance, even warns those kicking

SELF-ASSESSMENT FOR ALCOHOL ADDICTION

1. Have you ever decided to stop drinking for a week or so but only lasted for a couple of days?

2. Do you wish people would mind their own business about your drinking—stop telling you what to do?

3. Have you ever switched from one kind of drink to another in the hope that this would keep you from getting drunk?

4. Have you had to have an eye-opener upon awakening during the past year? Do you need a drink to get started or to stop shaking?

5. Do you envy people who can drink without getting into trouble?

6. Have you had problems connected with drinking during the past year?

7. Has your drinking caused trouble at home?

8. Do you ever try to get "extra" drinks at a party because you do not get enough?

9. Do you tell yourself you can stop drinking any time you want to, even though you keep getting drunk when you don't mean to?

10. Have you missed days of work or school because of drinking?

11. Do you have "blackouts?"

12. Have you ever felt that your life would be better if you did not drink?

Answers: Four or more yes answers suggest a problem with alcohol addiction.

Source: Alcoholics Anonymous; The preceding twelve questions have been excerpted from questions appearing in the pamphlet "Is A.A. For You?" and the Twelve Steps (later in this chapter) has been reprinted with permission of Alcoholics Anonymous World Services, Inc. Permission to reprint this material does not mean that Alcoholics Anonymous has reviewed and/or endorses this publication. A.A. is a program of recovery from alcohol only—use of A.A. material in any non-A.A. context does not imply otherwise.

← For more information on Alcoholics Anonymous, visit their Web site at www.alcoholics-anonymous.org.

the pot habit to be careful with prescription drugs and to be mindful of other ways addicts may react when quitting—be it raiding the refrigerator or going on a shopping spree they cannot afford.

Think about your past efforts at quitting smoking or kicking another addiction. Did you do anything in particular to compensate, from overeating sweets, spending money foolishly, or drinking more? Be honest with yourself, and remember that replacing addictive behaviors with healthy substitutes may bring you the rewards you seek, rather than providing a quick fix of excitement or happiness that carries a downside later.

Is there an addictive personality?

If you have multiple addictions or a particularly hard time quitting your sole addiction, the same could be true for relatives. Think about your family—does it include many smokers, alcoholics, or drug users? If the answer is yes, you've got company. And while environmental factors during your childhood could certainly predispose you to cigarettes and other addictions, the problem *could* in part be genetic.

The saying "the apple doesn't fall far from the tree" may have relevance when it comes to addictions. New research has focused on a gene that seems to suggest whether or not a person will start smoking and experience nicotine addiction. Two studies appearing in the January 1999 edition of the journal *Health Psychology* deal with the gene. The first study, conducted at Georgetown University Medical Center, notes that people with a certain version of a dopamine transporter gene called SLC6A3-9 are less likely to begin smoking before age 16, and, if they do, they are more likely to be able to quit.

The second study, by researchers at the National Cancer Institute, found that the gene was associated with certain personality characteristics—points capable of influencing a person's susceptibility to smoking. Those with the gene (which, remember, made someone less likely to have a smoking problem) showed lower novelty-seeking traits than those with the genotype. Study authors concluded that a low level of novelty seeking could predict success in smoking cessation. The amount of novelty seeking was quite a bit lower in those who were former smokers than in people who currently smoked, and those with the SLC6A3-9 gene were fully one-and-a-half times more likely to have quit smoking than people without the gene.

What does it mean to your life if you are genetically predisposed to addiction? It does not mean that you will become addicted, but it may mean you'll need to keep the potential tendency in mind and consciously avoid engaging in addictive behaviors or exposing yourself to temptation. A lot has yet to be learned about genetic correlations with addiction, and regardless of the outcome of more research, it's important not to use the concept as a crutch to avoid coping with addictive behaviors. Wherever addictive behavior originates, it's still largely up to you to address it in the best way possible.

Establish healthy boundaries that protect you in situations where you might be easily persuaded—by yourself or others—to partake. Rather than rigid rules, boundaries should be carefully thought-out guidelines based on what you know about your behavior. You should establish them as a way of looking out for yourself, as a way of helping yourself ahead of time.

Healthy boundaries may include:

- Limiting your contact with those who smoke, drink, or use drugs to just those situations where you know you will not feel temptation to join in the activity, and avoiding activities with

Timesaver
Make appropriate, interesting evening and weekend plans well in advance so that you'll find it less tempting to default to situations where your addictions may be encouraged.

them where you would be more likely to want to participate. (For instance, socializing with them early in the evening but making plans with others for later hours when your willpower might not be as strong.)

- Stepping away from stressful situations that can make you want to seek refuge in drugs, alcohol, or other addictive behaviors. (For instance, politely but firmly limiting contact with a difficult relative or looking for a job where you're treated well if that is not the case at your present one.)

- Knowingly exposing yourself to activities that may help you stay away from addictions. (For instance, goal setting, engaging in a fitness program and being health conscious in your diet, cultivating friendships with people who respect your boundaries, etc.)

Those who fail to have healthy boundaries may let situations and other people dictate what happens to them. In a sense, not setting healthy boundaries is an invitation to abuse. Although we'd all like to think others will look out for us, the best way to ensure that is to set a good example that assures others we have a healthy respect for ourselves, as well as for them.

What if you suspect you could be someone with high novelty-seeking traits? If you seem to crave excitement and new activities, use common sense. Rather than denying yourself rewarding experiences, make sure you include plenty of them in your life. Just take care to make sure that they are really beneficial experiences for you, rather than experiences where you are taking unnecessary risks, such as with smoking or using drugs. As you approach quitting smoking, rather than leaning on other potential addictions, think of something that you've always wanted to do and plan to do it. It could mean:

- Planning now for a vacation overseas next year

- Taking up a participatory sport

- Embarking on exploratory road trips every weekend

- Simply becoming more extroverted in your activities

- Starting a creative endeavor—painting, music, or something else

Essentially, creating a life with plenty of good novelty on its own may help keep you from subconsciously seeking thrills that carry a heavy price.

Quitting without feeding another habit

If you have a tendency to use addictive substances besides nicotine, why is it so bad to continue with them while you're kicking the tobacco habit—isn't it easier to concentrate on one problem at a time? Not always. Research has repeatedly found that using another addictive drug often leads to relapse using the first drug of choice. For this reason, addiction treatment professionals sometimes address multiple substance problems at once.

The philosophy is not commonly seen in treatment of nicotine abuse, but rather treatment of drug and alcohol dependence. A 1997 study in the *American Journal on Addictions* presented evidence that continued use of nicotine may be a factor in promoting relapse after drug or alcohol abuse treatment. At the one-year mark, recovery rates following in-patient treatment for drug or alcohol use were significantly higher in those who did not use

66
Of two evils, the
less is always to
be chosen.
—Thomas à
Kempis
(1380–1471),
*Imitation of
Christ*
99

tobacco than in those who did (especially if the drug of choice was a sedative like alcohol or narcotics).

Studies in animals have shown that the effects of one drug can stimulate use of another. After a while, the user becomes conditioned to want to use the second drug after he has taken the first. For instance, alcohol use has been found to stimulate cigarette cravings.

If you have multiple serious addictions, strongly consider getting involved in a 12-step or other support group, or look into addiction treatment and counseling. If you can't establish that you're addicted to anything but nicotine yet think you may have a casual tendency to lean on another habit when you give up cigarettes, thwart that possibility in advance.

What substance are you most likely to abuse in giving up nicotine? A common answer is alcohol. Some ways you can look out for yourself include:

- Make a promise to yourself that you will not increase the amount of alcohol you consume as you quit smoking.

- When you do drink, make sure you have a cigarette substitute with you—carrots or pretzel sticks, for instance.

- If you use nicotine replacement therapy, make sure it is available at the time you drink (bring gum or an inhaler or make sure you're wearing your patch).

- Try to steer yourself somewhat away from activities likely to involve alcohol to subtly reduce your exposure to it.

- If you're keeping a quitting journal, note how much alcohol you're consuming and any cravings for cigarettes during that time.

- When you're in a situation where you would usually be drinking, plan to have a snack or nonalcoholic beverages instead.
- Order drinks with a lower percentage of alcohol.

A typical drink contains half an ounce of alcohol, which is what you'll often find in a 12-ounce can of beer, a 4-ounce glass of table wine, or a 1-ounce shot of 100-proof distilled spirits (like whiskey or vodka). Half an ounce of alcohol is a broad rule of thumb for how much a person can metabolize in an hour, although weight, gender, and a host of other factors can change the equation. You should know your own limits.

You should be aware of how changing your mood with alcohol or other drugs could affect cravings for nicotine. At first, alcohol or another depressant could seem to quell the need for nicotine by taking the edge off anxieties in much the same way that nicotine can. However, once you are relaxed, it is possible you may feel the need for a nicotine pick-me-up. And after the effects of alcohol or depressant drugs wear off, you could well find yourself craving another hit of nicotine to help alleviate the hangover produced.

Beware of anything that is likely to speed you up or slow you down. The interruption in your normal daily cycles can easily set off a seeming need for nicotine to restore regulation. It is really a type of *stress*. If you're a coffee drinker, easing up on the number of cups you drink is probably a good idea. Beyond its ability to give you jittery nerves or insomnia if you've had too much, caffeine is also a dopamine mimic which over time can reduce the activity of dopamine in your brain—leaving you

Unofficially...
Caffeine can be
found in coffee,
tea, and a
number of soft
drinks, but there
is some in
chocolate, too.

potentially in need of even more stimulation, the kind that more caffeine, nicotine, or a host of other drugs could supply, but only at the cost of addiction.

Here are some ways you might consider handling the situation if you find yourself loading up on coffee or other sources of caffeine as you kick the cigarette habit:

- Restrict yourself to one morning cup of coffee
- Use nicotine-replacement therapy since the continuously supplied nicotine may quell caffeine cravings
- Try decaffeinated coffee, "half-caff," or use a coffee substitute (like chicory)
- If you drink sodas, switch to caffeine-free varieties (check the label)
- Begin an exercise program (which should improve your energy)
- Be especially sure to balance your diet for energy (see Chapter 11)
- Try an herbal energizer (an adaptogen-like one of the ginsengs described in Chapter 11, which helps build energy differently than stimulant herbs, like ma huang or guarana)
- Make a point to get plenty of sleep
- Take a little time off work or adjust your schedule not to be as demanding during the first few weeks that you're going without cigarettes
- Use weekends to putter, get fresh air, and recharge, rather than for strenuous activity
- Drink lots of water and nutritious juices

Prescription medication is another thing to watch when you're keeping an eye on potential addictions. By some estimates, several million

Americans have abused prescription drugs at one time or another. If you are afraid you could become reliant on a pharmaceutical, discuss options with your physician—a nonaddictive or less addictive alternative may be available.

Drugs are categorized by abuse potential by law under the Controlled Substances Act, part of the Comprehensive Drug Abuse Prevention and Control Act. They are divided into *schedules:*

- **Schedule I** drugs are those with a high potential for abuse, considered unsafe, and with no currently accepted medical use in treatment in the United States. *Examples: heroin, LSD, marijuana, and methaqualone.*

- **Schedule II** drugs are those with a high potential for abuse, which have a currently accepted medical use in treatment in the United States (or a currently accepted medical use with severe restrictions). *Examples: morphine, PCP, cocaine, methadone, and methamphetamine.*

- **Schedule III** drugs have abuse potential less than Schedules I and II, have a currently accepted medical use in treatment in the United States, and, when abused, may lead to low or moderate physical dependence or high psychological dependence. *Examples: anabolic steroids, codeine and hydrocodone with aspirin or Tylenol, and some barbiturates.*

- **Schedule IV** drugs have low potential for abuse, have currently accepted medical use in treatment in the United States, and, when abused, may produce limited physical or psychological dependence. *Examples: Darvon, Talwin, Equanil, Valium, and Xanax.*

Watch Out!
Talk with your pharmacist before buying any over-the-counter product if you have questions about its addictive potential and read the label carefully.

▪ **Schedule V** drugs are considered to have a low abuse potential and a currently accepted medical use in the United States. Abusing a Schedule V drug may lead to limited physical or psychological dependence. *Examples: over-the-counter cough medicines containing codeine.*

The following table includes examples of some commonly abused drugs noted under the act (excluding illicit Schedule I and less addictive Schedule V substances):

SOME PRESCRIPTION DRUGS WITH ADDICTIVE POTENTIAL

Schedule II Substances (abuse potential high):

Alfentanil (Alfenta)	Oxycodone (Percodan, Percocet, Tylox, Roxicodone)
Methamphetamine (Desoxyn)	Glutethimide
Amobarbital (Amytal)	Oxymorphone (Numorphan)
Methylphenidate (Ritalin)	Hydromorphodone (Dilaudid)
Amphetamine (Dexedrine)	Phenmetrazine (Preludin)
Mepridine (Demerol)	Levomethadyl (ORLAAM)
Codeine	Phenobarbital (Nembutal)
Morphine (MS Contin, Oramorph, Roxanol)	Levorphanol (Levo-Dromoran)
Dronabinol	Phenylacetone
Nabilone	Marinol (Dronabinol)
Etorphine Hydrochloride	Secobarbital (Seconal)
Opium (Pantopon)	Methadone (Dolophine)
Fentanyl (Duragesic, Sublimaze)	Sufentanil (Sufenta)

Schedule III Substances (some abuse potential):

Amobarbital Compounds	Phendimetrazine (Plegine)
Hydrocodone (Lorcet, Vicodin, Lortab, Tussionex)	Butalbital (Fiorinal, Fiorgen, Isollyl)
Anabolic Steroids	Phenobarbital Compounds
Methyprylon (Noludar)	Chlorphentermine
Benzphetamine (Didrex)	Secobarbital Compounds
Paregoric	Clortermine
Butabarbital (Butisol)	Tylenol with Codeine

Schedule IV Substances (abuse potential lower):	
Alprazolam (Xanax)	Pentazocine (Talwin)
Mephobarbital (Mebaral)	Ethchlorovynol (Placidyl)
Chloral Hydrate (Nortec)	Phenobarbital (Luminal)
Meprobamate (Equanil, Miltown)	Ethinamate (Valmid)
	Phentermine (Fastin)
Chlorazepate (Tranxene)	Fefluramine
Methohexital	Prazepam (Verstran, Centrax)
Chlordiazepoxide (Librium, Libritabs)	Flurazepam (Dalmane)
Midazolam (Versed)	Propoxyphene (Darvon, Darvocet)
Clonazepam (Klonapin)	Halazepam (Paxipam)
Oxazepam (Serax)	Quazepam (Dormalin, Doral)
Detropropoxyphene (Davron)	Lorazepam (Ativan)
Paraldehyde	Temazepam (Restoril)
Diazepam (Valium)	Mebutamate
Pemoline (Cylert)	Triazolam (Halcion)
Diethylpropion	

Source: Prescription Abuse.

If you are already addicted to a prescription drug, as difficult as the topic may be to bring up, tell your doctor immediately so he or she can help you with an appropriate way to cope with the situation.

Just the facts

- Dependencies on more than one substance are frequently seen in addictions counseling.
- There appears to be a genetic component to addiction, which may help explain why some people find it easier or harder to quit their habits.
- Continued use of nicotine may be a factor in promoting relapse after drug or alcohol abuse treatment.
- A high index of *novelty-seeking* traits is linked to increased potential for addiction.

Quitting and the Special Situation

PART VI

GET THE SCOOP ON...
Whether quit aids are safe in pregnancy ▪
Dangers of smoking when you're pregnant ▪ Why
quitting may help you get pregnant ▪ How
smoking causes damage during pregnancy

Smoking, Sex, and Pregnancy

Chapter 13

I f there's any time in a woman's day-to-day life when quitting smoking is most crucial, it's when she's pregnant and responsible for two lives. Though the desire to do what's best for your baby can spur your resolve immensely, anxieties about the impending blessed event can increase your desire to smoke. The changes your body goes through when you're pregnant may also affect your cravings for cigarettes.

What does quitting smoking do for your baby? It allows more oxygen and nutrition to reach her during development and assures a greater chance your child will be born healthy. But continuing to smoke during pregnancy allows toxins like nicotine, cyanide, and carbon monoxide to reach the baby through the placenta and deprives it of nutrients and the oxygen it needs. You are literally smoking for two.

This chapter discusses how to approach quitting if you're already pregnant. You should try to stop smoking without certain quit aids, and the reasons why will be explained. You can learn about the different risks that continuing to smoke poses to your baby and also why it's important to keep smoke away from your newborn. This chapter also talks about how quitting can potentially help you become pregnant.

Smoking and sex

The classic post-coitus cigarette break notwithstanding, smoking does not make you sexier, at least as far as your sex hormones are concerned. It can actually impair your hormonal balance, potentially leading to earlier menopause and reduced fertility. If you smoke while also using birth control pills, you run an increased risk of cardiovascular disease.

Smoking makes women less fertile

Smoking may inhibit fertilization by as much as two thirds, according to English research. A 1996 report in the journal *Fertility and Sterility* noted that of 13 relevant studies, all but one found smoking to work against fertility. It may do so in a number of ways, acting on the level of the hypothalamus and pituitary (which have important roles in hormonal signaling and regulation) and on the ovaries, Fallopian tubes, eggs, the embryo, and the lining of the uterus.

Heavy smoking—at least 20 cigarettes per day—has been associated in research studies with almost four times the risk of a shortened monthly cycle, as compared to not smoking at all. On average, women who smoked heavily had menstrual cycles shortened by almost three days, due almost wholly to a shortening of the first part of the cycle following menstruation, known as the *follicular phase*. This is the time of the month when estrogen builds and becomes the dominant sex hormone, readying the reproductive system for possible fertilization at the time of ovulation, around which time the follicular phase gives way to the second half of the cycle, known as the *luteal phase.*

Not only heavy smokers experienced changes in their cycle length. Women who smoked more than 10 cigarettes per day had more variation in the length of their cycles than did nonsmokers. The research data suggests that women who smoke more heavily could run an increased risk of *anovulation* (a cycle where ovulation does not occur) and a short luteal phase. And even ex-smokers have been found to exhibit altered cycle length, with shorter cycles and shorter luteal phases than those who had never smoked.

Studies show reduced levels of the body's main estrogen *estradiol* in smokers. This is the hormone that is released by developing egg sacs (called *follicles*) in the ovary during the first of two major phases—the follicular phase. Estradiol is necessary for an egg to develop and be released at ovulation. If that does not occur, the hormone *progesterone* may not be properly produced for the second half of the monthly cycle since it is actually secreted from the follicle once it has ruptured to release an egg. In this way, an interruption in the amount of estradiol in the ovary can influence other hormones and disrupt the entire fertility cycle.

How may smoking reduce estrogen? Through nicotine or its derivatives actually making it into the ovary, for one. A study at St. George's Hospital Medical School and the University of Bristol (England) identified nicotine's by-product *cotinine* concentrated in the follicles in the ovaries of smokers and, along with it, a reduced number of mature

Timesaver...
When counting days in a menstrual cycle, the first day of menstruation is day one. Keep track of your cycles as a help for your gynecologist in diagnosing ailments or predicting fertility.

eggs—thus, a potentially harder time maintaining normal fertility patterns.

The impact of smoking appears to increase with age. In one study, the number of mature eggs in older women was found to be reduced by half when cotinine was present. If you are quitting but live with a smoker, take note. Cotinine has been found in the follicular fluid of both smokers and nonsmokers exposed to passive smoke (though higher concentrations have been noted in smokers).

What smoking does to reduce fertility is still being explored, though its anti-estrogenic effects are well known. Beyond the presence of cotinine in ovarian follicles, research has focused on how constituents of cigarette smoke affect the *metabolization* of estrogen and estrogen receptors themselves. One thing is clear—smoking is not good for your menstrual cycle or, thus, your fertility.

Male problems

Women are not the only ones whose reproductive functions are compromised by smoking. You may have seen anti-smoking billboards featuring a cowboy smoking a notably flaccid cigarette. Smoking is a risk factor for erectile dysfunction, literally the inability to achieve an erection. There are several mechanisms by which smoking may cause erectile dysfunction, including by impeding blood flow in the penis.

There are other ways smoking may interfere with male potency, though it has not been shown to decrease male fertility per se. While smoking has been associated with higher levels of male hormones in women, conversely, it has also been associated with hormone level changes in males, such as increases in the levels of the female hormones estrone and estradiol (both of which are estrogens).

Scientists think smoking may alter the DNA of some sperm. And studies have shown smokers to have sperm that is more diluted, less viable, more abnormal, and with less ability to move than non-smokers' sperm. A British study suggests smoke-affected sperm could lead to cancer-causing cell mutations in offspring. Research at the University of Birmingham suggests as many as 15 percent of child-hood cancers might be due to smoking-related dam-age to the father's sperm. Interestingly, researchers did not find a link between mothers who smoke and childhood cancer.

Smoking, menopause, and aging

Research has found menopause to be hastened in women who smoke; skin wrinkling and tooth loss have increased, as well. Menopause arrived, on aver-age, two years earlier in smokers—at a mean age or 48.5 years instead of 50.5 years. Also, osteoporosis, a condition of brittle bones associated with meno-pause and low estrogen levels, shows up in greater proportion among smokers than nonsmokers, though lower estrogen levels in smokers do not appear to explain the whole story.

An English study of nearly 200 postmenopausal women found smokers and nonsmokers shared sim-ilar levels of the estrogens estradiol and estrone, as well as other hormones, but smokers showed higher levels of *androgens* (male hormones)—37 percent higher levels of DHEAS and 34 percent higher lev-els of androstenedione.

Women normally produce androgens in small quantities, just as men produce female sex hormones like estrogen in small quantities. However, excess lev-els of androgens in women can be responsible for masculinizing effects, such as deepened voice, dark

Bright Idea
Concerned about wrinkles? Quit smoking and go on a serious health kick aimed at balancing hormone levels. You may be surprised at what healthy living can do for you.

body and facial hair, added weight (especially around the midsection), and other unwanted changes.

Along with potentially throwing off hormonal balance, smoking visibly ages you. A 1998 Spanish study of postmenopausal women found that smokers got more wrinkles than nonsmokers; in fact, they were more than two-and-a-half times more likely to develop moderate to severe facial wrinkling. The longer and more intensely the women had smoked, the worse the wrinkles were.

As an interesting footnote to this study, researchers found that lifelong nonsmokers who used *hormone replacement therapy (HRT)*, which is estrogen and sometimes progesterone supplementation, had less wrinkling than lifelong nonsmokers who hadn't used HRT. Interestingly, the use of HRT didn't alter the wrinkling seen in current smokers.

The Pill and the cigarette

If you're on the Pill and you smoke, the older you are and the more you indulge your habit, the more danger you're putting yourself in. Risk of death among Pill users over 35 who smoke is much higher than for nonsmokers. Smoking accentuates the risk of cardiovascular problems in users of oral contraceptives.

If you're over 35 years old, you need to make a choice between taking the Pill and smoking—one should be given up (I suggest giving up smoking). Remember that other risk factors for heart attack or stroke (like diabetes, high blood pressure, or high cholesterol) make quitting even more important.

Smoking and reproductive disorders

Smoking is associated with increased risk of certain reproductive disorders, including cervical cancer. A 1997 Czech study found smokers tended to experience significantly more frequent heavy menstrual bleeding than nonsmokers, as well as more difficulty becoming pregnant and more complications during pregnancy.

A study by Britain's Imperial Cancer Research Fund has found that cervical abnormalities may be reversible some of the time when a woman stops smoking. Smokers whose Pap smear tests were mildly abnormal gave up smoking or drastically reduced their use of cigarettes for six months as part of the study, and at the end of that time, more than 80 percent of participants showed a reduction in the size of the abnormal looking area, compared with less than 20 percent of those who continued to smoke.

Research suggests nicotine can alter the activity of the hypothalamus and pituitary by stimulation of a number of hormones, which may account for changes in menstrual patterns seen in smokers. Epidemiologic studies show essentially that women who smoke can wind up with a relative estrogen deficiency, given that they experience earlier menopause and an increased risk of fractures from osteoporosis (estrogen is bone-protective). Women who smoke also may show lower risk of a number of ailments associated with excess estrogen, including endometrial cancer, endometriosis, uterine fibroids, and benign breast disease, as well as hyperemesis gravidarum (a condition of severe nausea and vomiting during pregnancy).

Unofficially...
Beyond smoking, other risk factors for cervical cancer include a history of sexually transmitted disease, multiple pregnancies beginning at an early age, sex before age 18, multiple partners, and having a mother who took the potent estrogen DES while pregnant with you.

Smoking, your pregnancy, and your baby

Most of us have heard that you should quit smoking and look out for your health when you become pregnant. But how much do you know about what smoking can do to your baby? Try this quiz to find out.

SMOKING AND YOUR BABY

1. Smoking during pregnancy can lead to premature delivery and lowered birthweight.

   TRUE or FALSE

2. The annual U.S. costs of complicated childbirth that have been attributed to smoking are:

   a. No costs have been attributed to smoking

   b. $96.3–$99.4 million

   c. $1.4–$2 billion

   d. $15.7 billion

3. What percentage of women who experienced miscarriage early in a pregnancy were found to have smoked during the pregnancy?

   a. 2 percent

   b. 7 percent

   c. 12.2 percent

   d. 34 percent

4. A man's smoking habits pose no risk to his baby's development.

   TRUE or FALSE

Answers: 1. True; 2. c; 3. d; 4. False.

Just how bad *is* it to smoke while you're pregnant? Pretty bad. The risks include:

- Miscarriage

- Stillbirth

- Premature labor

- Low birthweight

- Sudden infant death syndrome (SIDS)

- Asthma and breathing disorders

- Retardation

Remember these problems for a baby are in addition to the damage smoking is doing to the mother.

Your own health is reason enough to quit. Let's take a closer look at each of the risk issues above.

Miscarriage

Miscarriage is also called *spontaneous abortion*. It happens in nearly a third of first-time pregnancies. Miscarriages usually happen during the first 14 weeks of pregnancy and often so early that a woman is unaware both that she is pregnant and that a miscarriage has occurred.

What can cause miscarriage? A mother's use of certain drugs, as well as some kinds of infections and diseases, uterine and fetal abnormalities, and severe stress or poor nutrition.

Smoking appears to be a significant factor in the risk of miscarriage. Researchers link smoking to more than 140,000 miscarriages each year in the United States. A 1999 University of Pittsburgh study appearing in the *New England Journal of Medicine* found that 34 percent of women who experienced miscarriage had smoked during their pregnancy, while among women whose pregnancies continued beyond 22 weeks, just under 22 percent smoked.

Why might smoking contribute to the risk of miscarriage? One point, expressed by the researchers in this study, is that nicotine is a *vasoconstrictor*, an agent that triggers the narrowing of arteries, which can reduce blood flow to the fetus. Another is the deleterious effect smoking has on the placenta's ability to implant into the uterus, as described in a 1999 study in the journal *Placenta*.

To understand why smoking could cause difficulty with egg implantation, you can look at the issues surrounding smoking's supposed benefit in some gynecological conditions. Some research has suggested the risk of certain diseases may actually

Bright Idea
If you have an endocrine condition such as hypothyroidism or diabetes, visit your doctor and make sure your management of symptoms is up to par before you try to get pregnant since these disorders can spur miscarriage.

Watch Out!
When you're pregnant, seek your physician's okay for use of any medication, even non-prescription.

be reduced by smoking. Such has appeared to be the case with uterine cancer, endometriosis, and in a condition known as pre-eclampsia, which is characterized by blood pressure irregularity during pregnancy.

New findings are coming to light that to some degree counter the earlier, puzzling results. Researchers at Columbia University and the University of Florida noted that the tobacco smoke compound benzopyrene, which was earlier found to inhibit the cell overgrowth of endometriosis, may also inhibit the growth of normal tissue within the uterus. That means it could potentially cause fertility and miscarriage problems since an egg needs healthy uterine tissue to attach to and be sustained by as it implants in the womb. In the case of pre-eclampsia, frequently a condition of late pregnancy, the authors postulate that smoking may *appear* to be protective because a high miscarriage rate among smokers means fewer pregnancies even make it to the time when pre-eclampsia is prevalent.

It is also interesting to note that, as explained earlier, androgen (male hormone) levels have been found to be higher in postmenopausal women who smoke than in nonsmokers. Androgen levels are also higher in women who have recurrent miscarriages than in those with normal fertility patterns.

Stillbirth

Smoking accounts for about 10 percent of all infant deaths, including stillbirths. Stillbirths to smoking mothers can be accounted for wholly by the higher incidence of retarded growth and placental complications that occur in pregnancies of smokers, according to a 1994 study in the *British Journal of Obstetrics and Gynaecology*.

Many stillbirths that smoking mothers have are due to premature separation of a normally implanted placenta, which is known as *abruptio placentae*. A 1975 study in the journal *Biomedicine* found a substantial increase in stillbirths among smokers, with a large proportion of this increase due to abruptio placentae. The percentage of smokers in this category rose to 46 percent while it was only 12 percent in the group of livebirths.

Premature labor and low birthweight

Smoking is believed to account for up to 14 percent of preterm deliveries, which are often associated with reduced birthweight, particularly in pregnancies where the mother smoked. Smoking is responsible for 20 to 30 percent of the occurrences of low birthweight, according to the American Lung Association, though some estimates suggest the incidence of low birthweight infants is possibly nearly twice as high among smoking mothers.

Low birthweight brings an increased risk of breathing problems and other difficulties for a baby. A 1975 study in the *European Journal of Obstetrics, Gynecology and Reproductive Biology* noted that a mother's smoking reduces birthweight by 150 to 250 grams, even though carried through full term.

One reason for these lower weights in smokers' babies appears to be a lack of oxygen, as is sometimes seen in the infants of mothers who live at high altitude. Other studies point to compromised utilization of vitamins and minerals in the developing fetus since levels of some vitamins and minerals such as calcium, vitamin B_{12}, and vitamin C are lower in smokers.

Low birthweight babies do put on weight as infants, but by the age of seven, children of smokers

Unofficially...
An estimated
15 percent of
mothers smoke
during
pregnancy.

are still more likely than others to have reduced height, slower reading speed, and lower social adjustment scores than children of nonsmokers.

Sudden infant death syndrome

Sudden infant death syndrome, or *SIDS*, is a frightening specter for new parents. Seemingly healthy babies stop breathing and die without warning in SIDS, which is the leading cause of death in infants between one month and one year old. SIDS is not well understood, though recent studies have found a proportionately large number of SIDS infants are born tiny for their gestational age, and mothers of SIDS babies are often smokers.

Results of a 1996 English study suggested that deaths from the syndrome could be reduced by almost two thirds if parents did not smoke. The same study found that smoking in a household after a baby's birth contributed to the risk of SIDS from maternal smoking. While lying a baby on its back rather than its stomach is associated with a reduced rate of SIDS death, scientists are increasingly looking at prenatal cardiorespiratory development as a key factor in SIDS.

Asthma and breathing disorders

Babies of mothers who smoked during pregnancy are not only more likely to experience the breathing failure of SIDS, they are more likely to have breathing disorders in general. Infants of smoking mothers have been found to have reduced respiratory function and more tendency to develop wheezing. Environmental tobacco smoke once a baby is home from the hospital contributes to the problem. A 1997 study in the *European Respiratory Journal* found that babies born to mothers who smoked while pregnant actually have weaker lungs than babies born to non-smokers, and the more cigarettes the mother smoked, the greater the harm to a baby's lungs.

Mental retardation

The incidence of mental retardation in children and smoking in mothers has been linked in research. A 1996 study reported in the journal *Pediatrics* found women who smoked had more than a 50 percent greater chance of having a mentally retarded child than women who didn't smoke. Children whose mothers smoked at least a pack a day while they were pregnant showed more than a 75 percent increase in the rate of mental retardation.

The dramatic findings were not accounted for when researchers looked at the socioeconomics of the women involved, nor the well-known tendency of smokers to have lower birthweight babies. Researchers concluded that if their findings represent a causal relationship, then slightly more than one in three cases of otherwise unexplained retardation in children of women who smoke may be due to smoking during pregnancy.

Behavioral problems may also arise with greater incidence in children of women who smoked while pregnant. A 1996 study in the *American Journal of Psychiatry* found that 22 percent of the children with ADHD (attention deficit hyperactivity disorder) that they studied were born to mothers who smoked during pregnancy, compared with just eight percent of the normal subjects.

Quitting if you're pregnant (or trying to be)

Quitting altogether is the most preferable and really the only way to protect your child. Just cutting down

Bright Idea
The knowledge that you are indeed responsible for someone else's life can be overwhelming when you have to grapple with the urge to smoke. It makes the most sense to quit smoking altogether before you try to conceive.

on how much you smoke or switching to light cigarettes may not be helpful to your baby since many people who do so unknowingly compensate by inhaling more deeply or more often, and since smoking even a little may have some effect on your baby.

Kicking the cigarette habit before you conceive is the best plan, but if you've just found out you're going to have a baby, take heart. According to the American Lung Association, a woman who quits smoking in the first three to four months of her pregnancy can cut the chances of her child being born prematurely or with smoking-related health problems.

What about nicotine replacement and Zyban?

If you've used nicotine patches or gum before, you'll see on the package insert that you should check with your doctor before use, if you're pregnant or if you are breastfeeding. There is some division of opinion in medical circles over whether, in some cases, nicotine replacement *should* be used, if a woman has tried and cannot quit smoking any other way. She should *try* to quit smoking without the use of nicotine replacement if at all possible.

A 1996 study in the journal *Clinical Pharmacology & Therapeutics* looked at the concentrations of nicotine and its by-product cotinine in pregnant women and their fetuses. One group quit smoking using six pieces of 2mg nicotine gum daily, while the other group continued to smoke. Researchers found a significant reduction in nicotine and cotinine concentrations in the gum group as compared to the smoking group, lending some support to the idea that nicotine-replacement therapy might be appropriate in some cases. However, it's important to remember that nicotine can enter breast milk, and a nursing mother, in effect, is supplying nicotine to her suckling baby if using nicotine-replacement therapy (or smoking).

Zyban, the quit-smoking pill, should be used in pregnant women only if clearly needed, and pharmacological quit aids should not be the first thing a pregnant woman turns to in an effort to stop smoking. So states prescribing literature for Zyban, which also notes that the pill has not been found to impair fertility or harm the fetus in animal teratology studies (studies to evaluate potential for abnormal embryonic development). However, large scale human studies are lacking, and effects on labor and delivery in humans are still unknown. Bupropion (the chemical name for Zyban) and its metabolites are secreted in breast milk, however, and due to the potential for serious adverse reactions in a nursing infant, a new mother should make a choice whether to continue taking Zyban and not breastfeed, or to discontinue Zyban so she can breastfeed. If you're taking Zyban and have found out you're pregnant or if you're thinking of becoming pregnant, be sure to talk with your doctor.

Watch Out!
Continuing to smoke while using nicotine-replacement therapy can be dangerous to a fetus because of increased nicotine intake.

The quitting mom-to-be

Why would any woman keep smoking during pregnancy, given the risks to her baby? Researchers have looked at the reasons behind such continued cigarette use. What they've found out is that knowing about the dangers doesn't seem to affect the inclination to smoke while pregnant, but living with a smoker makes a huge difference.

An English study of new mothers found that while about half had never smoked and almost 3 of 10 still smoked, some 22 percent were former smokers, and of those, about half had given up smoking while they were pregnant. Women in all of the groups shared the same level of knowledge about the risks of maternal smoking; and about a third of the smokers had firsthand knowledge: They had themselves experienced problems associated with smoking during pregnancy—from miscarriage to premature birth to sudden infant death.

More than three quarters of the new moms who smoked said they wanted to quit, and most had tried. One of the most striking points of this study is the high percentage of smokers—75 percent—who had smoking partners, since only 30 percent of nonsmokers did.

Sharing a home with a smoker adds daily pressure for a mom-to-be who's trying hard to quit. But so may postpartum depression, or for any woman, PMS. It becomes more difficult to kick the habit in the face of depression or anxiety, and keeping that in mind may help you overcome quitting challenges.

If you've quit while pregnant, do everything you can in your life to make sure you don't succumb to temptation as a new mother, even if you experience a tough bout of postpartum depression (related to changing hormone levels). Preplan ways to make your life easier and more rewarding at that time, keep your nutrition good, and pamper yourself, as well as the new baby. Or at the very least try to plan ahead for extra help so you can keep the stress level as low as possible—not an easy task when your sleep schedule is disturbed by nighttime feedings and crying, along with all the other stresses of having a new baby.

Likewise, if you are prone to premenstrual mood difficulties, don't put yourself in the line of temptation at that time, and arrange your life so that you have the best emotional support at that time of the month. Don't let your healthy diet slip or stress catch up with you. With any kind of anxiety or depression—whether it is postpartum, premenstrual, or garden variety—use your head to think about its severity. Does it seem abnormal? Do you need help with it? Don't hesitate to talk to your physician or a counselor about it.

Women who quit smoking during their pregnancy are in the same boat as other quitting smokers—it's hard not to resume the habit. A Duke University study in *American Journal of Public Health* looked at three different groups of women who were given the booklet "Stop Now for Your Baby" while they were pregnant. One group also received counseling in the way of three phone calls encouraging them to quit smoking before their babies were born. Another group received phone counseling both before and after the birth of their babies, as well as parenting newsletters with information about quitting smoking. Researchers found that the program didn't prevent the women from resuming smoking, but it did delay their relapse. Six months after their babies were born, those who received postpartum treatment were less likely to be smoking than the other women, but at the one-year mark, the women in each group shared similar rates of smoking.

A 1999 study in the *American Journal of Public Health* suggests that keeping new moms from resuming smoking is *quite* a challenge and that ongoing and stronger interventions may be needed. Some 457 women received counseling (in varying levels) about smoking cessation. Counseling contact after a birth delayed relapse but didn't prevent it. The women in the study group who received the most

Bright Idea
If you're quitting for pregnancy, talk with other new moms about forming a buddy system to help you resist the urge to smoke once the baby's home. Keep focused on yourself, as well as your role as a new mom.

attention were also the least likely to be smoking again six months after giving birth. However, at one year the results for all levels of counseling were similar—more than half had begun to smoke again by the time the trial ended.

To guard against a relapse into your old smoking behaviors, use the *buddy system*, attend a smoking cessation support group regularly, and keep the necessity of being smoke-free high in your mind.

Smoking and dads-to-be

Moms are not in this alone! Prospective fathers need to quit smoking to protect their children, too. Paternal smoking has been found to increase both risk of respiratory infection in infants and sudden infant death syndrome, regardless of whether a child's mother smokes.

Men's smoking habits are probably one of the strongest influences on a woman's ability to quit while pregnant and not relapse following the birth of their child. But how many men realize how important their smoking behavior is around this time?

A 1998 Australian study found men largely unaware that their own smoking could endanger a fetus. They also thought their own smoking was unimportant when the mother smoked during pregnancy, though, in actuality, a smoking father adds risk even if the mother already smokes. Researchers found that the men in their study weren't well informed about the risks of secondhand smoke to a developing baby. They also found another interesting reason why fathers may have a hard time quitting: Early in a woman's pregnancy, the baby didn't seem real to the men in the study (given the lack of visible signs of impending birth) and thus the importance of quitting didn't sink in.

Armed with this knowledge, how do you as a mother-to-be convince dad-to-be that he needs to take quitting seriously? Show him the data on secondhand smoke, set a smoke-free example yourself, discuss the tobacco issue with him plainly, and involve him in your pregnancy so the reality that *this is a baby* hits home early.

Ask him to come with you if you have an ultrasound so he can see the resulting live picture of the baby (and ask him to attend other obstetrician visits). Involve him in preparations for the baby's arrival, capitalizing on his talents. Handyman? Put him to work building nursery furniture, *early*. Financial genius? Get him started on insurance papers and a safe investment fund for Junior's college education, *early*. At the very least, ask him to physically help you during all stages of your pregnancy—a brief but regular lower-back massage, shopping for healthy foods, a companion walk for exercise.

When you and the father of your baby are around other couples, ask other fathers about how they helped with, viewed, or came to terms with pregnancy. Some dads-to-be jump in, participating every step of the way in their child's development, and some are much less at ease with that idea. But with a little creativity, you can probably find some way the male in your life can participate in a way that is comfortable for them.

Fathers-to-be have been jokingly (or not so) said to go through four distinct phases upon learning of pregnancy: shock, denial, acceptance, and fear. Recognizing the stages may assist you in helping the father of your baby to quit smoking.

Telling him you're pregnant and in the same breath that he needs to quit smoking probably won't result in a recognition of anything you said beyond

Unofficially... Some fathers even experience sympathetic pregnancy, replete with weight gain, nausea, and slightly distended stomach.

the word "pregnant." It may take a few hours, a day, or longer for the concept to sink in. Denial is the phase where the pregnancy won't seem real to him. The doctor has confirmed your home pregnancy test, and you may notice the changes in your body, but to him, everything is eerily the same except that you have uttered the words "I'm pregnant."

At this stage, where you need to start involving him in your pregnancy so it can feel real to him, you can realistically start to talk about quitting for the baby's health, although a father and mother ideally should have quit before conception. However long it takes you to introduce the idea of his quitting for the baby's health, make sure you insist that he at least not smoke around you but keep his smoking activities outside the house and the car.

Once the baby's home

It's traditional for new fathers to pass out cigars to celebrate the birth of their child. Ironic? Sure...just make sure smokes don't make it home with the baby. Smoking has a huge impact on infants and kids. Children who live with cigarette smokers:

- Become ill more often

- Stay ill longer

- Have more frequent colds, coughs, ear infections, and asthma attacks

- Run an increased risk of breathing problems, lung cancer, or heart disease in adulthood

Smoking even affects breastfeeding, so refraining from smoking during the time you're lactating is important. The American Academy of Pediatrics lists nicotine among drugs of abuse contraindicated in breastfeeding, due to the possibility of shock, vomiting, diarrhea, rapid heart rate, restlessness, and decreased milk production. Smoking also apparently influences the amount of important antioxidants that a baby receives when feeding. A 1998 Spanish study found vitamin C levels were lower in the breast milk of smokers.

Is it possible that smoking while you're breast-feeding a baby could make him or her more likely to smoke as an adult? Researchers have found that smoking changes both the taste and scent of breast milk, and that could help to explain why children of smokers are more likely to take up the habit in adulthood. In a 1998 study reported in the *New England Journal of Medicine*, scientists at the Monell Chemical Senses Center in Philadelphia noted that milk samples collected half an hour to one hour after smoking carried a characteristic scent of cigarettes.

A word to new moms

If you're quitting smoking because you're pregnant or planning to have a baby in the near future, congratulations. This is one time that, since you're doing things for two, you have an extra impetus to stick with your quit plan. Throughout your pregnancy and after your baby is born, make sure you don't neglect your own needs—take very good care of yourself and don't let the possibility of relapse gain ground.

Remember that one of the biggest predictors of whether a woman will resume smoking again after the birth of her baby is sharing a home with a smoker, so if your partner can quit now, too, that is the ideal situation. For a mother considering her future as well as her child's, the benefit of remaining smoke-free is clear. Women who don't smoke live on average almost 16 years longer than women who do, and that's more time to spend as a mother or even a grandmother.

Just the facts

- Smoking while pregnant poses a greater risk of miscarriage, stillbirth, premature labor, low birthweight, sudden infant death syndrome (SIDS), infant asthma and breathing disorders, and retardation.

- Whether or not her partner smokes is the biggest statistical determinant of whether a woman will return to smoking after quitting during pregnancy.

- Smoking is associated with earlier menopause and infertility in women.

- Smoking is associated with sexual dysfunction in men.

GET THE SCOOP ON...
Ailments quitting can improve ▪ How quickly
your risks drop ▪ Drug interactions and
nicotine ▪ How quit aids affect some
specific health conditions

Chapter 14

Medical Conditions and Quitting

Quitting smoking is hard enough when you are *otherwise* in good health. Eventually, though, smoking can take its toll, and you could be faced with a medical condition for which it is absolutely imperative that you give up cigarettes.

This chapter walks you through some of the major ailments that may be improved when you give up cigarettes, and I'll caution you about which could potentially be affected for the worse—in these situations, it's important to discuss quitting plans with your physician. In some cases, it may be necessary to switch, add, or stop using certain medications.

What effect can quitting have on my condition?

Smoking is the number one preventable cause of death and illness in the United States, claiming more than 430,000 lives every year. It can make breathing harder, worsen asthma, and reduce the amount of oxygen all of your cells get, and it's linked to impotence and infertility. In the long run, smokers run greater risk of many cancers, heart attacks, strokes, and pulmonary diseases.

When you stop smoking, you reduce your risks. A study conducted by Rutgers University (funded by the Agency for Health Care Policy and Research) found that those who smoke are more than 30 percent more likely to wind up in the hospital than those who don't. Projecting from that research, hospital admissions might be cut by more than 12 percent if only middle-aged men in the United States quit smoking.

Smoking causes death most frequently in the following ways:

1. Cardiovascular disease

2. Cancer

3. Respiratory disease

Between the years 1990 and 1994, some 906,600 deaths from cardiovascular disease were attributed to smoking, and of 778,700 smoking-related cancer deaths, 616,800 fatalities were from lung cancer.

Is your serious health problem smoking related? Most cancers of the lung, trachea, bronchus, larynx, pharynx, oral cavity, and esophagus can be traced to the use of tobacco, and smoking also accounts for a sizable number of the incidences of cancer of the bladder, cervix, kidney, and pancreas. Cigarette smoking worsens atherosclerosis—hardening of, and the buildup of plaque deposits in—the arteries and greatly increases risk of heart attack and stroke, as well as coronary artery and vascular disease, and, obviously, respiratory disease. It also may be linked to increased risk of osteoporosis and can cause myriad problems in pregnancy (described in Chapter 13), among many other drawbacks. In all, the extra lifetime health-care cost that smokers pose could be as much as $500 billion.

Changing your risk

Quitting smoking can improve your risk profile with regard to many of the diseases it causes or worsens. Risk of some cancers, as well as heart attack, stroke, and coronary heart disease, drop dramatically when a person kicks the habit according to the U.S. Preventive Services Task Force. For example:

- **Heart attack (and fatal coronary heart disease).** 50 percent risk reduction one year after quitting

- **Oral and esophageal cancer.** 50 percent risk reduction five years after quitting

- **Lung cancer.** 30 to 50 percent risk reduction 10 years after quitting

Risk reductions can also improve with time; for instance, while the risk of heart attack drops by half within a year after quitting, after 15 years, it's similar to the better risk profile of nonsmokers. The same is true with regard to death rates from coronary heart disease and stroke (with improvements in stroke risk profiles seen about two years following the quit date. Risk for hemorrhage and peripheral vascular disease also drops after quitting.

After about 15 years without smoking, coronary heart disease risk drops to a level similar to that of people who have never smoked. In smokers already diagnosed with coronary heart disease, quitting seems to reduce risk of recurrent infarction and cardiovascular death by half or greater.

Those smokers with chronic obstructive pulmonary disease (COPD) typically experience improved pulmonary function—about 5 percent

> " ...To leave the world a little better; whether by a healthy child, a garden patch or a redeemed social condition; to know even one life has breathed easier because you have lived. This is the meaning of success.
> —Ralph Waldo Emerson "

better—in just a few months after quitting. Decline in pulmonary function does not continue at the rapid pace seen in continuing smokers, but rather slows.

Cutting out cigarettes lowers risk of laryngeal cancer and cuts to 50 percent the risk of mouth and esophageal cancer five years after cessation. In lung cancer, a former smoker's risk has declined 30 to 50 percent within 10 years of cessation, with improvements in risk as time goes on. Pancreatic cancer risk declines a decade after cessation and bladder cancer risk drops after several years, too.

There are myriad benefits to be found with kicking the habit. Smokers who quit also have lower risk of cervical cancer than those who continue to smoke, and they experience fewer respiratory problems like pneumonia, bronchitis, or just coughing and wheezing. Quitting can cut risk of developing duodenal and gastric ulcers. Those conditions, when seen in smokers, are typically worse than when they occur in nonsmokers, too.

Some research suggests, however, with regard to a small group of ailments, those who smoke may in some cases face a lower risk than the population at large. These diseases include:

- Parkinson's disease

- Alzheimer's disease

- Some cancers (certain breast and endometrial cancers)

- Endometriosis

- Uterine fibroids

Bright Idea
You can improve your risks of many diseases by eating a healthy diet and getting regular moderate exercise, as well as quitting smoking.

While smoking is in no way a justifiable way to prevent any of these diseases, if you have one of these conditions (or are at high risk) and are quitting, please discuss it with your doctor. What scientists are learning about smokers' apparent and puzzling reduced risk is leading to possible treatments for these diseases that do not carry the extreme health burden that smoking imposes. You may decide with your physician to modify medication dosing, start a new medication, schedule frequent screenings, or undertake preventative measures for these ailments as you quit.

Smokers may run a lower risk of Parkinson's disease and Alzheimer's disease due to nicotine's action in the body, and research is being conducted on the possible use of nicotinic drugs in the treatment of these diseases, as well as Tourette's Syndrome (a neuropsychiatric disorder characterized by movement and vocal tics, and obsessions and compulsions) and ulcerative colitis. In some study situations, the prolonged use of nicotine patches or the use of nicotine gum is already being tested.

Research showing smoking as a risk reduction factor in disease runs into problems, too, with quick assumptions—for instance, in the case of Parkinson's disease, which heavy smokers can run half the risk of getting. Though nicotine may prove helpful, a Singapore study suggests other possibilities:

■ Smokers prone to Parkinson's disease may deteriorate and die at an accelerated rate, leaving fewer smokers alive with Parkinson's disease and thereby skewing study results of smokers with Parkinson's.

■ The phase of Parkinson's disease prior to the appearance of symptoms could involve personality changes associated with an aversion to smoking, potentially due to progressive dopamine depletion eventually resulting in

Parkinson's disease (thus again potentially skewing study results).

Both possibilities, in other words, do not take for granted that someone with Parkinson's disease who smokes is just like anyone else who smokes. There could hypothetically be fewer Parkinson's patients who do smoke still alive or fewer Parkinson's patients who want to smoke and do smoke. It's not a farfetched idea, since both Parkinson's disease and the use of nicotine have in common a relationship with dopamine levels in the body.

While, technically speaking, smoking could mean reduced risk of certain diseases, the issue is clouded by the overwhelming negative health effects of smoking, health effects that quitting may improve. For instance, in one study following up for two years on patients with multi-infarct dementia, an impairment of brain function brought on by a series of cerebrovascular accidents, quitting smoking was associated with improving cognitive function. *Dementia,* a condition associated with the elderly, is really a broad classification which the World Health Organization sorts into nine main categories, for instance Alzheimer's disease.

While lung cancer kills about 50,000 women every year, breast cancer claims the lives of some 43,000 women annually. Breast cancer risk is generally increased by smoking, although in one surprising study, carriers of a certain gene mutation experienced reduced incidence of a particular kind of breast cancer if they smoked. Relatively heavy smokers had a 54 percent reduction in breast cancer when compared to women who had never smoked.

Researchers hypothesize that the risk reduction is due to smoking's reduction of estrogen in the

Unofficially...
Dementia occurring before age 65 is referred to as *early-onset.*

body. Many breast cancers are estrogen-related, and other diseases smoking decreases the risk of—uterine fibroids, endometriosis, and endometrial cancer—are all also linked to elevated estrogen levels.

However, an American Cancer Society study following the progress of more than 600,000 healthy women for six years indicates that women who smoke generally have a greater risk of death from breast cancer than do nonsmokers—about 25 percent greater. Women who smoked two packs or more daily elevated their risk to 75 percent above nonsmoker risk. Interestingly, women who quit smoking were able to reduce their risk levels down to that of nonsmokers. And other studies certainly support smoking's ability to increase breast cancer risk.

Why was breast cancer risk increased so much? There are no absolute answers yet, though past research has indicated smoking-related impairment of the immune system could be the culprit, causing the body to respond to cancer with less vigilance.

Surgery, hospitalization, and smoking

Amazing though it may sound, nearly three in five smokers who undergo an operation for heart disease keep smoking after the surgery, according to a multicenter study funded by the National Heart, Lung, and Blood Institute. Researchers were surprised at the high percentage of patients who chose to continue smoking, after either angioplasty to open blocked blood vessels or coronary artery bypass surgery.

Many of the patients had a long history of heart disease before having the surgery but still kept smoking. Those with a prior history of heart attack were among the groups most likely to keep smoking,

Timesaver
You can find out
more about good
heart health at
The American
Heart
Association's
Web site at www.
americanheart.
org.

and so were those who rated their general health "poor" or "fair," as well as African Americans and younger patients. Those with high blood pressure or diabetes were less likely to be die-hard smokers.

It is imperative if you have cardiovascular problems or any other serious illness potentially related to smoking that you discuss quitting with your physician since cessation may help prevent further deterioration and recovery prospects should be improved. Physicians are admonished to stress how important quitting smoking is to heart patients—for instance, Canadian medical guidelines on treatment of heart failure note that adequate management of risk factors like hypertension, diabetes mellitus, hyperlipidemia, and cigarette smoking must be vigorously undertaken.

If you are ill enough to be hospitalized, it is crucial that you attempt to quit smoking since continuing to smoke could interfere with your recovery. You should know, too, that all hospitals in the United States are required to be smoke free in order to receive accreditation (by the Joint Commission on Accreditation of Healthcare Organizations).

If you are in the hospital, you should have at least two motivators to quit:

- You will not be allowed to smoke in the hospital
- Your illness could be made worse by continuing to smoke

Patients with cancer of the lung, head, or neck remain at higher risk for another cancer incidence, even if one is successfully treated. Cardiac patients who don't quit are more likely to have a second heart attack. Smoking can also deter healing of wounds and bones.

Since smokers do wind up hospitalized and unable to continue their habit while they're convalescing, the Agency for Health Care Policy and Research (AHCPR) recommends in its *Clinical Practice Guideline on Smoking Cessation* that clinicians should consider providing nicotine patches for temporary nicotine replacement therapy during hospitalization to reduce the nicotine withdrawal symptoms a regular smoker is likely to experience.

Psychiatric considerations

If you smoke and are either diagnosed with a psychiatric disorder or are concerned you may have one, there are a few things you should know about quitting smoking. If you take medication for psychiatric conditions, your physician will need to monitor you since quitting may prompt the need for a change in dosage.

Psychiatric problems are quite common among those who smoke, more so than in the population at large. It's not surprising since some of the drive to use nicotine may be a form of self-medication for anxiety, depression, or other uncomfortable states. Between 30 and 50 percent of those who look into smoking cessation may have been depressed at least once in their life, and more than one in five may have a history of alcohol abuse.

However, quitting smoking in some cases has the potential to worsen a psychiatric condition. If you have a history of depression, for instance, there is plenty of evidence to suggest you may experience another bout of it as you kick the habit. You also run a greater risk of relapsing to old smoking behaviors.

When you have a psychiatric condition and are considering quitting, it is wise to discuss it with your

Moneysaver
Quitting smoking saves not only the dollars you're not spending on cigarettes, but also a potentially heavy burden in health-care costs and lost quality of life.

psychiatrist before proceeding. The good news is that nicotine replacement therapy can probably help by gradually lessening your exposure to nicotine rather than abruptly withdrawing it cold turkey, and the quit-smoking pill Zyban may also be an option.

Smoking, pregnancy, and reproduction

It is important that women quit smoking when they become pregnant—ideally before pregnancy (so should prospective fathers since some childhood diseases have been linked to paternal smoking). Even when a woman smokes up to her 30th week of pregnancy and then quits, she is likely to have a baby with higher birthweight than a woman who continues to smoke for the rest of her pregnancy.

Smoking's link to earlier menopause, impaired fertility, and altered hormone levels—such as reduced estrogen and increased androgens (male hormones) in women, and increased estrogen in men—is another important reason to give up cigarettes. Smoking-related impotence in males has much to do with altered blood flow from smoking, another good reason to quit cigarettes and improve cardiovascular health. And a lack of estrogen in postmenopausal women is often responsible for the development of the brittle bone disease osteoporosis. It's no surprise then that smoking has been associated with increased risk of osteoporosis.

Restoring hormone levels may lead to pleasant surprises—such as a slowing of visible aging. A 1998 Spanish study (discussed in Chapter 13) noted that not only were smokers two-and-a-half times more likely to have noticeable facial wrinkles, but also that the longer women smoked, the worse wrinkling became.

Quitting is also important to cut risk of those reproductive diseases smoking is associated with, such as invasive cervical cancer, which some smokers may be twice as likely as nonsmokers to get. Recent studies have shown risk drops when a woman stops smoking, though her chances of cervical cancer remain higher than if she had never smoked. As noted in Chapter 13, smokers with abnormal Pap smear tests who gave up smoking or even simply reduced the amount they smoked largely wound up with better Pap smear results after six months. In more than 80 percent, there was less abnormalcy found in the second set of Pap tests.

The conundrum of reproductive diseases for which smoking may present reduced risk may be largely explained by its estrogen-reducing effect. Endometrial cancer, endometriosis, uterine fibroids, and breast disease are all linked to estrogen. If you are at high risk of any of these conditions, rather than continuing to smoke and running much higher risk of other ailments, talk to your physician about more frequent screening and other options.

New and promising breast cancer treatments and preventions are being developed, for example. Researchers have found use of the *selective estrogen receptor modulator (SERM)* or "estrogen substitute" *raloxifene* makes for a dramatic drop in breast cancer risk among postmenopausal women who have taken it to prevent osteoporosis. A three-year study of more than 7,000 women taking it found 76 percent lower risk of breast cancer. Another SERM called *tamoxifen* has also been found to help reduce breast cancer in those at high risk.

Weighty issues

Quitting smokers are likely to gain a few to several pounds (but less than 10 according to predominant studies) as they give up nicotine, though using a

Watch Out!
Women should remember to get regular Pap tests. Many doctors recommend at least an annual test and gynecological exam. If you have had cancer or certain other conditions or if you show abnormal results, your doctor may advise more frequent Pap tests.

replacement therapy such as nicotine gum may delay it. Rather than going on a strict diet as you quit, you may be better off eating healthy foods but being careful not to overeat or use fattening foods as a quick fix when you have a nicotine craving. Dieting attempts have been known to foil attempts to quit smoking.

While most people do not gain an inordinate amount of weight when quitting, as many as 1 in 10 may gain as much as 30 pounds. Women tend to gain a bit more than men. Among African Americans, those who are heavy smokers and those under the age of 55 are likeliest to experience big gains.

Interestingly, not all of the weight gain appears related to increased food intake, but rather a portion appears possibly due to a change in the body's set point—that is the body's metabolism adjusts. And if a quitter relapses and begins smoking again, studies have shown some or all of the weight gained while trying to quit is likely to be lost again.

Drug interactions and quit aids

Are you taking a medication right now? Did you know its effectiveness may be affected by smoking? Smoking reduces the therapeutic benefit of many commonly-prescribed medications. When you quit, your medication's therapeutic effect may be increased—another reason to quit, and another reason to talk over *quitting* and *quit aids* with your doctor.

Nicotine is a drug that can change the *pharmacokinetics*—or absorption, distribution, metabolism, and excretion of—other medications. Whether in cigarettes or a nicotine-replacement aid, nicotine can interact with:

- Insulin
- Propoxyphene
- Propranolol
- Theophylline
- Warfarin

It is true that if you are smoking and then switch to a nicotine replacement, in theory, you should be getting a dose of nicotine not far from what you're used to. However, all forms of nicotine replacement are absorbed a little differently into the system, which may change nicotine's interaction with a medication you take. Also, since you'll be gradually weaning yourself away from nicotine when using nicotine replacement therapy, as you reduce the dose, the action of other drugs you take could change. Therefore, it's wise to talk with your doctor before starting nicotine replacement therapy to discuss your prescription and how it might need to be modified as you kick the smoking habit.

Some of the side effects of nicotine are noted in the following list. If the dose in your replacement aid is on the high side for what you're used to, you may run into these difficulties (which could also occur with cigarettes). They don't usually require medical attention, though you should tell your doctor if they continue or if they are bothering you:

- Appetite increase
- Belching
- Constipation
- Diarrhea
- Flushing
- Irritability

Bright Idea
Tell your doctor about all medicines you are taking, including nonprescription ones, nutrients, or herbal remedies. If you frequently use caffeine or alcohol, mention that, too, since all of these may affect the way your medicine works.

- Jaw ache
- Joint or muscle ache
- Menstrual irregularity
- Sleep problems
- Sore throat

However, some nicotine side effects can be serious. If you experience any of these, let your doctor know right away:

- Chest pain
- Confusion
- Convulsions
- Dizziness
- Fainting
- Headache
- Hearing problems
- Irregular heartbeat
- Nausea
- Salivation
- Stomach pain
- Tooth damage
- Vision alterations
- Weakness or faintness
- Vomiting

If problems continue with these serious side effects, you may need to discontinue using the nicotine replacement aid, switch to a different kind of aid, or reduce the dosage.

When using Zyban, you should be aware that it can interact with a number of other drugs, among them:

- Carbamazepine
- Cimetidine
- Levodopa
- Phenelzine
- Phenobarbital
- Phenytoin
- Rifampin

Watch Out!
Your physician should also be advised if you drink caffeine or alcohol frequently or use illegal drugs, since all of these may change how Zyban works in your system.

You should tell your doctor about any medicines you are taking, of course, including nonprescription medicines or herbal or nutritional supplements.

Zyban can cause side effects, including these rare or uncommon ones, which you should report to your doctor as soon as possible:

- Breathing difficulty
- Confusion
- Hallucinations
- Irregular or fast heartbeat
- Seizures
- Vomiting

Zyban use can also result in side effects that usually do not require medical attention:

- Agitation
- Alterations in sense of taste
- Anxiety
- Appetite loss
- Blurred vision
- Constipation
- Difficulty sleeping
- Dizziness
- Dry mouth

- Headache

- Increased sweating

- Menstrual cycle changes

- Nausea

- Restlessness

- Sex drive reduction

- Skin problems (such as itching, a rash, or hives)

- Tremors

You should report to your doctor any of these symptoms that you experience if they continue or become bothersome.

Quit aids and your health condition

Since nicotine can affect a number of systems in the body, it's important that your physician know when you're planning to use a nicotine replacement quit aid. Even though smoking provides you with nicotine, the nicotine delivered by a quit aid—for instance a patch—may behave somewhat differently. It will enter your bloodstream at a somewhat different rate and in a somewhat different quantity than the nicotine provided when you smoke a cigarette.

Tell your doctor prior to using a nicotine replacement quit aid if you have any of the following conditions:

- Allergic reaction to nicotine or other substances

- Angina

- Breastfeeding

- Dental disease

- Diabetes

- Heart attack (a history of)

- Heartbeat irregularity
- Pheochromocytoma
- Pregnancy (or if you are trying to become pregnant)
- Stomach problems
- Thyroid overactivity
- Ulcers

According to clinical guidelines by the U.S. Preventive Services Task Force, if you are pregnant or nursing, have severe or worsening angina (heart pain), a serious heart arrhythmia, vasospastic or endocrine disorders, or if you've had a recent heart attack, your doctor must weigh carefully the benefits of using nicotine to help you quit against the potential risks of causing problems in these conditions. Caution is also advised in using nicotine or replacement aids in people who have renal or hepatic insufficiency, accelerated hypertension, peptic ulcer disease, or claudication.

If you are using Zyban to quit smoking, follow your doctor's instructions and be sure to discuss any of the following conditions:

- Alcohol or drug abuse history
- Bipolar disorder
- Brain tumor
- Eating disorder (anorexia nervosa or bulimia)
- Heart attack history or current heart disease
- Head injury
- Kidney disease
- Pregnancy or breastfeeding (or desired pregnancy)
- Psychosis

- Seizures
- An unusual or allergic reaction to bupropion or other substances

Beyond noting on an information sheet if you have a history of one of the above, it's best to bring up the topic when talking to your physician so you can be assured your questions will be answered and nothing will be missed.

Pregnancy

Since a woman who smokes during pregnancy is providing her baby with doses of nicotine and other chemicals that can bring illness or death to the child, quitting is imperative. However, quitting without using nicotine-replacement therapy is considered best. According to guidelines set forth by the Agency for Health Care Policy and Research, pregnant smokers should initially be asked to try to quit without using pharmacologic aids. A nicotine patch should be used only if the likelihood and benefits of successful quitting by using it outweigh the risk of nicotine replacement with potential smoking during patch use. The same goes for nursing mothers.

It is recommended that doctors and other health-care providers suggest intensive counseling to their pregnant patients as a first-line step toward smoking cessation as this has been shown to have good results. Less intensive counseling is advised if in-depth counseling is not available. Also suggested are motivational messages about the effects of smoking on mother and baby.

Cardiovascular disease

Nicotine patches should be used by those with cardiovascular problems only after a physician considers

Timesaver
Chapter 13 discusses smoking and pregnancy, as well as the use of nicotine replacement, in detail.

the risks and benefits inherent in different groups of patients:

- Those who have had a myocardial infarction within the last month
- Those with serious arrythmias
- Those with severe or worsening angina pectoris

A different type of nicotine replacement

Your health condition could dictate which nicotine replacement aids you should or shouldn't use. For instance, if you have active temporomandibular joint disease, nicotine gum is contraindicated and shouldn't be used.

Skin problems may prevent use of a nicotine patch. As many as half of those who use a nicotine patch may experience some kind of localized reaction. Most of the time, the skin irritation is not serious, but there is the potential that they may worsen the longer patches are used. You can rotate patch sites and use a little hydrocortisone cream to address minor skin problems from the patch. It is only in less than 5 percent of patients that skin reactions are severe enough to require discontinuing use of the patch. However, this is something you may want to keep in mind if you have particularly sensitive skin and are prone to reactions from topically applied products. A different form of nicotine replacement therapy could be used.

Smoking, quitting, and surviving

People who kick the habit live longer than those who don't, even if they quit relatively late in life. Those who quit smoking before they are 50 have been found to have as little as half the risk of death in the following 15 years, as compared to those who continue to smoke. Even those who quit after the age of 70 cut their death-from-smoking risk notably.

Studies in Britain suggest quitting no matter your age increases life expectancy, as long as you kick the habit before cancer or other serious disease develops. And those who stop smoking relatively early in life—before age 35—enjoy a life expectancy rivaling that of people who have never smoked.

Just the facts

- The risk of a number of smoking-related diseases drops dramatically within a few years of quitting.

- In certain illnesses, such as Alzheimer's and Parkinson's disease, some research has suggested smokers may have substantially less risk than nonsmokers (but that's *not* a reason to smoke).

- In diseases where smoking has been found to correlate with reduced risk, nicotine or reduced estrogen levels may be responsible for lessened incidence of disease.

- Some cessation aids may be contraindicated when you take some drugs or have some health conditions—talk with your physician about both issues before you start.

GET THE SCOOP ON...
Whether you can help ▪ How *not* to intervene ▪
Dealing with problem quitters ▪ Whether
they're really ready to quit

Helping Someone Kick the Habit

Chapter 15

What if you've already mastered the art of quitting cigarettes, but your mate hasn't? Or maybe you're a nonsmoker whose best friend in the world is making noises—alternately coughing and swearing he or she will swear off cigarettes. Welcome to the wonderful world of becoming a quit aid yourself.

This is treacherous territory. Human relationships are not always easy. You may be able to offer a huge amount of help to a dear friend or loved one. You could just help to lengthen their life (maybe by the number of years you've known them)! But you could be in for a surprise because quitting smokers can be touchy. Anyone can become bristly if well-meaning advice comes off as criticism or an effort to control.

Take a deep breath and resolve to do your absolute best, to offer help where you can, to think before you speak, and to let go of the outcome—*that* is territory the quitter needs to handle. In this chapter, you'll find some guidance to maximize the effectiveness of the help you offer, as well as some tips and hints for dealing with difficult situations and people. Also, before you put on the hat of *helper,* you should assess for yourself the odds that your friend, mate, or other loved one is actually ready to quit for real.

Why and when to help a loved one quit

If the person who is quitting is your significant other, you certainly have a stake in seeing him quit smoking. Not only are *you* reducing risks for yourself posed by secondhand smoke, but also you're maximizing the chances he'll be around and *healthy* during your old age.

Before you go any further, however, think: Who really wants to quit? Is it you or he? If the other person doesn't think much about quitting, isn't that concerned when you bring up the topic, and mentions quitting only casually on his own, then it's probably *you* behind the effort, which will get you nowhere until *he* is ready.

All the world's a stage

Becoming *ready* to quit smoking, or any addiction, isn't something that happens on cue. It's a whole production. A popular current behavioral theory suggests at least five separate stages of kicking an addiction such as smoking—you start out offstage with no real intention to change. Then the curtain goes up: In stage two, your addiction enters the spotlight as you realize there is a *problem.* The third act could be entitled *Good Intentions*—it's the point from which you make initial forays into *trying* to quit (but this stage ends in a cliffhanger as you prepare to take action). The fourth stage is where the real plot twists happen, where you reach readiness and actually change behaviors, determining what the outcome of your personal drama will be. In the fifth and final stage, you take your bows for successfully thwarting your addiction, but stay vigilant to *keep your act together* and prevent relapse.

Without the theater metaphors, these stages (as introduced in Chapter 10) are known as:

1. Precontemplation

2. Contemplation

3. Preparation

4. Action

5. Maintenance

In the *precontemplation* phase, an addicted person isn't likely to make a significant change for the better. While nearly everyone who associates with him may be painfully aware of his problem, the addicted person can walk around in blissful ignorance of the aberrant behavior he presents. Or they may simply not *face* their addiction though it lurks beneath the surface. Someone who is in this stage can be a tough case for those who want to intervene. Rather than hitting the addict—in this case, ~~smoker~~—over the head with pleas of cessation, try nudging him along toward the next stage, contemplation, where he accepts that he actually has an addiction.

Stage two, the *contemplation* phase, is awareness short of the decision to actually *do* anything about one's addiction. The smoker is *contemplating* quitting. This stage can go on for a very long time as the smoker toys with the good points of quitting versus the bad points of smoking (and vice versa). Assisting a stage two individual can involve frustration that the smoker is dragging his feet about quitting—he

Timesaver
Cancer prevention researcher Prof. James Prochaska, of the University of Rhode Island, is a developer of the stage model of behavior change. You can read his book *Changing for Good* (Avon Books, 1995), if you'd like to learn more about it.

may talk about it, but try pinning him to a plan and all you're likely to do is spin *yourself* into a tizzy. Recognize that a stage two smoker may benefit from having a sounding board for his smoking conundrums. Offer to listen and help but don't heighten your expectations for an immediate quit.

In the third stage, *preparation*, you're likely to see increasing momentum toward quitting. The smoker is getting his feet wet and may have made half-hearted or seemingly sincere attempts at cessation, without actually reaching that goal yet. By being supportive and understanding how the process works, you can position yourself to *assist* a quitter in her path toward being smoke-free, rather than becoming annoyed that the person *failed* and thinking that the situation is *hopeless*. A person in the preparation stage typically intends to take action in the next month and has unsuccessfully tried to quit in the last year. He is poised on the brink of the next stage—*action*.

The *action* stage is characterized by real, noticeable changes in behavior and other life factors, to facilitate the outcome desired. This is what the wait was for. Focus and resolution in the quitting smoker should be clearly visible. It is a *motivated* time. As the desired outcome is reached, the benefits of cessation can reinforce to the quitting smoker that, yes, this *was* a very good idea. There is an understanding that success has been attained. There is reason for self-confidence.

In the months and years following a successful cessation program, the smoker resides in the *maintenance* stage. The rest of a smoker's life may be the maintenance phase, where he consciously efforts to keep himself away from his former vice.

Playing your part

How do you prompt someone to want to quit? First, it's necessary to realize that *you* are living *your* life, *he* is living *his*, and no one wants another person to live his life for him. You have no real power over whether the other person quits at all. So how do you handle a situation like this if you're feeling a nagging need to alert him to the dangers of smoking (that he is probably at least peripherally aware of already)?

We discussed healthy boundaries in the last chapter when talking about avoiding addiction, and they play a role here, too. To best help a smoker who is showing all signs of continuing to smoke, you need to delineate your life from hers.

Make a list, at least a mental list, of all the reasons why you want him to quit, but make the list a selfish one, since it really is. If you're tempted to say, "I want my loved one to quit because smoking is so bad for him," note instead how that pertains to your wants and needs—perhaps, "I want my loved one to quit smoking because it hurts me to think that someone I care about could wind up with tragic health problems." Or even, "I want to enjoy my retirement, not spend it taking care of someone who burdens me with being his caregiver just because he didn't watch out for his health." Be selfish when you make this list.

Some reasons why you want your loved one or friend to quit may be:

- If something happened to her because of smoking, I would feel guilty that I hadn't done more to help her stop.

- I am concerned about the health-care burden he could impose on me later in life.

Timesaver
Vow to give up nagging someone to quit since it is generally a waste of time and may only spur her to continue smoking.

- I'm just sick of all that secondhand smoke in the house.

- I want my child to have a healthy father and mother for years to come.

- I sometimes feel she only smokes to annoy me, or in spite of me, and I want more respect.

- I see his smoking as a way of saying he doesn't care about me, and I want to know I'm loved.

- Smoking is part of the image of my friend or partner that I don't like—it reflects poorly on me.

- We're on a budget, and I feel that my spouse's smoking is an unnecessary waste.

- I don't want my partner to leave me, especially not through disease or death.

- I'm a former smoker myself (or I'm trying to quit) and being around smokers this closely makes it hard for me to stay smoke-free.

- I'm not sure why I want her to quit, it just seems like one of so many things she does wrong.

- I don't really care that much about whether he continues smoking, but this is one relatively righteous thing I can ask him to do, which helps me even the score for something else.

- It's a power play, pure and simple. I want the power to tell my partner or friend what to do.

Now that you have a list, you should be better able to discern which reasons are legitimate needs and wants of yours (such as not having to be around secondhand smoke, or not wanting to play caregiver to a careless person) and which reasons may demonstrate a control issue (such as if this is part of a larger fault-finding mission). Think about your answers.

If you have a good relationship, it's okay to tell the other person all of your reasons for wanting him to quit. But if you discuss reasons related to control issues with your partner, use it as a springboard to examine in honesty and care the other aspects of the relationship which are the root cause of the control issue. In other words, *that* part is not really about smoking.

The 12-step group Al-Anon is for families and friends of alcoholics, though its tenets are applicable in many ways to those who are family or friend to a smoker. They often confront the same issues. The following quiz is designed to help a person see whether they could use Al-Anon's support. You can substitute the word drinking with smoking to help decide whether you may be preoccupied with your loved one's smoking habits.

Bright Idea
To find out more about the group Al-Anon—for families and friends of alcoholics, check out their Web site at www.al-anon.alateen.org.

1. Do you worry about how much someone else drinks?

2. Do you have money problems because of someone else's drinking?

3. Do you tell lies to cover up for someone else's drinking?

4. Do you feel if the drinker loved you, he or she would stop drinking to please you?

5. Do you blame the drinker's behavior on his or her companions?

6. Are plans frequently upset or canceled or meals delayed because of the drinker?

7. Do you make threats, such as, "If you don't stop drinking, I'll leave you?"

8. Do you secretly try to smell the drinker's breath?

9. Are you afraid to upset someone for fear it will set off a drinking bout?

10. Have you been hurt or embarrassed by a drinker's behavior?

11. Are holidays and gatherings spoiled because of drinking?

12. Have you considered calling the police for help in fear of abuse?

13. Do you search for hidden alcohol?

14. Do you often ride in a car with a driver who has been drinking?

15. Have you refused social invitations out of fear or anxiety?

16. Do you sometimes feel like a failure when you think of the lengths you have gone in order to control the drinker?

17. Do you think that if the drinker stopped drinking, your other problems would be solved?

18. Do you ever threaten to hurt yourself to scare the drinker?

19. Do you feel angry, confused, or depressed most of the time?

20. Do you feel there is no one who understands your problems?

Key to the Al-Anon concept is the idea of *detachment*—letting go of an obsession with another person's behavior and beginning to lead a happier and more manageable life. Another way of saying this might be "get your own house in order," rather than focusing on someone else's concerns. Are there addictions in your life that *you* should be addressing?

Detachment simply means separating yourself from the negative effects another person's addiction can have on your life and entails learning the life lessons in the following checklist.

This is not to say that you cannot help a smoker who wants to quit do so, nor that you should be forbidden from suggesting to a smoker reasons why she might consider quitting. Just don't make the latter

Detachment
Detachment includes learning...

____ Not to suffer because of the actions or reactions of other people

____ Not to allow ourselves to be used or abused by others in the interest of another's recovery

____ Not to do for others what they could do for themselves

____ Not to manipulate situations so others will eat, go to bed, get up, pay bills, not drink

____ Not to cover up for anyone's mistakes or misdeeds

____ Not to create a crisis

____ Not to prevent a crisis if it is in the natural course of events

Source: Copyright © Al-Anon Family Group Headquarters, Inc., 1981; Pamphlet S-19. Reprinted with permission of Al-Anon Family Group Headquarters, Inc.

your life's purpose. Make sure you understand your own motivations so you can help someone in your life to quit if she wants to without doing so in a subconsciously manipulative manner.

Avoiding codependency

Codependency is a psychology term used to describe a condition or relationship in which one person is controlled by another who has a pathological condition (such as an addiction). The buzzword has come into common usage and there are now many books on the topic.

How can you tell if you're codependent? This next quiz can alert you to behaviors suggestive of codependency. Some of these questions relate to smoking behaviors and some address other aspects of relationships.

ARE YOU CODEPENDENT?

1. Do you feel particularly hurt that your loved one continues to smoke?

2. Do you feel you lack self-confidence and are continually trying to please others?

3. Do you go beyond the call of duty to arrange a smoker's life so it should be easy for them to quit?

4. Do you feel unable to leave a situation with a smoker that you really can't tolerate?

5. Do you ever mislead other people to come across better or so they won't be upset with you?

6. If your smoker asks you to help him get cigarettes, do you have a hard time saying no, even though you hate his habit?

7. Do you feel responsible for a smoker's smoking behavior at least some of the time?

8. Do you focus on the wrongs others have done you rather than identifying your feelings about their behavior (and the root reasons you feel bad)?

9. Do you let other people make decisions for your life or ask their permission to do things when you really have no obligation to?

10. If you are or were a smoker, have you ever hidden your habit from someone else for fear he wouldn't approve (and not because you wanted to keep secondhand smoke away from him)?

11. Are you embarrassed about your loved one's smoking behavior because you're afraid it reflects poorly on you?

Answers: Every yes answer is a potential clue to codependent behavior.

Some people are not codependent until they run into a situation or person that evokes codependent behavior. Some of the attitudes that tend to foster codependency include:

- Expectations of perfection or unreasonably high standards

- Disdain for feelings

- Refusal to discuss things openly or validate others' positions
- Belittling and other passive-aggressive abuses
- Love only on certain conditions
- Demands that you take responsibility for someone else's emotions
- Directing behavior of others (ruling the roost)
- "Because I said so!" and other controlling comments
- Blaming others
- Sudden anger and moodiness when another expresses happiness
- Causing others to feel ashamed

Watch Out!
Many of these are also signs of a potentially physical abuser. Don't stand for poor treatment or risk violence!

If you find yourself in a situation illustrated by one of the phrases above, how do you prevent becoming codependent in the first place? Central to the idea is a very healthy dose of self-esteem.

According to EURAD (Europe Against Drugs), a grassroots organization dealing with many of the confusing aspects of substance addiction, a codependent is the person who in good faith tries to help an addict stop abusing a substance by trying to control both the addict and the drug. If you feel it is your responsibility to get your loved one to stop smoking and your responsibility to keep cigarettes away from him, this could be you.

As a well-meaning codependent embarks on her private temperance campaign, her life increasingly gets out of hand as she tries to control what she cannot. The emotional turmoil can leave her devastated, lacking self esteem, and frayed.

EURAD notes how the stages of drug abuse are often mirrored by the codependent in the situation:

Bright Idea
If you're looking for some help playing coach to a quitting smoker, consider these Internet options: Coaches Smoking Corner (by GlaxoWellcome) at www. ccsmoking.com. COMMIT at www.cyberisle. org/ commit/guide.

1. **Denial.** First you often deny that there is a problem. You might be the last person to realize that your husband is a drug addict, maybe even after he has realized it himself. You may be the last person in the neighborhood to realize that your own kid is using drugs.

2. **Anger.** The next stage often has to do with finding someone to blame. You might blame society, the drug addict, God, or life itself. You have tried to win over the drug by trying to control, and you have failed. In bitterness, you might ask yourself, "Why did I deserve this?" All this anger is normal, but if you don't get past this stage, your life will continue to be controlled by the drug abuser. In this anger, codependent persons have done everything from committing crimes to suicide, fastened in an uncontrolled rage or, maybe, more common, gotten stuck in an endless, devastating bitterness.

3. **Bargaining.** In this stage you try to tell yourself it is not so bad. Maybe if he gets help just one more time, everything will pass. Maybe if he'll just get this job, or this house, or this gift, the drug abuse will stop. You will pray for one last chance.

4. **Depression.** Depression is the stage where the codependent begins to realize the situation— that he is powerless over another person's drug abuse.

5. **Acceptance.** Acceptance does not mean liking drug abuse. It means that you still care for your loved one, but that you have realized that you are powerless over some things, such as drug

abuse. Acceptance means that you have realized that, as a codependent, you need help for your own sake. You must get well, whatever happens to the drug addict. You must be able to let the problem go and to let the drug addict learn from the consequences of his own actions. To reach this stage, the 12-step groups are of great help.

← Some books on codependency include Melody Beattie's *Codependent No More* (Hazelden Information Education, 1996) and Robert Subby's *Lost in the Shuffle: the Co-dependent Reality* (Health Communications, 1987).

Getting started as a quitting buddy

If a loved one or friend has expressed a desire to quit smoking and an openness to or desire for your assistance, how do you proceed? Once again, making sure your own house is in order is important.

Think about your relationship with the person who wants to quit. What do you mean to each other? What activities do you do together? Look for any ways you could be contributing to her problem before you help her solve it.

Do you:

■ Introduce her to situations where others are smoking or where temptation might be great?

■ Engage in controlling or other behaviors that could be adding stress to her life, reinforcing her need to smoke?

■ Fail to lead by good example in your life?

■ Facilitate her smoking by a condoning attitude or smooth over her worries about health problems?

■ Become lazy about the relationship and fail to look for fun things to do together?

The sooner you identify and try to correct these kinds of behaviors in yourself, the sooner you will be able to help a relative, significant other, or a friend

Unofficially...
Remember, you don't want to approach the buddy talk as an interrogation in a small room with a single table and a bright overhead light! Don't push.

to quit. In fact, making these important changes can be a help toward quitting.

Once your loved one has come to terms with the need to quit, it's time for a conversation. You can start now to do a little looking out for her without crossing over into codependent territory. Be wise in hitting the timing right for a quit-smoking talk. Don't do it when the other person is rushed, tired, not in a good mood, or otherwise distracted.

When's a good time? Next time you're having lunch at a quiet restaurant where you have some privacy to talk and something else to do (eating) that doesn't require a lot of thought but may help a person feel relaxed and not uncomfortably focused on the subject at hand.

Another choice might be on the way back from an early evening out, when the mood is jovial. Or over midmorning coffee. Use your instincts to time the talk, perhaps taking advantage of the next time she brings up the need to quit smoking.

If you need to bring up the topic, do so in a non-confrontational way. Ask if she's still thinking about quitting smoking. Use the opportunity to find out a little background. Following are some questions you may want to ask casually:

- How long have you been smoking?

- Why do you think you smoke?

- Have you tried to quit before? How? How long ago?

- Why do you think you started smoking again?

- What do you like about smoking?

- Is there anything really keeping you from quitting now?

- What's the top reason you're considering quitting?
- What are other reasons?
- Do you think you're addicted to smoking?
- Have you had or has anyone else in your family had another addiction?

Please don't press the issue. You might need to ask these background questions over two separate sessions. It's important to *validate* a person's feelings and opinions—not just in this discussion but every one you have. That means even if you disagree with a person's position on something, taking care to state that you understand that she feels how she does and not passing judgment on her.

If you need to disagree, make sure you state it clearly as your opinion and make it clear you're not attacking her. For instance, if your smoker says, "I didn't have a chance not to smoke; everyone in my family smoked while I was growing up. You can't fight that," let her know first that you understand her position. You can say, "Wow, everyone? I can see how a person would feel it's natural to smoke in that situation." You aren't condoning smoking by saying this, just letting your smoker know you see her point of view.

What if you also came from a household full of smokers and found the courage never to smoke because you saw firsthand what it did to the health of your family? What if your opinion is exactly the opposite of "You can't fight that?" After you've validated the other person's comments, make a transition to your own situation—you may phrase it first in the form of a question: "If everybody smoked, did you ever worry about their health—did anybody get sick?"

Moneysaver
As a buddy, start a piggy bank for your quitting smoker where she can deposit every week the money she's saved not smoking. Plan with her to spend the money on a needed but fun project you can help her with.

   This gives your smoker a chance to bring up the other side of the issue on her own and makes it less likely that expressing your opinion on the matter will come across as high-handed. Your smoker may respond, "Well, my uncle did get emphysema really bad, and my dad tried to quit then, but he couldn't." It's then that your side of the story is best heard: "You know, I know what you mean. My grandmother smoked like a chimney and died early. I miss her a lot, and when I saw what it was doing to her, I never wanted to touch the stuff."

   By indirectly getting to your point, or rather by *prefacing* it with some appropriate context, you are engaging in a conversation where the other person is likely to be more receptive to your point of view. You have not *invalidated* hers by simply stating an opposing opinion.

   Once your smoker has opened up a little bit about her habit and stated with some resolve that she wants to quit, you can offer your assistance. Simple ways of approaching this territory include statements like the following:

- You mentioned that you could use help quitting—I'd be happy to help you, like the buddy system, if you want.

- Do you want a friend to help coach you to quit?

- Have you looked into a good step-by-step quitting plan? I know the American Lung Association has a terrific one. Shall I get the number for you? It's (800) LUNG-USA.

- Well, if you're ready to quit, I'd be happy to help. How can I be supportive?

- Well, if you're going to quit smoking, I'm resolving to lose five pounds. I'll try to persuade you not to smoke if you ask, if you'll try to persuade me to keep away from the sweets. Deal?

■ It's got to be hard to quit by yourself. If I were quitting, I would want someone to call me every day and give me a pep talk.

■ There has to be something to do in this town that doesn't involve being around smokers, and I'm tired of secondhand smoke. I'm going to try to go do some new activities in the evening. Want to come along?

At this point, you should be looking for some sign of a go-ahead from the other person. If it doesn't come, say "Well, let me know" and change the subject. You don't want to set up a resistance pattern where a person feels compelled to take the opposite course of action because she feels as if an issue is being forced on her.

Being a good buddy—tactics

If your smoker gives you the go-ahead to help, it's your job to be supportive, introduce him to important points about quitting, and listen to him when he needs to talk. You can also look out for him a bit by heading off at the pass activities that you're sure would lead him toward relapse. But only if he okays it.

For example, say your friend has asked you sincerely to help him kick the habit in any way you can. Say he uses nicotine patches. Say the two of you are going away for the weekend but he forgets to bring his. "Oh, well. I can do without for two days," he says. Since you've already come to agreement that you will help him quit, you should feel alright about taking a stand, encouraging him to purchase new patches. You can say, "That's running a big chance you'll relapse and smoke. Since you asked me to help you

Watch Out!
Quitting smokers can be cranky, and it's easy to step on their toes. Before you say something, think, "Would I appreciate hearing this if I were trying to quit?"

quit, I'm asking you to go buy the patches. If money's tight, let's skip a big dinner out tonight, get sandwiches, and go buy your patches."

Using the buddy system when quitting smoking has been shown to result in better success rates, sometimes notably so. Refer back to Chapter 10 for more details. But there are different things you can do as a buddy. It may be up to you to bring up these things to your smoker, and then you need to decide together, concretely, what is being asked of you (and what you are willing to do within the constraints of involvement and time).

As a buddy, you can:

- Empathize with your smoker and realize how tough kicking an addiction can be

- Agree to be available to talk whenever your smoker needs support to keep from lighting up

- Help your smoker clarify his goals

- Help him plan his quit

- Provide affirmations to help strengthen your smoker and his resolve

- Introduce him to negative aspects of smoking

- Set a regular schedule for quitting pep talks or check-ins

- Help your smoker engage in activities that won't make him likely to relapse

- Offer observations about why you think your smoker may be choosing to have a cigarette at a certain time

- Help your smoker to consider her quit plan as a very important step in her life

- Offer praise for success

- Believe in your smoker's ability to quit successfully

- Accompany your smoker to group quitting support meetings

- Introduce your smoker to materials that could be helpful in his quit attempt

- Provide a reward for a successful quit at appropriate intervals

If you are a smoker's buddy, you can also help him extend his circle of support. Sit down with pen in hand with your smoker and make a list of different people he knows and feels are potentially reliable buddies. Next to each person's name, list how they may be able to help support your smoker. For instance, a close coworker may be able to provide reinforcement during breaks when smoking is tempting, or a son or daughter may be able to remind the smoker that he's dearly loved and his company is wanted for a long time to come.

Leave it up to your smoker to approach the other members of the circle but encourage him to do so. You can remain his number one buddy, most responsible for offering support, but there's no reason to skimp on support that could be widely available.

Set up a contact schedule with your smoker. You might consider:

- Daily calls (offer encouragement, get updates on cravings and potential problems, review tips)

- Weekly progress reviews (total up money saved not smoking, go over health benefits and dangers of smoking, mark calendar days abstinent)

- Monthly celebrations for abstinence (dinner out, a shopping expedition or road trip, or

Bright Idea
Consider sending occasional cards illustrating how proud of your quitting smoker you are, or planning special surprises you know your quitting smoker will like, as a reward for success and reinforcement to continue smoke-free.

just a few moments with family and breakfast in bed)

Of course, being on call for times that your smoker needs a shoulder to lean on is important. You may want to consider tying the reinforcement to the benefit of not smoking—for instance, packing lunch for a picnic in the park (fresh air) or scheduling a free or inexpensive beauty treatment at a local salon for a female friend who's quitting and looking forward to a healthier look, as well as a healthier body.

Only you know the level of silliness your quit assist should rise to with the smoker in question. If your quitting smoker is particularly open for amusement, you can always schedule a day of horseback riding to show that cowboys don't necessarily smoke or an ultra-chic evening out sans cigarettes to show 1940s film stars who chain-smoked aren't in vogue anymore.

When the smoker is your main squeeze

Anyone can act as a quitting buddy, but one of the single biggest determinants of success in kicking the habit is having a supportive partner—not just a quitting partner, but a life partner. Studies have shown cessation is most successful when a smoker's quitting buddy is his or her significant other.

Why is this and what should you do about it? If you're the smoker, talk to your spouse or romantic partner about your request for support and ask if he will be your buddy. If you are the partner, realize that your influence may be strongest in helping your smoker quit. You also have the most stake in whether your partner quits, given the distinct possibility you will be spending your retirement together, either in good health or poor, and also you're the most likely to be exposed to secondhand smoke if she does not give up the habit.

Significant others are people with whom we have a special dynamic and often the most frequent contact. Help your partner identify what makes her tick in life and what she wants from it. Smoking is not always about having a cigarette—sometimes, it is a reaction to a feeling of failure or frustration.

You can encourage smoking cessation in the context of your relationship and future togetherness. However, it's important not to demand that your partner quit for your benefit, but to distinguish that you are there to support her in improving her life. Always let the quitting smoker lead the way.

You are in a prime place to set a good example, too. If you truly hate cigarettes, don't be afraid to let your partner know that, just make sure she knows it's the cigarettes you dislike and not her. She must know you love her in spite of the smoking habit and that the relationship is not dependent on her quitting. A relationship that *is* dependent on one party quitting is on shaky ground. As a non-smoker, you should protect your health by asking that if your partner continues to smoke, she doesn't do it around you or inside the main areas of your home.

All in all, the buddy system approach comes down to rapport—knowing someone is there to help you, knowing someone cares for you, and knowing that your relationship boundaries are healthy. It is only with the dignity of personal freedom that a quitting smoker can choose to give up cigarettes on her own and not under the weight of others' expectations of her.

66
I think the absolute best way to quit smoking is to literally fall in love with someone who abhors cigarettes. You would probably choose the relationship.
—Brenda
99

Just the facts

- Detachment from another's smoking problem is a necessary for your own health.

- Loved ones who take on responsibility for another person's quit attempt may be codependent.

- Insisting that someone who doesn't want to quit should quit can springboard him toward smoking all the more, so be careful.

- There are many ways to be a quitting buddy, and smokers are more likely to succeed in quitting when they have one.

Fresh Air

PART VII

GET THE SCOOP ON...
Body changes you may notice when you quit ▪
Don't relapse—relax ▪ What to do about
secondhand smoke ▪ Getting medical checkups

Taking Care of Your Smoke-Free Self

Chapter 16

Congratulations! If you're well on your way to being smoke-free by now, there's a lot more good news in store. You may already have begun to notice that you're *feeling different*, with less dependence on nicotine and less impact from toxins in cigarettes.

What to do now? You have a lifetime of health ahead of you, and the more you focus on that, the *less* you may be inclined to focus on smoking ever again. In this chapter, you'll learn a bit about how to take care of your health—and why if you're feeling a bit odd instead of better, it could actually be a *good sign*. Read on.

How your body changes when you quit

In past chapters, you've read about how soon after quitting your body begins to change and how risk of many diseases goes down the longer you remain smoke-free. What are you experiencing in the way of positive changes right now? You can note them in the following checklist.

Checklist

Positive Post-Quit Changes

_____ I feel like I can breathe more easily, with less obstruction.

_____ My heart's not racing anymore.

_____ My blood pressure isn't as easily overelevated.

_____ I can think more clearly.

_____ I feel cleaner.

_____ I have more energy.

_____ My hands and feet aren't cold anymore.

_____ My circulation has improved.

_____ I am sleeping better.

_____ My skin looks and feels healthier.

_____ I am not short of breath anymore.

_____ Wound-healing has improved.

_____ I'm not feeling fatigued as easily.

_____ My moods are generally brighter.

_____ (Women:) My menstrual cycle is more normal.

_____ (Men:) I am functioning better sexually.

_____ Other.

The items you checked in the checklist are typical signs that your body is healing itself from the damage and impairment cigarette smoking caused. It is marvelous impetus to continue smoke-free.

After a person quits, negative symptoms sometimes show up before things improve. Has this happened to you? Use the following checklist to note the less-than-good effects you've run into since quitting.

Negative Post-Quit Changes

_____ I feel depressed and/or anxious more often or more severely.

_____ I feel foggy and tired.

_____ I've gained unwanted weight.

_____ I'm coughing _more_.

_____ My sinuses are clogged.

_____ Other.

It may seem paradoxical, now that you've taken steps to ensure your health, that you may be feeling worse. Don't feel discouraged, though. You may be in what is referred to in alternative medicine circles as a *healing crisis* or *detox reaction*. Always report any serious symptoms to your physician, of course, so he or she can take steps to determine the cause and appropriate treatment. Serious symptoms should be reviewed by a physician no matter *what* their source.

A crisis or reaction like this is what happens when the body begins to clean up a real mess. You've probably experienced something analogous yourself, when spring cleaning, remodeling your house, or excavating the junk in your garage. *Things can seem to get worse before they get better.*

Mild negative symptoms may be your body simply starting to function better again—well enough to start its cleanup. As it escorts toxins from deep inside your cells to the outside world to be disposed of, you may naturally feel their effects more strongly—they are being pulled out of deep storage.

Detox reactions can show up in a number of ways. Your skin can become a little troubled as toxins are excreted through your pores to literally be sweated out of the body. In fact, a popular kind of *Ayurvedic* (Indian wellness and medicine) therapy involves controlled sweating just to rid the body of noxious items.

Coughing and mucus production or sinus congestion is another typical detox symptom. Your body's immune system wraps debris in containers made from white blood cells to produce mucus, then brings it out through your respiratory system for disposal. An increase in this activity means your immune system is healthy enough to start cleaning

> **"**
> Without a struggle, there can be no progress.
> —Frederick Douglass
> **"**

house, now that it is no longer simply trying to keep the level of new incoming smoke toxins at bay.

Feeling foggy and tired may be part of a detox reaction or it may be a reaction to the reduction or elimination of nicotine from your daily diet. Depression and anxiety can also occur as your body marshals its resources to deal with cleanup but can be linked to the lack of nicotine in your system.

A detox reaction is often likened to having the flu since it may feel reminiscent of your last bout. Instead of fighting to rid the body of an invading virus, your immune system is at work trying to rid the body of toxins that have already invaded it.

Watch Out!
Post-quit is not the time to succumb to junk food or overindulge in alcohol. Instead, give your body the good stuff it deserves to become feeling healthy again as soon as possible.

Nutrient and herbal detox helps

If you are feeling less optimal than you expected following quitting, two things may be helpful—patience and nutrition. Drink plenty of water since the body uses it to wash away what it doesn't want to keep. You should also pay attention to basic nutrition as described in Chapter 11.

Beyond a balance of healthy proteins, carbohydrates, fats, vitamins, and minerals across the board, there are specific ways to help your body continue its tobacco cleanup. You can concentrate on fresh vegetables and fruits—raw where possible. Not only are these wonderful suppliers of vitamins and other nutrients, they also provide water and fiber, which can help your digestive system's efficiency.

pH balance is about more than your shampoo

Some alternative medicine practitioners contend that eating more *alkaline* foods instead of *acidic* foods aids healing. Fresh vegetables and some other complex carbohydrates are typically more alkalinizing in the system, whereas proteins are more acidifying.

The terms alkaline and acidic have to do with the body's *pH balance* or *acid-base balance.*

At it's most basic level, literally the level of the atom, this is a description of how many hydrogen ions are present versus the number of hydroxyl ions (hydrogen and oxygen). More hydroxyl means more alkaline. More hydrogen means more acidic.

The scale used to measure pH runs from 0 to 14. Most organisms have a narrow range of pH levels they can function at effectively. For the human body, it is right around 7.4 (7.35– 7.45). Even a little variation from this prevents survival. The body has mechanisms that allow it to keep tight control on levels.

Pure water has a pH of 7, which is considered neutral, since it's midway on the scale. Numbers lower than 7 are thought of as acidic (progressively so as numbers decrease to 0), and numbers above 7 are considered alkaline (progressively so to 14).

The pH level is important in many things—even haircare. You may have heard of "pH-balanced" shampoos that are supposed to leave your hair feeling soft and shiny. They are adapted to the specific pH level of hair. Hair colorants often work by *alkalinization,* while the old-fashioned idea of using vinegar to rinse your hair after a shampoo has a lot to do with vinegar's acidic pH, which helps neutralize the alkalinity of water and many soap products.

Specific nutrients for healing

Ideally, what you are looking for is good balance and nutritional adequacy—enough and in the right ratio. Nutritionists often recommend that certain nutrients be particularly well provided when the body is healing because the process can require greater quantities of that nutrient or because its presence is vital to restoring health.

Unofficially...
The pH scale is *logarithmic,* which means each number increase is actually a *tenfold* increase in alkalinity. A pH of 9 is actually 10 times more alkaline than a pH of 8, and a pH of 10 would be a *hundredfold* more alkaline than a pH of 8.

The liver is a major organ of detoxification, filtering unwanted chemicals from the blood and turning them into innocuous substances that can be readily excreted by the kidneys. To support the liver's function in this capacity, nutritionists often recommend the vitamins A, B_3, B_6, C, E, as well as beta-carotene (the vitamin A precursor) and the amino acids L-cysteine and L-glutamine.

The function of the kidneys may be particularly supported by vitamins A, C, and B_6, as well as the minerals magnesium and potassium. For good kidney health, it's important to drink plenty of fluids.

The intestines have a massive digestive job, and their balance can be greatly affected by the ratio of good bacteria that normally inhabit them to other unfavorable bacteria that can cause ill health. If you've ever experienced constipation after taking antibiotics, it may be because the antibiotics, whose job is to kill bacteria, have killed off the good bacteria your intestines needed. To support the "good bacteria" (or *flora*) of the intestines, a supplement of acidophilus and other *probiotic* microorganisms (by supplement or as they're found in yogurt) can be taken. Vitamin B_5, zinc, and the amino acid L-glutamine also support intestinal health.

Herbs for healing

Some herbs are well known in natural medicine circles for their help in detoxifying the body. Some, like milk thistle, are believed to be especially beneficial to detoxifying a number of substances in the blood and protecting the liver so it can do its work better. Beyond the herbs to support health discussed in Chapter 11, here are some specifically used in detoxing and their suggested properties:

- **Alfalfa:** helps to eliminate body odors, contains chlorophyll, somewhat diuretic and laxative
- **Blessed thistle:** heart and lung tonic, helps heal lung and liver disorders, increases circulation to the brain
- **Burdock root:** blood purifier, aids in skin healing
- **Cascara sagrada:** a fast-acting laxative that stimulates secretions of the liver and other internal organs
- **Comfrey:** helps healing in respiratory ailments, benefits mucous membranes and lungs, digestive aid
- **Dandelion:** a potent detoxifier for the liver, stimulatory to the gallbladder and other organs, immune-booster
- **Echinacea:** an effective blood and lymph system cleaner, antibiotic, assists in removal of mucus buildup and sweetens bad breath (not usually used for long periods)
- **Garlic:** blood purifier and antibiotic, helps regulate cholesterol and fats in the blood, normalizing to blood pressure
- **Hyssop:** helps in blood pressure regulation, promotes circulation, a blood purifier, helpful to relieve mucus buildup in the lungs, and an aid in nervous disorders
- **Irish moss:** used to treat coughs, bronchitis, and intestinal problems, anti-inflammatory, aids in expelling mucus
- **Licorice:** considered a rejuvenator, nourishing to the adrenal glands, soothing to mucous membranes, tonic to the respiratory system, and somewhat laxative

Moneysaver
Try garlic as a detox herb. It's inexpensive and available in an odorless variety.

- **Marshmallow root:** considered rejuvenative, soothing to digestive tract and moisturizing to tissues, somewhat diuretic and laxative

- **Rose hips:** infection-fighting, high in vitamin C and related nutrients, antioxidant

- **Sarsaparilla:** blood purifier, helps reduce mucus buildup, relieves inflammation

- **Slippery elm bark:** anti-inflammatory that aids in tissue healing and soothing

- **Witch hazel bark and leaves:** beneficial to healing blood vessels, anti-inflammatory and antiseptic

- **Gentian root:** helps to stimulate digestive secretions, reduces inflammation and infection

- **Mullein leaf:** soothing to irritated tissues, particularly of the respiratory system, somewhat diuretic

Alfalfa, dandelion, licorice root, and marshmallow root are considered *alteratives.* That is, they cleanse the blood. Particularly helpful in getting rid of expelling mucus from the lungs are the herbs comfrey, garlic, licorice root, and mullein. Comfrey, garlic, Irish moss, and marshmallow are helpful to eliminate mucus conditions and are considered *anticatarrhals.*

Getting a little fresh air and exercise

As a new nonsmoker, you may be surprised at the energy level you experience now that you're not hampered by tar and other chemicals impeding your respiration. A successful quit is often just the impetus a person needs to embark on a fitness kick. So put your new energy to work making your body even better—it will thank you.

Watch Out!
If you are pregnant or nursing (or anticipating pregnancy), or if you have a serious health condition, get your physician's approval before using any medicinal herbs.

Exercise and disease risk

Why exercise? There are a host of health reasons. Exercise may help to lower the risk of many diseases that smoking increases the risk of. Research has shown protective effects of varying degree with respect to physical activity and risk for several chronic diseases, including:

- Coronary heart disease
- Hypertension
- Noninsulin-dependent diabetes mellitus
- Osteoporosis
- Colon cancer
- Anxiety and depression

According to the U.S. Centers for Disease Control and Prevention, low levels of habitual physical activity and low levels of physical fitness are associated with markedly increased death rates from all causes. As many as 250,000 deaths annually in the United States—12 percent of total deaths—can be attributed to a lack of regular physical activity.

There are a number of aspects of health that fitness has been found to better. Exercise training has been found to improve risk factors for:

- Coronary heart disease
- Blood lipid profile
- Resting blood pressure in borderline hypertensives
- Body composition (fat to muscle ratio)
- Glucose tolerance and insulin sensitivity
- Bone density
- Immune function
- Psychological function

In the case of coronary heart disease, the relative risk posed by being physically inactive is similar to the risk increase seen when people either smoke or have high cholesterol or hypertension. Exercise improves coronary factors potentially by increasing good cholesterol, reducing triglyceride levels, lowering blood pressure, altering the function of platelets, making for better blood sugar control, and making the heart less likely to experience stress damage.

How much exercise is enough? Government guidelines on improving health suggest that half an hour of moderate physical activity—enough to burn about 200 calories—every day is a good rule of thumb. Many of the health benefits described above, researchers say, can be attained with that level of exercise, for instance walking two miles daily.

Getting started with fitness

It is important to remember that in the weeks and even months after a quit date, your body is still healing. You should not be overly ambitious in your regimen—remember heart attack and stroke risk take awhile to drop. Start modestly and get to know your body again.

Many smokers aren't avid exercisers, and if you were in that category, try introducing yourself to different kinds of exercise:

- Aerobic (that which gets your heart pumping and increases breathing)
- Stretching
- Muscle toning (or muscle-building)

You don't have to begin a formal plan. You can improve your aerobic capacity and get your lungs

Unofficially...
Statistically, smokers are more likely to drop out of fitness programs than nonsmokers.

working better simply by walking more. Make it an enjoyable experience, not a task—perhaps an after-dinner walk around the neighborhood with your spouse, or a stroll through a park, or to do some errands on your lunch break.

Bicycling, swimming, and dancing are all good aerobic activities. Aerobic activity is a natural for the quitting smoker since it not only addresses the health of the heart and lungs, but also can help address post-quit weight gain since aerobic activity is a major calorie burner.

Just how many calories can a healthy adult burn off during aerobic activity? You can compare different forms of exercise using the following table.

Bright Idea
Moderate weight-bearing exercise (such as walking, lifting light weights, or dancing) helps preserve bone density and prevent osteoporosis, a disease the risk of which is associated with older age and smoking.

ACTIVITY AND CALORIES

Light <4 kcal/min	Moderate 4–7 kcal/min	Hard/Vigorous >7 kcal/min
Walking, slowly (strolling) (1–2 mph)	Walking, briskly (3–4 mph)	Walking, briskly uphill or with a load
Cycling, stationary	Cycling for pleasure or transportation (<=10 mph)	Cycling, fast or racing (>10 mph)
Swimming, slow treading	Swimming, moderate effort	Swimming, fast treading or crawl
Conditioning exercise, light stretching	Conditioning exercise, light calisthenics	Conditioning exercise, stair ergometer, ski machine
Racquet sports, table tennis	Racquet sports, singles tennis, racquetball	
Golf, power cart	Golf, pulling cart or carrying clubs	
Bowling		
Fishing, sitting	Fishing, standing/casting	Fishing in stream
Boating, power	Canoeing, leisurely (2.0–3.9 mph)	Canoeing, rapidly (>=4 mph)

Watch Out!
If you have either chronic disease or risk factors for chronic disease, consult your physician before beginning a fitness program of moderate intensity.

ACTIVITY AND CALORIES *(cont.)*

Light <4 kcal/min	Moderate 4– 7 kcal/min	Hard/Vigorous >7 kcal/min
Home care, carpet sweeping	Home care, general cleaning	Moving furniture
Mowing lawn, mower riding mower	Mowing lawn, power mower	Mowing lawn, hand
Home repair, carpentry	Home repair, painting	

Source: Centers for Disease Control and Prevention.

Your target heart rate

Another way you can measure your level of aerobic activity is by *target heart rate*. This is an effective means to measure your initial fitness level and then monitor your progress once you begin exercising more. To use this method, you need to measure your pulse periodically as you work out and try to stay within 50 to 75 percent of your maximum heart rate. That range is your target heart rate.

You can use the following table to find your estimated target heart rate. Just look for the age closest to yours and read across to find your target rate.

TARGET HEART RATE ZONES

Age	Target HR Zone 50–75%	Average Maximum Heart Rate 100%
20 years	100–150 beats per minute	200
25 years	98–146 beats per minute	195
30 years	95–142 beats per minute	190
35 years	93–138 beats per minute	185
40 years	90–135 beats per minute	180
45 years	88–131 beats per minute	175
50 years	85–127 beats per minute	170
55 years	83–123 beats per minute	165
60 years	80–120 beats per minute	160

Some high ➜ blood pressure medications lower the maximum heart rate and thus lower the target zone rate. If you are taking high blood pressure medicine, check with your physician to see if your program should be adjusted.

Age	Target HR Zone 50–75%	Average Maximum Heart Rate 100%
65 years	78–116 beats per minute	155
70 years	75–113 beats per minute	150

Source: American Heart Association.

To find your approximate maximum heart rate, take the number 220 minus your age. The figures in the following table are averages only and should be used simply as general guidelines. When you start a fitness program, you can try to meet just the lowest part of your target zone (50 percent) for the first few weeks and gradually build toward the higher part of your zone (75 percent).

If measuring your target heart rate seems like too much hassle during your exercise sessions, you can use a rule of thumb to check your probable range during activities like walking. (However, for faster activities like brisk walking or jogging, it's probably better to use pulse as an indicator.) The American Heart Association suggests if you can talk and walk at the same time, you are not working too hard. However, if you can sing and maintain your level of effort, you're probably not working hard enough. Also, if you get out of breath quickly or have to stop and catch your breath, you're probably working too hard.

Beyond aerobics

While simply walking more, jogging, or bicycling certainly can put your muscles to work more than sitting behind a desk or in an easy chair, they are mainly *aerobic* activities, helping to burn calories and tone the cardiovascular and pulmonary systems. Toning your muscles is important, too. Having good

Timesaver
You may find aerobic exercise equipment at your gym has built-in heart rate monitoring. You can also buy small devices to check it yourself when exercising.

Timesaver
You can estimate your *body fat percentage* on the Internet using a special calculator at www.phys.com.

muscles can help prevent injuries in falls. Muscle burns more calories than fat—and is much denser—an important point for those coping with post-cessation weight gain. So while aerobic activity is good at burning off the calories while you're doing it, muscle-toning and muscle-building exercise will help your metabolism stay up so that it can burn more calories *all the time.* (After following an exercise program you may find your weight up slightly from muscle gains that make you look leaner—remember muscle is denser than fat.)

An often-overlooked part of fitness is *stretching.* This is very important to keep you limber and flexible, particularly when you are undertaking muscle-toning activities. Think how good it feels to stretch as you wake up in the morning. Don't stretch too aggressively or twist unnaturally when you stretch, but do stretch gently before and after you exercise.

If you're a member of a health club, ask a trainer to show you some stretching exercises appropriate for your level of fitness (joining a club is a good idea to keep you focused on fitness and progressing with supervision). If you use a chiropractor for occasional back trouble, discuss with him your desire to learn some good stretching exercises. It is natural for him to instruct you and a good part of back health. If you're thinking of joining a gym, consider joining with a buddy, so you can motivate each other and have some company. One of you may even get a lower rate for referring the other.

Exercise can be stress-reducing in addition to its other benefits. Many people report relaxation after a certain amount of exertion—a *runner's high,* for instance. You may be surprised at how quickly your anxieties evaporate when you increase your activity

Bright Idea
You can work simple stretches into your day easily—while you're sitting at your desk or when you get up in the morning, for example.

level. By supporting your metabolism, circulation, and other activities, regular exercise can leave you feeling better and less anxious or depressed all the time. You may sleep better, as well.

Yoga is a form of exercise and meditation with its roots in ancient India. Actually considered a spiritual practice, conventional yoga concentrates on continued breathing through different exercises—many of them floor exercises—designed to stretch and tone the muscles, allowing better energy flow through the body. Relaxation and meditation is a big part of yoga practice, and many who try it find it leads to better *balance*, both in terms of physical coordination and emotional state. The Asian practice of *Tai Chi* is another option with stress-reducing benefits as well as other benefits along the lines of yoga. Look into different forms of exercise and see which you feel most at home with. Variety is good too.

That half an hour of daily, moderate, physical activity recommended by government scientists *is not* a lot to work into your schedule. How much benefit will *you* get? The good news is that the less active you are now, the more benefit you're likely to extract from starting a fitness regimen, as the following figure shows.

Going to the doctor

Once you have successfully quit and some time has passed, you can expect some medical tests to begin reflecting your improved health status. You should still get regular medical checkups and discuss with your doctor regular intervals for screening of those diseases past smoking may still have left you with increased risk for.

Timesaver
You can check your local Yellow Pages for yoga centers or check in at some health clubs that offer yoga classes.

This curve ➡ shows the best estimate of the relationship between physical activity and health benefits. The lower the baseline physical activity status, the greater will be the health benefit associated with an increase in physical activity.

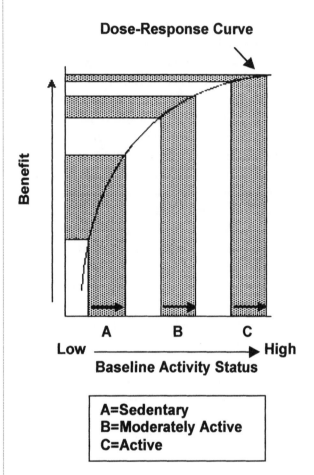

Dose-Response Curve

Benefit

Low ————————➤ High

Baseline Activity Status

A=Sedentary
B=Moderately Active
C=Active

Next time you visit your physician or the time after that, you may find your blood pressure has dropped into normal range, your triglyceride levels have dropped along with your level of so-called bad cholesterol, LDL cholesterol. Many other factors of basic blood tests may begin to normalize—from red and white blood cell counts to bilirubin, a measure of liver function.

Preventative efforts pay off. For instance, deaths from stroke have decreased by more than half since

1972, and part of the trend is attributed to earlier detection and treatment of hypertension. Regular blood pressure checks and routine blood panels with cholesterol counts are a good idea for everyone, and women should also have at least annual Pap smears during gynecological exams—perhaps more frequently if abnormalities are noticed. There, too, screening has paid off—the use of Pap tests has dramatically reduced incidence of invasive cervical cancer. Other screenings may be appropriate, and that is something to discuss with your doctor in light of past medical history and risk factors.

Cancer will eventually develop in about 30 percent of Americans, and many cancers can be cured if they are detected early and treated in the early stages. Breast cancer screening is important for women, and monthly self breast exams are recommended. You can find out how to do this by asking your gynecologist or family doctor at your next visit. Clinical breast exams are recommended as frequently as every year for women in good health without major risk factors, though opinion on when mammography should be done and for women of which age groups varies. It is a good topic for discussion with your gynecologist.

Generally, adults should have at least annual physical exams, and it's not a bad idea to schedule a visit to your physician a month or two after your quit date to reassess how you're doing. You may be pleasantly surprised at how quickly your health is improving.

Just the facts

- If your symptoms are slightly worse right after quitting, it may be a normal detoxification reaction.

- Many herbs, such as milk thistle and garlic, are used to support the liver and help clean the blood during detoxification.

- Renewed depression or anxiety following quitting may be related to nicotine discontinuance and is not uncommon.

- Finding new and healthy ways to reduce stress and fatigue is important since you won't be relying on cigarettes for that role.

GET THE SCOOP ON...
Coping with secondhand smoke ▪ Balancing
smokers' and nonsmokers' rights ▪ How times
are changing for smokers ▪ The future
of smoking cessation

You and Smokers

Chapter 17

S moking has become a dividing line in society.
There are many such lines which change how
we interact with people—those on the *other
side of the fence*. How many times before have you
been asked if you're a smoker?

The impact is in the choice of words. *I'm a smoker*
or *I'm a nonsmoker* starts to identify who we are,
though what it seems like we really want to know is
do you smoke? It would sound a bit odd if someone
asked whether you ate chocolate and you described
yourself as a non-chocolate-eater. But rather than
just being described as people who smoke, smokers
are described as...*smokers*.

Now that you're becoming a nonsmoker, how
will you interact with your friends who still smoke.
How will you interact with strangers who smoke? Are
you becoming someone different? In this chapter,
we'll examine the rights of smokers and those of
nonsmokers and how to respect both. We'll also take
a look at what may change in the future of smoking.

The smokers in your life

It's clear that smoking around others has become much less acceptable in recent years, with nonsmokers feeling more comfortable to assert their rights—in a climate of increasing intolerance to secondhand smoke exposure. Yet smokers still feel the urge to light up.

What has resulted is a delicate balance of wills that sometimes can get out of hand. Case in point, as noted in Chapter 3, are some commercial airline pilots' pleas that nicotine replacement therapy be offered to plane passengers, in order to quell so-called *air rage* that has been increasing, by some estimates at alarming rates. Smokers being prevented from smoking on long airline flights is cited as among the major reasons for in-flight unruliness.

What to do in the air and on the ground? In general it may be helpful to think of not being *passive*, but *assertive* about your rights, still without being aggressive and advancing your wants without regard for other people.

What about your inner circle? Like it or not, one of the things you probably had in common with some of those close to you was that you smoked. That meant you could spend time together smoking freely and not offending the other person. It may have meant a chance for bonding—"Hey, let's go have a cigarette"—that separated you from non-smokers in your social circle. It was a chance to chat, perhaps an opportunity to share secrets or thoughts you wouldn't share with a larger group of people.

Now that you're a nonsmoker, how do you feel about losing that opportunity, about subtly changing your place in a group? You may not have thought about this, but what happens next time you go out for an evening with smokers, and you're no longer leaving the table with them to share a smoke outside?

Don't minimize the influence those around you can have. Though you've kicked the habit for plenty of valid reasons, you may find yourself tempted to have just one more cigarette purely for social reasons. And smoking *is* a very social activity, as some part-time smokers, those who may not be very physically addicted, like Holly, can attest.

> There was a time when I did consider myself addicted to cigarettes, and perhaps in some ways I still am. While I do not smoke on a regular basis, I find that I cannot resist the offer of a cigarette when I am at a bar or out with friends who smoke. It seems that cocktails and cigarettes just go together for me, and in order to quit one I'd probably have to quit the other. Either that or find a new group of friends. At any rate, I don't think it's the nicotine I'm addicted to, it's everything else about smoking— the having something to do with your hands, the deep inhalation that gives you a brief moment of relaxation before turning into the head rush that the first drag gives you, even the feeling of pseudo-sophistication holding a cigarette gives.

Just as having one drink can be very dangerous for an alcoholic, having one smoke can lead to relapse for a former smoker with a strong addiction to nicotine or even an addiction to the behavior of smoking. You can ask your friends to be supportive of your quit effort and spend time around them when they smoke, if you wish. However, if you find yourself in the company of those who would only

Bright Idea
Find something else to do when you're with smokers who are smoking. Bring carrot sticks or gum so you won't feel like you're just sitting or standing there.

egg you on into having just one cigarette, you may need to set better boundaries—not spending time with them when they smoke or even not spending time with them at all.

While looking out for nonsmokers' rights, the Environmental Protection Agency (EPA) advises that smokers take an active role in helping to protect those close to them, with these suggestions:

- **Don't smoke around children.** Their lungs are very susceptible to smoke. If you are expecting a child, quit smoking.

- **Take an active role in the development of your company's smoking policy.** Encourage the offering of smoking cessation programs for those who want them.

- **Keep your home smoke free.** Nonsmokers can get lung cancer from exposure to your smoke. Because smoke lingers in the air, people may be exposed even if they are not present while you smoke.

- **If you must smoke inside, limit smoking to a room where you can open windows for cross-ventilation.** Be sure the room in which you smoke has a working smoke detector to lessen the risk of fire.

- **Test your home for radon.** Radon contamination in combination with smoking is a much greater health risk than either one individually.

- **Don't smoke in an automobile with the windows closed if passengers are present.** The high concentration of smoke in a small, closed compartment substantially increases the exposure of other passengers.

Although living with a smoker can be difficult for a nonsmoker, living with a nonsmoker can be tough on a smoker, too. You can encourage those you care about to give up their habit, but you can't do it for them. A supportive attitude allowing them to make their own decisions for their own life and setting a good smoke-free example yourself may be the best policy.

How do you feel about secondhand smoke?

Secondhand smoke, as you may recall from earlier chapters, is dangerous. According to the EPA, it has been estimated to cause approximately 3,000 lung cancer deaths in nonsmokers each year (though that figure has been challenged by some factions). It is particularly dangerous to children and, in adults, can—according to the EPA:

- Cause irritation of the eye, nose, and throat

- Irritate the lungs, causing coughing, excess phlegm, chest discomfort, and reduced lung function

- Possibly affect the cardiovascular system and cause chest pain

As a new nonsmoker very aware of the health implications of smoking, only you can decide how hard a line to take to keep yourself from the dangers of secondhand smoke. You will find yourself exposed to it in a number of different situations.

In the home

If you have quit smoking but your spouse or someone else in your household has not, you are faced with health dangers and so is anyone else under the same roof. Be kind but also set appropriate boundaries to

Moneysaver
Whenever the weather permits, leave windows open in a household with smokers and use overhead paddle fans to help dispel smoke without incurring a high electric bill.

minimize exposure to secondhand smoke in what is, after all, your home. Some suggestions from the Environmental Protection Agency are:

- Don't smoke in your house or permit others to do so.

- If a family member insists on smoking indoors, increase ventilation in the area where smoking takes place. Open windows or use exhaust fans.

- Don't allow baby-sitters or others who work in your home to smoke in the house or near your children. Infants and toddlers are particularly susceptible to the effects of passive smoking.

To further protect your children from second-hand smoke risks, you can ask about smoking policies of the daycare providers, preschools, schools, and others who provide care for your children. You can help other parents to understand the dangers of secondhand smoke to children and work to make your child's environment smoke-free through parent-teacher associations, your school board and school administrators, community leaders, and other concerned citizens.

When you're out

The push for nonsmokers' rights has resulted in laws against smoking in many public places. Get to know your area's standards. Some communities have entirely banned smoking in places such as restaurants. Others require that restaurants provide smoking areas separate from other patrons, and some simply ask that smokers and nonsmokers be separated within the same space in restaurants. That can help cut down on secondhand smoke, but not eliminate it.

The EPA advises:

- You ask to be seated in a nonsmoking area as far from smokers as possible.

- If your community does not have a smoking control ordinance, urge that one be enacted or that an ineffective ordinance be beefed up.

Bars and lounges can be a problem when it comes to avoiding secondhand smoke. There are relatively few restrictions, and drinking and smoking often go hand in hand. If your state or locality does not have laws restricting smoking in bars, patronize those establishments that look out for nonsmokers by voluntarily providing a nonsmoking area.

In some areas, there *are* laws against smoking in bars. For instance, in 1998, California enacted a ban on smoking in bars, casinos, and nightclubs, dramatically reducing the secondhand smoke exposure of many spending an evening out. In the Canadian city of Toronto, a similar law was passed in 1996 restricting smoking in all restaurants, bars, and entertainment facilities. Though it was short-lived, it is being resurrected with modifications that try to accommodate both smokers and nonsmokers.

Where in the United States will you find preemptive laws enforcing indoor air quality? The following figure maps it for you. Preemptive legislation is legislation that prevents a local jurisdiction from enacting laws stricter than, or at odds with, state mandated law.

Many states have laws that prohibit smoking in public facilities like schools, hospitals, airports, bus terminals, and other public buildings. Smoking is prohibited on all airline flights of six hours or less within the United States and on all interstate bus travel.

Timesaver
Ask bartenders, waiters, and waitresses where the least smoky and best ventilated areas of their establishment is before you are seated—they will know.

Bright Idea
You can read up
on Toronto's
tough stance on
smoking in
Chapter 301 of
their municipal
code, online at
old.city.toronto.
on.ca.

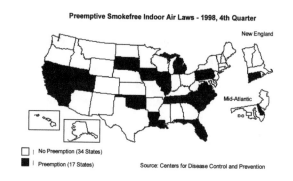

Preemptive Smokefree Indoor Air Laws - 1998, 4th Quarter

New England

Mid-Atlantic

☐ │ No Preemption (34 States)
■ │ Preemption (17 States)   Source: Centers for Disease Control and Prevention

At work

What about the workplace? Many businesses have
smoking policies in place, and the EPA recommends
every company have one and suggests that if your
company does not have a smoking policy that effectively controls secondhand smoke, work with appropriate management and labor organizations to
establish one.

For private workplaces, California is the only
state with laws on the books calling for designated
smoking areas with separate ventilation—it has the
toughest legislation. Most states have no restrictions
though some call for designated smoking areas.
There are laws restricting smoking at state government work sites in 41 states and the District of
Columbia. Smoking is also limited at commercial
daycare centers in 28 states and the District of
Columbia. Hawaii, Massachusetts, Vermont, New
Jersey, and Tennessee have all strengthened their
laws on smoke-free indoor air since 1995, according
to the Centers for Disease Control.

What works in the workplace? Consider these
points from the EPA:

▪ Simply separating smokers and nonsmokers
within the same area, such as a cafeteria, may

reduce exposure, but nonsmokers will still be exposed to recirculated smoke or smoke drifting into nonsmoking areas

■ Prohibiting smoking indoors or limiting smoking to rooms that have been specially designed to prevent smoke from escaping to other areas of the building are two options that will effectively protect nonsmokers. The costs associated with establishing properly designated smoking rooms vary from building to building and are likely to be greater than simply eliminating smoking entirely.

If smoking is permitted indoors, the EPA also suggests it should be in a room that meets certain conditions:

1. Air from the smoking room should be directly exhausted to the outside by an exhaust fan. Air from the smoking room should not be recirculated to other parts of the building. More air should be exhausted from the room than is supplied to it to make sure ETS (environmental tobacco smoke) doesn't drift to surrounding spaces.

2. The ventilation system should provide the smoking room with 60 cubic feet per minute (CFM) of supply air per smoker. This air is often supplied by air transferred from other parts of the building, such as corridors.

3. Nonsmokers should not have to use the smoking room for any purpose. It should be located in a nonwork area where no one, as part of his or her work responsibilities, is required to enter.

If the designated smoking area is outdoors, smoking should not be allowed immediately outside the doors where nonsmokers may have to pass or near ventilation system air intakes for the building.

The future of smoking

Anti-smoking efforts have already altered smoking. The most noticeable changes in everyday life recently may be the restrictions on smoking in bars and restaurants some localities have started to slap on.

Timesaver
To find out about regulations on smoking in various establishments in your state, check out the CDC's State Tobacco Activities Tracking and Evaluation (STATE) System on the Internet at www2.cdc.gov/ nccdphp/osh/ state.

The state of California's 1998 ban on smoking in bars, nightclubs, and casinos is of note. While more establishments are truly smoke-free, there is pressure on bar owners to allow smoking, and some establishments openly violate the ban, relying on a lack of complaints from patrons and a lack of resources to enforce the code, among local authorities.

According to a survey of 300 establishments, almost 4 percent said they did not actively enforce the ban, while another 23 percent said customers simply ignored the ban. Most businesses experienced a decrease in business since the ban went into effect. However, many bartenders may not be complaining—or coughing as much—since, on average, they have gone from 28 hours a week of smoke exposure down to 2.

A month before the ban went into effect, researchers tested the lungs of some California bartenders. About 74 percent reported respiratory problems like wheezing and cough, and 77 percent said they suffered eye, nose, or throat irritation. When tested again, one to two months after the ban, 59 percent of those who had complained about respiratory problems no longer had the symptoms. Nearly 80 percent of those who had reported eye, nose, or throat irritation reported their symptoms had cleared up.

Aside from tighter restrictions on smoking in public places, you can expect to see a lot of anti-smoking advertising. The 46-state legal settlement with the tobacco industry is resulting in a huge amount of funding for such efforts, aimed at countering youth tobacco use and educating consumers about the causes and prevention of tobacco related diseases.

Four states—Florida, Minnesota, Mississippi, and Texas—were the first to settle with big tobacco companies in a $40 billion deal. Then in November 1998, attorneys general representing 46 states, the District of Columbia, and five U.S. territories signed an agreement with major tobacco companies in settlement of all the state lawsuits that sought to recover Medicaid costs of treating smokers. By contract, the Master Settlement Agreement imposes restrictions on how tobacco can be advertised, marketed, and promoted. It also requires the tobacco firms to make yearly payments that will total some $200 billion through the year 2025. On September 22, 1999, the U.S. Attorney General's office filed its suit against the tobacco industry for the excess costs of medical care the government paid for smokers' ailments. (See Chapter 3 for more on the topic.)

Cigarette prices have been on their way up, with the costs of the tobacco settlement being passed on to consumers.

States aren't required to spend their portion of the legal settlement any particular way, though more support for those kicking the habit can be expected, with a huge push to keep cigarettes from catching on with children and teens. In exchange for not having to reimburse federal Medicaid monies from their portion of the settlement, states could agree to spend all settlement proceeds on public health pro-grams of which anti-tobacco components would be a large part.

The future of quitting smoking

The enormous settlement between states and the tobacco industry could easily mean more widely available, free-of-charge smoking cessation services. Free help in kicking the habit is something that is already advocated. Clinical guidelines from the Agency for Healthcare Policy and Research call for including smoking-cessation treatments as paid ser-vices in all health benefits packages:

> Smoking cessation treatments (both pharma-cotherapy and counseling) are not consistently provided as paid services for subscribers of health insurance packages. The level of coverage is par-ticularly surprising given that studies show that physician counseling against smoking is at least as cost-effective as several other preventive med-ical practices, including the treatment of mild or moderate hypertension or high cholesterol.
>
> The national health promotion and disease prevention objectives for the year 2000 as set forth in Healthy People 2000 propose to increase to 100 percent the proportion of health plans that offer treatment of nicotine addiction, such as tobacco-use cessation counseling by health care providers, tobacco-use cessation classes, pre-scriptions for nicotine replacement therapies, and/or other cessation services.
>
> Action: Provide coverage to all insurance subscribers for effective smoking-cessation treat-ments, including pharmaco-therapy (nicotine-replacement therapy) and counseling.

Free access to help in quitting smoking is also an objective of Healthy People 2000, a preventative health agenda of the U.S. Department of Health and Human Services. Tobacco use is a priority area, and specific objectives include:

- Reduce coronary heart disease deaths
- Slow the rise in lung cancer deaths
- Slow the rise in chronic obstructive pulmonary disease deaths
- Reduce cigarette smoking
- Reduce initiation of cigarette smoking by children and youth
- Increase smoking cessation
- Increase smoking cessation during pregnancy
- Reduce child exposure to tobacco smoke at home
- Reduce smokeless tobacco use
- Establish tobacco use prevention programs in schools
- Increase restrictive smoking policies at worksites
- Enact clean indoor air laws
- Enact and enforce laws prohibiting the sale of tobacco products to minors
- Increase states with plans to reduce tobacco use
- Eliminate or restrict tobacco advertising and promotion to youth
- Increase smoking cessation counseling and follow-up by providers
- Reduce oral cavity and pharynx cancers

- Reduce stroke deaths
- Increase average age of first use of cigarettes, alcohol, and marijuana
- Reduce past-month substance abuse among young people
- Increase proportion of high school seniors who disapprove of substance use
- Increase proportion of high school seniors who associate physical or psychological harm with substance use
- Increase the average tobacco excise tax
- Increase proportion of health plans offering treatment for nicotine addiction
- Reduce the number of states with preemptive clean indoor air laws
- Enact laws banning youth access to cigarette vending machines

No matter what laws are enacted against smoking, no matter how many advertising dollars are spent dissuading teenagers from taking up smoking, and no matter how bad the health effects of continued tobacco use, quitting smoking still comes down to an individual decision and a lifelong commitment to take good care of yourself and the people you love. Chances are you'll be around longer for them.

Just the facts

- Secondhand smoke is dangerous, especially to children.
- Smoking is not allowed in many public facilities, though it can be tough to find a smoke-free nightspot.

- Smoke-free policies help service workers, such as waiters, waitresses, and bartenders who are exposed to secondhand smoke at their job.

- It is possible for nonsmokers and smokers to live side by side, peaceably, with a little common courtesy.

Glossary

addiction A chronic, relapsing disease, characterized by compulsive drug seeking and use and by neurochemical and molecular changes in the brain.

carcinogen A cancer-causing substance.

craving A strong, nagging desire for a particular substance.

dopamine A neurotransmitter found in areas of the brain that regulate movement, emotion, motivation, and the feeling of pleasure.

emphysema A lung disease involving tissue deterioration, difficult breathing, and shortness of breath. Often caused by smoking.

neurotransmitter Chemicals that carry signals from one neuron to another over a synapse.

nicotine An alkaloid chemical in the tobacco plant that is psychoactive and addictive. Toxic at high doses but can be used safely and effectively as a medication at lower doses (as in nicotine replacement therapy).

nicotine patch An adhesive patch worn on the body which releases nicotine slowly into the system *transdermally* (through the skin). Used in smoking cessation.

passive smoking Inhaling smoke that is either exhaled by a smoker or released from the burning tip of a cigarette, cigar, or pipe.

physical dependence A physiological adaptation to recurrent drug use characterized by withdrawal symptoms when use of the substance is discontinued.

secondhand smoke (also *environmental smoke*) Smoke from the burning tip of a cigarette, cigar, or pipe, or smoke exhaled by a smoker.

sidestream smoke Smoke from the burning tip of a cigarette, cigar, or pipe.

tolerance A physiological state following the initial use of an addictive substance in which higher doses of a drug are required to produce the same effect as during initial use.

withdrawal A range of symptoms occurring when use of an addictive substance is reduced or stopped.

Recommended Reading

Amen, Daniel G. *Change Your Brain Change Your Life: The Breakthrough Program for Conquering Anxiety, Depression, Obsessiveness, Anger, and Impulsiveness.* Random House, 1999.

American Cancer Society. *The American Cancer Society's "Freshstart": 21 Days to Stop Smoking (cassette).* Simon & Schuster, 1986.

American Lung Association; Fisher, Edwin B., Jr.; C. Everett Koop. *7 Steps to a Smoke-Free Life.* John Wiley & Sons, 1998.

Chopra, Deepak. *Overcoming Addictions: The Spiritual Solution.* Three Rivers Press, 1998.

Fahs, John. *Cigarette Confidential: The Unfiltered Truth About the Ultimate American Addiction.* Berkley Publishing Group, 1996.

Gebhardt, B. Jack. *The Enlightened Smoker's Guide to Quitting.* Element, 1998.

Naparstek, Belleruth. *A Meditation to Help You Stop Smoking* (hypnosis and guided imagery cassette). Warner Elektra Atlantic Corp., 1997.

Pringle, Peter. *Cornered: Big Tobacco at the Bar of Justice.* Henry Holt & Company, Inc., 1998.

Rustin, Terry A. *Keep Quit: A Motivational Guide to a Life Without Smoking.* Hazelden Information Education, 1996.

Stevic-Rust, Lori, Ph.D.; Anita Maximin. *The Stop Smoking Workbook.* Fine Communications, 1997.

Whelan, Elizabeth M. *Cigarettes: What the Warning Label Doesn't Tell You: The First Comprehensive Guide to the Health Consequences of Smoking.* Prometheus Books, 1997.

Resource Guide

Organizations

These organizations have information about smoking and how to quit, or health conditions linked to smoking.

Health- and cessation-related organizations

American Heart Association
7272 Greenville Avenue
Dallas, TX 75231
(800) AHA-USA1 or (800) 242-8721
www.americanheart.org

American Cancer Society
1599 Clifton Road, NE
Atlanta, GA 30329
(404) 320-3333
www.cancer.org

American Lung Association
1740 Broadway, 14th Floor
New York, NY 10019
(212) 315-8700
www.longusa.org

National Cancer Institute
Office of Cancer Communications
Bldg. 31, Room 10A24
9000 Rockville Pike
Bethesda, MD 20894
(800) 4-CANCER or (800) 422-6237
www.nci.nih.gov

American College of Obstetricians and Gynecologists
409 12th Street, SW
Washington, DC 20024
(202) 638-5577

Nicotine Anonymous World Services
P.O. Box 126338
Harrisburg, PA 17112-6338
(415) 750-0328
www.nicotine-anonymous.org
e-mail: info@nicotine-anonymous.org

Government organizations

A number of government agencies provide information and materials related to smoking, including those listed here.

Centers for Disease Control and Prevention (CDC)
National Center for Chronic Disease Prevention
and Health Promotion (NCCDPHP),
Office on Smoking and Health (OSH)
Mail Stop# K-50
4770 Buford Highway, NE
Atlanta, GA 30341-3724
(770) 488-5705 (general information and
publication requests)
www.cdc.gov/tobacco/

Agency for Health Care Policy and Research (AHCPR)
AHCPR Publications Clearinghouse
P.O. Box 8547
Silver Spring, MD 20907-8547
(800) 358-9295
www.ahcpr.gov

Environmental Protection Agency (EPA)
Indoor Air Quality Information Clearinghouse
P.O. Box 37133
Washington, DC 20013-7133
(800) 438-4318
www.epa.gov/iaq/

The EPA offers publications and information on the adverse effects of environmental tobacco smoke and indoor air pollution.

Federal Trade Commission (FTC)
Public Reference Branch
600 Pennsylvania Avenue, NW
Washington, DC 20580
(202) 326-2222 (publications)
(202) 326-3090 (tobacco-related questions)
www.ftc.gov

Produces a report that contains data on the tar, nicotine, and carbon monoxide of domestic cigarettes.

Food and Drug Administration (FDA)
Office of Consumer Affairs, HFE-50
5600 Fishers Lane
Rockville, MD 20857
(301) 827-4420
(301) 443-9767 (fax)
www.fda.gov

National Clearinghouse for Alcohol and Drug Information (NCADI)
P.O. Box 2345
Rockville, MD 20847-2345
(301) 468-2600
(800) Say-No-To
www.health.org

National Health Information Center (NHIC)
P.O. Box 1133
Washington, DC 20013-1133
(800) 336-4797
(301) 565-4167
(301) 984-4256 (fax)
nhic-nt.health.org

Uses a database containing descriptions of health-related organizations to refer inquirers to the most appropriate resources.

Canadian organizations
Health Canada
A.L. 0913A
Ottawa, Ontario K1A 0K9
(613) 941-5366
www.hc-sc.gc.ca

National Cancer Institute of Canada
10 Alcorn Avenue, Suite 200
Toronto, Ontario M4V 3B1
(416) 961-7223
www.ncic.cancer.ca

Canadian Cancer Society
10 Alcorn Avenue, Suite 200
Toronto, Ontario M4V 3B1
(888) 939-3333 (Cancer Information Service)
(416) 961-7223
(416) 961-4189 (fax)
www.cancer.ca

Canadian Lung Association
1900 City Park Drive, Suite 508
Gloucester, Ontario K1J 1A3
(613) 747-6776
(613) 747-7430 (fax)
www.lung.ca

Quit-smoking materials

Looking for more ready resources you can turn to
for smoking cessation help? Here are a few from
the American Lung Association and Nicotine
Anonymous.

American Lung Association materials

For more information about obtaining these materials, call the American Lung Association at (800)
LUNG-USA or (800) 586-4872 or visit their Web site
at www.lungusa.org.

Freedom From Smoking® (ALA Item #0055)—This
self-help manual, which combines cessation and
maintenance programs, targets a broad range of
smokers; its goal is to help smokers at different stages
in the quitting process. The manual includes a quitting calendar and easy-to-use records to help people
get to know their own smoking habit. Messages
include the effects of secondhand smoke, identifica-
tion of nicotine dependence, use of nicotine replacement products, and specific relapse strategies.

7 Steps To A Smoke-Free Life (published by John
Wiley & Sons, Inc.; available through retail book
stores and the ALA Web site www.lungusa.org)—
This straightforward book carefully guides smokers
through the seven steps that will lead to a longer,
healthier life. The book provides guidance and support smokers need to cope with cravings, manage

stress, keep off extra weight, avoid setbacks, and stick with their plans to quit smoking.

A Lifetime of Freedom From Smoking® (ALA Item #0026)—Targeted toward the new ex-smoker, this maintenance manual gives suggestions on how to stay quit and to deal with issues such as controlling weight and coping with social situations as a non-smoker. Staying quit is the hardest part of quitting, and this manual helps the ex-smoker develop a non-smoking habit that will last a lifetime.

Nicotine Anonymous materials
Nicotine Anonymous World Services
P.O. Box 126338, Harrisburg, PA 17112-6338
(415) 750-0328
www.nicotine-anonymous.org
e-mail: info@nicotine-anonymous.org

Available materials include:

Nicotine Anonymous THE BOOK
Our Path to Freedom

Pamphlets are also available including:

Introducing Nicotine Anonymous
The Serenity Prayer for Smokers
The Serenity Prayer for Smokers (Spanish)
A Smoker's View of the Twelve Steps
Tips for Gaining Freedom from Nicotine
To the Newcomer & Sponsorship
To the Medical Profession
Facing the Fatal Attraction
Our Promises
To the Dipper & Chewer
Slogans
Worldwide Meeting Directory
The By-Laws of Nicotine Anonymous

Facts on Smoking and Kicking the Habit

American Lung Association Smoking Fact Sheet

Smoking-related diseases claim an estimated 430,700 American lives each year, including those affected indirectly, such as babies born prematurely due to prenatal maternal smoking and some of the victims of "secondhand" exposure to tobacco's carcinogens. Smoking costs the United States approximately $97.2 billion each year in health-care costs and lost productivity.

- Cigarettes contain at least 43 distinct cancer-causing chemicals. Smoking is directly responsible for 87 percent of lung cancer cases and causes most cases of emphysema and chronic bronchitis. Smoking is also a major factor in coronary heart disease and stroke; may be causally related to malignancies in other parts of the body; and has been linked to a variety of other conditions and disorders, including slowed healing of wounds, infertility, and peptic ulcer disease.

- Smoking in pregnancy accounts for an estimated 20 to 30 percent of low-birth weight babies, up to 14 percent of preterm deliveries, and some 10 percent of all infant deaths. Even apparently healthy, full-term babies of smokers have been found to be born with narrowed airways and curtailed lung function. Only about 30 percent of women who smoke stop smoking when they find they are pregnant; the proportion of quitters is highest among married women and women with higher levels of educational attainment. In 1996, 13.6 percent of women who gave birth smoked during pregnancy.

- Smoking by parents is also associated with a wide range of adverse effects in their children, including exacerbation of asthma, increased frequency of colds and ear infections, and sudden infant death syndrome. An estimated 150,000 to 300,000 cases of lower respiratory tract infections in children less than 18 months of age, resulting in 7,500 to 15,000 annual hospitalizations, are caused by secondhand smoke.

- Secondhand smoke involuntarily inhaled by nonsmokers from other people's cigarettes is classified by the U.S. Environmental Protection Agency as a known human (Group A) carcinogen, responsible for approximately 3,000 lung cancer deaths annually in U.S. nonsmokers.

- Approximately 22.5 million American women are smokers. Current female smokers aged 35 years or older are 12 times more likely to die prematurely from lung cancer than nonsmoking females. More American women die annually from lung cancer than any other type of cancer; for example, lung cancer will cause an estimated 68,000 female deaths in 1999, compared with 43,300 estimated female deaths caused by breast cancer.

- As smoking has declined among the white non-Hispanic population, tobacco companies have targeted both African Americans and Hispanics with intensive merchandising, which includes billboards, advertising in media targeted to those communities, and sponsorship of civic groups and athletic, cultural, and entertainment events.

- The prevalence of smoking is highest among Native Americans/Alaskan Natives (36.2 percent), next highest among African Americans (25.8 percent) and whites (25.6 percent), and lowest among Asians and Pacific Islanders (16.6 percent). Hispanics (18.3 percent) are less likely to be smokers than non-Hispanic blacks and whites.

- Tobacco advertising plays an important role in encouraging young people to begin a lifelong addiction to smoking before they are old enough to fully understand its long-term health risk. It is estimated that 4.5 million U.S. teenagers are cigarette smokers; 22.4 percent of high school seniors smoke on a daily basis. Approximately 90 percent of smokers begin smoking before the age of 21.

- The American Lung Association coordinates the Smoke-Free Class of 2000 in response to former Surgeon General C. Everett Koop's call for a smoke-free society by the Year 2000. We are focusing on the three million children who entered the first grade in 1988, to increase students' awareness and education, to focus media attention on a tobacco-free society, and to place tobacco-use prevention education programs in school health curricula. These students are now in high school and the focus is on empowering them to become peer educators on the dangers of tobacco and tobacco control advocates in their communities.

- Workplaces nationwide are going smoke-free to provide clean indoor air and protect employees from the life-threatening effects of second-hand smoke. According to a 1992 Gallup poll, 94 percent of Americans now believe companies should either ban smoking totally in the workplace or restrict it to designated areas.

- Employers have a legal right to restrict smoking in the workplace, or implement a totally smoke-free workplace policy. Exceptions may arise in the case of collective bargaining agreements with unions.

- Nicotine is an addictive drug, which when inhaled in cigarette smoke reaches the brain faster than drugs that enter the body intravenously. Smokers become not only physically addicted to nicotine; they also link smoking with many social activities, making smoking a difficult habit to break.

- In 1995, an estimated 44.3 million adults were former smokers. Of the current 47 million smokers, more than 31 million persons reported they wanted to quit smoking completely. Currently, both nicotine patches and nicotine gum are available over the counter, and a nicotine nasal spray and inhaler, as well as a non-nicotine pill, are currently available by prescription; all help relieve withdrawal symptoms people experience when they quit smoking. Nicotine replacement therapies are helpful in quitting when combined with a behavior change program such as the American Lung Association's Freedom From Smoking® (FFS), which addresses psychological and behavioral addictions to smoking and strategies for coping with urges to smoke.

For more information call the American Lung Association at (800) LUNG-USA (586-4872), or visit their Web site at www.lungusa.org.

Source: American Lung Association.

American Lung Association Smoking and Pregnancy Fact Sheet

Cigarette smoking during pregnancy can cause serious health problems to an unborn child. Smoking during pregnancy has been linked to premature labor, breathing problems, and fatal illness among infants. An estimated 430,700 Americans die each year from diseases caused by smoking. Smoking is responsible for an estimated 1 in 5 U.S. deaths and costs the U.S. at least $97.2 billion each year in health-care costs and lost productivity.

- Smoking during pregnancy is estimated to account for 20 to 30 percent of low birth-weight babies, up to 14 percent of preterm deliveries, and some 10 percent of all infant deaths. Maternal smoking during and after pregnancy has been linked to asthma among infants and young children.

- In 1996, 13.6 percent of mothers were reported to have smoked during pregnancy, a 26 percent decline from the 1990 level.

- Smokers inhale nicotine and carbon monoxide, which reach the baby through the placenta and prevent the fetus from getting the nutrients and oxygen needed to grow. Secondhand smoke also adds a risk to pregnancy. Breast milk often contains whatever is in the woman's body. If the woman smokes, the baby ingests the nicotine in her breast milk.

- Reducing frequency of smoking may not benefit the baby. A pregnant woman who reduces her smoking pattern or switches to lower tar cigarettes may inhale more deeply or take more puffs to get the same amount of nicotine as before.

- The most effective way to protect the fetus is to quit smoking. If a woman plans to conceive a child in the near future, quitting is essential. A woman who quits within the first three or four months of pregnancy can lower the chances of her baby being born premature or with health problems related to smoking.

- Pregnancy is a great time for a woman to quit. No matter how long she has been smoking, her body benefits from her quitting because it lessens her chances of developing future tobacco-related health problems, such as lung and heart disease, and cancer.

For more information call the American Lung Association at (800) LUNG-USA (586-4872), or visit their Web site at www.lungusa.org.

Source: American Lung Association.

FTC Report on "Tar," Nicotine, and Carbon Monoxide

"Tar," Nicotine, and Carbon Monoxide of the Smoke of 1252 Varieties of Domestic Cigarettes for the Year 1997: A Federal Trade Commission Report to Congress

Issued 1999

This report contains data on the "tar," nicotine, and carbon monoxide yields of 1252 varieties of cigarettes manufactured and sold in the United States in 1997. [1]

Limitations of the Cigarette Test Method

Cigarette ratings for "tar," nicotine, and carbon monoxide are currently determined by machine testing conducted in accordance with a methodology adopted by the Commission in 1967. The "tar" and nicotine testing program was intended to provide smokers seeking to switch to lower "tar" cigarettes with a single, standardized measurement with which to choose among the then-existing brands.[2]

Over the past 30 years that the current system has been in place, there have been dramatic decreases in the machine-measured "tar" and nicotine yields of cigarettes. Since 1968, the average sales-weighted machine-measured "tar" yield has fallen from 21.6 mg. to 12.0 mg. Today, 70% of all cigarettes sold have machine-measured "tar" yields of 15 mg. or less.

Despite these substantial decreases in machine-measured yields, the Commission has been concerned for some time that the current test method may be misleading to individual consumers who rely on the ratings it produces as indicators of how much "tar" and nicotine they actually get from their cigarettes. In fact, the current ratings tend to be relatively poor predictors of "tar" and nicotine exposure. This appears to be due primarily to compensation—the tendency of smokers of lower rated cigarettes to take bigger or more frequent puffs, or otherwise alter their smoking behavior to get the amount of nicotine they need. Such variations in the way people smoke can have significant effects on the amount of "tar," nicotine, and carbon monoxide they get from any particular cigarette. The Commission is concerned that smokers may incorrectly believe, for example, that they will get three times as much "tar" from a 15 mg. "tar" cigarette as from a 5 mg. "tar" cigarette. In fact, if compensation is sufficiently great, it is possible for smokers to get as much "tar" and nicotine from relatively low rated cigarettes as from higher rated ones. Although these limitations have been present in the system since its initiation in 1967, they have become of substantial concern more recently because of changes in modern cigarette design and a better understanding of the effects of compensatory smoking behavior.

Some public health agencies have also expressed concerns that new studies may question the basic assumption underlying cigarette testing—that cigarettes with lower machine-measured "tar" and nicotine ratings are less harmful than ones with higher ratings. For example, in 1997, the National Cancer Institute issued a monograph noting that the apparent mortality risk among current smokers has risen in the last forty to fifty years, even though machine-measured "tar" and nicotine yields have fallen during the same period.[3] In attempting to understand this fact, the monograph suggested that the increased mortality risk might be due to increases in current smokers' lifetime exposure to cigarette smoke or that the reduced "tar" levels of modern cigarettes may have less benefit than previously believed. In addition, a number of studies have also found that changes in smoking behavior and cigarette design appear to have resulted in an increase in a type of cancer that occurs deeper in the lung than the lung cancer traditionally associated with smoking.[4]

In light of these concerns, in 1998 the Commission requested that the Department of Health and Human Services ("HHS") conduct a complete review of the FTC's cigarette testing methodology.[5] This review will be completed in September 2000.

While that review is underway, the Commission believes that all smokers should know the following facts:

- "Tar" and nicotine ratings were never intended to reflect what any individual consumer would get from any particular cigarette;

- How much "tar" and nicotine an individual gets from a cigarette depends on how he or she smokes it—smokers of cigarette brands with lower "tar" and nicotine ratings who take larger or more frequent puffs may get as much "tar" and nicotine as smokers of higher rated brands;

- Many cigarettes have ventilation holes that, when blocked, substantially increase exposure to the harmful constituents in smoke;

- There is no such thing as a safe smoke, no matter what the "tar" and nicotine ratings are; and

- People who are concerned about the health effects of smoking should quit.

The Commission also believes it is vital that there be a mechanism for implementing the recommended changes once the HHS review is completed. Although the Commission brings a strong, market-based expertise to its scrutiny of consumer protection matters, it does not have the specialized scientific expertise needed to design scientific test procedures. Indeed, when evaluating medical or other scientific issues, the Commission often relies on other government agencies and outside experts with more knowledge in the relevant areas. Therefore, in its July 1999 "Report to Congress for 1997, Pursuant to the Cigarette Labeling and Advertising Act," the Commission recommended that Congress consider giving authority over cigarette testing to one of the Federal government's science-based, public health agencies.

The Source of the Data in This Report

The FTC obtained the test results published in this report from the five largest cigarette manufacturers in the United States. These companies are: Brown & Williamson Tobacco Corporation; Liggett Group, Inc.; Lorillard, Inc.; Philip Morris, Inc.; and R.J. Reynolds Tobacco Company, Inc.

The Tobacco Institute Testing Laboratory (TITL), a private laboratory operated by the cigarette industry, conducted much of the "tar," nicotine, and carbon monoxide testing for these varieties.[6] The Commission collected the results of the TITL testing directly from the individual companies under compulsory process. Generic, private label, and other brands not widely available were not tested by TITL. The Commission obtained the information on these other brands directly from the manufacturers, pursuant to compulsory process. Results of such non-TITL testing are indicated by asterisks. The methodology, processes, and procedures that the five cigarette companies and TITL employ are identical to those the Commission, in its own testing lab, had followed in the past.[7] Harold Pillsbury, the former director of the FTC laboratory and currently a contractor to the Commission, had unrestricted access to the TITL laboratory to review TITL's testing methodology and protocols and to monitor the actual testing process. TITL provided the results to the respective cigarette companies, which then provided TITL's data regarding their own brands to the Commission in response to compulsory process.

A Description of the Cigarette Test Method

The cigarettes were tested using the Cambridge Method. The Commission approved this methodology, and it has been the standard for cigarette testing since 1966. The testing was conducted under conditions originally prescribed by the Commission in 1967, 32 Fed. Reg. 11,187 (1967), as modified by the Commission's 1980 adoption of procedures for measuring carbon monoxide yields.[8] The conditions prescribed in the FTC's 1967 announcement were:

1. Smoke cigarettes to a 23mm. butt length, or to the length of the filter and overwrap plus 3mm. if in excess of 23mm.;

2. Base results on a test of 100 cigarettes per brand, or type;

3. Cigarettes to be tested will be selected on a random basis, as opposed to "weight selection";

4. Determine particulate matter on a "dry" basis employing the gas chromatography method published by C.H. Sloan and B.J. Sublett in Tobacco Science [9], page 70, 1965, as modified by F.J. Schultz' and A.W. Spears' report published in Tobacco Vol. 162, No. 24, page 32, dated June 17, 1966, to determine the moisture content;

5. Determine and report the "tar" yield after subtracting moisture and alkaloids (as nicotine) from particulate matter;

6. Report "tar" yield to the nearest whole milligram and nicotine yield to the nearest ⅒ milligram.[9]

TITL reported, and the FTC's contractor confirmed, that an independent company under contract to TITL obtained the tested cigarette samples. Under its contract, this company purchased two packages of every variety of cigarettes in 50 geographical locations throughout the United States. If not all varieties were available in every location, one or more additional packages of cigarettes were purchased in the areas where the respective varieties were available. Cigarettes used in the test represented cigarettes sold in the U.S. at the time of purchase in 1997.

"Tar" and carbon monoxide ratings are rounded to the nearest milligram (mg.); those with 0.5 mg. or greater are rounded up, while those with 0.4 mg. or less are rounded down. The nicotine figures are rounded to the nearest tenth of a milligram. Those with 0.05 mg. or greater are rounded up; those with 0.04 mg. or less are rounded down.

Cigarette varieties with assay results for "tar" or carbon monoxide below 0.5 mg. per cigarette and for nicotine below 0.05 mg. are recorded in the table as <0.5, and <0.05, respectively. The table does not differentiate, nor are actual ratings provided for these cigarettes, because the currently approved testing methodology is not sufficiently sensitive to report these components at lower levels.

Table 1 of this report displays the average "tar" and nicotine values, calculated on a sales-weighted basis, from 1968 through 1997.[10]

1 This report is the most recent in a series that the Federal Trade Commission (FTC) has prepared since 1967.

2 When the test method was adopted, the public health community believed that "[t]he preponderance of scientific evidence strongly suggests that the lower the "tar" and nicotine content of cigarette smoke, the less harmful would be the effect." U.S. Dep't of Health and Human Services, *The Health Consequences of Smoking: The Changing Cigarette* 1 (1981) (quoting 1966 Public Health Service statement).

3 *Smoking and Tobacco Control Monograph 8: Changes in Cigarette-Related Disease Risk and Their Implications for Prevention and Control*, National Institutes of Health, National Cancer Institute (1997).

4 *See* Thun, M.J., et al., "Cigarette Smoking and Changes in the Histopathology of Lung Cancer," 89 *J. of the Nat'l Cancer Inst.* 1580 (1997); Ernster, V.L., "The Epidemiology of Lung Cancer in Women," 4 *Annals of Epidemiology* 102 (1994); Levi, F.S., et al., "Lung Carcinoma Trends by Histologic Type in Vaud and Neuchatel, Switzerland, 1974-1994," 79 *Cancer* 906 (1997).

5 Among other things, HHS's review is designed to reconcile the findings of recent studies suggesting that cigarettes with lower "tar" ratings may not be less harmful with the findings of other studies suggesting that there may be some risk reduction from the use of lower "tar" cigarettes. *See* Parish, H., et al., "Cigarette smoking, tar yields, and non-fatal myocardial infarction: 14,000 cases and 32,000 controls in the UK," 311 *Brit. Med. J.*, 471 (1995); Tang, J., et al., "Mortality in relation to tar yield of cigarettes: a prospective study of four cohorts," 311 *Brit. Med. J.* 1530 (1995).

6 In early 1999, the Tobacco Institute was disbanded pursuant to the multi-state tobacco settlement. The Tobacco Institute Testing Laboratory's facilities have continued operation under the name Tobacco Industry Testing Laboratory.

7 The Commission decided in early 1987 to close its laboratory. The Commission found that closing the laboratory was necessary for several reasons: chiefly, the cost of the laboratory was significant, and the Commission would have had to commit significant additional funds to continue the program. The Commission was also persuaded that the information could be obtained from other sources, and other means were available to verify the accuracy of industry testing results.

8 On April 13, 1983, the Commission announced it had determined that its testing methodology understated the measured deliveries for Brown & Williamson's Barclay cigarettes. Therefore, Barclay cigarettes were removed from the Commission's reports for "tar," nicotine, and carbon monoxide until a new, accurate methodology could be tested and adopted. The Commission found that there was also a significant likelihood that the same problem existed with two other Brown & Williamson varieties—Kool Ultra and Kool Ultra 100's.

On July 25, 1986, the Commission informed Brown & Williamson that as a result of a review of data presented by Brown & Williamson regarding "tar" and nicotine rating for two varieties of Barclay cigarettes with a new filter, the Commission would authorize, under certain conditions, the following legends for advertising purposes:

1. For Barclay King size:
   3 mg. "tar," .2 mg. nicotine avg. per cigarette as authorized by FTC.

2. For Barclay 100's:
   5 mg. "tar," .4 mg. nicotine avg. per cigarette as authorized by FTC.

9 The Commision's 1980 announcement, 45 Fed. Reg. 46,483 (1980), adopted a new testing methodology to determine cigarettes' carbon monoxide (CO) yields, and modified the existing specifications for determining nicotine yields:

1. Determine CO concentration using a 20-port smoking machine described by H.C. Pillsbury and G. Merfeld at the 32nd Tobacco Chemists Research Conference, October 1978;

2. The concentration of CO will be reported as milligrams per cigarette;

3. The present method for "tar" and nicotine determination will be modified to use the method described in an article entitled, "Gas Chromatographic Determination of Nicotine Contained on Cambridge Filter Pads," by John R. Wagner, et al., as presented at the annual meeting of the Association of Official Analytical Chemists, October 1978.

10 Several issues should be noted with regard to the collection and tabulation of the data in Table 1. First, the underlying "tar" and nicotine ratings were obtained using smoking machine parameters (puff frequency, puff volume, etc.) that have not changed since they were first adopted in 1967. Although this consistency allows for comparison of the data over time, it also means that the test has not been modified to reflect possible changes in the way people smoke. For example, research indicates that smokers of lower rated cigarettes may tend to smoke them more intensively than they smoke cigarettes with higher ratings. Thus, while Table 1 suggests a decline in average "tar" and nicotine yields of cigarettes, this might not correspond to a similar reduction in "tar" and nicotine ingestion by smokers.

Second, the source of the data in Table 1 has changed over time. From 1967 through 1985, the Commission's laboratory provided practically all of the "tar" and nicotine ratings reported by the Commission. As noted supra, the Commission decided in 1987 to close its cigarette testing laboratory. Since then, the TITL has continued to test most branded cigarettes; the companies report the results to the Commission pursuant to compulsory process and the Commission publishes the results. The companies test their own generic and private label cigarettes—which today represent a significant part of the overall cigarette market—brands not widely available, and new brands. While the companies are required to follow the FTC method for testing their cigarettes, staff does not directly monitor the company tests (as it does the TITL tests).

Third, although the Commission did not publish "tar" and nicotine reports during some of the years covered by Table 1, reliable data for those years are still available. Beginning with cigarettes sold in calendar year 1985, the Commission required the major cigarette companies to report annually the "tar," nicotine, and carbon monoxide ratings of all cigarettes they sold in the United States. These data were incorporated as needed into the database that was used to compute the sales-weighted "tar" and nicotine figures in Table 1.

Finally, when the FTC created its computerized database for "tar" and nicotine figures in 1982, various problems resulted in missing observations for between four and eight percent of the data for the years 1982 through 1984. Although these missing observations do not appear to generate systemic biases in the data, they suggest that the data in Table 1 may be more useful for gauging long term trends than for evaluating changes over very short time spans.

TABLE 1: SALES WEIGHTED "TAR" AND NICOTINE YIELDS (1968–1997)

Year	"Tar" (mg.)	Nicotine (mg.)
1968	21.6	1.35
1969	20.7	1.38
1970	20.0	1.31
1971	20.2	1.32
1972	19.9	1.39
1973	19.3	1.32
1974	18.4	1.24
1975	18.6	1.21
1976	18.1	1.16
1977	16.8	1.12
1978	16.1	1.11
1979	15.1	1.07
1980	14.1	1.04
1981	13.2	0.92
1982	13.5	0.89
1983	13.4	0.88
1984	13.0	0.89
1985	13.0	0.95
1986	13.4	0.93
1987	13.3	0.94
1988	13.3	0.94
1989	13.1	0.96
1990	12.5	0.93
1991	12.6	0.94
1992	12.4	0.92
1993	12.4	0.90
1994	12.1	0.90

Year	"Tar" (mg.)	Nicotine (mg.)
1995	12.0	0.87
1996	12.0	0.88
1997	12.0	0.89

TABLE 2: VARIETIES WITH THE LOWEST "TAR" YIELD

Brand Name	Description				Tar	Nic	CO
Carlton	King	F	HP	Ultra-Lt	<0.5	<0.05	<0.5
Now	King	F	HP		<0.5	<0.05	<0.5
Now	100	F	HP		<0.5	<0.05	<0.5
Carlton	King	F	SP	Lt	<0.5	.1	1
Cambridge	King	F	SP	Lowest	1	.1	1
Carlton	100	F	HP	Lt Menthol	1	.1	1
Carlton	King	F	HP		1	.1	1
Carlton	King	F	SP	Lt Menthol	1	.1	1
Carlton	100	F	HP	Lt	1	.1	1
Bristol	King	F	SP	Lowest	1	.1	2
Merit	King	F	HP	Ultima	1	.1	2
Now	King	F	SP		1	.1	2
Now	King	F	SP	Menthol	1	.1	2
Merit	King	F	SP	Ultima	1	.1	3
Carlton	100	F	SP	Lt	1	.2	2

NOTE: F—Filter, HP—Hard Pack, SP—Soft Pack, Lt—Light

TABLE 3: VARIETIES WITH THE HIGHEST "TAR" YIELD

Brand Name	Description				Tar	Nic	CO
Bristol	King	NF	SP		27	1.7	16
Commander	King	NF	SP		27	1.7	15
Basic	King	NF	SP		26	1.7	15
English Ovals	King	NF	HP		25	2.0	15
Old Gold	King	NF	SP	Straight	25	1.8	17
Pyramid	King	NF	SP	FF	25	1.5	18
Camel	Reg	NF	SP		24	1.7	16
All American Value*	King	NF	SP		24	1.6	NA
Best Buy*	King	NF	SP	Generic	24	1.6	NA

TABLE 3: VARIETIES WITH THE HIGHEST "TAR" YIELD (cont.)

Brand Name	Description				Tar	Nic	CO
Bronson*	King	NF	SP	Generic	24	1.6	NA
Genco*	King	NF	SP	Generic	24	1.6	NA
Generals*	King	NF	SP	Generic	24	1.6	NA
Gridlock*	King	NF	SP	Generic	24	1.6	NA
Premium Buy*	King	NF	SP	Generic	24	1.6	NA
Shenandoah*	King	NF	SP	Generic	24	1.6	NA
Shield*	King	NF	SP	Generic	24	1.6	NA
Top Choice*	King	NF	SP	Generic	24	1.6	NA
Lucky Strike	Reg	NF	SP		24	1.5	17
Chesterfield	King	NF	SP	FF	24	1.4	17
Tareyton	King	NF	SP		24	1.4	16

NOTE: NF—Non-Filter, HP—Hard Pack, SP—Soft Pack, FF—Full Flavor

* indicates brand tested by the manufacturer rather than by TITL.

"TAR," NICOTINE & CARBON MONOXIDE REPORT

Brand Name	Description				Tar	Nic	CO
All American Value*	100	F	SP	Lt	11	.8	NA
All American Value*	100	F	SP	Lt Menthol	11	.8	NA
All American Value*	100	F	SP	FF	15	1.0	NA
All American Value*	King	F	SP	Lt Menthol	11	.7	NA
All American Value*	King	F	SP	Ultra-Lt	6	.5	NA
All American Value*	100	F	SP	Ultra-Lt	6	.5	NA
All American Value*	King	F	SP	F	15	1.0	NA
All American Value*	King	NF	SP		24	1.6	NA
All American Value*	King	F	SP	Lt	11	.7	NA
Alpine	King	F	HP	Lt Menthol	9	.7	10
Alpine	100	F	SP	Lt Menthol	9	.8	11

Brand Name	Description				Tar	Nic	CO
Alpine	100	F	SP	Menthol	15	1.1	14
Alpine	King	F	HP	Menthol	16	1.0	15
Alpine	King	F	SP	Menthol	15	1.0	15
Alpine	King	F	SP	Lt Menthol	9	.7	10
American	100	F	SP	FF	15	.9	17
American	100	F	SP	Lt	9	.7	12
American	King	F	SP	Lt	10	.8	11
American*	King	F	S	FF	16	.9	16
American*	King	F	HP	FF	16	.9	NA
Austin*	100	F	SP	Lt Menthol	10	.7	12
Austin*	King	F	SP	Lt Menthol	9	.6	12
Austin*	King	F	SP	Lt	9	.6	12
Austin*	100	F	SP	FF	13	.8	17
Austin*	100	F	SP	Ultra-Lt	4	.4	7
Austin*	King	F	SP	Ultra-Lt	4	.3	6
Austin*	King	F	SP	FF	14	.8	16
Austin*	100	F	SP	Lt	9	.7	12
Austin*	King	F	SP	FF Menthol	14	.8	16
Austin*	100	F	SP	FF Menthol	14	.9	18
Austin*	King	F	HP	Lt	10	.7	13
Austin*	King	NF	SP		20	1.1	16
Austin*	King	F	HP	FF	15	.9	16
Barclay*	King	F	HP		3	.3	3
Barclay*	King	F	SP		3	.3	3
Barclay*	100	F	SP		5	.4	5
Bargain Buy*	100	F	SP	FF Menthol	14	.9	18
Bargain Buy*	King	F	SP	FF Menthol	14	.8	16
Bargain Buy*	King	NF	SP		20	1.1	16
Bargain Buy*	100	F	SP	Ultra-Lt	4	.4	7
Bargain Buy*	King	F	SP	Ultra-Lt	4	.3	6
Bargain Buy*	100	F	SP	Lt Menthol	10	.7	12
Bargain Buy*	King	F	SP	Lt Menthol	9	.6	12
Bargain Buy*	100	F	SP	Lt	9	.7	12
Bargain Buy*	King	F	SP	Lt	9	.6	12
Bargain Buy*	100	F	SP	FF	13	.8	17

"TAR," NICOTINE & CARBON MONOXIDE REPORT *(cont.)*

Brand Name	Description				Tar	Nic	CO
Bargain Buy*	King	F	SP	FF	14	.8	16
Basic	King	F	HP		16	1	16
Basic	King	F	SP		16	1	16
Basic	100	F	SP		15	1	18
Basic	100	F	SP	Lt Menthol	10	.8	14
Basic	King	F	SP	FF Menthol	15	1	16
Basic	King	NF	SP		26	1.7	15
Basic	King	F	SP	Lt	10	.7	13
Basic	King	F	SP	Lt Menthol	10	.7	13
Basic	100	F	SP	Lt	10	.8	14
Basic	King	F	HP	Lt	10	.7	13
Basic	100	F	SP	Ultra-Lt	6	.5	9
Basic	100	F	SP	FF Menthol	15	1	17
Basic	King	F	HP	Menthol	16	1	16
Basic	King	F	SP	Ultra-Lt	6	.5	8
Basic*	100	F	HP		16	1	NA
Basic*	100	F	HP	Lt	11	.8	NA
Beacon*	100	F	SP	Lt Menthol	10	.7	12
Beacon*	King	F	SP	Lt Menthol	9	.6	12
Beacon*	King	F	SP	Ultra	4	.3	6
Beacon*	100	F	SP	FF Menthol	14	.9	18
Beacon*	King	NF	SP		20	1.1	16
Beacon*	King	F	SP	FF Menthol	14	.8	16
Beacon*	King	F	SP	Lt	9	.6	12
Beacon*	100	F	SP	Lt	9	.7	12
Beacon*	King	F	SP	FF	14	.8	16
Beacon*	100	F	SP	FF	13	.8	17
Beacon*	100	F	SP	Ultra	4	.4	7
Bee	King	F	HP	Lt	10	.9	12
Bee	King	F	HP		15	1.1	14
Belair	King	F	SP	Menthol	10	.8	9
Belair	100	F	SP	Menthol	9	.8	10
Benson & Hedges	King	F	HP		16	1.1	13

Brand Name	Description				Tar	Nic	CO
Benson & Hedges	100	F	SP	Lt Menthol	10	.8	12
Benson & Hedges	100	F	HP	Ultra-Lt Dlx	6	.5	7
Benson & Hedges	100	F	SP	Lt	10	.8	12
Benson & Hedges	100	F	HP	Menthol	15	1.1	15
Benson & Hedges	100	F	HP		15	1.1	15
Benson & Hedges	100	F	SP		15	1.1	15
Benson & Hedges	100	F	HP	Lt Menthol	10	.8	10
Benson & Hedges	100	F	HP	Lt	10	.9	11
Benson & Hedges	100	F	HP	Ultra-Lt Menthol Dlx	6	.5	7
Benson & Hedges	King	F	SP	M-fi	10	.8	10
Benson & Hedges	100	F	SP	Menthol	15	1.1	15
Best Buy*	Reg	F	HP	FF Generic	15	1.0	NA
Best Buy*	100	F	SP	FF Generic	15	1.0	NA
Best Buy*	King	NF	SP	Generic	24	1.6	NA
Best Buy*	100	F	SP	Ultra-Lt Generic	6	.5	NA
Best Buy*	King	F	SP	Ultra-Lt Generic	6	.5	NA
Best Buy*	100	F	SP	Lt Generic	11	.8	NA
Best Buy*	King	F	SP	Lt Menthol Generic	11	.7	NA
Best Buy*	King	F	SP	Lt Generic	11	.7	NA
Best Buy*	100	F	SP	FF Generic	15	1.0	NA
Best Buy*	King	F	SP	FF Generic	15	1.0	NA
Best Buy*	100	F	SP	FF Menthol Generic	16	1.0	NA
Best Buy*	King	F	SP	FF Menthol Generic	16	1.0	NA

"TAR," NICOTINE &
CARBON MONOXIDE REPORT (cont.)

Brand Name	Description				Tar	Nic	CO
Best Buy*	100	F	SP	Lt Menthol Generic	11	.8	NA
Best Choice*	King	F	SP	Lt	9	.6	12
Best Choice*	King	F	SP	Lt Menthol	9	.6	12
Best Choice*	100	F	SP	FF	13	.8	17
Best Choice*	King	F	SP	FF	14	.8	16
Best Choice*	King	F	HP	Lt	10	.7	13
Best Choice*	100	F	SP	Lt Menthol	10	.7	12
Best Choice*	King	F	SP	Ultra-Lt	4	.3	6
Best Choice*	100	F	SP	Ultra-Lt	4	.4	7
Best Choice*	King	F	SP	FF Menthol	14	.8	16
Best Choice*	100	F	SP	Lt	9	.7	12
Best Choice*	King	NF	SP		20	1.1	16
Best Choice*	100	F	SP	FF Menthol	14	.9	18
Best Choice*	King	F	HP	FF	15	.9	16
Best Value	King	F	SP	Ultra-Lt	4	.3	6
Best Value	King	F	SP	FF	14	.8	16
Best Value	100	F	SP	FF	13	.8	17
Best Value	King	F	SP	Lt	9	.6	12
Best Value	100	F	SP	Lt	9	.7	12
Best Value	King	F	SP	Lt Menthol	9	.6	12
Best Value	100	F	SP	Lt Menthol	10	.7	12
Best Value	100	F	SP	FF Menthol	14	.9	18
Best Value	King	F	SP	FF Menthol	14	.8	16
Best Value	100	F	SP	Ultra-Lt	4	.4	7
Best Value	King	NF	SP		20	1.1	16
Big Money*	100	F	SP	Lt Menthol Generic	11	.8	NA
Bonus Value*	King	F	SP	FF	14	.8	16
Bonus Value*	King	F	HP	FF	15	.9	16
Bonus Value*	100	F	SP	Lt	9	.7	12
Bonus Value*	100	F	SP	FF	13	.8	17
Bonus Value*	King	F	HP	Lt	10	.7	13
Bonus Value*	100	F	SP	Lt Menthol	10	.7	12

Brand Name	Description				Tar	Nic	CO
Bonus Value*	King	F	SP	FF Menthol	14	.8	16
Bonus Value*	King	F	SP	Lt Menthol	9	.6	12
Bonus Value*	100	F	SP	FF Menthol	14	.9	18
Bonus Value*	King	F	SP	Ultra	4	.3	6
Bonus Value*	King	F	SP	Lt	9	.6	12
Bonus Value*	King	NF	SP		20	1.1	16
Bonus Value*	100	F	SP	Ultra	4	.4	7
Brandon*	100	F	SP	FF Menthol	14	.9	18
Brandon*	King	F	SP	FF Menthol	14	.8	16
Brandon*	100	F	SP	Lt Menthol	10	.7	12
Brandon*	King	F	HP	Lt	10	.7	13
Brandon*	100	F	SP	Ultra-Lt	4	.4	7
Brandon*	100	F	SP	FF	13	.8	17
Brandon*	King	F	HP	FF	15	.9	16
Brandon*	King	F	SP	Ultra-Lt	4	.3	6
Brandon*	100	F	SP	Lt	9	.7	12
Brandon*	King	F	SP	Lt	9	.6	12
Brandon*	King	F	SP	FF	14	.8	16
Brandon*	King	F	SP	Lt Menthol	9	.6	12
Brentwood*	100	F	SP	FF Menthol	14	.9	18
Brentwood*	100	F	SP	Ultra-Lt	4	.4	7
Brentwood*	100	F	SP	FF	13	.8	17
Brentwood*	King	F	SP	FF	14	.8	16
Brentwood*	King	F	SP	FF Menthol	14	.8	16
Brentwood*	100	F	SP	Lt	9	.7	12
Brentwood*	King	F	SP	Lt	9	.6	12
Brentwood*	King	F	SP	Ultra-Lt	4	.3	6
Brentwood*	King	F	SP	Lt Menthol	9	.6	12
Brentwood*	100	F	SP	Lt Menthol	10	.7	12
Bristol	100	F	SP	Lowest	2	.2	3
Bristol	King	F	SP	Lt Menthol	10	.7	12
Bristol	100	F	SP	Lt Menthol	10	.8	14
Bristol	King	F	SP		16	1.0	16
Bristol	King	F	SP	Lt	10	.7	12
Bristol	100	F	SP		15	1.0	17

"TAR," NICOTINE & CARBON MONOXIDE REPORT (cont.)

Brand Name	Description				Tar	Nic	CO
Bristol	King	NF	SP		27	1.7	16
Bristol	100	F	SP	Ultra-Lt	5	.5	8
Bristol	King	F	SP	Lowest	1	.1	2
Bristol	100	F	SP	Lt	11	.8	13
Bronson*	100	F	SP	Lt Generic	11	.7	NA
Bronson*	King	F	SP	FF Menthol Generic	16	1.0	NA
Bronson*	King	F	SP	Lt Generic	11	.7	NA
Bronson*	King	F	SP	Ultra-Lt Generic	6	.5	NA
Bronson*	100	F	SP	Lt Menthol Generic	11	.8	NA
Bronson*	100	F	SP	Ultra-Lt Generic	6	.5	NA
Bronson*	King	F	SP	Lt Menthol Generic	11	.7	NA
Bronson*	King	F	HP	Generic	14	.9	NA
Bronson*	King	NF	SP	Generic	24	1.6	NA
Bronson*	100	F	SP	FF Generic	15	1.0	NA
Bronson*	King	F	SP	FF Generic	15	1.0	NA
Bronson*	King	F	HP	Lt Generic	11	.7	NA
Bronson*	100	F	SP	FF Menthol Generic	16	1.0	NA
Bucks	King	F	SP	Lt	10	.8	12
Bucks	King	F	SP		14	1.0	13
Cambridge	King	F	SP	FF	15	1.0	16
Cambridge	100	F	SP	Lt	10	.7	14
Cambridge	King	F	SP	Lt	10	.7	13
Cambridge	King	F	SP	Lowest	1	.1	1
Cambridge	100	F	SP	FF	15	1.0	17
Cambridge	100	F	SP	Ultra-Lt	5	.5	8
Cambridge	100	F	SP	Lowest	2	.2	3
Cambridge	100	F	SP	Lt Menthol	10	.7	13
Cambridge	King	F	SP	Lt Menthol	10	.7	13
Camel	King	F	HP		17	1.1	16
Camel	100	F	HP	Lt Special	10	.9	11

Brand Name	Description				Tar	Nic	CO
Camel	King	F	SP		17	1.2	18
Camel	100	F	SP		16	1.2	17
Camel	100	F	SP	Lt	10	.8	14
Camel	Reg	NF	SP		24	1.7	16
Camel	100	F	HP		16	1.2	18
Camel	King	F	HP	Lt Special	9	.8	11
Camel	King	F	SP	Lt	11	.9	12
Camel	100	F	HP	Ultra-Lt	5	.5	7
Camel	King	F	HP	Ultra-Lt	5	.5	8
Camel	King	F	SP	Ultra-Lt	5	.4	7
Camel	King	F	HP	Lt Wides	11	.9	12
Camel	King	F	HP	Wides	17	1.2	18
Camel	King	F	HP	Lt	11	.9	12
Camel	100	F	HP	Lt	9	.8	10
Camel	King	F	SP	Lt Special	11	.9	13
Camel	King	F	HP	Lt Menthol	9	.8	12
Camel	King	F	HP	Menthol	17	1.1	17
Canadian Players*	Reg	F	HP	Lt	13	1.3	NA
Canadian Players*	Reg	F	HP	Extra-Lt	9	1.1	NA
Canadian Players*	King	F	HP	Extra-Lt	12	1.4	NA
Canadian Players*	Reg	F	HP	Lt Smooth	13	1.2	13
Canadian Players*	King	F	HP	Lt Smooth	13	1.3	16
Canadian Players*	King	F	HP	Lt	14	1.5	NA
Canadian Players*	Reg	F	HP	Medium	13	1.2	15
Canadian Players*	Reg	F	HP		15	1.5	NA
Capri	100	F	HP	Ultra-Lt	5	.5	4
Capri	100	F	HP	Lt Menthol Sup-Slim	9	.7	5
Capri	100	F	HP	Ultra-Lt Menthol	5	.5	4
Capri	100	F	HP	Sup-Slim	9	.7	6

"TAR," NICOTINE & CARBON MONOXIDE REPORT *(cont.)*

Brand Name	Description				Tar	Nic	CO
Capri	120	F	HP	Sup-Slim	13	1.0	9
Capri	120	F	HP	Menthol Sup-Slim	12	1.0	7
Cardinal*	King	NF	SP		20	1.1	16
Cardinal*	100	F	SP	Lt Menthol	10	.7	12
Cardinal*	King	F	SP	Lt	9	.6	12
Cardinal*	King	F	SP	FF	14	.8	16
Cardinal*	100	F	SP	FF	13	.8	17
Cardinal*	100	F	SP	Ultra	4	.4	7
Cardinal*	King	F	HP	FF	15	.9	16
Cardinal*	100	F	SP	FF Menthol	14	.9	18
Cardinal*	King	F	SP	FF Menthol	14	.8	16
Cardinal*	King	F	HP	Lt	10	.7	13
Cardinal*	100	F	SP	Lt	9	.7	12
Cardinal*	King	F	SP	Ultra-Lt	4	.3	6
Cardinal*	King	F	SP	Lt Menthol	9	.6	12
Carlton	100	F	SP	Lt Menthol	2	.2	2
Carlton	King	F	HP		1	.1	1
Carlton	King	F	SP	Lt Menthol	1	.1	1
Carlton	100	F	HP	Lt	1	.1	1
Carlton	100	F	HP	Lt Menthol	1	.1	1
Carlton	King	F	HP	Ultra-Lt	<0.5	<0.05	<0.5
Carlton	King	F	SP	Lt	<0.5	.1	1
Carlton	100	F	SP	Lt	1	.2	2
Carlton	120	F	SP	Lt Menthol	5	.5	4
Carlton*	King	F	HP	Menthol	5	.5	6
Carlton*	120	F	SP	Lt	4	.4	3
Cavalier*	100	F	SP	Ultra-Lt	4	.4	7
Cavalier*	King	F	SP	Ultra-Lt	4	.3	6
Cavalier*	King	F	SP	Lt Menthol	9	.6	12
Cavalier*	100	F	SP	FF	13	.8	17
Cavalier*	King	F	SP	FF Menthol	14	.8	16
Cavalier*	100	F	SP	FF Menthol	14	.9	18
Cavalier*	King	NF	SP		20	1.1	16

Brand Name	Description				Tar	Nic	CO
Cavalier*	King	F	SP	FF	14	.8	16
Cavalier*	100	F	SP	Lt Menthol	10	.7	12
Cavalier*	100	F	SP	Lt	9	.7	12
Cavalier*	King	F	SP	Lt	9	.6	12
Century	100	F	SP	25-pk	14	.9	17
Century	King	F	SP	Lt 25-pk	7	.5	12
Century	King	F	SP	25-pk	13	.7	16
Century	100	F	SP	Lt 25-pk	9	.7	12
Century	100	F	SP	Lt Menthol 25-pk	9	.6	12
Charter	100	F	SP	Ultra-Lt	4	.4	7
Charter*	King	F	SP	Ultra-Lt	4	.3	6
Charter*	King	F	SP	Lt Menthol	9	.6	12
Charter*	100	F	SP	Lt Menthol	10	.7	12
Charter*	King	F	HP	FF	15	.9	16
Charter*	King	F	SP	Lt	9	.6	12
Charter*	100	F	SP	Lt	9	.7	12
Charter*	King	F	HP	Lt	10	.7	13
Charter*	King	F	SP	FF	14	.8	16
Charter*	100	F	SP	FF	13	.8	17
Chesterfield	King	NF	SP	FF	24	1.4	17
Chesterfield	Reg	NF	SP	FF	20	1.1	14
Chesterfield*	King	F	SP	Lt	11	1.1	9
Chesterfield*	100	F	SP	Lt	11	1.1	9
Chesterfield*	King	F	SP	FF	17	1.4	2
Cimarron*	100	F	SP	Ultra	4	.4	7
Cimarron*	100	F	SP	Lt Menthol	10	.7	12
Cimarron*	King	F	SP	Lt	9	.6	12
Cimarron*	King	F	HP	Lt	10	.7	13
Cimarron*	King	F	SP	Ultra	4	.3	6
Cimarron*	King	F	HP	FF	15	.9	16
Cimarron*	100	F	SP	FF	13	.8	17
Cimarron*	King	F	SP	FF	14	.8	16
Cimarron*	100	F	SP	Lt	9	.7	12
Cimarron*	100	F	SP	FF Menthol	14	.9	18
Cimarron*	King	F	SP	Lt Menthol	9	.6	12

"TAR," NICOTINE &
CARBON MONOXIDE REPORT (cont.)

Brand Name	Description				Tar	Nic	CO
Cimarron*	King	F	SP	FF Menthol	14	.8	16
Cimarron*	King	NF	SP		20	1.1	16
Citation*	100	F	SP	Lt	9	.7	12
Citation*	100	F	SP	Ultra	4	.4	7
Citation*	King	F	SP	FF	14	.8	16
Citation*	King	F	SP	Ultra	4	.3	6
Citation*	100	F	SP	Lt Menthol	10	.7	12
Citation*	King	F	SP	FF Menthol	14	.8	16
Citation*	King	NF	SP		20	1.1	16
Citation*	King	F	SP	Lt	9	.6	12
Citation*	100	F	SP	FF Menthol	14	.9	18
Citation*	King	F	SP	Lt Menthol	9	.6	12
Citation*	100	F	SP	FF	13	.8	17
City	100	F	HP		16	1.3	15
City	100	F	HP	Lt	10	.9	12
Class A*	King	F	SP	Lt	10	.6	14
Class A Dlx*	100	F	SP	Lt Menthol	10	.6	15
Class A Dlx*	100	F	SP	Ultra-Lt	6	.4	8
Class A*	King	F	SP	Ultra-Lt	6	.4	6
Class A*	King	F	SP	Lt Menthol	10	.6	14
Class A*	100	F	SP	FF Menthol	15	.8	20
Class A*	100	F	SP	Lt	10	.6	15
Class A*	100	F	SP	Lt Menthol	10	.6	15
Class A*	100	F	SP	Ultra-Lt	6	.4	8
Class A*	100	F	SP	Ultra-Lt Menthol	6	.4	8
Class A Dlx*	100	F	SP	FF	15	.8	20
Class A Dlx*	100	F	SP	Lt	10	.6	15
Class A*	King	NF	SP	FF	23	1.4	15
Class A*	100	F	SP	FF	15	.8	20
Class A Dlx*	King	F	SP	FF	14	.7	18
Class A Dlx*	King	F	SP	FF Menthol	14	.7	18
Class A Dlx*	King	F	SP	Lt	10	.6	14
Class A Dlx*	King	F	SP	Lt Menthol	10	.6	14

Brand Name	Description				Tar	Nic	CO
Class A Dlx*	King	F	SP	Ultra-Lt	6	.4	6
Class A Dlx*	King	NF	SP	FF	23	1.4	15
Class A*	King	F	SP	FF	14	.7	18
Class A*	King	F	SP	FF Menthol	14	.7	18
Commander	King	NF	SP		27	1.7	15
Commander	Reg	NF	SP		22	1.4	13
Courier*	King	F	SP	Lt	9	.6	12
Courier*	100	F	SP	Lt	9	.7	12
Courier*	King	F	SP	Lt Menthol	9	.6	12
Courier*	100	F	SP	Lt Menthol	10	.7	12
Courier*	King	F	SP	Ultra-Lt	4	.3	6
Courier*	100	F	SP	Ultra-Lt	4	.4	7
Courier*	King	F	HP	FF	15	.9	16
Courier*	King	F	SP	FF	14	.8	16
Courier*	100	F	SP	FF	13	.8	17
Courier*	King	F	HP	Lt	10	.7	13
Covington*	100	F	SP	Ultra-Lt	6	.4	8
Covington*	King	F	SP	Lt	10	.6	14
Covington*	King	F	SP	FF Menthol	14	.7	18
Covington*	100	F	SP	Lt	10	.6	5
Covington*	100	F	SP	Lt Menthol	10	.6	15
Covington*	100	F	SP	FF	15	.8	20
Covington*	King	F	SP	FF	14	.7	18
Daves	King	F	HP	Lt	10	.7	13
Daves	King	F	HP		16	1.0	17
Director's Choice*	King	NF	SP		20	1.1	16
Director's Choice*	King	F	SP	Lt	9	.6	12
Director's Choice*	100	F	SP	Lt	9	.7	12
Director's Choice*	King	F	SP	Lt Menthol	9	.6	12
Director's Choice*	100	F	SP	FF	13	.8	17
Director's Choice*	King	F	HP	Lt	10	.7	13

"TAR," NICOTINE &
CARBON MONOXIDE REPORT *(cont.)*

Brand Name	Description				Tar	Nic	CO
Director's Choice*	King	F	SP	FF Menthol	14	.8	16
Director's Choice*	King	F	HP	FF	15	.9	16
Director's Choice*	King	F	SP	FF	14	.8	16
Director's Choice*	100	F	SP	FF Menthol	14	.9	18
Director's Choice*	100	F	SP	Lt Menthol	10	.7	12
Director's Choice*	King	F	SP	Ultra-Lt	4	.3	6
Director's Choice*	100	F	SP	Ultra-Lt	4	.4	7
Doral	King	F	SP	FF Menthol	13	.8	15
Doral	100	F	SP	FF	12	.8	16
Doral	King	F	HP	Lt	8	.5	12
Doral	King	F	HP	FF	13	.8	15
Doral	100	F	SP	Ultra-Lt	4	.4	8
Doral	King	F	SP	Ultra-Lt	4	.3	6
Doral	King	NF	SP		19	1.0	16
Doral	100	F	SP	FF Menthol	13	.8	16
Doral	100	F	HP	Lt	12	.8	14
Doral	King	F	SP	FF	13	.8	15
Doral	100	F	HP	FF	13	.8	16
Doral	King	F	SP	Lt	8	.6	12
Doral	King	F	SP	Lt Menthol	8	.6	12
Doral	100	F	SP	Lt Menthol	10	.7	14
Doral	100	F	SP	Lt	10	.7	14
Doral	King	F	HP	FF Menthol	13	.9	15
Eclipse*	King	F	HP	Mild	2	.1	7
Eclipse*	King	F	HP		3	.1	8
Eclipse*	King	F	HP	Menthol	3	.1	9
Eclipse*	King	F	HP	Mild Menthol	2	.1	7
English Ovals	King	NF	HP		25	2.0	15
Eve	120	F	HP	Ultra-Lt	5	.5	5

Brand Name	Description				Tar	Nic	CO
Eve	120	F	HP	Lt Menthol	11	.8	11
Eve	120	F	HP	Lt Menthol	11	.8	11
Eve	120	F	HP	Lt	11	.9	12
Eve	120	F	HP	Lt	11	.9	12
Eve	120	F	HP	Ultra-Lt Menthol	5	.4	5
Eve*	100	F	HP	Lt Slim	5	.5	4
Eve*	100	F	HP	Ultra-Lt Menthol Slim	6	.6	4
Extra Value*	King	F	SP	FF Menthol	14	.8	16
Extra Value*	100	F	SP	Ultra-Lt	4	.4	7
Extra Value*	King	F	SP	Ultra-Lt	4	.3	6
Extra Value*	King	F	SP	Lt	9	.6	12
Extra Value*	100	F	SP	Lt	9	.7	12
Extra Value*	King	NF	SP		20	1.1	16
Extra Value*	100	F	SP	FF	13	.8	17
Extra Value*	King	F	SP	Lt Menthol	9	.6	12
Extra Value*	100	F	SP	FF Menthol	14	.9	18
Extra Value*	100	F	SP	Lt Menthol	10	.7	12
Extra Value*	King	F	SP	FF	14	.8	16
F&L*	100	F	SP	Lt Menthol Generic	11	.8	NA
F&L*	100	F	SP	FF Generic	15	1.0	NA
F&L*	100	F	SP	Ultra-Lt Generic	6	.5	NA
F&L*	100	F	SP	FF Menthol Generic	16	1.0	NA
F&L*	King	F	HP	Lt Generic	11	.8	NA
F&L*	100	F	SP	Lt Generic	11	.8	NA
F&L*	King	F	SP	Ultra-Lt Generic	6	.5	NA
F&L*	King	F	SP	FF Menthol Generic	16	1.0	NA
F&L*	King	F	SP	Lt Generic	11	.7	NA
F&L*	King	F	SP	FF Generic	15	1.0	NA
First Choice*	King	F	SP	FF	14	.8	16
First Choice*	100	F	SP	Lt	9	.7	12

"TAR," NICOTINE &
CARBON MONOXIDE REPORT *(cont.)*

Brand Name	Description				Tar	Nic	CO
First Choice*	100	F	SP	Ultra	4	.4	7
First Choice*	King	F	SP	Lt	9	.6	12
First Choice*	100	F	SP	Lt Menthol	10	.7	12
First Choice*	King	NF	SP		20	1.1	16
First Choice*	King	F	SP	Lt Menthol	9	.6	12
First Choice*	100	F	SP	FF	13	.8	17
First Choice*	King	F	SP	Ultra-Lt	4	.3	6
Focus*	King	F	HP	FF	15	.9	16
Focus*	King	F	SP	Lt Menthol	9	.6	12
Focus*	King	F	SP	Ultra-Lt	4	.3	6
Focus*	100	F	SP	FF Menthol	14	.9	18
Focus*	King	F	HP	Lt	10	.7	13
Focus*	100	F	SP	Lt Menthol	10	.7	12
Focus*	King	F	SP	Lt	9	.6	12
Focus*	100	F	SP	Ultra-Lt	4	.4	7
Focus*	King	NF	SP		20	1.1	16
Focus*	King	F	SP	FF	14	.8	16
Focus*	100	F	SP	Lt	9	.7	12
Focus*	100	F	SP	FF	13	.8	17
Focus*	King	F	SP	FF Menthol	14	.8	16
Gen/Private Label*	King	F	SP	Lt	10	.6	14
Gen/Private Label*	100	F	HP	Lt Menthol	10	.6	15
Gen/Private Label*	King	NF	SP	FF	23	1.4	15
Gen/Private Label*	King	F	SP	Lt Menthol	10	.6	14
Gen/Private Label*	King	F	SP	Ultra-Lt	6	.4	6
Gen/Private Label*	100	F	HP	Lt	10	.6	15
Gen/Private Label*	100	F	HP	Ultra-Lt	6	.4	8
Gen/Private Label*	100	F	SP	FF	15	.8	20

Brand Name	Description				Tar	Nic	CO
Gen/Private Label*	100	F	SP	FF Menthol	15	.8	20
Gen/Private Label*	100	F	SP	Lt	10	.6	15
Gen/Private Label*	100	F	SP	Lt Menthol	10	.6	15
Gen/Private Label*	100	F	SP	Ultra-Lt	6	.4	8
Gen/Private Label*	King	F	HP	FF	14	.7	18
Gen/Private Label*	King	F	HP	Lt	10	.6	14
Gen/Private Label*	King	F	SP	FF	14	.7	18
Gen/Private Label*	King	F	SP	FF Menthol	14	.7	18
Genco*	King	F	SP	Generic	15	1.0	NA
Genco*	King	NF	SP	Generic	24	1.6	NA
Genco*	King	F	SP	FF Menthol Generic	16	1.0	NA
Genco*	100	F	SP	Generic	15	1.0	NA
Genco*	King	F	SP	Lt Menthol Generic	11	.7	NA
Genco*	100	F	SP	FF Menthol Generic	16	1.0	NA
Genco*	100	F	SP	Lt Menthol Generic	11	.8	NA
Genco*	100	F	SP	Ultra-Lt Generic	6	.5	NA
Genco*	100	F	SP	Lt Generic	11	.8	NA
Genco*	King	F	SP	Lt Generic	11	.7	NA
Genco*	King	F	SP	Ultra-Lt Generic	6	.5	NA
Generals*	100	F	SP	FF Menthol Generic	16	1.0	NA
Generals*	100	F	SP	Lt Menthol Generic	11	.8	NA
Generals*	King	F	SP	Lt Menthol Generic	11	.7	NA
Generals*	King	F	SP	FF Menthol Generic	16	1.0	NA

"TAR," NICOTINE & CARBON MONOXIDE REPORT (cont.)

Brand Name	Description				Tar	Nic	CO
Generals*	100	F	SP	Lt Generic	11	.8	NA
Generals*	King	F	SP	FF Generic	15	1.0	NA
Generals*	100	F	SP	FF Generic	15	1.0	NA
Generals*	King	F	SP	Lt Generic	11	.7	NA
Generals*	100	F	SP	Ultra-Lt Generic	6	.5	NA
Generals*	King	F	SP	Ultra-Lt Generic	6	.5	NA
Generals*	King	NF	SP	Generic	24	1.6	NA
Gold Coast*	King	F	SP	Lt Menthol	9	.6	12
Gold Coast*	King	F	SP	FF	14	.8	16
Gold Coast*	100	F	SP	Lt	9	.7	12
Gold Coast*	100	F	SP	FF	13	.8	17
Gold Coast*	King	F	SP	Lt	9	.6	12
Gold Coast*	100	F	SP	Ultra-Lt	4	.4	7
Gold Coast*	100	F	SP	Lt Menthol	10	.7	12
Gold Coast*	King	F	SP	Ultra-Lt	4	.3	6
GPC	King	NF	SP		22	1.2	14
GPC	100	F	SP	Ultra-Lt	5	.4	6
GPC	100	F	SP	Lt	10	.7	12
GPC	King	F	HP	FF	15	.9	15
GPC	King	F	SP	Ultra-Lt	5	.4	7
GPC	King	F	SP	FF	15	.9	15
GPC	100	F	HP	Lt	9	.7	12
GPC	100	F	SP	FF Menthol	13	.9	14
GPC	King	F	SP	FF Menthol	14	.9	13
GPC	100	F	SP	FF	15	.9	16
GPC	King	F	SP	Lt	9	.6	11
GPC	100	F	SP	Ultra-Lt Menthol	5	.4	5
GPC	100	F	SP	Lt Menthol	8	.7	8
GPC	100	F	HP	FF	15	.9	16
GPC	King	F	HP	Lt	9	.6	11
GPC	King	F	SP	Ultra-Lt Menthol	5	.4	6

Brand Name	Description				Tar	Nic	CO
GPC	King	F	SP	Lt Menthol	9	.7	9
GPC*	King	F	HP		11	.6	11
GPC*	100	F	HP		12	.7	13
GPC*	100	F	SP	Ultra-Lt	6	.5	NA
Gridlock*	King	NF	SP	Generic	24	1.6	NA
Gridlock*	100	F	SP	FF Generic	15	1.0	NA
Gridlock*	King	F	SP	FF Generic	15	1.0	NA
Gridlock*	100	F	SP	Lt Generic	11	.8	NA
Gridlock*	100	F	SP	Ultra-Lt Generic	6	.5	NA
Highway*	100	F	SP	FF Menthol	14	.9	18
Highway*	King	F	SP	Lt Menthol	9	.6	12
Highway*	100	F	SP	Lt	9	.7	12
Highway*	100	F	SP	Ultra-Lt	4	.4	7
Highway*	King	F	SP	Ultra-Lt	4	.3	6
Highway*	100	F	SP	Lt Menthol	10	.7	12
Highway*	King	F	SP	FF Menthol	14	.8	16
Highway*	King	NF	SP		20	1.1	16
Highway*	King	F	SP	FF	14	.8	16
Highway*	100	F	SP	FF	13	.8	17
Highway*	King	F	SP	Lt	9	.6	12
Hogshead	King	F	HP	FF Wides	17	1.2	19
Horizon	100	F	SP	Lt	11	.9	12
Horizon	100	F	SP	Lt Menthol	11	1.0	11
House Blend*	King	F	HP		15	1.2	14
House Blend*	King	F	HP		11	.8	12
Icebox	King	F	HP	Lt Menthol	11	.9	12
Icebox	King	F	HP	FF Menthol	18	1.3	16
Jacks*	King	F	SP	Lt	9	.6	12
Jacks*	King	F	SP	Lt Menthol	9	.6	12
Jacks*	100	F	SP	Lt	9	.7	12
Jacks*	100	F	SP	FF	13	.8	17
Jacks*	King	F	SP	Ultra-Lt	4	.3	6
Jacks*	100	F	SP	Ultra-Lt	4	.4	7
Jacks*	King	NF	SP		20	1.1	16
Jacks*	King	F	HP	Lt	10	.7	13

"TAR," NICOTINE &
CARBON MONOXIDE REPORT *(cont.)*

Brand Name	Description				Tar	Nic	CO
Jacks*	King	F	SP	FF Menthol	14	.8	16
Jacks*	King	F	SP	FF	14	.8	16
Jacks*	100	F	SP	Lt Menthol	10	.7	12
Jacks*	King	F	HP	FF	15	.9	16
Jacks*	100	F	SP	FF Menthol	14	.9	18
Jasmine*	100	F	HP	Lt Slim	7	.5	8
Jumbos	King	F	HP	Lt	11	.9	12
Jumbos	King	F	HP		16	1.2	18
Kamel	King	F	HP	Red	15	1.2	16
Kamel	King	F	HP	Lt Menthol	12	1.0	12
Kamel	King	F	HP	Menthol	17	1.2	16
Kamel	King	F	HP	Lt Red	10	.8	12
Kent	King	F	HP		11	.8	12
Kent	100	F	SP		13	1.0	13
Kent Golden Lights	100	F	SP	Lt Menthol	9	.8	11
Kent Golden Lights	King	F	SP	Lt	8	.7	10
Kent	King	F	SP		12	.9	12
Kent Golden Lights	King	F	SP	Lt Menthol	8	.7	10
Kent Golden Lights	100	F	SP	Lt	9	.8	10
Kent Golden Lights	100	F	HP	Lt	9	.8	11
Kent Golden Lights	King	F	HP	Lt	7	.6	9
Kent III	King	F	SP	Ultra-Lt	3	.4	4
Kent III	100	F	HP	Ultra-Lt	5	.5	6
Kent III	100	F	SP	Ultra-Lt	5	.5	7
Kool	King	F	HP	Menthol	16	1.2	14
Kool	King	F	SP	Mild Menthol	11	1.0	11
Kool	100	F	SP	Mild Menthol	10	.9	11
Kool	King	F	SP	Lt Menthol	7	.7	8
Kool	King	F	HP	Menthol	16	1.2	14
Kool	King	F	HP	Menthol	16	1.2	14

Brand Name	Description				Tar	Nic	CO
Kool	100	F	HP	FF Menthol	15	1.2	15
Kool	100	F	SP	Lt Menthol	8	.7	9
Kool	100	F	SP	Super Menthol Long	16	1.2	15
Kool	Reg	NF	SP	Menthol	19	1.2	12
Kool	King	F	HP	Mild Menthol	11	.9	10
Kool	King	F	SP	Menthol	16	1.2	14
Kool*	King	F	SP	Ultra Menthol	6	.5	7
Kool*	100	F	SP	Ultra Menthol	6	.5	7
Kool*	100	F	HP	Mild Menthol	12	.9	12
L & M*	100	F	SP	Lt 30-pack	7	.6	17
L & M	100	F	SP	FF Super	10	.7	15
L & M	100	F	SP	Lt Long	7	.6	8
L & M*	King	F	SP	FF 6-pack Ctn	14	.9	17
L & M	King	F	HP	FF	13	.8	16
L & M	King	F	SP	FF	14	.8	17
Lark	100	F	SP	FF Long	15	1.1	17
Lark	100	F	SP	Lt	12	.9	12
Lark	King	F	SP	FF	14	1.0	16
Lark	King	F	SP	Lt	11	.8	11
Legend*	King	F	SP	Ultra-Lt	4	.3	6
Legend*	100	F	SP	Ultra-Lt	4	.4	7
Legend*	King	NF	SP		20	1.1	16
Legend*	100	F	SP	Lt Menthol	10	.7	12
Legend*	100	F	SP	FF	13	.8	17
Legend*	100	F	SP	Lt	9	.7	12
Legend*	King	F	SP	Lt Menthol	9	.6	12
Legend*	King	F	SP	Lt	9	.6	12
Legend*	100	F	SP	FF Menthol	14	.9	18
Legend*	King	F	SP	FF	14	.8	16
Legend*	King	F	SP	FF Menthol	14	.8	16
Lucky Strike	Reg	NF	SP		24	1.5	17
Lucky Strike*	King	F	SP		12	1.0	
Lucky Strike*	100	F	HP		11	.8	11
Lucky Strike*	King	F	HP		6	.5	5
Lucky Strike*	King	F	HP	Lt	11	.8	11

"TAR," NICOTINE &
CARBON MONOXIDE REPORT (cont.)

Brand Name	Description				Tar	Nic	CO
Lucky Strike*	King	F	SP	FF	15	1.1	14
Magna	King	F	HP		15	.9	17
Magna	King	F	SP	Lt	9	.7	12
Magna	King	F	SP		15	.8	16
Magna	King	F	HP	Lt	10	.6	13
Manchester*	King	F	SP	Lt	9	.6	12
Manchester*	100	F	SP	FF Menthol	14	.9	18
Manchester*	100	F	SP	Lt Menthol	10	.7	12
Manchester*	King	F	SP	FF Menthol	14	.8	16
Manchester*	King	F	SP	Ultra-Lt	4	.3	6
Manchester*	100	F	SP	FF	13	.8	17
Manchester*	King	F	SP	FF	14	.8	16
Manchester*	King	F	SP	Lt Menthol	9	.6	12
Marker*	100	F	SP	Ultra-Lt	4	.4	7
Marker*	King	F	SP	FF	14	.8	16
Marker*	100	F	SP	FF Menthol	14	.9	18
Marker*	King	NF	SP		20	1.1	16
Marker*	King	F	SP	Ultra-Lt	4	.3	6
Marker*	100	F	SP	Lt Menthol	10	.7	12
Marker*	100	F	SP	Lt	9	.7	12
Marker*	King	F	SP	Lt	9	.6	12
Marker*	King	F	SP	Lt Menthol	9	.6	12
Marker*	100	F	SP	FF	13	.8	17
Marker*	King	F	SP	FF Menthol	14	.8	16
Marlboro	King	F	SP	Medium	11	0.9	12
Marlboro	King	F	HP		16	1.1	14
Marlboro	King	F	SP		16	1.1	15
Marlboro	King	F	SP		15	1.1	14
Marlboro	King	F	SP	Menthol	16	1.1	15
Marlboro	100	F	SP	Gold	15	1.2	15
Marlboro	100	F	HP	Gold	15	1.1	15
Marlboro	100	F	HP	Medium	13	1.0	13
Marlboro	King	F	SP	Lt	10	.8	12
Marlboro	100	F	HP	Red	15	1.1	14

Brand Name	Description				Tar	Nic	CO
Marlboro	King	F	SP	Lt Menthol	9	.8	10
Marlboro	100	F	SP	Lt	10	.8	12
Marlboro	100	F	HP	Lt	10	.8	12
Marlboro	100	F	HP	Lt Menthol	9	.7	11
Marlboro	King	F	HP	Lt Menthol	9	.8	9
Marlboro	King	F	HP	Ultra-Lt	5	.4	7
Marlboro	100	F	HP	Ultra-Lt	6	.5	8
Marlboro	King	F	HP	Menthol	16	1.1	14
Marlboro	King	F	HP	Medium	11	0.9	12
Marlboro	King	F	HP	Lt	11	.8	12
Marlboro	100	F	SP	Red	15	1.2	14
Marlboro	King	F	SP	Lt	10	0.8	12
Marlboro	100	F	SP	Medium	12	0.9	13
Maverick	King	F	HP	Lt	10	0.8	9
Maverick	King	F	HP		13	0.9	14
Maverick	100	F	SP		14	1.1	15
Maverick	King	F	SP	Lt	8	0.6	9
Maverick	King	F	SP		14	1.0	14
Maverick	100	F	SP	Lt	9	0.7	11
Maverick*	100	F	HP	Menthol Special	19	1.3	19
Maverick*	King	F	HP	Menthol Special	15	1.1	16
Maverick*	King	F	HP	Lt Menthol Special	10	0.7	12
Maverick*	100	F	HP	Lt Menthol Special	8	0.7	12
Max	120	F	SP	Menthol	16	1.3	16
Max	120	F	SP		16	1.3	17
Medley*	King	F	SP	Lt Menthol	12	.8	NA
Merit	King	F	HP	Ultima	1	.1	2
Merit	100	F	SP	Ultra-Lt	6	.6	8
Merit	100	F	HP	Ultima	2	.2	4
Merit	100	F	SP	Ultima	2	.2	5
Merit	King	F	SP		7	.6	9
Merit	King	F	SP	Ultima	1	.1	3
Merit	100	F	SP		9	.8	11

"TAR," NICOTINE &
CARBON MONOXIDE REPORT *(cont.)*

Brand Name	Description				Tar	Nic	CO
Merit	100	F	SP	Menthol	9	.7	10
Merit	King	F	SP	Ultra-Lt	5	.5	7
Merit	King	F	SP	Menthol	7	.6	9
Merit	100	F	SP	Ultra-Lt Menthol	5	.5	7
Merit	King	F	HP	Ultra-Lt	5	.5	7
Merit	100	F	HP	Ultra-Lt	6	.5	7
Merit	King	F	SP	Ultra-Lt Menthol	4	.4	6
Merit	King	F	HP		7	.6	9
Metro	100	F	HP	Lt Slims	9	.8	9
Metro	100	F	HP	Lt Slims	9	.9	9
Misty Slims	100	F	HP	Ultra-Lt Slim	5	.5	5
Misty Slims	100	F	HP	Ultra-Lt Menthol Slim	5	.5	5
Misty Slims	100	F	HP	FF Slim	14	1.0	13
Misty Slims	120	F	HP	Lt Menthol Slim	11	.9	9
Misty Slims	100	F	HP	Lt Menthol Slim	7	.6	7
Misty Slims	100	F	HP	Lt Slim	7	.6	8
Misty Slims	120	F	HP	Lt Slim	11	.9	10
Misty Slims	100	F	HP	FF Menthol	13	1.0	13
Misty Slims	100	F	HP	Ultra-Lt Menthol Slim	5	.5	NA
Monaco*	100	F	SP	Lt	9	.7	12
Monaco*	King	F	SP	FF	14	.8	16
Monaco*	King	F	SP	Lt	9	.6	12
Monaco*	100	F	SP	FF Menthol	14	.9	18
Monaco*	King	F	SP	FF Menthol	14	.8	16
Monaco*	100	F	SP	Lt Menthol	10	.7	12
Monaco*	King	F	SP	Lt Menthol	9	.6	12
Monaco*	King	NF	SP		20	1.1	16
Monaco*	King	F	SP	Ultra-Lt	4	.3	6
Monaco*	100	F	SP	Ultra-Lt	4	.4	7

Brand Name	Description				Tar	Nic	CO
Monaco*	100	F	SP	FF	13	.8	17
Monarch	King	F	SP	FF	14	.8	16
Monarch	100	F	SP	FF	13	.8	17
Monarch	King	F	HP	Lt	10	.7	13
Monarch	King	F	HP	Lt Menthol	9	.7	12
Monarch	100	F	SP	Lt	9	.7	11
Monarch	King	F	HP	FF	15	.9	16
Monarch	King	F	HP	Menthol	14	.8	16
Monarch	King	F	SP	Lt Menthol	9	.6	12
Monarch	100	F	SP	Lt Menthol	10	.7	12
Monarch	100	F	SP	Ultra-Lt	4	.4	8
Monarch	King	F	SP	Ultra-Lt	4	.3	6
Monarch	King	F	SP	Menthol	14	.8	17
Monarch	100	F	SP	Menthol	14	.8	18
Monarch	King	NF	SP		20	1.0	17
Monarch	King	F	SP	Lt	9	.6	12
Money*	King	F	SP	Lt Menthol Generic	11	.7	NA
More	120	F	SP		14	1.2	21
More	100	F	HP	Lt	10	.9	10
More	120	F	SP	Lt	10	.8	16
More	100	F	HP	Lt Menthol	9	.8	9
More	120	F	SP	Menthol	14	1.2	20
More	120	F	SP	Wht-Lt	12	1.0	16
More	120	F	SP	Lt Menthol	10	.9	16
More	120	F	SP	Wht-Lt Menthol	12	1.1	15
Mustang*	King	F	SP	FF	14	.8	16
Mustang*	100	F	SP	Lt	9	.7	12
Mustang*	King	F	SP	Lt	9	.6	12
Mustang*	100	F	SP	FF Menthol	14	.9	18
Mustang*	100	F	SP	Lt Menthol	10	.7	12
Mustang*	King	F	SP	Ultra-Lt	4	.3	6
Mustang*	King	F	SP	FF Menthol	14	.8	16
Mustang*	100	F	SP	FF	13	.8	17
Mustang*	King	F	HP	FF	15	.9	16

"TAR," NICOTINE & CARBON MONOXIDE REPORT *(cont.)*

Brand Name	Description				Tar	Nic	CO
Mustang*	King	F	HP	Lt	10	.7	13
Mustang*	100	F	SP	Ultra-Lt	4	.4	7
Mustang*	King	F	SP	Lt Menthol	9	.6	12
Newport Stripes	100	F	HP	Lt	12	.9	14
Newport	100	F	SP	Menthol 10-pk	18	1.3	17
Newport	100	F	SP	Menthol 25-pk	18	1.4	18
Newport	King	F	SP	Menthol 25-pk	17	1.3	16
Newport	100	F	SP	Menthol	18	1.4	18
Newport	King	F	SP	Menthol	17	1.2	17
Newport	King	F	SP	Menthol 10-pk	17	1.2	16
Newport	100	F	HP	Menthol	18	1.4	18
Newport Ice	King	F	HP	Lt Menthol	9	.7	13
Newport Ice	King	F	SP	Menthol	16	1.1	17
Newport Ice	100	F	SP	Menthol	18	1.3	19
Newport Lights	100	F	SP	Lt Menthol	9	.8	11
Newport Lights	100	F	HP	Lt Menthol	10	.8	11
Newport Lights	King	F	SP	Lt Menthol	8	.7	11
Newport Lights	King	F	HP	Lt Menthol	8	.7	11
Newport Slim	100	F	HP	Slim-Lt Menthol 10s	9	.8	10
Newport	King	F	HP	Menthol	16	1.1	15
Newport Stripes	100	F	HP	Lt Menthol	11	.9	14
No Frills*	100	F	SP	Lt Generic	11	.8	NA
No Frills*	100	F	SP	Ultra-Lt Generic	6	.5	NA
No Frills*	100	F	SP	FF Generic	15	1.0	NA
No Frills*	King	F	SP	Ultra-Lt Generic	6	.5	NA

Brand Name	Description				Tar	Nic	CO
No Frills*	King	F	SP	Lt Menthol Generic	11	.7	NA
No Frills*	King	F	SP	Lt Generic	11	.7	NA
North Star	King	F	HP		15	1.2	16
North Star	King	F	HP	Lt	9	.8	10
Now	100	F	SP		2	.2	3
Now	100	F	HP		<0.5	<0.05	<0.5
Now	King	F	SP	Menthol	1	.1	2
Now	King	F	HP		<0.5	<0.05	<0.5
Now	King	F	SP		1	.1	2
Now	100	F	SP	Menthol	2	.2	3
Old Gold	King	NF	SP	Straight	25	1.8	17
Old Gold	King	F	SP	Lt	8	.8	10
Old Gold*	100	F	SP	Lt Menthol	9	0.7	10
Old Gold*	100	F	SP	Lt	4	0.5	5
Old Gold	King	F	HP		14	1.0	15
Old Gold	100	F	HP		15	1.1	18
Old Gold	King	F	SP		15	1.1	16
Old Gold	100	F	SP	Lt	12	.9	14
Old Gold	100	F	SP		14	1.1	18
Old Gold	King	F	HP	Lt	7	.7	10
Pace*	100	F	SP	Lt	9	.7	12
Pace*	King	F	SP	Lt Menthol	9	.6	12
Pace*	100	F	SP	Ultra-Lt	4	.4	7
Pace*	King	F	SP	Ultra-Lt	4	.3	6
Pace*	King	F	SP	FF	14	.8	16
Pace*	100	F	SP	Lt Menthol	10	.7	12
Pace*	100	F	SP		13	.8	17
Pace*	King	F	SP	Lt	9	.6	12
Pall Mall*	Reg	NF	SP		23	1.5	15
Pall Mall	King	F	SP	Red	14	1.1	13
Pall Mall*	100	F	SP	FF	16	1.1	15
Pall Mall	King	NF	SP		23	1.5	15
Pall Mall	100	F	SP	Lt	11	.9	11
Pall Mall	100	F	SP	FF Gold	15	1.1	14
Pall Mall	100	F	SP	FF Red	15	1.1	15

"TAR," NICOTINE & CARBON MONOXIDE REPORT *(cont.)*

Brand Name	Description				Tar	Nic	CO
Parliament	King	F	HP	Lt	9	.7	10
Parliament	100	F	SP	Lt	12	1.0	13
Parliament	100	F	HP	Lt Menthol	11	.9	13
Parliament	King	F	SP	Lt	9	.7	10
Parliament	King	F	HP	Lt Menthol	10	.7	11
Picayune	Reg	NF	SP	FF	18	1.2	15
Pilot*	King	F	SP	Ultra-Lt	4	.3	6
Pilot*	100	F	SP	Ultra-Lt	4	.4	7
Pilot*	100	F	SP	Lt Menthol	10	.7	12
Pilot*	King	F	HP	Lt	10	.7	13
Pilot*	King	F	SP	Lt Menthol	9	.6	12
Pilot*	100	F	SP	FF	13	.8	17
Pilot*	King	NF	SP		20	1.1	16
Pilot*	100	F	SP	Lt	9	.7	12
Pilot*	King	F	SP	Lt	9	.6	12
Pilot*	King	F	HP	FF	15	.9	16
Pilot*	King	F	SP	FF Menthol	14	.8	16
Pilot*	100	F	SP	FF Menthol	14	.9	18
Pilot*	King	F	SP	FF	14	.8	16
Planet	King	F	HP	Lt Menthol	11	.9	12
Planet	King	F	HP	Menthol	15	1.1	14
Planet	King	F	HP		15	1.1	13
Planet	King	F	HP	Lt	10	.8	12
Players	Reg	NF	HP		23	1.6	13
Players	King	F	HP	Menthol	11	.8	11
Players	100	F	HP		13	1.0	13
Players	King	F	HP		11	.9	11
Players	King	F	HP	Lt	9	.7	10
Players	King	F	HP		15	1.1	15
Players	King	F	SP	Lt	10	.7	12
Players	King	F	SP	Lt Menthol	10	.7	12
Players	100	F	SP	Lt	10	.8	13
Players	100	F	SP	Lt Menthol	10	.8	13
Players	100	F	HP	Menthol	13	1.0	14

Brand Name	Description				Tar	Nic	CO
PM International	100	F	HP	Intl	14	1.1	14
PM International	100	F	HP	Menthol Intl	14	1.1	14
Politix	King	F	HP		16	1.2	17
Politix	King	F	HP	Lt	10	.8	11
Premium Buy*	King	F	SP	Ultra-Lt Generic	6	.5	NA
Premium Buy*	100	F	SP	Ultra-Lt Generic	6	.5	NA
Premium Buy*	100	F	SP	Lt Generic	11	.8	NA
Premium Buy*	King	F	SP	FF Generic	15	1.0	NA
Premium Buy*	100	F	SP	Lt Menthol Generic	11	.8	NA
Premium Buy*	King	F	SP	Lt Menthol Generic	11	.7	NA
Premium Buy*	King	F	SP	Lt Generic	11	.7	NA
Premium Buy*	100	F	SP	FF Generic	15	1.0	NA
Premium Buy*	King	NF	SP	Generic	24	1.6	NA
Price Master*	King	F	SP	FF	14	.8	16
Price Master*	100	F	SP	FF	13	.8	17
Price Master*	100	F	SP	Lt	9	.7	12
Price Master*	100	F	SP	Lt Menthol	10	.7	12
Price Master*	King	F	SP	Ultra-Lt	4	.3	6
Price Master*	King	F	SP	FF Menthol	14	.8	16
Price Master*	100	F	SP	FF Menthol	14	.9	18
Price Master*	King	F	SP	Lt	9	.6	12
Price Master*	King	NF	SP		20	1.1	16
Price Master*	King	F	HP	FF	15	.9	16
Price Master*	King	F	HP	Lt	10	.7	13
Price Master*	100	F	SP	Ultra-Lt	4	.4	7
Price Master*	King	F	SP	Lt Menthol	9	.6	12
Prime	100	F	SP	FF Menthol	13	.9	15
Prime	King	F	HP	FF	13	.9	13
Prime	King	F	SP	Lt	9	.7	11
Prime	King	F	SP	Ultra-Lt	5	.5	7
Prime	King	F	SP	FF Menthol	14	1.0	13

"TAR," NICOTINE &
CARBON MONOXIDE REPORT *(cont.)*

Brand Name	Description				Tar	Nic	CO
Prime	100	F	SP	FF	13	.9	15
Prime	100	F	SP	Ultra-Lt	4	.4	6
Prime	King	F	SP	FF	15	.9	15
Prime	King	F	SP	Lt Menthol	9	.8	10
Prime	King	NF	SP		22	1.3	15
Prime	100	F	SP	Lt Menthol	8	.7	8
Prime	100	F	SP	Lt	9	.7	12
Prime*	King	F	HP	Lt	10	.6	12
Private Stock	100	F	SP	Ultra-Lt	5	.4	6
Private Stock	King	F	SP	FF	15	.9	14
Private Stock	King	F	HP	Lt	10	.7	11
Private Stock	King	F	SP	Ultra-Lt	6	.5	8
Private Stock	100	F	SP	Lt Menthol	8	.7	8
Private Stock	100	F	SP	Lt	10	.7	12
Private Stock	King	NF	SP		21	1.2	14
Private Stock	King	F	SP	Lt Menthol	9	.7	9
Private Stock	King	F	SP	FF Menthol	14	1.0	13
Private Stock	King	F	SP	Lt	9	.7	11
Private Stock	King	F	HP	FF	15	.9	15
Private Stock	100	F	SP	FF	15	.9	17
Private Stock	100	F	SP	FF Menthol	13	.9	14
Pyramid	100	F	SP	Lt	10	.7	16
Pyramid	100	F	SP	FF	15	.9	22
Pyramid	100	F	SP	FF Menthol	15	.8	22
Pyramid	100	F	SP	Lt	10	.7	16
Pyramid	100	F	SP	Lt Menthol	9	.6	15
Pyramid	100	F	SP	Ultra-Lt	5	.4	7
Pyramid	King	F	SP	FF	14	.7	18
Pyramid	King	F	SP	FF Menthol	14	.7	18
Pyramid	King	F	SP	Lt	10	.7	15
Pyramid	King	NF	SP	FF	25	1.5	18
Quality Smokes*	King	F	SP	Ultra-Lt	4	.3	6
Quality Smokes*	King	F	SP	Lt	9	.6	12

Brand Name	Description				Tar	Nic	CO
Quality Smokes*	100	F	SP	FF	13	.8	17
Quality Smokes*	King	F	SP	FF	14	.8	16
Quality Smokes*	King	F	HP	Lt	10	.7	13
Quality Smokes*	King	F	SP	FF Menthol	14	.8	16
Quality Smokes*	100	F	HP	Lt	10	.8	13
Quality Smokes*	100	F	SP	Lt	9	.7	12
Quality Smokes*	100	F	SP	FF Menthol	14	.9	18
Quality Smokes*	100	F	SP	Lt Menthol	10	.7	12
Quality Smokes*	King	F	SP	Lt Menthol	9	.6	12
Quality Smokes*	King	NF	SP		20	1.1	16
Quality Smokes*	King	F	HP	FF	15	.9	16
Quality Smokes*	100	F	SP	Ultra-Lt	4	.4	7
Rainbow*	100	F	SP	Lt	9	.7	12
Rainbow*	100	F	SP	Ultra-Lt	4	.4	7
Rainbow*	King	F	SP	Lt Menthol	9	.6	12
Rainbow*	100	F	SP	Lt Menthol	10	.7	12
Rainbow*	King	F	SP	Lt	9	.6	12
Rainbow*	King	F	SP	FF	14	.8	16
Rainbow*	100	F	SP	FF	13	.8	17
Raleigh Extra	King	F	SP	Extra-Lt	9	.6	11
Raleigh	100	F	SP		16	1.1	15
Raleigh	Reg	NF	SP	Plain	21	1.2	14
Raleigh	100	F	SP	Lt	12	1.0	12
Raleigh	King	F	SP	Lt	10	.8	10
Raleigh	King	F	SP		16	1.0	15
Raleigh Extra	100	F	SP		9	.7	13
Raleigh Extra	100	F	SP	Extra-Lt Menthol	8	.7	9

"TAR," NICOTINE & CARBON MONOXIDE REPORT *(cont.)*

Brand Name	Description				Tar	Nic	CO
Raleigh Extra	King	NF	SP		21	1.2	14
Raleigh Extra	King	F	SP		15	.9	15
Raleigh Extra	100	F	SP		15	.9	17
Raleigh Extra	100	F	SP	Ultra-Lt	4	.4	5
Reno*	100	F	SP	FF Menthol	17	.9	22
Reno*	100	F	SP	Lt	12	.7	17
Reno*	100	F	SP	Lt Menthol	12	.7	17
Reno*	King	F	HP	FF	17	.8	22
Reno*	King	F	HP	FF Menthol	17	.8	22
Reno*	King	F	SP	FF	17	.8	22
Reno*	100	F	SP	FF	17	.9	22
Richland 20's	King	F	SP		15	1.1	13
Richland 20's*	King	F	HP		15	1.1	13
Richland 20's	King	F	SP	Menthol	15	1.1	14
Richland 20's	100	F	SP		16	1.2	15
Richland 20's	100	F	SP	Menthol	15	1.2	14
Richland 20's*	King	F	HP	10-pk	15	1.1	13
Rothmans*	King	F	HP		16	1.2	NA
Rothmans*	King	F	HP	Spec-Mild	13	1.1	NA
Rothmans*	King	F	HP	Extra-Lt	10	1.1	NA
Rothmans*	King	F	HP		15	1.3	15
Rothmans*	King	F	HP	Spec-Mild	13	1.2	12
Salem	King	F	SP	Menthol	17	1.2	17
Salem	100	F	HP	Slim-Lt Menthol	9	.8	9
Salem	King	F	SP	Lt Menthol	10	.8	12
Salem	100	F	HP	Lt Menthol Cus-Case	12	1.0	11
Salem	100	F	SP	Lt Menthol	8	.7	10
Salem	100	F	SP	Menthol	17	1.3	18

Brand Name	Description				Tar	Nic	CO
Salem	King	F	HP	Menthol Gold	17	1.3	17
Salem	100	F	SP	Ultra-Lt Menthol	5	.5	8
Salem	King	F	SP	Ultra-Lt Menthol	5	.5	7
Salem	100	F	SP	Lt Menthol Preferred	7	.6	8
Salem	100	F	SP	Menthol Preferred	15	1.2	17
Salem*	King	F	HP	FF Menthol	17	1.2	17
Salem*	King	F	HP	Lt Menthol	10	.8	12
Salem*	100	F	HP	FF Menthol	17	1.3	18
Saratoga	120	F	HP	Menthol	14	1.1	14
Saratoga	120	F	HP		14	1.1	14
Satin	100	F	SP		11	1.0	14
Satin	100	F	SP	Menthol	12	1.0	15
Scotch Buy*	King	F	SP	Ultra-Lt	4	.3	6
Scotch Buy*	100	F	SP	Ultra-Lt	4	.4	7
Scotch Buy*	King	F	SP	FF	14	.8	16
Scotch Buy*	100	F	SP	Lt Menthol	10	.7	12
Scotch Buy*	100	F	SP	Lt	9	.7	12
Scotch Buy*	King	F	SP	Lt Menthol	9	.6	12
Scotch Buy*	King	F	SP	Lt	9	.6	12
Scotch Buy*	100	F	SP	FF	13	.8	17
Sebring*	King	F	SP	FF Menthol	14	.8	16
Sebring*	King	NF	SP		20	1.1	16
Sebring*	100	F	SP	FF Menthol	14	.9	18
Sebring*	100	F	SP	Ultra-Lt	4	.4	7
Sebring*	100	F	SP	Lt Menthol	10	.7	12
Sebring*	King	F	SP	FF	14	.8	16
Sebring*	King	F	SP	Ultra-Lt	4	.3	6
Sebring*	King	F	SP	Lt Menthol	9	.6	12
Sebring*	100	F	SP	Lt	9	.7	12
Sebring*	100	F	SP	FF	13	.8	17
Sebring*	King	F	SP	Lt	9	.6	12
Sedona	King	F	HP	Lt	10	.9	12

"TAR," NICOTINE &
CARBON MONOXIDE REPORT *(cont.)*

Brand Name	Description				Tar	Nic	CO
Sedona	King	F	HP		14	1.1	14
Shenandoah*	King	F	SP	Lt Menthol Generic	11	.7	NA
Shenandoah*	King	F	SP	Lt Generic	11	.7	NA
Shenandoah*	King	F	SP	FF Generic	15	1.0	NA
Shenandoah*	100	F	SP	Menthol Generic	16	1.0	NA
Shenandoah*	100	F	SP	Lt Generic	11	.8	NA
Shenandoah*	King	F	SP	Menthol Generic	16	1.0	NA
Shenandoah*	100	F	SP	Lt Menthol Generic	11	.8	NA
Shenandoah*	King	NF	SP	Generic	24	1.6	NA
Shenandoah*	100	F	SP	Ultra-Lt Generic	6	.5	NA
Shenandoah*	King	F	SP	Ultra-Lt Generic	6	.5	NA
Shenandoah*	100	F	SP	Generic	15	1.0	NA
Shield*	King	F	SP	FF Menthol Generic	16	1.0	NA
Shield*	100	F	SP	Ultra-Lt Generic	6	.5	NA
Shield*	King	F	SP	Ultra-Lt Generic	6	.5	NA
Shield*	100	F	SP	Lt Menthol Generic	11	.8	NA
Shield*	100	F	SP	Lt Generic	11	.8	NA
Shield*	King	F	SP	Lt Menthol Generic	11	.7	NA
Shield*	100	F	SP	Generic	15	1.0	NA
Shield*	King	NF	SP	Generic	24	1.6	NA
Shield*	100	F	SP	FF Menthol Generic	16	1.0	NA
Shield*	King	F	SP	Generic	15	1.0	NA
Shield*	King	F	SP	Lt Generic	11	.7	NA
Signature*	100	F	SP	Lt Menthol	10	.7	12
Signature*	King	F	SP	FF Menthol	14	.8	16

Brand Name	Description				Tar	Nic	CO
Signature*	King	F	SP	Lt Menthol	9	.6	12
Signature*	King	F	SP	Ultra-Lt	4	.3	6
Signature*	100	F	SP	Lt	9	.7	12
Signature*	King	F	SP	Lt	9	.6	12
Signature*	100	F	SP	Ultra-Lt	4	.4	7
Signature*	100	F	SP	FF Menthol	14	.9	18
Signature*	100	F	SP	FF	13	.8	17
Signature*	King	F	SP	FF	14	.8	16
Silva Thins	100	F	HP	Menthol	11	.9	11
Silva Thins	100	F	HP		11	.9	11
Skyline*	King	F	SP	FF	15	.9	NA
Slim Price*	King	F	SP	FF Menthol	14	.8	16
Slim Price*	100	F	HP	Lt	10	.8	13
Slim Price*	100	F	SP	FF Menthol	14	.9	18
Slim Price*	100	F	SP	FF	13	.8	17
Slim Price*	King	F	SP	Lt	9	.6	12
Slim Price*	100	F	SP	Lt	9	.7	12
Slim Price*	100	F	SP	Lt Menthol	10	.7	12
Slim Price*	King	F	SP	Lt Menthol	9	.6	12
Slim Price*	King	NF	SP		20	1.1	16
Slim Price*	King	F	SP	Ultra	4	.3	6
Slim Price*	100	F	SP	Ultra	4	.4	7
Slim Price*	King	F	SP	FF	14	.8	16
Smoke One*	King	F	HP		15	.9	16
Smoke One*	100	F	SP	Menthol	10	.7	12
Smoke One*	King	F	SP		9	.6	12
Smoke One*	100	F	HP		10	.8	13
Smoke One*	King	F	HP		10	.7	13
Smoke One*	King	F	SP		4	.3	6
Smoke One*	100	F	SP		9	.7	12
Smoke One*	100	F	SP		13	.8	17
Smoke One*	100	F	SP		4	.4	7
Smoke One*	King	F	SP	Menthol	14	.8	16
Smoke One*	100	F	SP	Menthol	14	.9	18
Smoke One*	King	F	SP	Menthol	9	.6	12
Smoke One*	King	F	SP		14	.8	16

"TAR," NICOTINE & CARBON MONOXIDE REPORT (cont.)

Brand Name	Description				Tar	Nic	CO
State	King	F	HP	FF	15	1.4	16
State	King	F	HP		15	1.4	16
State	100	F	HP	FF	14	1.4	14
State	King	F	HP	Lt	12	1.2	11
Sterling	100	F	SP		13	.8	17
Sterling	100	F	SP	Ultra-Lt	4	.3	7
Sterling	100	F	SP	Ultra-Lt Menthol	4	.4	8
Sterling	100	F	SP	Menthol	13	.8	17
Sterling	100	F	HP	Slim-Lt	7	.5	9
Sterling	100	F	HP	Slim-Lt Menthol	7	.5	9
Sterling	100	F	SP	Lt	9	.7	11
Sterling	100	F	SP	Lt Menthol	10	.8	12
Stockton*	King	F	SP	Ultra-Lt	4	.3	6
Stockton*	King	F	SP	Lt Menthol	9	.6	12
Stockton*	100	F	SP	Lt	9	.7	12
Stockton*	100	F	SP	Lt Menthol	10	.7	12
Stockton*	King	F	SP	Lt	9	.6	12
Stockton*	100	F	SP	FF	13	.8	17
Stockton*	King	F	SP	FF	14	.8	16
Stockton*	100	F	SP	Ultra-Lt	4	.4	7
Stride*	100	F	SP	FF	16	1.3	21
Stride*	King	F	SP	FF	14	1.1	18
Style	100	F	HP	Slim-Lt Menthol	8	.7	9
Style	100	F	HP	Slim-Lt	9	.8	10
Style	100	F	SP	Lt	11	.9	14
Style	100	F	HP	Lt	11	.9	14
Style	100	F	HP	Lt Menthol	11	.9	14
Style	100	F	SP	Lt Menthol	11	.9	13
Summit	100	F	SP	FF	15	1.0	17
Summit	King	NF	SP		22	1.2	15
Summit	King	F	SP	Ultra-Lt	6	.6	8
Summit	100	F	SP	Ultra-Lt	4	.4	6

Brand Name	Description				Tar	Nic	CO
Summit	100	F	SP	Lt Menthol	8	.6	8
Summit 100	F	SP	FF	Menthol	14	1.0	15
Summit	King	F	SP	Lt	9	.7	11
Summit	King	F	SP	Lt Menthol	10	.7	11
Summit	King	F	SP	FF	15	.9	15
Summit	100	F	SP	Lt	9	.7	11
Summit	King	F	HP	Lt	9	.7	11
Summit*	King	F	HP	FF	15	.9	15
Summit*	King	F	SP	FF Menthol	15	.9	14
Sundance*	King	NF	SP		20	1.1	16
Sundance*	100	F	SP	Ultra-Lt	4	.4	7
Sundance*	King	F	SP	FF	14	.8	16
Sundance*	King	F	HP	Lt	10	.7	13
Sundance*	100	F	SP	FF	13	.8	17
Sundance*	King	F	SP	Lt	9	.6	12
Sundance*	100	F	SP	Lt	9	.7	12
Sundance*	King	F	SP	Lt Menthol	9	.6	12
Sundance*	King	F	HP	FF	15	.9	16
Sundance*	King	F	SP	Ultra-Lt	4	.3	6
Sundance*	100	F	SP	FF Menthol	14	.9	18
Sundance*	King	F	SP	FF Menthol	14	.8	16
Sundance*	100	F	SP	Lt Menthol	10	.7	12
Tall	120	F	SP	FF Menthol	19	1.4	19
Tall	120	F	SP	FF	18	1.4	20
Tareyton	King	F	SP	FF	14	.9	14
Tareyton	King	F	SP	Lt	6	.5	6
Tareyton	100	F	SP	Lt Long	8	.7	8
Tareyton	100	F	SP	FF	14	1.0	16
Tareyton	King	NF	SP		24	1.4	16
Tempo*	100	F	SP	Ultra-Lt	4	.4	7
Tempo*	King	NF	SP		20	1.1	16
Tempo*	King	F	SP	FF	14	.8	16
Tempo*	King	F	SP	Ultra-Lt	4	.3	6
Tempo*	King	F	SP	Lt Menthol	9	.6	12
Tempo*	100	F	SP	Lt Menthol	10	.7	12
Tempo*	King	F	SP	FF Menthol	14	.8	16

"TAR," NICOTINE & CARBON MONOXIDE REPORT *(cont.)*

Brand Name	Description				Tar	Nic	CO
Tempo*	100	F	SP	FF Menthol	14	.9	18
Tempo*	King	F	SP	Lt	9	.6	12
Tempo*	100	F	SP	Lt	9	.7	12
Tempo*	100	F	SP	FF	13	.8	17
Top Choice*	100	F	SP	Lt Generic	11	.8	NA
Top Choice*	100	F	SP	Ultra-Lt Generic	6	.5	NA
Top Choice*	100	F	SP	Lt Menthol Generic	11	.8	NA
Top Choice*	King	F	SP	Lt Menthol Generic	11	.7	NA
Top Choice*	King	F	SP	Lt Generic	11	.7	NA
Top Choice*	King	NF	SP	Generic	24	1.6	NA
Top Choice*	King	F	SP	FF Generic	15	1.0	NA
Top Choice*	100	F	SP	FF Generic	15	1.0	NA
Top Choice*	100	F	SP	FF Menthol Generic	16	1.0	NA
Top Choice*	King	F	SP	Ultra-Lt Generic	6	.5	NA
Tri-brand*	100	F	SP	Lt	9	.7	12
Tri-brand*	King	F	SP	Lt Menthol	9	.6	12
Tri-brand*	100	F	SP	Lt Menthol	10	.7	12
Tri-brand*	King	NF	SP		20	1.1	16
Tri-brand*	King	F	SP	Ultra-Lt	4	.3	6
Tri-brand*	100	F	SP	FF	13	.8	17
Tri-brand*	King	F	SP	FF	14	.8	16
Tri-brand*	100	F	SP	Ultra-Lt	4	.4	7
Tri-brand*	King	F	HP	Lt	10	.7	13
Tri-brand*	King	F	SP	Lt	9	.6	12
Triumph	King	F	SP	Menthol	4	.4	5
Triumph*	King	F	SP		4	.4	4
True	100	F	SP		6	.6	7
True	100	F	SP	Menthol	6	.6	7
True	King	F	HP		4	.4	4
True	100	F	HP		6	.6	7

Brand Name	Description				Tar	Nic	CO
True	King	F	SP		4	.4	5
True	King	F	SP	Menthol	4	.4	5
Value & Quality*	100	F	SP	Ultra-Lt	4	.4	7
Value & Quality*	100	F	SP	FF Menthol	14	.9	18
Value & Quality*	King	F	SP	Ultra-Lt	4	.3	6
Value & Quality*	King	F	SP	Lt	9	.6	12
Value & Quality*	King	F	SP	Lt Menthol	9	.6	12
Value & Quality*	100	F	SP	Lt	9	.7	12
Value & Quality*	100	F	SP	Lt Menthol	10	.7	12
Value & Quality*	King	F	SP	FF	14	.8	16
Value & Quality*	100	F	SP	FF	13	.8	17
Value & Quality*	King	F	SP	FF Menthol	14	.8	16
Value & Quality*	King	NF	SP		20	1.1	16
Value Pride*	King	F	SP	Lt	9	.6	12
Value Pride*	King	F	HP	FF	15	.9	16
Value Pride*	King	F	SP	FF Menthol	14	.8	16
Value Pride*	King	F	SP	FF	14	.8	16
Value Pride*	100	F	SP	FF	13	.8	17
Value Pride*	100	F	SP	Lt Menthol	10	.7	12
Value Pride*	King	NF	SP		20	1.1	16
Value Pride*	100	F	SP	Lt	9	.7	12
Value Pride*	King	F	SP	Lt Menthol	9	.6	12
Value Pride*	100	F	SP	Ultra-Lt	4	.4	7
Value Pride*	100	F	SP	FF Menthol	14	.9	18
Value Pride*	King	F	SP	Ultra-Lt	4	.3	6
Value Pride*	King	F	HP	Lt	10	.7	13
Value Sense*	King	F	SP	Ultra-Lt	4	.3	6
Value Sense*	100	F	SP	Lt Menthol	10	.7	12

"TAR," NICOTINE &
CARBON MONOXIDE REPORT *(cont.)*

Brand Name	Description				Tar	Nic	CO
Value Sense*	King	F	SP	Lt Menthol	9	.6	12
Value Sense*	King	F	SP	FF Menthol	14	.8	16
Value Sense*	King	F	SP	FF	14	.8	16
Value Sense*	100	F	SP	FF	13	.8	17
Value Sense*	King	F	SP	Lt	9	.6	12
Value Sense*	100	F	SP	FF Menthol	14	.9	18
Value Sense*	King	NF	SP		20	1.1	16
Value Sense*	100	F	SP	Lt	9	.7	12
Value Sense*	100	F	SP	Ultra-Lt	4	.4	7
Value Time*	King	F	SP	FF Menthol	14	.8	16
Value Time*	King	F	SP	FF	14	.8	16
Value Time*	100	F	SP	FF Menthol	14	.9	18
Value Time*	100	F	SP	Lt	9	.7	12
Value Time*	King	F	SP	Lt	9	.6	12
Value Time*	100	F	SP	Lt Menthol	10	.7	12
Value Time*	King	F	SP	Lt Menthol	9	.6	12
Value Time*	King	NF	SP		20	1.1	16
Value Time*	100	F	SP	Ultra	4	.4	7
Value Time*	King	F	SP	Ultra	4	.3	6
Value Time*	100	F	SP	FF	13	.8	17
Vantage	King	F	HP	Ultra-Lt	5	.5	8
Vantage	King	F	SP	Ultra-Lt	4	.4	6
Vantage	100	F	SP	Ultra-Lt	4	.4	7
Vantage	100	F	SP	Menthol	8	.7	10
Vantage	King	F	SP	Menthol	9	.8	9
Vantage	100	F	SP		8	.7	8
Vantage	King	F	SP		9	.8	9
Vantage	100	F	HP	Ultra-Lt	5	.5	7
Venture Gold*	100	F	SP	Lt Menthol	9	.6	11
Venture Gold*	King	F	HP	FF	14	.8	16
Venture Gold*	100	F	SP	Ultra-Lt	6	.5	7
Venture Gold*	100	F	SP	FF	15	.9	18
Venture Gold*	100	F	SP	Lt	8	.6	9
Venture Gold*	King	F	HP	Lt	8	.5	7

Brand Name	Description				Tar	Nic	CO
Viceroy	King	F	HP		14	1.1	13
Viceroy	King	F	SP		15	1.1	13
Viceroy	King	F	HP	Lt	10	.8	11
Viceroy	100	F	SP		16	1.3	15
Viceroy	King	F	SP		15	1.1	13
Viceroy	100	F	SP	Ultra	6	.5	6
Viceroy	100	F	SP		16	1.3	15
Viceroy	King	F	SP	Lt	10	.8	11
Viceroy	100	F	SP	Lt	11	.9	11
Viceroy	King	F	HP		14	1.1	13
Viceroy	King	F	HP	Lt	10	.8	11
Viceroy*	King	F	HP	10-pk	14	1.1	13
Virginia Slims	100	F	HP	Sup-Slim	6	.5	5
Virginia Slims	100	F	HP	Ultra-Lt Slim	5	.5	6
Virginia Slims	100	F	HP	Ultra-Lt Menthol Slim	6	.5	6
Virginia Slims	100	F	HP	Menthol Sup-Slim	5	.5	5
Virginia Slims	120	F	HP	Lt Menthol Slim	14	1.1	15
Virginia Slims	120	F	HP	Lt Slim	15	1.1	15
Virginia Slims	100	F	HP	Lt Menthol Slim	8	.7	9
Virginia Slims	100	F	HP	Lt Slim	8	.7	9
Virginia Slims	100	F	SP	Slim	14	1.1	13
Virginia Slims	100	F	SP	Menthol	15	1.1	14
Vista*	King	F	SP	Lt	11	.7	NA
Winston	King	F	SP		16	1.1	14
Winston	100	F	SP		16	1.2	17
Winston	King	F	SP	Ultra-Lt	5	.5	8
Winston	100	F	SP	Lt	10	.8	13
Winston	100	F	HP	Lt	8	.7	10
Winston	100	F	HP	Ultra-Lt	6	.5	8

"TAR," NICOTINE &
CARBON MONOXIDE REPORT (cont.)

Brand Name	Description				Tar	Nic	CO
Winston	King	F	HP		16	1.1	16
Winston	King	F	HP	Lt	10	.9	12
Winston	King	F	SP	Lt	10	.8	11
Winston	100	F	SP	Ultra-Lt	4	.4	7
Winston	King	F	SP	Select	16	1.2	15
Winston	King	F	HP	Ultra-Lt	5	.5	8
Winston	King	F	HP	Select	15	1.2	16
Winston	100	F	SP	Lt Select	9	.8	11
Winston	100	F	HP	Slim-Lt Select	9	.8	9
Winston	King	F	HP	Lt Select	9	.8	10
Winston	King	F	SP	Lt Select	10	.8	12
Winston	100	F	SP	Select	16	1.3	15
Winston	100	F	HP	Select	16	1.3	15
Worth*	King	NF	SP		20	1.1	16
Worth*	King	F	SP	FF	14	.8	16
Worth*	100	F	SP	FF	13	.8	17
Worth*	King	F	SP	Lt	9	.6	12
Worth*	100	F	SP	Lt	9	.7	12
Worth*	King	F	SP	Lt Menthol	9	.6	12
Worth*	100	F	SP	Lt Menthol	10	.7	12
Worth*	King	F	SP	Ultra-Lt	4	.3	6
Worth*	100	F	SP	Ultra-Lt	4	.4	7
Worth*	King	F	HP	Lt	10	.7	13
Worth*	King	F	SP	FF Menthol	14	.8	16
Worth*	100	F	SP	FF Menthol	14	.9	18
Worth*	King	F	HP	FF	15	.9	16

Source: Federal Trade Commission.

1 Commonwealth Of Pennsylvania By D. Michael Fisher, In His Official Capacity As Attorney General Of The Commonwealth Of Pennsylvania Plaintiff, v. Philip Morris, Inc.; R.J. Reynolds Tobacco Company; Brown & Williamson Tobacco Corporation; B.A.T. Industries, P.L.C.; The American Tobacco Company, Inc. c/o Brown & Williamson Tobacco Corporation; Lorillard Tobacco Company; Liggett Group, Inc.; United States Tobacco Company; The Tobacco Institute,

Inc.; The Council For Tobacco Research–U.S.A., Inc.; Smokeless Tobacco Council, Inc.; And Hill And Knowlton, Inc. Defendants Civil Action Complaint; "The Defendants' Wrongful Conduct And Conspiracy In Concealing And Misrepresenting The Addictive And Harmful Nature Of Tobacco/Nicotine"; E. The Defendants' Knowledge That Tobacco Use Is Harmful and Their Suppression Of The Truth. (http://www.attorneygeneral.gov/tobacco/tablit/tldefn.html)

A

The *Unofficial Guide*™ Reader Questionnaire

If you would like to express your opinion about quitting smoking or this guide, please complete this questionnaire and mail it to:

The *Unofficial Guide*™ Reader Questionnaire
IDG Lifestyle Group
1633 Broadway, floor 7
New York, NY 10019-6785

Gender: ___ M ___ F

Age: ___ Under 30 ___ 31–40 ___ 41–50
___ Over 50

Education: ___ High school ___ College
___ Graduate/Professional

What is your occupation?

_____

How did you hear about this guide?
___ Friend or relative
___ Newspaper, magazine, or Internet
___ Radio or TV
___ Recommended at bookstore
___ Recommended by librarian
___ Picked it up on my own
___ Familiar with the *Unofficial Guide*™ travel series

Did you go to the bookstore specifically for a book on quitting smoking? Yes ___ No ___

Have you used any other *Unofficial Guides*™?
Yes ___ No ___

If Yes, which ones?

_____
_____
_____

What other book(s) on quitting smoking have you purchased? _____

_____

_____

Was this book:
___ more helpful than other(s)
___ less helpful than other(s)

Do you think this book was worth its price?
Yes ___ No ___

Did this book cover all topics related to quitting smoking adequately?
Yes ___ No ___

Please explain your answer:

_____

_____

_____

Were there any specific sections in this book that were of particular help to you? Yes ___ No ___

Please explain your answer:

_____

_____

_____

On a scale of 1 to 10, with 10 being the best rating, how would you rate this guide? ___

What other titles would you like to see published in the *Unofficial Guide*™ series?

_____

_____

Are *Unofficial Guides*™ readily available in your area? Yes ___ No ___

Other comments:

_____

_____

_____

_____